FOURTH EDITION

BASKETBALL

SKILLS & DRILLS

JERRY V. KRAUSE

CRAIG NELSON

HUMAN KINETICS

Library of Congress Cataloging-in-Publication Data

Names: Krause, Jerry, 1936- author. | Nelson, Craig, 1984- author.
Title: Basketball skills & drills / Jerry V. Krause and Craig Nelson.
Other titles: Basketball skills and drills | Basketball skills and drills.
Description: Fourth Edition. | Champaign, Illinois : Human Kinetics, [2019] |
 Originally published: Champaign, Illinois : Leisure Press, c1991. |
 Includes bibliographical references and index.
Identifiers: LCCN 2018020668 (print) | LCCN 2018023641 (ebook) | ISBN
 9781492568353 (ebook) | ISBN 9781492564102 (print)
Subjects: LCSH: Basketball--Coaching.
Classification: LCC GV885.3 (ebook) | LCC GV885.3 .K68 2018 (print) | DDC
 796.323--dc23
LC record available at https://lccn.loc.gov/2018020668

ISBN: 978-1-4925-6410-2 (print)

The web addresses cited in this text were current as of July 2018, unless otherwise noted.

Developmental Editor: Anne Cole; **Copyeditor:** Tom Tiller; **Proofreader:** Leigh Keylock; **Indexer:** Dan Connolly; **Permissions Manager:** Martha Gullo; **Graphic Designers:** Sean Roosevelt and Dawn Sills; **Cover Designer:** Keri Evans; **Cover Design Associate:** Susan Rothermel Allen; **Photograph (cover):** PhotoAlto/Sandro Di Carlo Darsa/Brand X/ Getty Images; **Photographs (interior):** © Human Kinetics; **Photo Production Coordinator:** Amy M. Rose; **Photo Production Manager:** Jason Allen; **Senior Art Manager:** Kelly Hendren; **Illustrations:** © Human Kinetics; **Printer:** Sheridan Books

We thank the Sanford Pentagon in Sioux Falls, South Dakota, for assistance in providing the location for the photo and video shoot for this book.

The video contents of this product are licensed for private home use and traditional, face-to-face classroom instruction only. For public performance licensing, please contact a sales representative at **www.HumanKinetics.com/SalesRepresentatives.**

Printed in the United States of America   10 9 8 7 6 5 4 3 2 1

Human Kinetics
P.O. Box 5076
Champaign, IL 61825-5076
Website: www.HumanKinetics.com

In the United States, email info@hkusa.com or call 800-747-4457.
In Canada, email info@hkcanada.com.
In the United Kingdom/Europe, email hk@hkeurope.com.

For information about Human Kinetics' coverage in other areas of the world, please visit our website: **www.HumanKinetics.com**   E7294

Coaches often learn much from their players. One of my former players, Don Meyer, spent his 40-year career at the small-college level and became an eight-time hall of fame coach. We both had roots in the small town of Wayne, Nebraska; he grew up there, and I graduated from Wayne State College. Years later, our paths crossed at Colorado State College, where I was fortunate to coach Don as an assistant basketball coach. We became lifelong friends and coaching brothers who shared a passion for the game as well as for giving back to coaches and players through the sharing of knowledge.

For more than 30 years we collaborated on clinics, DVDs, and books to share basketball coaching ideas with other coaches and players. Don and I shared the belief that a coach's good example as a role model isn't just one way to teach players life lessons—it is the *only* way. Here are three life lessons we learned together:

1. **Always take notes.** My "Never stop learning" mantra is based on Don's belief that we should "get all good ideas" (learn) but pick out those that are best for you and your team. His rule is still true today, particularly thanks to the ease with which coaches can share ideas in this age of technology. Learning is more effective with handwritten note-taking compared to using electronic devices.

2. **Always say *please* and *thank you*.** This was his way to teach players civility and kindness. I used this rule to develop my theme of *respect*: develop your own self-respect and earn the respect of others.

3. **Always pick up trash.** This was Don's way of making our world better. My approach to this lesson is this: Practice leaving your personal world better than you found it on a daily basis. This can be accomplished even with the simple act of picking up trash around your personal or business space.

Don, thank you for helping me model these values for others to learn. Your extraordinary example set a high standard of excellence for coaching knowledge, and you shared so much with so many. You were incredible! Thank you, my coaching brother; you taught me well, and I learned with you as best I could.

In respect, love, and gratitude,
Your friend, Jerry Krause

CONTENTS

Drill	Level	Specific focus	Warm-up component	Conditioning component	Page
Basic Body Control					
Quick-Stance Check	Basic	Basic stance			22
Quick-Stance Mirror	Basic	Basic stance			22
Mass Quick Moves ▶	Intermediate	Basic stance	✓	✓	22
Line Drill: Quick Starts, Steps, Turns, and Stops ▶	Basic	Starting, stepping, turning, stopping, PPF footwork, and EPF footwork	✓	✓	24
Line Drill: Quick Jumps	Basic	Jumping skills for rebounding and shooting	✓	✓	26
Line Drill: Rebound Jumping and Turns	Basic	Jumping skills for rebounding	✓	✓	27
Line Drill: Quick Stance, Starts, Steps, Jumps, Turns, and Stops	Basic	Body-control movements	✓		27
Line Drill: Starts, Stops, and Turns	Intermediate, advanced	Quick stance, quick starts, quick stops, quick turns, and passing and catching skills	✓	✓	27
Full-Court Team Rebounding	Intermediate, advanced	Two-handed rebounding, tapping ball on backboard		✓	28
Advanced Body Control					
Line Drill: Moving Without the Ball ▶	Basic	Basic moves without the ball	✓		45
V-Cut	Basic	Basic moves without the ball in 2on-0 and 2-on-2 situations			46
2-on-2 Offense and Defense	Intermediate, advanced	All two-player scoring moves (live ball, back cuts, pass-and-cut, ball screen), plus varied defense		✓	48
4-on-4 Half-Court Offense and Defense	Intermediate, advanced	Concentrated half-court team offense and defense		✓	48
4-on-4 Defense-to-Offense Transition	Advanced	Half-court team offense option, offensive and defensive rebounding, controlled defense-to-offense transition, offense-to-defense transition		✓	48
One-Minute Continuous Game	Advanced	Use of all offensive moves without the ball and applying full-court defense (no over-the-top breakaway cuts allowed); one-minute games	✓	✓	49
Pick-and-Roll ▶	Intermediate, advanced	Screening and cutting options for on-the-ball screens	✓		49
3-on-0 Motion	Advanced	Scoring options on screens away from the ball; two-ball shooting	✓	✓	50
3-on-3 Motion Screen	Advanced	Screening and cutting options for off-the-ball screens	✓		50
Ballhandling					
Ballhandling	Basic, advanced	Controlling the ball, becoming familiar with the ball, developing an individual ballhandling warm-up and skill-practice routine	✓	✓	77
Line Drill: Passing and Catching	Basic	Passing and catching techniques (all basic passes)	✓		79

(continued)

Drill Finder *(continued)*

Drill	Level	Specific focus	Warm-up component	Conditioning component	Page
Ballhandling (continued)					
Two-Player Passing and Catching ▶	Basic	Passing and catching using a one-handed push pass with either hand after a dribble	✓		79
Coach Beilein's Perfect Passing	Intermediate, advanced	2-on-2 half-court passing and catching with correct fundamental passing technique (30 seconds, at least 10 passes to score)	✓	✓	80
Gonzaga Team Pass–Catch (Around the World)	Advanced	4-on-0 pass–catch sequence performed correctly and quickly (1 minute, layup numbers)	✓	✓	81
2-on-1 Keepaway Passing	Advanced	Passing and catching between partners who must pass by a defender		✓	81
Moving Pairs Passing ▶	Basic, intermediate	Partner passing and catching skills while moving and against a defender; spacing and timing	✓		82
Wall Passing	Basic	Individual ballhandling skills of passing and catching	✓		82
Line Drill: Stance, Starts, and Skill Breakdown	Basic	Selected footwork skills from a quick stance and a quick start	✓		82
Line Drill: Starts, Stops, and Turns ▶	Basic, intermediate, advanced	Combining footwork, dribbling, starting, stopping, passing, catching, and turning skills in four lines	✓	✓	83
Mass Dribbling ▶	Basic, intermediate	Basic ballhandling skills of dribbling	✓		83
Full-Court Dribbling	Basic	Ballhandling skills of dribbling		✓	84
Wall Dribbling	Intermediate, advanced	Ballhandling skills with one ball and two balls	✓		85
Basic Ballhandling Drill ▶	Intermediate, advanced	Individual and pair dribbling, passing, and catching skills with basketballs and tennis balls	✓		85
Gonzaga Full-Court Footwork and Layup (Peer-Pressure Drill) ▶	Basic, intermediate, advanced	EPF footwork and two-handed passing and catching	✓	✓	86
Shooting					
Line Drill: Shooting Addition (Without Ball, With Ball) ▶	Basic	Shooting in a simulated game situation	✓		122
Layup Shooting Progression ▶	Intermediate, advanced	Proper and quick execution of game-type layups; dribble-chase layups	✓		123
Gonzaga Full-Court Team Layup	Basic, intermediate, advanced	PPF and EPF options (peer-pressure shooting drill)	✓	✓	124
Field-Goal Progression ▶	Basic, intermediate, advanced	Improved shooting through feedback; self-teaching	✓		125
Shoot-the-Line and Soft-Touch Shooting	Basic, intermediate, advanced	Shooting mechanics and confidence building	✓		128
Groove-It Spot Shooting	Intermediate	Evaluating shooting effectiveness and range	✓		129
Pairs In-and-Out Shooting ▶	Intermediate, advanced	Shooting in a 2-on-0 game simulation (all shooting situations)		✓	130

Drill	Level	Specific focus	Warm-up component	Conditioning component	Page
Outside Offensive Moves (continued)					
Partner Passing and Shooting	Basic, intermediate, advanced	Combination drill using all offensive skills and various shots and addressing ballhandling goals	✓	✓	163
Timed Layups ▶	Basic	Ballhandling and layup shooting (V and reverse V)	✓	✓	163
Perimeter Game	Intermediate, advanced	All perimeter moves with the ball; individual PR competition; game moves at game spots at game speed	✓	✓	164
Five-Spot Dribble and Finish	Basic, intermediate	Live-ball and finish moves in a timed situation	✓	✓	164
Diamond Dribble Moves (Full-Court)	Intermediate, advanced	Rebounding and perimeter skills with dummy defenders	✓	✓	165
Continuous Pass-and-Trap	Intermediate, advanced	Passing and catching against defensive traps	✓	✓	166
Finish the Play ▶	Intermediate, advanced	Offensive attack moves and basket finishes	✓	✓	167
Three-Lane-Rush Pass–Catch (Peer-Pressure Drill) ▶	Intermediate, advanced	Full-court layups; team peer-pressure drill	✓	✓	168
Inside Offensive Moves: Playing the Post					
Post Warm-Up ▶	Basic	Basic post skills	✓		187
Line Drill: Post-Player Starts, Turns, and Stops	Basic	Proper footwork	✓		187
Post Pairs	Basic	Post stance, passing and catching, and chinning the ball	✓		188
Spin-Pass Post Moves ▶	Basic	Individual offensive post moves; back-to-basket moves	✓		189
Post Progression	Basic, intermediate, advanced	Offensive post moves	✓	✓	190
Big Spacing and Post Feeding ▶	Intermediate, advanced	Triangle spacing; big spacing	✓		190
All-American Post Workout	Advanced	All offensive post moves	✓	✓	192
2-on-2 Feeding the Post	Intermediate, advanced	Offensive and defensive post-play skills; passing to post players; movement after pass for return pass			192
Mikan	Basic, intermediate, advanced	Footwork, ballhandling, layup shooting close to basket; regular, reverse, and power Mikans	✓	✓	193
5-on-5 Post Passing	Advanced	Post players: getting open, catching, post moves, passing from post position while reading and reacting to defenders. Defensive players: double-teaming post players, rotating to ball on passes from post	✓	✓	193
Post Score Through Defense	Intermediate, advanced	Capturing and chinning the ball; scoring through contact		✓	194
1-on-1 Post Cutthroat	Basic, intermediate, advanced	Post offense and defense in 1-on-1 live format		✓	194
Perimeter–Post Progression	Basic, intermediate, advanced	Perimeter and post players working together as outside–inside units	✓		195

(continued)

Drill	Level	Specific focus	Warm-up component	Conditioning component	Page
Rebounding (continued)					
Garbage ▶	Basic, intermediate	Scoring on the offensive rebound	✓	✓	251
No-Babies-Allowed (NBA) or Survival Rebounding ▶	Advanced	Aggressiveness as a rebound skill		✓	252
Individual Rebounding	Basic	Rebounding skills	✓		252
Rebound Progression: 3-on-0, 3-on-3	Intermediate, advanced	Rebounding skills	✓		253
Cutthroat Rebounding: ▶ 3-on-3, 4-on-4	Intermediate, advanced	Offensive and defensive rebounding		✓	253
War Rebounding	Advanced	Aggressive defensive or offensive rebounding		✓	254
Team Offense					
Skeleton Offense: ▶ 5-on-0 (Dry Run)	Basic	Basic team offensive formation	✓		272
Team Offense and Defense: ▶ 4-on-4, 5-on-5	Intermediate, advanced	Team offense and defense		✓	272
Blitz Fast Break ▶	Intermediate, advanced	Two-lane and three-lane fast-break plays (offense and defense)		✓	273
Transition Fast Break ▶	Intermediate, advanced	Transition basketball		✓	275
Defense-to-Offense Transition	Basic, intermediate, advanced	Teach defense-to-offense transition (2-on-0, 3-on-0, 5-on-0) to score and then get back	✓	✓	275
Team Defense					
Half-Court Basic Defense: ▶ 3-on-3, 4-on-4	Intermediate, advanced	Two-person and three-person offensive play		✓	288
Half-Court to Full-Court: 3-on-3, 4-on-4, 5-on-5	Intermediate, advanced	Half-court defense and transition to offense; half-court offense and transition to defense		✓	289
Full-Court: 3-on-3, 5-on-5	Intermediate, advanced	All phases of defense		✓	289
2-on-2 Avoid the Screen	Basic, intermediate, advanced	2-on-2 ball screen defense: fight through and switch up		✓	289
Sprint to Low-I Help Position	Basic, intermediate, advanced	Perimeter closeout and sprint to protect basket (low-I position)		✓	290

The ▶ symbol indicates which drills can also be found in the online video.

ACCESSING THE ONLINE VIDEO

This book includes access to online video that includes 41 clips demonstrating some of the most dynamic drills from the book. In the drill finder and throughout the book, exercises marked with this play button icon indicate where the content is enhanced by online video clips: ◉

Take the following steps to access the video. If you need help at any point in the process, you can contact us by clicking on the Technical Support link under Customer Service on the right side of the screen.

1. Visit www.HumanKinetics.com/BasketballSkillsAndDrills.

2. Click on the **View online video** link next to the book cover.

3. You will be directed to the screen shown in figure 1. Click the **Sign In** link on the left or top of the page. If you do not have an account with Human Kinetics, you will be prompted to create one.

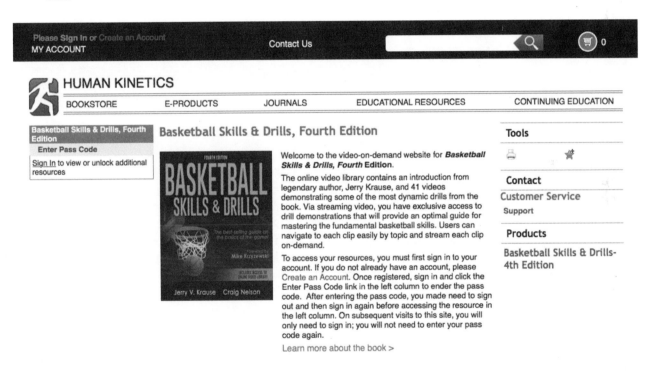

Figure 1

4. If the online video does not appear in the list on the left of the page, click the **Enter Pass Code** option in that list. Enter the pass code exactly as it is printed here, including all hyphens. Click the **Submit** button to unlock the online video. After you have entered this pass code the first time, you will never have to enter it again. For future visits, all you need to do is sign in to the book's website and follow the link that appears in the left menu.

Pass code for online video: **KRAUSE-43TD-OV**

5. Once you have signed into the site and entered the pass code, select **Online Video** from the list on the left side of the screen. You'll then see an Online Video page with information about the video, as shown in the screenshot in figure 2. You can go straight to the accompanying videos for each topic by clicking on the blue links at the bottom of the page.

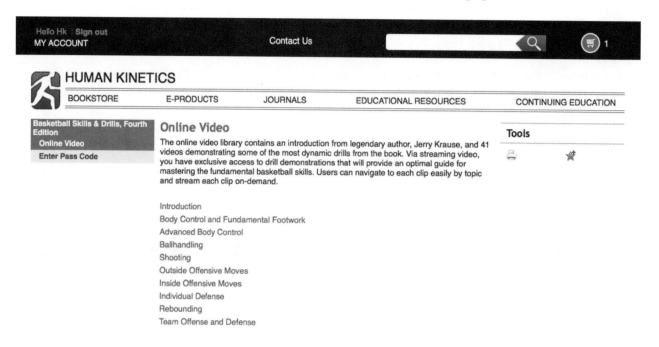

Figure 2

6. You are now able to view video for the topic you selected on the previous screen, as well as all others that accompany this product. Across the top of the page, you will see a set of buttons that correspond to the topics in the text that have accompanying video. Once you click on a topic, a player will appear. In the player, the clips for that topic will appear vertically along the right side. Select the video you would like to watch and view it in the main player window. You can use the buttons at the bottom of the main player window to view the video full screen, to turn captioning on and off, and to pause, fast-forward, or reverse the clip.

FOREWORD

It is a real honor for me to write the foreword for the fourth edition of *Basketball Skills & Drills*. For more than 25 years, this book has stressed basketball fundamentals. More than 250,000 copies have been sold, and it continues to be translated and published around the globe. To say the least, all of us in the game should feel a great sense of pride for the work that Jerry Krause and Don Meyer have done to enhance teaching, learning, and coaching the fundamental skills of basketball.

In order to be a good player and to have a good team, fundamentals must be stressed. *Basketball Skills & Drills* breaks the game into its simplest form. It is easy to understand for both coaches and individual players at any level. I enthusiastically recommend the book to everyone who wants to become a better player, coach, or teacher.

I believe that all coaches take great pride in being called Coach. I also believe that all coaches feel that they are teachers. The ability to fundamentally teach this game is essential for a coach to become better. I have benefitted greatly from reading this book and using many of its ideas as I have taught the game for the past four decades. Please take the time to study each of the pages in this treasured book. You will benefit greatly from it!

No coach in the history of the game has taught this great game better than Don Meyer. As I read the pages in this book, I can visualize Don teaching these fundamentals. He loved this game as much as anyone could ever love it.

Finally, I want to thank Jerry Krause, Don Meyer's coach and mentor, whose love of the game is unmatched. Jerry, thank you for this fabulous book and video library and for what you have done for the game throughout your life!

Mike Krzyzewski, Head Men's Basketball Coach at Duke University
and U.S. Olympic Coach (2008, 2012, 2016)

"I seek to leave the world a little better place than I found it."

James Naismith, inventor of basketball

Basketball Skills & Drills rests on a foundation laid by *Better Basketball Basics* (Leisure Press), which focused only on fundamental skills of the game. That 1983 publication featured 550 sequential pictures, became extremely popular with coaches, and sold out its two editions. In 1991, its main concepts were refined and developed into the first edition of *Basketball Skills & Drills* (Human Kinetics). That book quickly became a best-selling reference for teaching and learning basketball. Today, nearly a quarter-million players and coaches around the world agree that this book is the simplest, most comprehensive treatment of basketball basics—the fundamental skills of the sport.

For the second edition of *Basketball Skills & Drills* (1999), the addition of Don Meyer and Jerry Meyer as co-authors brought expertise in successful playing and coaching from two more generations of linked experts who built their careers around successful execution of basketball fundamentals. The book's third edition (2008) had significant innovations. Specifically, it included two hours of video demonstrations on DVD, thus adding a new component for those who prefer visual learning for key skills and drills. In fact, that package provided a legacy for future basketball players and coaches and became the basis for a new video library made exclusively for *Skill & Drills* readers for this fourth edition. Readers will gain special access to an array of video clips covering all of the fundamental skills and the critical cues for teaching and learning them, plus selected drills for developing all of the basketball basics. See instructions on how to view the video clips located on the previous page titled Accessing the Online Video.

Thus, *Basketball Skills & Drills* has become the definitive source of fundamentals for coaches, players, and parents. Improvements in this edition include the following:

- Updated and expanded primary and secondary concepts for the fundamental skills (integrating insights from the Krause–Meyer basketball family tree, as well as drills derived from Dennis Hutter that are direct offshoots of our philosophy)

- Additions to the teaching methods and alternative ways to teach and learn skills more effectively for all players

- References to players and coaches who also place a special emphasis on fundamental skills

- Addition and modification of court diagrams to ensure clear, accurate illustrations

- New focus on developing a teaching and learning community

- Addition of advanced either-pivot-foot (EPF) footwork and facing-the-basket post play with new "Zak-attack" techniques designed to help players attack the basket from the high post and short corners

- Expansion of the sequential, progressive drills for each chapter

- Revised troubleshooting sections addressing common problems and remedies

- Skill assessments, including both observational measures (in the troubleshooting sections) and quantitative measures of status and improvement through development and addition of "peer-pressure" shooting drills (presented in chapter 4). These drills originated in Krause's year spent with Naismith Hall of Fame coach Ralph Miller of Oregon State University in 1982-1983. Miller used this self-assessment technique with offensive fundamentals to set scoring goals, as well as related drills, so that players and teams could compete against the game. He developed a complete self-assessment system of teaching individual and team offense and defense through the careful selection of six drills. These peer-pressure self-training drills are very useful for coaches. This technique greatly enhances coaches' and players' ability to help each other in practicing game moves at game speed.

- A special emphasis on the International Basketball Federation (FIBA) rules with the inclusion of EPF footwork and greater emphasis on facing-the-basket post play. FIBA footwork differences are noted, and the difference between U.S. and FIBA fundamentals are discussed.

One further note about the book's history from the lead author, Jerry Krause. The origins of its first edition date back to 1982, when hall of fame player and coach John Wooden, one of my mentors (and the mentor of my primary coach mentor, George Sage of the University of Northern Colorado), hosted me at UCLA. Wooden was a gracious host and mentor, especially to young coaches—a lesson I never forgot. When asked how he learned the fundamentals, he told me of a continual yearly process of updating and researching other coaches' ideas about fundamental skills and adapting these ideas for his program and teams. I adopted this approach and began compiling key concepts in each skill area. By 1984, this work led to the creation of my first book on the fundamental skills (*Better Basketball Basics*, mentioned earlier). In recognition of Wooden's contribution to the game and the fact that he inspired me to author my first book, each chapter in this edition ends with a John Wooden quote—a nugget of Wooden Wisdom—that has been especially meaningful in my career. Without Coach Wooden's example, I would not have become the most prolific author in basketball history.

The basic skills lay the foundation for success at all levels of basketball. For example, Michael Jordan, Tim Duncan, LeBron James, and Stephen Curry—four of the greatest male players ever, as well as female greats Courtney Vandersloot, Sue Bird, and Diana Taurasi—have all combined great natural ability with proper and quick execution of exceptional fundamental skills. These superior skills were developed through years of dedication to continuous improvement. Coach Wooden stated that all players must learn to execute the fundamental skills properly and quickly in order to succeed, both individually and as a team. *Basketball Skills & Drills* can help all coaches and players reach this goal, as coaches strive to become more effective master teachers who make the game of basketball simple and easy to learn, so that players can learn more effectively and efficiently, as well as develop their love of the game.

Wooden Wisdom

"It isn't what you do, but how well you do it."

—John Wooden

INTRODUCTION

DEVELOPING A TEACHING—LEARNING COMMUNITY

"I'm a teacher and coach. Teaching is what I love most, the heart of my coaching style. The best thing about my profession is that I can teach."

Mike Krzyzewski, Duke University, U.S. Olympic coach, Naismith Hall of Fame coach

Learning is one of the most valuable ways to spend time. In fact, life is about learning, and players and coaches need to develop lifetime habits of learning. More specifically, they need to commit themselves to learning constantly in order to make progress, avoid repeating their mistakes, benefit from others' experience, and improve their performance—both in basketball and in life.

The value of learning should be appreciated both by players and by coaches. It can be natural, enjoyable, productive, and satisfying when approached with a positive attitude. When we are open to learning and growth, we will learn, and that learning enables us to achieve. We need to make connections between what we want to achieve and what we need to learn in order to be successful. In basketball, coaches need to make the game simple and easy to learn, and players need to be ready and open to learning in order to develop the foundation for success.

Knowing *how* to learn effectively helps both players and coaches make the most of the instruction offered in this book. The essential concepts are as follows:

- **Admit mistakes or ignorance.** Acknowledge that you don't know something and even be willing to look foolish while you learn and make mistakes. Fear of failure is a common trait and must be overcome in order to maximize learning and become a lifelong learner. Develop a *mistake mentality* by asking questions and taking risks. You must make mistakes in order to learn. It is a necessary part of the learning process.

- **Begin learning with questions.** Let what you already know about basketball skills be a starting point each day. Start with a challenge, problem, or question that propels you to learn more. Muster the humility to use your limited knowledge as a starting point for further learning.

- **Bring your knowledge to life.** If you learn why you are using a skill, then that skill will hold more meaning for you. Every skill or concept can be learned better when you know the reason for developing and using it. As a learner, discover the "why"; then, if you are a teacher-coach, communicate that "why" to your student-players. This process enhances learning as well as providing motivation for the learning process.

- **Take responsibility both for your own learning and for the learning of those around you.** The resulting synergy enables much faster learning and deeper learning on the individual and team levels. When a team (including both players and coaches) becomes a teaching–learning community, learning is dramatically increased because it serves as a central focus for both teachers and learners. A teaching–learning community facilitates learning in all situations—coach to player (and vice versa), player to player, and player to all other sources. These learning situations help develop a positive attitude that can move everyone along the path to becoming a lifelong learner.

- **Learn from experience.** Turn information into knowledge by applying it and working with it. Use drills to develop skills that can be used to play the game better. In turn, play the game to discover weaknesses that can be addressed through drills focused on specific skills.

- **Learn from other people, especially those who are successful.** Coaches can study the lives of hall of fame coaches to learn the best ideas from the best people. For example, hall of fame coach John Wooden identified the attributes associated with success and created his Pyramid of Success based on the cornerstones of *hard work* and *enthusiasm* for learning. Players can also learn from each other, including, of course, from players who are older and more skilled. Seeing skills from someone else's perspective is a great way to learn.

  Wooden's definition of success was developed over a long period of time during an illustrious teaching and coaching career. This definition came from his frustration with academic grades, which, in his opinion, did not allow all students who strived to do their best to achieve the success that they desired. He concluded that all students and athletes needed a definition for success where all could become successful if they learned to become their best. Thus, his success definition became the following: "Success is peace of mind that is the direct result of self-satisfaction in knowing you did your best to become the best you are capable of becoming" (Wooden and Jamison 2004, 86-87) Our interpretation of this learning mantra could be stated as "Do your best to become your best." What more can we ask than to have all players and coaches doing their best to become their best (in learning *and* in life)?

- **Learn by teaching others.** Players should be encouraged to teach and learn from each other (through buddy coaching) and teach younger, less experienced players. One of the best ways to teach others is by doing our own best, because others tend to be more interested in what we do than in what we say. At the same time, we ourselves never fully know something until we teach it to, or share it with, others. When players teach other players, the player serving as teacher-coach learns more than the student-player does, because serving in the role of teacher requires one to prepare and learn more in order to help the learner become more effective.

- **Just as the teacher-coach must be prepared to teach, players must be open to learning and ready to learn in order to accomplish learning objectives in a teaching–learning community.** As John Wooden stated, "The teacher hasn't taught until the student has learned" (Nater and Gallimore 2010, 103). The real objective is for the student-player to learn and improve, which is the ultimate test of teaching effectiveness.

- **Learning is one of the keys to living a satisfying life, and learning to live (well) is best done by living to learn.** Humans are naturally curious early in life, and they almost always respond well to the opportunity to learn. This philosophy is well expressed in the following simple statement: Learn to live by living to learn.

- **Never stop learning.** When you integrate learning into all you do, you benefit immensely. Every moment that you make learning a priority, you can bring something positive into your life.

BASKETBALL SKILLS AND DRILLS

Basketball Skills & Drills focuses on the fundamental skills of basketball that coaches teach and players learn. The acquisition of basic skills depends greatly on optimizing the teaching and learning process to generate a successful end product—namely, athletes who have learned basketball skills at the highest level.

Because movement skills are learned over time, patience is essential. Any athlete brings to the game certain genetically inherited movement traits, which we often refer to as *abilities*. These fundamental movement components—such as reaction time, predominant type of muscle fibers, and depth perception—serve as the building blocks for an athlete's movement potential. Teaching and learning, however, must focus not on these abilities themselves but on the skills developed from them.

Coaches and basketball experts often assert that too many players focus on style over substance and prefer to use inherited abilities (the quick fix) rather than develop fundamental skills (the slow process). For instance, many players find it easier to dunk the ball than to execute a challenging pass and catch for a team basket. This book focuses on the controllable and gradual process required to teach and learn basic basketball skills—a process that depends on the substance of the skilled athlete rather than the flash of the stylistic athlete who relies primarily on individual movement abilities. Coaches and players need to focus on teaching and learning the basic skills of basketball and emphasize the process more than the product (i.e., single performance). They need to build on each player's inherent ability base for developing basketball skills, by which we mean learned movements built on inherited abilities. This long, slow process provides the basis for individual and team success in basketball.

Coaches and players often use drills as necessary tools to enhance skill learning. Drills, however, are only tools—not the end result. Thus, the focus should always be placed not on the drills themselves but on the desired skills. The drills presented in this book have been carefully selected to help players and coaches improve fundamental basketball skills. All coaches can benefit from helping their players develop or modify skills that best fit their philosophy and system of play. Skills are best developed by careful selection of and proper use of drills that enhance learning.

Coaches and players can modify and develop their own drills to learn basketball skills that eventually result in performing game moves at game speed. As expressed by Naismith Hall of Fame coach Henry "Hank" Iba of Oklahoma State University, "Practice the game in the manner in which it is to be played" (personal communication, September 1969).

LEVELS OF LEARNING

Movement learning experts have found that basketball skills are learned in three stages.

1. *Cognitive stage:* The player forms a mental picture of the skill, usually based on a demonstration or explanation from a teacher or coach. Because vision is usually the dominant sense, especially for this stage of learning, coaches should "paint perfect pictures" through their demonstrations and explanations.

2. *Practice stage:* The player imitates the demonstration, the imitations are corrected and reinforced by the coach, and the skills are performed repeatedly. John Wooden emphasized this critical step when he stated that the five final learning steps are repetition, repetition, repetition, repetition, and repetition.

3. *Automatic stage:* The player can perform skills without thinking; the movements have become habits and can be performed as game moves at game speed.

Drills should use this repetitive process to reach the final goal of achieving game moves at game speed.

Basic skill learning in stages can involve the senses of sight, sound, and feel.

1. The sight, or *look*, of a skill: A player needs to know what a skill looks like when performed properly, and this need can be met through partner or buddy coaching—that is, watching teammates perform a skill, reinforcing what they are doing correctly, and correcting their mistakes. To maximize team learning of basic skills, coaches should convince all players to take responsibility for their teammates' basic skill learning. A team is only as strong as its weakest link, and its strength also depends on each player teaching all of the other players (e.g., through echo calls [repeating back the coaches' instructions or "critical cues"], as discussed later), thus enabling all players to learn more efficiently. To coach such demonstrations effectively, coaches must provide explanations that are precise, concise, correct, and understood by all players.

2. The *sound* of a skill: After players know the look of a proper skill, their focus can shift to sound—for instance, the sound of a dribble on the floor or of proper passing (*ping*) and catching (*click*).

3. The *feel* of a skill: Feeling is the highest sensory development of a skill—for example, when shooting a free throw in practice with one's eyes closed or dribbling a basketball while keeping one's eyes focused on the net or rim with big vision (head up to see the whole floor).

Visualization is a mental tool that can be applied in all three sensory areas. When a player mentally practices a skill by *picturing perfect performance* of it, the player learns in a relaxed state. This approach works best when players focus on mentally reviewing their *own* successful performance—how it looks, sounds, and feels. Thus, players need to become aware of the look, sound, and feel of a skill through both physical practice and mental practice.

COMMUNICATION

One of the paramount components of teaching and learning is communication. The ability to disseminate palatable information is a valuable tool—one that both players and coaches need to sharpen every day. What matters is not what coaches teach but what players learn. Players do not all learn in the same way or at the same speed, and what is effective for one player may not be effective for all. For coaches, the challenge is to know how to teach players in a way that allows them to learn best. Communication, like learning itself, requires patience, open-mindedness, and a common goal (usually that of gaining knowledge). When these elements are present, coaches, players, and teams create the greatest opportunity to grow and succeed through learning.

One example of an effective communication tool can be found in a practice known as *echo calls*, in which players repeat a critical teaching or learning cue or other communication from a coach to ensure that all players learn. This audible communication creates an environment in which players interact with each other. Players learn more efficiently when they teach and communicate with each other, and players on the floor can never communicate too much.

In order to develop communication skills, focus on the following six key areas identified by Rainer Martens in his best-selling book *Successful Coaching* (1997):

1. Credibility

2. Positive approach

3. Information over emotion

4. Consistency

5. Listening skills

6. Nonverbal communication

Let's briefly examine each of these areas. First, credibility with players is based on respect. Each player should be allowed the opportunity to build self-respect and confidence during the basketball experience. In fact, developing self-respect while earning respect from others should be the norm for both players and coaches.

Second, communication between players and coaches should generally be positive—that is, emphasizing praise and rewards more than punishment and criticism. In short, coaches should tell players what *to do* rather than what *not* to do. For example, when teaching shooting, coaches might tell players to shoot up rather than telling them that the shot is too low. Coaches should also look for what players are doing right instead of focusing on what they are doing wrong; this approach is a challenge common to most coaching paradigms or individual styles.

Third, messages to players should be filled with factual information rather than emotional outbursts. Players need to know what to do correctly; they do not need to be yelled at for making mistakes. Positive emotion or praise tends to be more helpful, especially when players can gather needed information from it in order to learn skills or correct mistakes. Coaches can use negative emotion and punishment sparingly and only when the negative approach is the best or last alternative. For instance, the "feedback sandwich" described later offers an excellent way to provide necessary information. In addition, information is used best by players when it is specific. Thus the statement "Your head is centered" may be more effective for learning than "Great balance!" In short, reducing judgment and increasing information are good guidelines for coaches.

Fourth, coaches should practice consistency of communication. Players are looking for consistent messages and feedback, which provide them with a comfort zone for communication, whether verbal or nonverbal. Moreover, whenever possible, what coaches say should match what they do. Athletes are quick to sense hypocrisy, and they expect coaches to be honest and real. As Martens (1997, 31) states, "Be as good as your word."

The next area of communication development—listening—is one of the most challenging. Good listeners maintain eye contact, constantly search for meaning, exhibit respect for the communicator, and practice active listening. Coaches should focus on two-way communication in which players can interact and voice their concerns and questions. Players' acceptance of a mistake mentality is helpful for enhancing listening and reducing the fear, doubt, and worry that can accompany coaching communication. Finally, effective listening also depends on nonverbal communication in the form of positive body language, such as gestures, appropriate touching, and voice quality.

The primary measure of communication is not what coaches know but what players learn. In order to enhance learning, coaches must improve their own listening skills and those of their players. One of the most effective tools for improving communication in teaching-learning communities is the SLANT strategy, which is used in many educational settings. This approach rests on the foundation of body language that facilitates active learning.

As shown in figure 1, the SLANT strategy, as suggested by the acronym that provides its name, includes the following elements: sit up (or stand up), listen, ask questions, nod, and track the speaker. On the first level, *sit up or stand up* and lean into learning; in other words, be open to learning. On the second level, do not just hear but purposefully *listen* to sounds from coaches, teachers, and teammates. To invoke this level, we often use the phrase

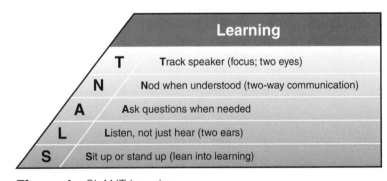

Figure 1 SLANT learning.
Adapted from E.S. Ellis, "A Metacognitive Intervention for Increasing Class Participation," *Learning Disabilities Focus* 5 no. 1 (1989): 36-46.

"Give me two ears." To ensure involvement, the player must also feel free to *ask questions*, thus developing an open attitude toward learning and following up when he or she does not understand what is being taught. The fourth level calls for the player to give feedback with a *nod* of the head when she understands and feels connected through two-way communication. Finally, the best learning tip is for the player to actively *track* the speaker (i.e., coach or teammate) with both eyes. By applying these SLANT techniques, student-players and teacher-coaches can enable more effective teaching and learning.

FEEDBACK

The learning process goes faster when appropriate feedback about skills is provided according to the following guidelines:

- **Feedback can best be provided by an experienced coach, but players also need to learn how to provide their own feedback whenever possible.** For example, a player can observe the starting point and landing spot of the feet before and after a jump shot, both of which are important factors in shooting with quickness and balance (the shooter should land slightly forward of the takeoff spot).

- **Players must be told what is correct (i.e., given reinforcement) and incorrect (i.e., given information about mistakes).** Mistakes should be known, acknowledged, and understood by players; then, a specific plan should be made for correcting those mistakes.

- **Correction of player errors should be consistent.** For players, the best learning approach to mistakes is to recognize them (with the coach's help), acknowledge them (to other players), learn from them, and then forget them.

- **Specific information is better than general feedback.** For instance, "Great full follow-through" is better than "Nice shot."

- **Provide feedback as soon as possible after performance.** Individual feedback can be given in this manner during practice by pulling a player aside. Players readily adapt to this coaching technique as a personal approach to learning that gives them necessary information; they are also motivated by the individual attention. This technique works well for both informational feedback about mistakes and reinforcement feedback for correct performance. One exception might be postgame situations, when emotions can run high for both coaches and players; in such cases, it may be more effective to provide feedback during the next meeting or practice.

- **Use "feedback sandwiches."** As recommended by Dennis Docheff, teaching expert from Central Missouri University, this type of feedback includes three parts: reinforcement (something done correctly), information (correction regarding a skill or behavior that needs improvement), and praise (encouragement). For example, you might say, "Jim, on your last shot, great follow-through at the elbow, but you need to get lower and have your feet wider for better balance. That's the way to keep working at game speed." Another way to conceive of this technique is provided by champion college coach Mike Dunlap of Loyola Marymount University:

  1. Praise—find a positive.
  2. Talk and tell—prompt, correct, and tell the player the next step. Talk and tell—prompt, correct, and tell the player the next step.
  3. Leave—give the player room and time to learn and absorb information.

Feedback helps players learn faster and retain skills better.

General Tips on Teaching and Learning

1. Coaching is teaching.
   - Know why you teach a skill; knowing helps both teacher and learner.
   - Focus on the skill first (not on the drill or strategy).
   - Focus on how well something is done rather than on what is done (execution over repetition; quality over quantity).
   - When teaching or coaching, preview first (tell what you are going to teach), then "view" (teach it), and then review (tell what you taught).
   - Help players remove emotional obstacles to learning: fear, doubt, and worry.

2. Demonstrate and explain as follows:
   - Make sure that all players can see and hear you.
   - Demonstrate, correctly, to show the big mental picture.
   - Repeat the demonstration; provide two angles, two repetitions, or more.

- Explain precisely and concisely (don't talk players to death).
- Use only critical cues (don't talk too much).
- Practice immediately—players learn by doing and may forget the demonstration and explanation unless they apply it right away.
- Emphasize repetitive practice to make behavior permanent (and beware: this process works for both good and bad habits).

3. Use teaching progressions.
   - Go from slow to fast. Do it right, then do it quickly (the final goal is game moves at game speed).
   - Go from simple to complex; for instance, often start with footwork, then go to the whole body.
   - Teach in sequence (from start to finish), then reverse it.

4. Both players and coaches need to remain open to learning; be green and growing, not ripe and rotten.
   - Adopt the whole skill or concept as a beginner or adapt one idea to improve if experienced.
   - Improve every day of the year (can't maintain—must progress).
   - Look for the lesson; there is always a lesson to learn (search for it).
   - Learn from others—both good and bad experiences offer lessons.
   - Communicate and encourage teammates (generally, coaches should criticize when necessary, whereas players praise and encourage each other).
   - Control what you can (all people have total control of their attitudes, actions, and responses) and let go of the rest.

5. Know how each player learns best.
   - Visually (seeing the skill)—reading about it or seeing a demonstration
   - Auditorily (hearing the skill)—getting more explanation or listening for sounds
   - Kinetically (feeling the skill)—walking through the skill

6. Use the following tools:
   - Word pictures (e.g., *footfire* for moving the feet)
   - Analogies and metaphors (e.g., *start quick like a sprinter*)
   - Critical cues (e.g., *full follow-through, freeze the follow-through*)

7. Teach fundamental skills and more:
   - Conditioning
   - Toughness and effort
   - Life and character lessons
   - Communication (early, loud, and often)
   - How to compete
   - Competitive greatness (Wooden's Pyramid of Success)

8. Become a full-package coach who helps players learn and develop in a well-rounded fashion.
   - Physically (conditioning and skill)
   - Mentally (psychologically)
   - Socially (teamwork)

9. Evaluate all that you do as a player or coach. One quick and effective evaluation tool—the one-minute assessment—can be used to gather information and feedback about what players are doing on and off the court. For instance, it can be used by coaches to evaluate a practice session, team strategy (offense or defense), or team rule. The tool consists of three parts: one quality, action, or performance that is praiseworthy (and why); one element that could be improved (and how); and relevant insights or comments. This simple format allows coaches to print the relevant questions on index cards or plain paper or distribute them electronically for use in a variety of settings.

One-Minute Assessment

a. What was *excellent* and *why?*

b. What could be *improved* and *how?*

c. Comments:

---

10. Coaches and players both need to know themselves, develop their own unique talents, and serve others—which is the ultimate personal lesson.

In order to develop an effective teaching–learning community, we must focus on the athletes and on their learning and improvement, both on and off the court. More specifically, in order to structure a strong development program built on a foundation of basketball fundamentals, a coach must develop a philosophy of teaching and learning and become a master teacher. The coach truly is the difference maker in any program—both as a leader and as a teacher.

Figure 2 depicts a step-by-step pathway to help coaches address critical areas in becoming a master teacher; this model has been developed over my lifetime of teaching and coaching. The essential elements for success are as follows.

1. Expectations: Set goals that are high but realistic.

2. Teaching–learning community: Build a community focused on student-athletes' learning.

3. Emphasis: Match teaching and learning with the time you spend through your words and actions. What you teach and spend time on in practice should reflect your coaching philosophy and emphasis.

4. Assessment: Provide measurements of status and progress for individual athletes, for the team, and for members of the coaching staff in all that you do.

5. Inspiration: Motivate all to become their best by living in spirit (i.e., your emotion should reflect your basic philosophy and intent).

6. Demand: Inspire and, as a final step, draw the leader's line in the sand—that is, hold everyone accountable.

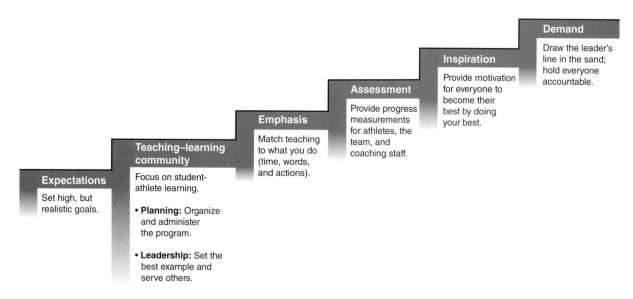

Figure 2 Becoming a master teacher.

This book provides considerable instruction and information. The potential for teaching and learning basketball skills depends on developing the skills to teach and learn effectively. To gain the most from the basketball skills and drills presented in this book, coaches and players can use the following guidelines:

- Develop a teaching-learning community.

- Make the game simple and easy to learn through diligent, purposeful practice of fundamental skills.

- Become a master teacher and learner to become the best you can be.

Wooden Wisdom

"It's what you learn after you know it all that counts."

—John Wooden

KEY TO DIAGRAMS

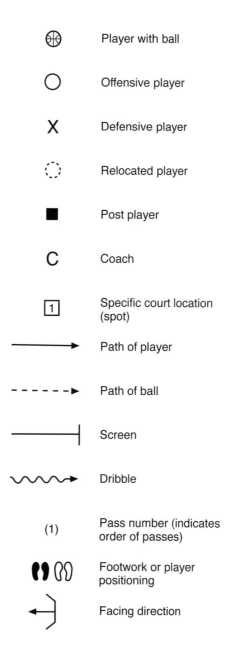

⊕ Player with ball

○ Offensive player

X Defensive player

⚬ Relocated player

■ Post player

C Coach

1 Specific court location (spot)

———▶ Path of player

- - - ▶ Path of ball

———| Screen

∿∿∿▶ Dribble

(1) Pass number (indicates order of passes)

👣 Footwork or player positioning

⤆ Facing direction

CHAPTER 1

BODY CONTROL AND FUNDAMENTAL FOOTWORK

"Footwork and balance are necessary every moment of a game, while ballhandling is needed less than 10 percent of the game."

Pete Newell, Naismith Hall of Fame coach and former head coach at University of California, Berkeley

One of the foremost tasks of a coach is to teach players how to move and control their bodies. Fundamental movements, sometimes referred to as *basketball basics*, are essential tools for all players. Coaches need to teach players to move both effectively (getting the job done) and efficiently (moving in the best way); they need to teach players to conserve time and space and to move with purpose, thus reducing wasted motion. In essence, basketball is a game of balance and quickness, and all movements should focus on these qualities. Players should strive to "tighten" their game, which means playing at top speed (being quick at the right time) while maintaining body control.

As a result, developing balance and quickness should be the overall focus for coaches and players at all levels. Balance hinges on footwork; it begins with the feet and ends with the head. Because of the human head's size (nearly 10 pounds, or 4.5 kilograms) and location on the body, it is crucial to balance, and it should be centered over the base of support. From there, the head moves in the desired direction to become unbalanced, thus committing the player to quick movement in that direction. Quickness is also related to the head and the feet, but in the opposite order. Quickness is first and foremost a state of mind (*think quick, then be quick*); thus it starts in the head and ends in the feet (it depends on footwork). Both balance and quickness, then, depend on proper footwork and relate closely to head position and state of mind.

Basketball requires quickness (of hand and foot) and speed (in overall body motion) to be used at the proper time. Therefore, coaching should continually emphasize the principle of doing things right, then quickly—making the right move quickly at the right time—while developing and maintaining individual, physical, emotional, and team balance and correct offensive and defensive position. Here again, we see that basketball is a game of balance and quickness. This idea can also be applied to learning for all skills—first do the skill properly (slowly), then do it quickly (progress toward game moves at game speed).

The six fundamental positions and movements of basketball are stance, starts, steps, turns, stops, and jumps. Because quickness is so important, these basic positions are all designated by the author with the word *quick*.

QUICK STANCE

Players need to develop the habit of assuming a good basic basketball position in order to ready themselves for quick movements. Quick stance requires adequate levels of muscle strength and endurance in the core area (abdominal muscles in front, lower-back muscles behind). Teaching quick stance on offense and defense is a challenging task, and patience is essential with younger players who may not have the strength and muscle endurance to stay in this position very long. The most important part of a quick stance is to achieve and maintain bent-knee and bent-elbow positions. All joints should be flexed and ready so that the game is played low to the floor. The lower players get, the higher they can jump, the more explosive their moves to the basket are, the quicker they are on defense, and the better they can protect the ball. Thus *play low and stay low* is a critical concept for all players.

Coaches should also teach players the *feeling* of quick stance—being ready for anything and feeling quick. Maintaining this basic position requires hard work because players must become comfortable in an awkward, unnatural, monkey-like position. Players should sit into the stance—get low—and stay in it. Consistent and early emphasis on quick stance teaches athletes to assume it automatically. Quickness is a combination of thinking quick, feeling quick, and becoming quick by improving one's skills. A good test for quick stance is to imagine sitting in a chair with the head positioned behind the knees, as shown in figure 1.1.

Foot Position

The best foot placement in most situations is that of a slightly staggered stance with the toes pointing slightly outward, not straight ahead. The feet should be about shoulder-width apart, with the instep of the front foot along the same horizontal line as the big toe of the other foot (see figure 1.2). Players should use this position when they need to move in any direction. To get into this foot position, players should put the feet together, move the preferred foot forward until the big toe of the back foot is next to the instep of the forward foot, and then step sideways with the preferred foot until the feet are about shoulder-width apart for balance and quickness.

The parallel stance shown in figure 1.3 is best used for side-to-side movement, as well as for catching the ball and stopping, stopping after dribbling, and responding defensively when a defender moves laterally. It is also important to use for shooting because it produces the body mechanics best suited to ensure that the shot goes straight and deep into the basket. In time, players will become equally adept at using either stance when needed.

Figure 1.1 Quick-stance test: Sit into the stance (side view).

CRITICAL CUE
Quick stance: Stagger the stance with the toes pointed slightly outward.

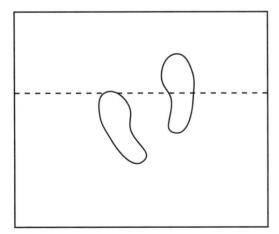

Figure 1.2 Staggered stance (top view), based on instep-and-toe relationship with the feet shoulder-width apart and the back foot toed slightly outward. The figure shows offensive quick stance (right-handed player).

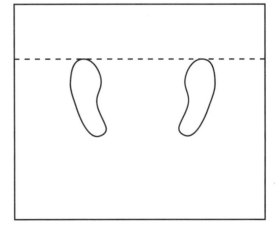

Figure 1.3 Parallel stance (top view), based on a toe-to-toe relationship with the feet shoulder-width apart and the toes pointed slightly outward.

Weight Distribution

Body weight should be evenly distributed from side to side, from front to back, and between the feet. The heels should be down, with most of the weight (60 percent) on the balls of the feet, although pressure should also be felt on the toes and heels. The toes should be curled and the heels kept down on the floor.

Players may incorrectly place all of their weight on the balls of the feet with the heels off the floor; this position is slower because the heel has to be brought down before forceful movement can be made. A good way to teach the feeling of proper position is to ask players to take an "eagle-claw" position, with the heels down and the toes curled (flexed), so that they can feel the floor with their toes.

When players are on defense, they should add "footfire" to their basic quick-stance position. Footfire involves keeping the feet active and in constant motion without having them leave the floor by alternately lifting the weight off each foot slightly while keeping the whole foot in contact with the floor—a technique that helps keep the leg muscles stretched and ready for action and thus enables a defender to be quicker. Players can imagine that they are standing on a bed of hot coals, using an alternating foot motion without letting their feet leave the floor. The weight must be on the whole foot for either offensive or defensive quick stance.

Head and Trunk Position

For proper balance, players should keep the head centered over the support base—at the apex of a triangle, with the legs as two equal sides and a line between the feet as the base when viewed from the front (figure 1.4). They should also center the head from front to back, assuming an erect trunk position, with the shoulders back and the trunk slightly forward of vertical. The back is straight, the chest is out, and the head is slightly behind the knees. Players should sit into this stance.

Figure 1.4   Offensive quick stance (triple-threat position): *(a)* Front view—the head, the key to balance, is carried up and alert at the apex of the triangle. *(b)* Side view—sit into the stance with the back straight, the chest out, and the head up. *(c)* Pit and protect the ball.

Arms and Legs

Teach players to keep their joints (ankles, knees, hips, shoulders, elbows, and wrists) bent and ready. Coach John Wooden suggested that all joints should be bent for quickness. Players on offense can tighten their game by bending the joints and keeping the ball close to the body—that is, pitting and protecting the ball in or near the shooting pocket. The shooting hand is behind the ball, and the offensive player is in triple-threat position, ready to shoot, pass, or drive quickly. Defensive players can also tighten their game (i.e., their movements) by bending the joints, keeping the arms close to the body (with elbows bent), and adding footfire to their footwork (figure 1.5). Keeping the hands and arms bent and close to the body enables balance and quickness. The entire sole of each foot should be touching or close to the floor. Coaches should remind players to stay low; in order to maintain the low center of gravity needed for quickness and balance, the angle at the knee joint in back of the legs should be 90 to 120 degrees.

Figure 1.5 Defensive quick stance with joints bent: *(a)* front view, *(b)* side view.

COACHING POINTS FOR QUICK STANCE

- Be ready for action: feet ready, hands ready.
- Keep all joints bent.
- Play low and stay low; sit into the game.
- Get in and stay in a quick stance.
- Keep the head up, the chest out, and the back straight.
- Keep body weight on the whole foot with the heels down (eagle-claw position).
- On defense, keep feet moving (footfire).

QUICK STARTS, STEPS, TURNS, AND STOPS

Starting, stepping, turning (pivoting), and stopping are the fundamental motions used in moving effectively and efficiently in and out of quick stance for both offensive and defensive purposes. Players should be taught to execute a skill correctly, quickly, and at the right time every time. To do so, they need to go slow, get a feel for executing the skill properly, find a rhythm, and then speed up progressively until they make a mistake. At that point, they learn from the mistake and then keep moving toward developing game moves at game speed.

A player's overall speed—that is, ability to move the body from point A to point B—is important in basketball, but it is not as critical as quickness, or hand and foot speed. Therefore, coaches should strive to improve the quickness of each player. Thinking quick and being quick should be the constant focus for both players and coaches.

Quick Starts

Starting is the first skill that players must learn using quick stance. To start quickly, players shift body weight (and the head) in the desired direction of movement. For example, to move to the left, body weight is shifted over the left foot by leaning to the left. The weight shift is always led by the head, which is critical to balance (see figure 1.6).

To be quick at the right time, players must remember that all motion change begins on the floor. This means taking short, choppy steps whenever a change of motion or quick start is needed. Players should keep their feet in contact with the floor as much as possible and use the floor to their advantage by staying close to it.

Front (Lead) Foot First From basic (quick stance) position, players should shift weight in the direction of the intended movement and take the first step with the foot nearest to that direction. This movement is shown in figure 1.6, in which the left foot is the lead foot after moving to the left. Likewise, to move to the right, take the first step with the right foot. To move forward, take the first step with the front foot (push from the back foot and step with the lead foot). This lead foot technique is used most often when a player needs to focus on quick movement on offense or defense.

Sometimes, it is quicker on defense to step across with the trail (back) foot first and run or sprint in the desired direction of movement, particularly when a defensive player is beaten by the opponent and must run to recover. This technique (stepping across with trail foot to lead with the back foot) can also be used on offense for moving with the ball (i.e., making a live-ball move) when the ball handler uses a jab step with the front foot (i.e., a shot fake) and a crossover step (break) with the lead foot.

Figure 1.6 Moving laterally to the left: Move body weight toward the desired direction of movement (i.e., over the left foot).

Defensive Quick Start and Steps On defense, players should more often use a sliding motion. Specifically, they should keep the feet shoulder-width apart and use short, quick shuffle steps that allow the head to remain level. This technique is called the *push step* or *step-and-slide* (stepping with the lead foot, sliding with the rear foot). The lead foot moves in the desired direction from the force of the trail foot at the same time that a short, quick push step (lead foot first) is taken (figure 1.6). The force for the push step comes from a power push from the trail foot, which moves the body and transfers the weight to the lead foot. It is quickly followed by a pulling slide step taken with the trail foot to regain basic position without bringing the feet together. Players should keep their feet wide at all times. The lead step and the pull and slide steps are short (1 to 2 feet, or 0.3 to 0.6 meters), and the stance is low and wide: *Step and slide, low and wide; can't get too low, can't get too wide.*

Players should learn to execute defensive starts and slides in side-to-side, forward, backward, and diagonal directions (figure 1.7)—all while keeping the head level. Head bounce shows that a player is rising out of the stance instead of using a push step or slide step. Such a bounce, known as a *bunny hop*, brings the feet together in the air, thus losing the advantage of floor contact for producing motion change, wasting time and space, and reducing quickness of motion. The head must be kept level. Players can imagine a steel plate above the head during all push-step motions to help them stay down in defensive quick stance, which produces low and level motion in which the head remains in a horizontal plane.

One exception to the step-and-slide footwork technique for defense occurs when a defender on the dribbler cannot stay in proper position ahead of the dribbler. When this happens, the defender guarding the dribbler should turn to face the direction of the sliding movement, sprint ahead of the dribbler in correct ball–defender–basket position, then return to basic stance and the step-slide technique. This method, also referred to as *run-to-recover*, is preferred by some coaches as their basic defensive movement to cover change-of-direction dribble moves. Consequently, they teach run-to-recover instead of step-and-slide.

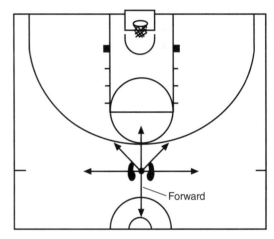

Figure 1.7 Defensive directions for starts and steps.

Offensive Quick Start (Permanent Pivot Foot) On offense, players with a live ball (i.e., who still can dribble) can execute a quick start from triple-threat position using the lead foot first. On live-ball moves, offensive players should establish a permanent pivot foot (PPF; left foot for right-handed players, right foot for lefties) and a permanent stepping foot for use either in dribble-driving past a defender or when the ball is held. Using the PPF, a player can do a quick start with the stepping foot (front foot first). These live-ball moves can be either direct drives (to the strong or preferred side) or crossover drives (to the nonpreferred side); these two types of moves are shown in figures 1.8 and 1.9, respectively.

The primary advantage of PPF footwork in live-ball situations is that it is simpler and easier for younger players to learn with the ball in triple-threat position. Also, using the PPF direct drive and crossover drive to get past a defender on the dribble relies on the safest driving footwork on the crossover drive (by protecting the ball from the defender with the crossover leg), which requires dribbling with the nonpreferred hand (figure 1.9). The PPF direct-drive move uses a direct step forward with the lead foot (figure 1.8). In contrast, when executing the PPF footwork on the crossover drive, the offensive player must move the ball across to the opposite side of the body (from pit to pit) while also making the crossover step to the nonpreferred side of the body in order to dribble-drive past the defender (figure 1.9). Either way, PPF provides a simple, quick method for attacking the front foot of the defender.

Figure 1.8 Live-ball move—direct drive (PPF footwork): *(a)* offensive quick stance (triple-threat position), *(b)* first step—long and low.

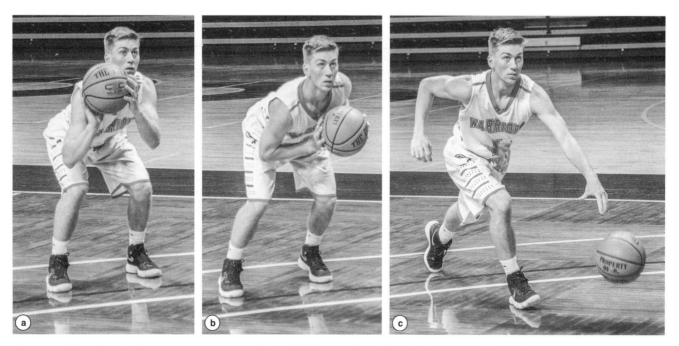

Figure 1.9 Live-ball move—crossover drive (PPF footwork): *(a)* triple-threat position, *(b)* circle-tight with ball (pit to pit), *(c)* long and low crossover step.

Figure 1.10   PPF direct drive: *(a)* win the battle, and *(b)* win the war.

The advantages and disadvantages of PPF technique are shown in figures 1.10 and 1.11 and summarized in the following list.

• **Direct drive:** Quick-step forward to "win the battle" of the first step; get the foot by on the side of the defender's front foot (preferred). As shown in figure 1.10, this technique allows the driver to win the battle but *not* the war (establishing inside hip protection of the ball). For beginning players, however, this disadvantage of less ball protection is offset by the more comfortable advantage of using the preferred stepping foot and the preferred dribbling hand.

• **Crossover drive:** A quick crossover step to the nonpreferred side of the ball handler allows him or her to attack the defender's front foot (figure 1.11). Even though the nonpreferred driving side is not as comfortable, the crossover driver uses the recommended footwork to get the nonpreferred foot past or to the side of the defender's front foot, thus winning both the battle of the first step and the war of inside hip contact and ball protection on the first dribble by the front foot.

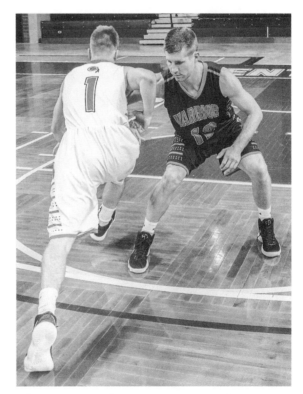

Figure 1.11   PPF crossover drive (*win the battle and the war*).

CRITICAL CUE
Live-ball moves: Attack the front foot.

COACHING POINTS FOR LIVE-BALL MOVES (PPF)

- Start from offensive quick stance or triple-threat position.
- PPF direct drive: Go long and low on the first step past the defender by using the front foot and straight-line movement. The driver must *win the battle* on the first step—getting the head and shoulders past the defender—and then *win the war* on the second step with hip contact on the defender to prevent recovery of the defensive position.
- PPF crossover drive: Circle tight from pit to pit (armpit to armpit in front of the body) while changing hands behind the ball without a foot fake. Step long and low, with the stepping foot in a straight line, and drive past the opposite side of the defender, all in the first step. The PPF crossover drive more easily allows the driver to *win the battle and the war* through inside hip contact and ball protection on the first step.

COACHING POINTS FOR QUICK STARTS

- Be ready to start by getting into and maintaining a quick stance.
- Using the floor works to your advantage—keep the feet on the floor when starting.
- Shift body weight in the desired direction and lead with the head.
- Stay down and pump the arms when starting (arms lead the action).
- Use the principle of front (lead) foot first.
- On direct or crossover drives with the ball, use a long and low first step to move in a straight line toward the basket and by the defender. Reduce lateral motion.
- For defensive slides, use the push-step technique. Slide, don't hop, and keep the feet wide. *Step and slide, low and wide*: push (from trail foot), step (with lead foot), and slide (with trail foot to quick stance) unless using run-to-recover movement to regain correct defensive position.
- Start and move in straight lines when possible.

Quick Steps

Quick steps are the basic motion changes that allow players to use speed and quickness to complete plays and execute offensive and defensive strategies. They consist of changes in speed or pace and in direction (usually at 90 or 180 degrees to the original motion direction). Quick steps are usually slow-to-quick moves that use quickness at the right time.

Change of Pace and Change of Direction Change-of-pace steps, including running or sliding at different speeds, are important skills of body control designed to apply the concept of quickness at the right time. For example, an offensive player might be running or dribbling at a moderate speed and then use a burst of speed to get past a defender. Likewise, a defender could be sliding along and then accelerate quickly to establish a legal position in the path of an offensive player in order to disrupt movement or take the charge.

Change-of-direction steps are also designed to apply quickness at the right time. For instance, when players are running down the floor on offense and then need to change to defense, they can use a stride stop, change direction by 180 degrees (i.e., make a 180-degree cut), and sprint quickly back in the opposite direction. Another change-of-direction step is the V-cut, which is a sharp side movement performed by going into the cut slowly, changing direction at a sharp angle, and accelerating quickly out of the cut. V-cuts are also called *L-cuts*, *7-cuts*, and *fake-and-break* moves, depending on the angle of change and on how they are used. They can be used on either offense or defense.

CRITICAL CUE
Change-of-pace steps require changes of speed, especially slow-to-quick moves.

Live-Ball Moves (PPF) A player with the ball who hasn't dribbled can execute quick steps called live-ball moves: direct drives (to the preferred or dominant side; figure 1.10) and crossover drives (to the nonpreferred or nondominant side; figure 1.11) (see chapter 5 for a full description). From a quick stance, live-ball moves allow the player with the ball to move quickly past the defender on the dribble drive. This is a straight-line move to the basket to penetrate the defensive perimeter with the use of a long, low, quick first step. By rule, the player with the ball needs to get the head and shoulders past the defender's trunk in order to gain an advantage legally on the quick first step. The driver then tries to get near-hip contact with the defender in order to maintain the positional advantage while moving past the defender to penetrate the defense and force another defender to help, thus creating an advantageous 2-on-1 for the offense. Note that PPF technique requires two steps to use the inside hip with a direct drive (i.e., strong-side dribble) but only one step to get inside hip contact with a weak-side dribble.

Offensive Quick-Start Live-Ball Moves (Either Pivot Foot) This footwork alternative is recommended for advanced players and coaches who prefer the approach of using either pivot foot (EPF). It offers the advantage of using a protection (or inside) foot as the primary stepping foot to move past the defender guarding the ball. The recommended footwork for EPF moves begins with a more parallel stance (figure 1.12), which is conducive to attacking either side of the defender with a preferred crossover move. The critical cue for the live-ball offensive player is to attack the front or forward foot of the defender, and this goal can be accomplished by using a jab step forward and toward the defender's back foot. If there is no defensive response, drive past the front foot with a crossover move while protecting the first dribble with the stepping leg and getting the head and shoulders by the defender in order to dribble-drive to the basket (figures 1.13 and 1.14). This move allows strong ball protection by the crossover leg to "win the battle and the war" by using EPF techniques to either the left or the right.

Figure 1.12 Triple-threat starting stance and footwork.

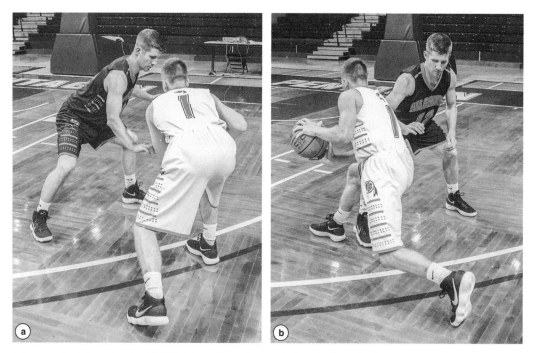

Figure 1.13 Live-ball EPF drive. Attack the defender's right front foot: *(a)* jab right, and *(b)* cross over to the left to drive.

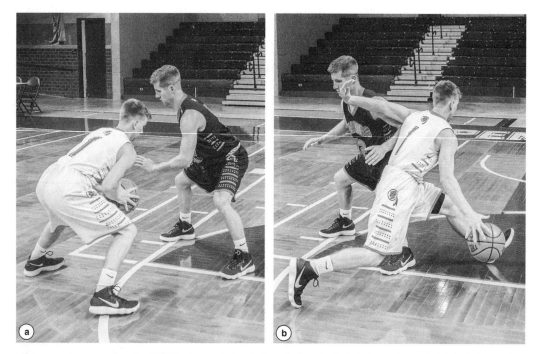

Figure 1.14 Live-ball EPF drive. Attack the defender's left front foot: *(a)* jab left, and *(b)* cross over to the right to drive.

Quick Turns and Pivots

Turning, or pivoting, rotates the body in a circular fashion around the ball of one foot while the player maintains basic position, or quick stance (figure 1.15). Sixty percent of body weight should be on the ball of the pivot foot as the heel of the turning foot is lifted slightly to pivot on the ball of the foot. Players on offense should use a PPF and a permanent stepping foot, especially when they have the ball as beginners.

As the basic skill used for initiating all changes in motion, the pivot, or turn, is one of the most important tools for quickness and balance. It is also one of the least-used and most poorly learned skills in basketball. Pivoting can be done with either foot serving as the stationary center of rotation, but a PPF is recommended for beginners with the ball. When the body is rotated toward the front—a pivoting motion that moves the trunk forward around the pivot—the pivot is a front turn (see figure 1.16). Similarly, a rear turn is used to pivot a player's backside to the rear (figure 1.17).

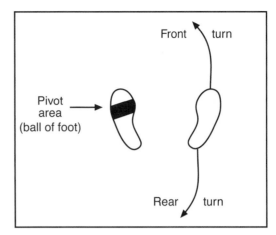

Figure 1.15 Pivot or turn: Rotate the body around the ball of the turning foot (lift the heel of the turning foot and put more weight on that foot).

Players on offense must learn to make pivots both with and without the ball. For instance, when a player with the ball is closely guarded but wants to face the basket, a rear turn on the nondominant foot (as the PPF) is usually used to clear space, though some coaches prefer a front turn. On defense, players use the pivot as the first move when changing from one position to another and when rebounding, as shown in figure 1.18; this move is sometimes called a *swing step*.

Figure 1.16 Right-foot pivot—front turn: *(a)* starting position, *(b)* ending position.

Figure 1.17 Left-foot pivot—rear turn: *(a)* starting position, *(b)* ending position.

COACHING POINTS FOR QUICK TURNS

- Stay down in basic stance and keep the head level and low for quickness.
- Lead with the elbow of the stepping foot (for a rear turn) or punch into the turn with the fist (for a front turn).
- Keep the feet shoulder-width apart for balance.
- Maintain balance and keep the head up.
- Pivot quickly but properly.
- Use the pivot to go as far as half a turn (180 degrees); use repeat pivots as necessary.
- Use a rear turn to face the basket when closely guarded (to clear space).
- With the ball, use a front or rear turn to face the basket.
- When catching the ball, face the basket with a front or rear turn while using big vision before dribbling (*pass first, dribble last*).

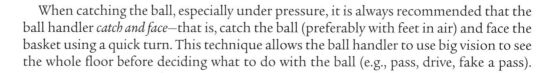

When catching the ball, especially under pressure, it is always recommended that the ball handler *catch and face*—that is, catch the ball (preferably with feet in air) and face the basket using a quick turn. This technique allows the ball handler to use big vision to see the whole floor before deciding what to do with the ball (e.g., pass, drive, fake a pass).

When in shooting range, the ball handler can quickly use small vision to focus on the shot target (i.e., back of the rim or upper corner of the backboard) and shoot the ball. When catching and facing the basket, players should follow the rim–post-action (RPA) vision progression:

R: Use big and then small vision to see the *rim*.

P: Use big and then small vision to look inside for a teammate *posting* up or cutting to the basket.

A: Use big vision and respond to what is seen by taking appropriate *action*— shooting, driving, or passing.

Players should learn this progression and follow it quickly and automatically when catching the ball anywhere except the low post (with the back to the basket).

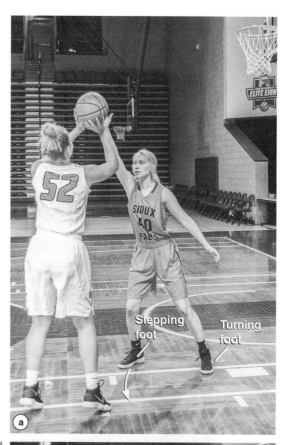

Figure 1.18 Defensive rebounding: *(a)* front turn, *(b)* rear turn, *(c)* blockout contact.

Quick Stops

To be quick with balance and control, players must be able to use quick stance, start properly and quickly, move quickly (by stepping, running, turning, or sliding), and stop quickly in a balanced position. The two recommended basic basketball stops are the one-count quick stop and the two-count stride stop.

Quick Stop The preferred stop for most situations—the quick stop—is executed at the end of a running or sliding motion. It should not be called a *jump stop* (jumping results in slower stops and too much air time). When running, a player does a quick stop by hopping slightly from one foot, skimming the floor surface, landing in a parallel or slightly staggered stance (basic position, or quick stance; figure 1.19), and sticking the landing with *soft feet*. Both feet hit the floor at the same time in a one-count motion: Hop from and skim the floor with one foot and land on two feet simultaneously.

The quick stop conserves time and space and can be used on either defense or offense (and with or without the ball); it complements the quick turn, which is one of the primary tools of body control and movement. Basketball rules allow a player with the ball to use either foot for pivoting after a quick stop. This freedom gives players a wide variety of motion possibilities with control and balance and prevents them from traveling with the ball if the incorrect foot is chosen as the turning foot. For instance, the quick stop is important for getting players into a quick stance for shooting, passing, or dribbling when receiving a pass. The critical cue on the quick-stop landing is to stick the stop (similar to a gymnastics dismount) with soft feet, which means landing on the whole foot while stopping firmly but softly in a balanced position.

Stride Stop The stride stop, shown in figure 1.20, is a two-count stop executed by landing on the rear foot (first count) with the front foot hitting immediately afterward (second count). Its primary use is to reverse direction when players are running forward (and in certain other situations, for advanced players). For all other motion situations, players should use the quick stop. When using the stride stop, players should keep the body weight back and sit on the rear foot.

Figure 1.19 Quick stop: (a) Hop from one foot (left or right) and (b) land softly on two feet.

Figure 1.20 Stride stop: *(a)* back-foot plant to pivot (staying low to slow down) and *(b)* shooting (planting and pivoting or using a step-plant move).

COACHING POINTS FOR QUICK STOPS AND STRIDE STOPS

- Use the quick stop unless changing direction (180 degrees) when running; in that case, use the stride stop.
- On a quick stop, stick the landing with soft feet (land on the whole foot).
- On a quick stop, hop from one foot and land in quick stance on two feet at once (one count). Stay close to the floor.
- On a stride stop, stay low and sit on the back foot. The rear foot (which hits first) must be used as the pivot foot when the player turns with the ball after using a stride stop.
- In most cases, players should use the quick-stop technique even though some coaches prefer the stride stop for outside shooting, in which case it is called the *plant-and-pivot* (planting the back foot and pivoting into the shot with the stepping foot) or the *step-plant jump shot*.

QUICK JUMPS

Jumping is an especially important skill in a sport that uses an elevated goal. Coaches often consider jumping a natural ability that cannot be taught and that players either do or do not have. Nothing could be further from the truth.

The basic principles for improving jumping skill include being in quick stance and ready to jump in order to jump quickly in any situation. In addition, players can jump higher if they increase the muscle strength in their legs. Therefore, coaches should help players improve leg strength through resistance training as well as improve the jumping skill.

How players land after a jump determines how quick and how high the next immediate jump will be. It is best to land in quick stance with balance and a wide base, which readies the player to jump again with balance and quickness. Body position and control are best taught when players have first learned to jump using both feet and both arms. The sections that follow explain how to execute two-foot power jumps, quick jumps, and one-foot jumps; they also address when to use each type of jump in game situations.

Two-Foot Power Jumps

A two-foot takeoff for jumping is slower but more stable than jumping from one foot on the move. As a slow but strong explosive move from a balanced position, it is best used in high-traffic situations (such as battling for a rebound) or on power layups with close defenders.

In the jumping position for power jumps (figure 1.21a), the arms are ready to be swung forcefully forward and up. The feet should be planted firmly before the jump (players should visualize stamping their feet through the floor) to enable maximum contraction of

Figure 1.21 Power jump for 2-and-2 rebounding: *(a)* preparation; *(b)* two hands, two feet (tall and small); and *(c)* landing on two feet (big and wide)

the leg muscles. It is even better to quick-stop into the jump. In fact, whenever possible (i.e., whenever time and space permit), players should use the forward momentum of a running jump with forceful quick-stop contact on the takeoff and swing the arms forcefully upward to add to the body's momentum.

Two-foot power jumps are almost always required for successful rebounding. The players who are best at rebounding do so from two feet with two hands, which is called *2-and-2 rebounding*. The critical cue for this technique is combined with another critical cue for teaching proper technique: "go up tall and small" (i.e., with two hands fully extended toward the ball) and "come down big and wide" (doing a quick stop on two feet). See figure 1.21*b* and 1.21*c*.

Quick Jumps

Quick jumps are the best compromise between conserving time and space and maintaining body position and control. A quick jump should be used wherever there is congestion, contact, or a contested jump around the basketball. For instance, repeated jumps in rebounding are usually quick jumps. Before performing a quick jump, the player should hold the hands near shoulder height, the upper arms nearly horizontal, and the forearms vertical. Figures 1.22 and 1.23 show two-foot jumps that use two hands (i.e., 2-and-2 jumps) and start without momentum from a quick stance.

In addition to rebounding using the quick-jump technique, John Wooden emphasized one basic rule for both offensive and defensive rebounding: Get the hands up (at least to shoulder height) to be ready to rebound.

The critical cue for successive quick jumps is a *circle-tight move* to add arm momentum to the quick jump. From the ready position (figure 1.22*a*), the hands are circled slightly down, inside, and up (figure 1.22*b*) to the "tall and small" jumping position.

Figure 1.22 Quick jumps: *(a)* hands up, *(b)* inside circle move with the hands for momentum.

Figure 1.23 Quick-jump rebounding: *(a)* blockout with hands up, *(b)* 2-and-2 rebounding to pursue the ball, *(c)* capture and protect the ball, and *(d)* pivot to turn away from pressure.

One-Foot Jumps

Jumping from one foot is beneficial when a player needs maximum forward momentum to produce higher vertical jumping movement and maximum height. Players should know how to use one-foot takeoffs in order to attack the basket on layups and jump high toward the basket or backboard (jumping high, not long). One-foot jumps involve opposition, stamping hard on the jumping foot and raising the opposite foot or knee; for a high jump, stamping the jumping foot and using the opposite leg drive to produce a vertical rather than a horizontal or long jump. The shooting hand and knee are connected as though on a string; both of them come up together. The ball is brought up with two hands, and the finish or shot is performed with one hand (usually).

COACHING POINTS FOR JUMPS

- Get in quick stance to be ready to jump, then land in quick stance for best rebounding in contested and congested situations.
- For power jumps and quick jumps, jump from two feet with two hands (i.e., use 2-and-2 jumps) most of the time, especially when rebounding.
- Whenever possible, use quick jumps with a tight circle-hand movement for repeated jumping efforts.
- For power, balance, and control, use a two-foot takeoff (2-and-2 rebounding); for speed and height, use a one-foot takeoff (layups).
- Whenever time allows, maximize power jumps by using momentum transfer from running forward and swinging the arms upward.
- When taking a jump shot, use a quick stop and a quick jump.
- For maximum height and quickness, use a one-foot opposition jump.

TROUBLESHOOTING

Most problems in learning and teaching basic body-control moves relate to balance and quickness—that is, unbalanced moves executed too quickly. Therefore, in the beginning, players should slowly imitate the demonstration (focusing on doing it right) and get the feel of the move (get a rhythm). Then they can increase quickness until they make mistakes. Players should note and acknowledge mistakes, correct them, learn from them, and then forget them (i.e., develop a *mistake mentality*). This process is the best way to learn basketball skills, and it must be taught and retaught until it becomes automatic.

BASIC BODY-CONTROL DRILLS

These drills can be used to develop and maintain the basic athletic stance for basketball—the quick stance—and to teach players to move and stop quickly during basketball play. The idea is to move with balance and quickness while maintaining control. Achieving the goal of performing game moves at game speed always requires proper skill development.

QUICK-STANCE CHECK

Purpose: To develop the skills of recognizing various basic stances, getting into a basic stance quickly, and maintaining that stance

Equipment: Half-court floor space (minimum)

Procedure: Players spread out on the court facing the coach, assume a basic stance variation as directed (offensive or defensive quick stance on the *ready* command), and maintain the stance while it is checked by a coach or learning partner. Players need to respond quickly to the command, know the look of a quick stance, and know how to get in and stay in the stance. When learning partners are used, they should focus on *one* critical cue each time the stance is assumed.

Coaching Points

- Sit into the stance with the head behind the knees.
- Keep body weight on the whole foot with the toes pointed slightly outward.
- Keep the butt down, the chest out, the back straight, and the arms ready.
- When using defensive quick stance, add footfire.
- When using offensive quick stance, pit and protect the ball (or imaginary ball) while keeping the hands (and ball) close to the trunk.

QUICK-STANCE MIRROR

Purpose: To self-evaluate variations in stance by recognizing the look of a correct stance

Equipment: Player and a full-length mirror or a partner

Procedure: Each player checks all stance variations in front of a mirror or with a learning partner. Each basic stance is held for at least five seconds and evaluated from both a front and side view. If a mirror is not available, a partner system can be used.

Coaching Points

- Match what you think you are doing with what you are actually doing.
- Sit into the stance with the head behind the knees.
- Keep body weight on the whole foot with the toes pointed slightly outward.
- Keep the butt down, the chest out, and the back straight.
- When using defensive quick stance, add footfire.
- When using offensive quick stance, pit and protect the ball (or imaginary ball).

MASS QUICK MOVES ▶

Purpose: To develop the skills of recognizing various basic stances, getting into a basic stance quickly, and maintaining that stance

Equipment: Half-court floor space (minimum)

Procedure: Players spread out on the court facing the coach, assume a basic stance variation as directed (offensive or defensive quick stance on the *ready* command), and maintain the stance while it is checked by a coach or partner. Players need to respond quickly to the command by getting into a quick stance. The coach should evaluate each player's ability to get into a quick stance by implementing the quick-stance critical cues: weight on whole foot, leg and arm joints bent, head up and centered over base, back straight, and chest out. To check the look of the stance and test balance, the coach can push on a player's shoulder area (push forward, back, right, and left). The coach can evaluate the stance by *look* and *sound* (e.g., the quick stop) while the player focuses on the *feel* of the stance. This approach can help players develop more awareness of the skill.

Players can be directed by specific commands to carry out the basic quick moves.

1. **Live-ball PPF direct and crossover moves:** ready, direct drive with long and low step, move, crossover drive with long and low step, move (see figures 1.8 and 1.9 earlier in this chapter)

   Coaching Points for Live-Ball PPF Direct and Crossover Moves

   - Start from triple-threat position.
   - Focus on quickness and balance with economy of motion.
   - Step long and low past the imaginary defender.
   - Use a straight-line attack (to the basket or toward the coach) and make contact with the imaginary defender.
   - Use the following commands:
     - Direct drive, long and low, go
     - Crossover drive, circle tight (ball), long and low, go

2. **Live-ball EPF drives to left and right:** jab step and opposite-side crossover moves (see figures 1.13 and 1.14 earlier in this chapter)

   Coaching Points for Live-Ball EPF Drives to Left and Right

   - Start from a quick-stop triple-threat position while catching a pass (from self or a passer). Catch the ball with the feet in the air, land with parallel stance at a spot 15 to 18 feet (4.6 to 5.5 meters) from the basket or at three-point field-goal distance, and use RPA vision progression.
   - Focus on quickness and balance.
   - Jab-step and recover to shoot or use a crossover live-ball move to the opposite side (offensive player is limited to one or two dribbles).
   - Complete the play with a jump shot after a jab step or one dribble or with a basket-completion move after one or two dribbles. A step-back move requires at least two dribbles.

3. **Quick jumps (three consecutive jumps) and power jumps:** quick-jump position, jump; power-jumping position, jump (see figures 1.21, 1.22, and 1.23 earlier in this chapter). For power jumps, add an imaginary ball and 2-and-2 rebounding. Go up tall and small and come down big and wide. This drill can also be done with a partner toss-up to simulate a rebound or a toss against the wall or backboard.

   Coaching Points for Quick Jumps and Power Jumps

   - Circle tight with the hands for quick jumps (keep the arms up and the elbows at right angles).
   - Jump quickly with a pop; land ready to repeat for quick jumps.

- Coil and gather with the arms low; the arm explosion triggers the leg explosion for power jumps.
- Commands: quick jump or power jump position, jump.

4. **Quick stops:** Step right (with right foot) and low-hop into a quick stop (command is *move*); step left (with left foot) into a quick stop (command is *move*); see figure 1.19 earlier in this chapter.

Coaching Points for Quick Stops

- Stick the landing with soft feet (*stick the stop*).
- Land on a one-count (both feet at the same time).
- Land in a balanced quick stance.
- Commands: right-foot step, move; left-foot step, move.
- Add half turns (front, rear) and increase the pace of turns until mistakes are made.

5. **Quick turns:** ready, front turn, move; ready, rear turn, move. See figures 1.16 and 1.17 earlier in this chapter.

Coaching Points for Quick Turns

- Front turn: Lead with a punch.
- Rear turn: Lead with an elbow.
- Stay low and keep the head level.
- Commands (PPF or EPF footwork): front turn, move; rear turn, move.

LINE DRILL: QUICK STARTS, STEPS, TURNS, AND STOPS

Purpose: To develop skill in starting, stepping, turning, and stopping

Equipment: Full court (preferred) or half court

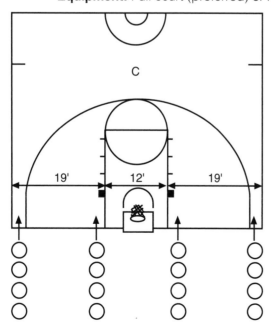

Figure 1.24 Line drill: starts, steps, turns, and stops.

Procedure: Players are divided into four groups behind the baseline at one end of the court with the coach in the middle of the court (figure 1.24). The groups are spaced 15 to 18 feet (4.6 to 5.5 meters) apart from each other from side to side along the baseline. The coach calls out options for players to perform. Coaches teach offensive spacing and timing concepts before and during the drill using the 12-by-19-foot (3.7-by-5 8-meter) free-throw lane as a reference. Coaches start the first four players (first player from each line) together; for optimal spacing, the next four players start when the players ahead have moved 15 to 18 feet up the court.

Options

- All players use a quick-start technique from a quick stance. When players step on the court, they should be ready and in a quick stance. They can use PPF or EPF footwork.

- Stutter steps: Players start from the baseline and go to the half-court line opposite end line, keeping the hands up and making the shoes squeak. Instruct players to use the floor to their advantage by taking short, choppy steps.

- Change-of-pace moves: Players alternate two or three slow and fast moves after a quick start. They should be quick and use a varied number of steps (avoid following the same pattern).

- Quick stops: Players perform quick stops at the free-throw line, half-court line, opposite free-throw line, and opposite base line (if full court).

- Quick turns: Players perform full front and rear turns (i.e., two half turns) after quick stops.

- Split-vision jog: Four players start simultaneously and jog at half speed, focusing on the far basket while using big vision to stay in a straight line from side to side.

- Stride stops and 180-degree change of direction moves: Four players move down the court in four lines. On the command "change," all four make a stride stop and 180-degree change of direction until the players finish at the opposite baseline.

- Progressive stride stops: Players make progressive forward stride stops and backward moves from the baseline to the free-throw line (stride stop, reverse), back to the baseline (reverse), from the baseline to the half-court line (reverse), back to the free-throw line, to the opposite free-throw line, back to the half-court line, and then to the opposite baseline (figure 1.25).

- Spacing jog (advanced skill that can be used with change-of-pace moves): The first four players start on command and move at their own pace, staying even with the leader (usually from the left or right outside line). For proper spacing, the next person in each line starts when the player ahead has moved 15 to 18 feet (4.6 to 5.5 meters) away and maintains that distance. This spacing jog is especially challenging in combination with change-of-pace moves. The four players stay in a line from left to right and are spaced 15 to 18 feet apart from side to side and behind the group ahead of them.

The coach can hold players in any quick-stop position to check position and correct mistakes. For offensive quick stops, players may simulate dribbling a ball or sprinting without the ball. If defensive quick stops are used, the feet should be active at all times.

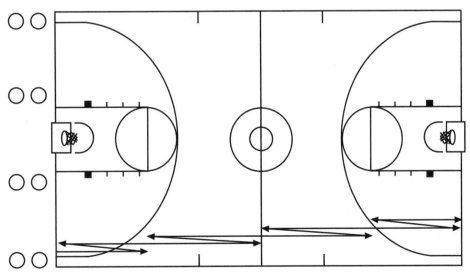

Figure 1.25 Progressive stride stops.

The coach can also advance to a whistle-stop drill: Four players start and, on each short whistle, stride-stop (or quick-stop), then reverse (on quick stops follow with a half-turn) and sprint until the next whistle. The next group of four players always starts on the second whistle after the previous group's start. The drill continues until a player reaches the opposite baseline and all players have run the floor. This is an excellent conditioning drill.

Coaching Points

- Each variation is done in one circuit (down and back).

- The first player in each line should come to a quick-stance position on the baseline and be ready before being asked to move. Players should listen for the *go* command and direction from the coach.

- When initiating movement, players should keep proper floor spacing, both from side to side and down the court.

- Unless directed otherwise, subsequent groups of four begin moving when the previous group reaches the near free-throw line (i.e., about 15 to 18 feet, or 4.6 to 5.5 meters, apart).

- All groups move to the opposite baseline and re-form; the first player in each group gets into a quick stance, ready to come back in the opposite direction.

- Review critical cues for starts, steps, stops, and turns.

LINE DRILL: QUICK JUMPS

Purpose: To develop basic jumping skills for rebounding and shooting

Equipment: Half-court floor space (minimum)

Procedure: Players are grouped in four lines on the baseline with the coach near the half-court line. One down-and-back circuit of quick jumps at the free-throw line, half line, opposite free-throw line, and opposite baseline can be completed as a warm-up. Then the first wave of four players sprints forward from basic position on the *go* command. Whenever the coach gives a thumbs-up signal, players execute a quick stop into a quick jump. They continue to repeat quick jumps in place until the coach signals them to run forward again. On that signal, the first group sprints again, and the next group starts from basic position on the end line. This pattern is repeated until all groups reach the opposite end line. The coach must be in front and visible so that all groups of players can see the signals. One alternative approach is to require a quick jump at the free-throw line, the half-court line, and the opposite free-throw line. Another option is for players to perform a regular power-rebound jump and chin the ball (with both hands under the chin) at the free-throw line, half-court line, opposite free-throw line, and opposite baseline, thus resulting in four rebounds for each floor length.

Coaching Points

- For quick jumps, circle tight inside with the hands.

- For power jumps, use arm pumps (down and up) followed by 2-and-2 power jumps.

- Jump quickly with a pop and land ready to repeat.

LINE DRILL: REBOUND JUMPING AND TURNS

Purpose: To develop jumping skills for rebounding situations

Equipment: Ball for each line

Procedure: The first person in each line steps forward with a ball. Using basic jumping techniques, players toss a ball in the air in front of them, pursue and capture the ball using the 2-and-2 rebounding technique and angle jumping to rebound out of their area to capture and chin the ball. The players' elbows should be up and out in order to protect the ball while they land in a quick stance. They should then execute a rear turn or front turn (using either PPF or EPF footwork) before stepping and passing to the next player in the line.

Coaching Points

- Coil and gather with the arms low; arm explosion triggers leg explosion for power jumps.
- Capture and chin the ball.
- Rear turn: Lead with an elbow; front turn; punch into the turn. Use a front or rear turn after the rebound using PPF or EPF footwork.
- Stay low and level on all turns.

LINE DRILL: QUICK STANCE, STARTS, STEPS, JUMPS, TURNS, AND STOPS

Purpose: To develop body-control movements by executing all skills properly, quickly, and at the right time (an ideal practice warm-up drill)

Equipment: Full-court floor space (preferred) or half-court space

Procedure: Players stand in three or four lines on the baseline. The coach is positioned in the midcourt area and commands a half or full circuit of body-control moves. Players get into and maintain a quick stance, then play and stay low as they execute a variety of combinations as directed by the coach. The step choices are change-of-pace and V-cut fake-and-break moves (i.e., slow-to-quick moves).

Coaching Points

- Emphasize the appropriate critical cues for the chosen skills.
- Start all variations with an offensive quick stance.

LINE DRILL: STARTS, STOPS, AND TURNS

Purpose: To set the foundation of quick stance, quick starts, quick stops, quick turns, and passing and catching skills without the ball in a combination warm-up drill (ball added later)

Equipment: Baseline area and floor space to the top-of-the-key area

Procedure: Players stand in four lines on the baseline with at least two players per line. On the *ready* command, the first player in each line steps onto the court in an offensive quick stance (an imaginary triple-threat position) without the ball. To start the action, the coach specifies the drill as either *direct drive, go* or *crossover drive, go* using either PPF footwork or EPF footwork with jab and crossover (right or left). The first player executes a direct drive (long and low) with an imaginary dribble using the preferred hand for two dribbles, then makes a quick stop (chinning the ball or staying in triple-threat position). The player then executes a rear turn and an imaginary one-handed push pass (stepping and passing, then freezing the follow-through). The next player in line is in a quick stance with the hands near their respective shoulders, thus providing two targets for the imaginary pass. The player assumes the two-handed catch position with both feet in the air (i.e., ball in the air, feet in the air), then repeats the direct-drive move. Next, the coach moves on to the crossover drive, dribble, and pass. For a right-handed player, this sequence involves a crossover drive to the left side, a left-handed dribble, a quick stop, a rear turn on the PPF, and a crossover imaginary one-handed push pass using the nonpreferred hand. After teaching or reviewing passing and catching, the coach should use starts, stops, and turns in a progression drill when the ball is added. The rule for learning body-control movement on the nonpreferred side is to perform three times as many repetitions as on the preferred side. Advanced players might use EPF footwork in this drill.

Coaching Points

- Passing: Pass with the feet on the floor, pass with a step, pass with a ping to a hand target, and freeze the follow-through.

- Catching: Catch with the feet in the air, catch with a click (two hands and two eyes), and land in a quick stance.

- Emphasize the critical cues for starts, steps, stops, and turns.

FULL-COURT TEAM REBOUNDING

Purpose: To develop body control (spacing and timing) using rebounding jumps (from one or both feet) to keep the ball live with consecutive two-handed tips by all players. A quick stop and quick turn can be added between jumps.

Equipment: Full-court space, two baskets, two balls, and at least ten players

Procedure: Start with one player and half of the other players spaced evenly facing one basket. The remaining players form a line and face the other basket (toward the opposite end of the court). The two players with a ball start the drill simultaneously by using a two-handed tip to the upper corner of the basket (right side counter-clockwise and left side clockwise when all team members are moving counterclockwise or vice versa). After executing the two-handed controlled tip to the backboard, players can be asked to move toward the opposite side of the free-throw lane and execute a quick stop and rear turn before sprinting toward the opposite basket. Depending on the number of players, the coach can add one or more body-control moves between baskets. The object is to keep the two balls in play on each backboard with continuous two-handed controlled tips. Keep the ball in play for a designated minimum period of time (1 to 5 minutes) or until any team member is unsuccessful at completing any assigned body-control move. The drill setup is shown in figure 1.26.

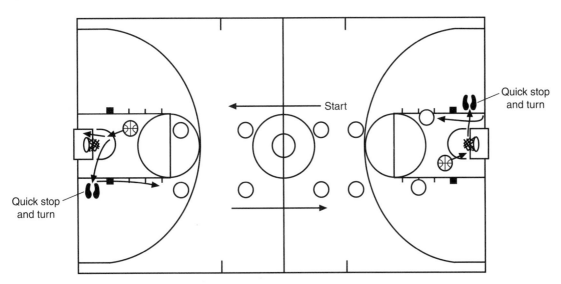

Figure 1.26 Team-rebounding tip drill.

Coaching Points

- Control each two-handed tip near the upper corner of the backboard (using a power jump or a one-foot quick jump).
- Complete each body-control move properly and quickly.
- Team goals: Don't let your teammates down (have their back).
- Skills and goals can be adapted as appropriate for players' age level (e.g., younger players might use correct layup technique on the backboard: one-handed speed or two-handed power layins).

Wooden Wisdom

"If you don't have time to do it right, when will you have time to do it over?"

—John Wooden

CHAPTER 2

ADVANCED BODY CONTROL

"Players who concentrate on the little things get better little by little. One of those little things is moving without the ball (100 percent on defense and at least 20 percent on offense). The little things are the big things."

Dan Hays, hall of fame coach and former head coach at Oklahoma Christian University

One of the most difficult coaching tasks is to teach players to carry out actions that don't involve the basketball—the magnet of the game. This is no small matter: An individual player on offense plays without the ball more than 80 percent of the time. With that reality in mind, this chapter addresses the importance of individual skills that do not involve possession of the ball.

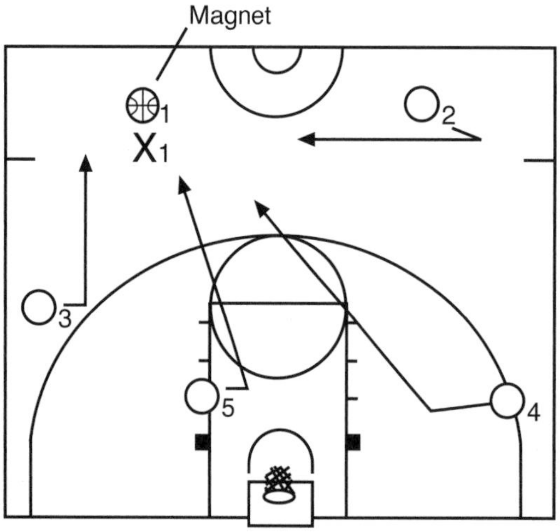

Many coaches find that young players on offense are almost obsessively attracted to the ball (figure 2.1). Therefore, time must be spent teaching them that movement without the ball and proper offensive spacing and timing can be just as important as moves made with the ball in terms of setting up scoring opportunities. If coaches help players understand that proper spacing and timing are crucial to successful team offense, then they can motivate players to move purposefully without the ball.

Figure 2.1 Ball magnet and team spacing.

CONCEPTS OF MOVING WITHOUT THE BALL ON OFFENSE

To move effectively without the ball, players must master and remember certain fundamentals on the court:

- Be alert and remember that all moves begin *on the floor*.

- Move with authority (make distinct moves) and with balance and quickness.

- Move with purpose and with proper spacing and timing. Be aware of teammates' movements and maintain focus on the offensive strategies of the whole team.

- Read the defense and the ball. All individual movement, which is dictated by the team-play situation, must be carried out in relation to the position and movement of both the ball and the defense. Get open by moving to clear areas on the court for receiving passes.

- Communicate all cuts and moves both by voice and with the hands. Players cannot talk too much.

- Get open or get out. The primary purpose of movement without the ball is to get open to receive a pass from the ball handler. Try to get open; if that is not possible, get out of the way. Maintain proper spacing—at least 15 to 18 feet (4.6 to 5.5 meters) apart (12 to 15 feet [3.7 to 4.6 meters] for younger players; 18 to 21 feet [5.5 to 6.4 meters] for college or professional players).

- Get open in the perfect catching position—again, generally 15 to 18 feet (4.6 to 5.5 meters) from the ball handler—and, ideally, in a floor position that affords the option to pass, shoot, or dribble. Catch the ball facing the basket or catch the ball and then use a turn (pivot) to face the basket. Players should be taught catch-and-face technique for use in the frontcourt in the following sequence: *rim* (look at the rim for the shot and see the whole floor), *post* (look inside to feed the post or a cutter in the post area), and *action* (move the ball or dribble-drive to the basket). To be effective, this rim–post–action (RPA) sequence must become automatic and be executed very quickly in proper order. Players should use it with big vision every time they catch the ball.

- Be an actor. Movement without the ball amounts to a continuous competition between offensive and defensive players. To keep opponents guessing in this ongoing contest, players must use believable fakes (and give the opponent time for reaction), thus baiting the defender and playing the role of decoy.

- Lose the defenders. Move out of their field of vision and force them to turn their heads. Most defenders have their backs to the basket and their eyes on the ball; therefore, offensive players should move behind them to the baseline and away from the ball (see figure 2.2). Cuts can best be made from this position, where defenders cannot easily anticipate moves. This technique is especially effective against zone defenses that focus on the ball.

- Run through the ball. When moving to catch a pass, players should maintain the open position by moving toward and meeting the pass, unless they are making a breakaway move ahead of the defender or a back cut to the basket behind the defender (figure 2.3). Beat the defender to the ball.

- Get close to get open. Because this rule goes against common sense, players often make the mistake of trying to free themselves by staying away from a defender. It is actually more effective to stay close and then break away quickly to get open, as shown by players O_2 and O_3 in figure 2.4. This technique allows the offensive player to execute an action move that precedes and is quicker than the defender's reaction move. This kind of move—such as an effective fake-and-break V-cut or L-cut to get open—are often slow-to-quick moves.

- While applying all concepts, keep proper spacing (more than 15 to 18 feet, or 4.6 to 5.5 meters, apart unless cutting or screening) and make moves at the right time (better late than early). On offense, proper spacing starts with big vision to see the whole court (*keep the head up and face the big part of the court*).

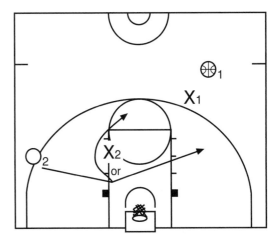

Figure 2.2 Lose the defenders (move behind or out of their field of vision), then make a quick cut to get open.

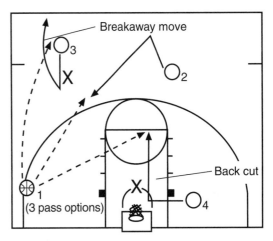

Figure 2.3 Run through the ball and meet the pass (player O_2 in the diagram).

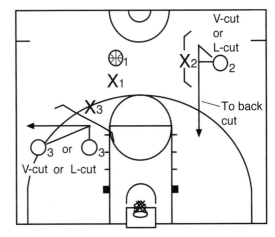

Figure 2.4 Get close to get open. O_3 moves close to X_3, then makes a quick V-cut or L-cut move to get open to receive a pass. Elsewhere, O_2 moves toward X_2, who overplays the pass from O_1, whereupon O_2 back-cuts to the basket.

BASIC MOVES OR STEPS WITHOUT THE BALL

Basic moves without the ball require players to be deceptive in order to fool the defense. When first learning these moves, players need to go slow and be correct, then they move progressively quicker until they make mistakes, then correct their mistakes, and continue until they can make correct game moves at game speed.

V-Cuts

Special-purpose cuts or moves (quick steps) include fake-and-break moves or V-cuts—basic zigzag or change-of-direction cuts that form the shape of a V. To execute a V-cut, place body weight on the foot opposite the desired direction of movement (sink the hips into the cut), point the lead foot, and step with that opposite foot in the desired direction. For example, *plant* and push from the right foot and *step* to the left with the left foot. Usually, one side of the V involves a move to the basket, away from the basket, or to the defender. The other side of the V involves the quick change-of-direction cut to get open. Beginners can also use short stutter steps during the fake (for balance), followed by a quick plant-and-break step at a right angle.

When teaching young players, use the term *fake-and-break* for the V-cut to get open. The first part of the V-move (the fake) goes toward the basket or the defender; it should be carried out slowly (the fake) and quickly (the break to get open) followed by the last part of the V (the break) to get open. On the break, both hands are usually thrown up in the direction of movement. This motion is needed in order to catch the ball—and to communicate that the player is open by holding the open hand up and away from the defender—when using a screen or preparing for a shot. The break move usually goes toward the ball but can also go toward the basket, as shown earlier in figure 2.4 (O_2's back-cut move on X_2's overplay). The V-cut is a sharp change-of-direction cut ranging from 60 to 90 degrees (the 90-degree version is called an L-cut).

Because the head leads a weight shift as a key to balance, the head leads the change of direction. For example, on a fake-and-break or V-cut move, the head first moves slightly in one direction (the fake) and then moves quickly in the direction of the intended movement (the break) to lead the desired cut.

As shown in figure 2.4, back cuts are important moves—made 15 to 18 feet (4.6 to 5.5 meters) away from the ball—when defenders overplay the passing lane. To execute this type of move, the cutter should get close to get open, make a slow-to-quick V-cut or L-cut move directly to the basket (i.e., a rim cut), and communicate with the outside hand (arm down and fist closed) on the fake and with the lead hand on the break (elbow bent, hand open, and shoulder high). This move is shown clearly in figure 2.5, where the cutter moves inside-out on a V-cut and is still overplayed. The cutter needs to create enough space on the perimeter for the back cut by baiting the defender, at least to the three-point arc, while maintaining 15 to 18 feet of spacing from the passer. Players should *make* back

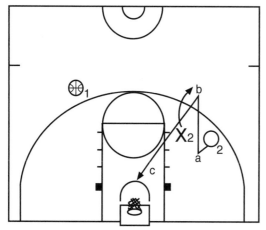

Figure 2.5 Backdoor cuts: *(a)* V-cut to get open; *(b)* "baiting" the defender and signaling the fake before the back cut (outside fist closed and pointed down); *(c)* back cut to rim and signaling open with the lead hand up.

cuts (hard and fast) but never *fake* back cuts; faking them usually confuses the passer and can lead to a turnover. To execute effectively, they should *make* a sharp, quick back cut on the fake-and-break move.

Front and Rear Cuts

These types of V-cut moves are made after a player has passed the ball to a teammate and wants to challenge the defense by cutting to the basket (making a rim cut) for a possible return pass. The pass-and-cut move—sometimes called a *give-and-go*—was the first two-player offensive move developed in the game, and it remains one of the most valuable offensive moves. The give-and-go takes two forms: the preferred front cut, which allows the offensive player to receive the ball in front of the defender (an excellent scoring position), and the rear cut, which lets the offensive player cut behind the defender to gain an advantage going to the basket (figure 2.6). A front cut uses a V-cut to set up the defense, whereas a rear

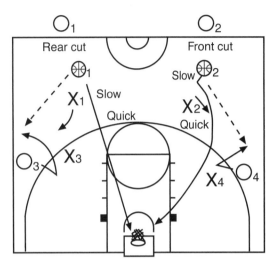

Figure 2.6 Front and rear cuts—give-and-go basketball.

cut is a direct, straight-line cut used as a change-of-pace or slow-to-quick move. Both front and rear cuts go to the rim and end exactly in front of the basket. The front or lead hand on the cut is held out in front at shoulder height to indicate the cutter's intention to the passer (i.e., communicate the cut with the lead hand), as shown in figure 2.7. On the rim cuts, advanced players can finish with either hand on either side of the basket using the rim to protect the shot from the defender.

CRITICAL CUE
Communicate cuts with the hands—lead hand open and up.

Figure 2.7 Rear cut: *(a)* Communicate the cut with the lead (open) hand, and *(b)* receive the pass.

Decoy Moves

Decoys are basic moves used to keep defenders busy—for example, distracting defensive players from helping to defend against a ball handler or trap the ball. Players should learn to be actors and distracters, misleading defenders with deceptive eye movements, physical bluffs, and other visual or auditory distractions. They should also use unpredictable change-of-pace moves.

Shot Moves

When the ball is in the air on a shot attempt, all offensive players either should move to a rebounding position or go to a defensive assignment, depending on their position and role. Players need to make decisive moves when a shot is taken rather than merely standing and watching the ball. Spectators are rightly ball watchers, but players should be movers. They should always assume that the shot will be missed and that they need to either rebound or get back on defense in order to do their job every time a shot is taken on offense. These offensive rebounding or offense-to-defense transition moves are explained in chapter 8 and utilize fake-and-break moves to execute the appropriate task.

Assigned Moves

Assigned moves are individually designated cuts in a system of play for special situations. Coaches make specific assignments for rebounding, jump balls, out-of-bounds plays, free throws, and set patterns. All players must carry out individual assignments properly, quickly, and at the right time. How *well* this is done matters just as much as *what* is done; proper spacing and timing are essential.

SCREEN MOVES

Setting a screen to get a teammate open for a pass or drive is an unselfish team move and an essential skill of individual offense. Instruction in setting and using screens should usually not begin until the secondary school level; elementary school players should concentrate instead on learning more basic moves and concepts without the ball.

Types of Screens

Screens can be classified according to three criteria (figure 2.8):

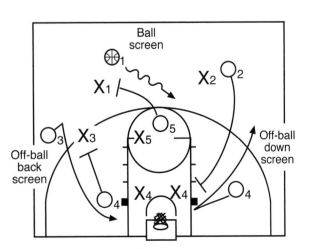

- Location—on or off the ball
- Type of body contact—front or rear
- Use—back screen (back to the basket, set behind or on the blind side of a defender) or down screen (back to the ball, set in front of or to the side of a defender)

Coaches should develop their own theories for how screens should work: screening a certain spot or area on the floor (position screen) or screening the defender (player screen). A player screen is usually more effective in freeing the offensive player, but it may result in more fouls for illegal screens, or *blocks*. Overall, the authors prefer player screens: Screen an opponent rather than a certain spot on the court or location near a teammate.

Figure 2.8 Types of screens.

Setting Screens

Setting a screen is a basic move. Players should use a noisy quick stop with the feet shoulder-width apart and the hands out of the screen (figure 2.9). The screen should be set perpendicular to the expected path of the defender and be forceful enough for the defender to see and hear it. Screening players should be loud, low, and legal—the screen should be set with a quick stance after a quick stop and should be heard when it is set and when the defender makes contact with it. The screening player should play and stay low, sit into the screen, and be ready for contact. A legal screen includes correct position (being stationary) and legal use of the hands. A down screen can be set skin-to-skin, but a back screen should allow at least one step for the defender to change direction. To avoid illegal hand contact, a player should use one hand to grasp the other wrist (usually of the shooting hand, for protection) and place the hands in front of the body over the vital parts (crotch area for men, chest area for women). Against good defensive teams, the cutter is usually covered, but the screener is often open during a defensive switch or help move when cutting back to an open spot.

Other tips include using down screens (toward the basket) when defenders are sagging, back screens (away from the basket) when the defense is exerting pressure or defenders are overplaying, and flare screens (away from the ball and the basket) when defenders are collapsing inside. Players should alert teammates that they are screening by giving a hand or voice signal.

Figure 2.9 Front screen: Use a noisy quick stop with a wide base and keep the arms out of the screen. *(a)* Men grab the shooting wrist over the groin area; *(b)* women cross the arms over the chest area (with the shooting arm next to the body for protection).

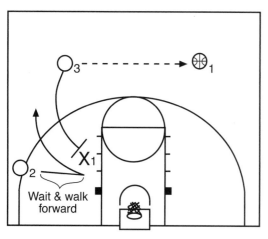

Figure 2.10 Using the screen: O₂ waits before the V-cut is made.

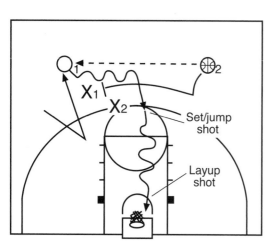

Figure 2.11 Pick-and-roll with defenders staying (no switched assignments).

Using Screens

The most difficult screening skill is that of preparing or setting up the defender to run into the screen (players should use a teammate as a screen or obstacle) with a V-cut, which usually starts toward the basket as shown in figure 2.10. An important cue is to wait for the screen. Coaches can require the cutter to wait until the screener calls *go* as the user comes to the screen on a V-cut. This move is advocated by Tommy Lloyd of Gonzaga University. Other coaches insist that the cutter grasp the jersey or trunk of the screener before cutting. These techniques force the cutter to wait and read the screen. This aspect of screening is so important that some coaches teach the screener to say "wait, wait, wait" before using or cutting by the screen.

Players should cut razor close so that they brush shoulders with the screener. On screens away from the ball, players should be in a low position with the hands up as they go by the screen, ready to receive a pass. Players should throw the hands up as they move past the screener on the break. Timing is crucial in effective screen plays: Players must wait for the screen to be set before making moves; they must also read the defender's position with big vision to make the correct cut opposite the defender's stance and position.

When two players set and use a screen, they both represent scoring options. The cutter reads the defender's position while waiting, then cuts accordingly to get open. For example, a defender trying to get through a screen causes a pop-cut (outside-shot) move with a reaction inside (a low cut) by the screener. The two scoring options are usually inside-and-low and outside-and-high moves by the cutter and screener (in response to the cut). With less determined or less skilled defenders, the cutter is usually open. With great defenders, the screener is usually open for the score on a screen-and-flash (or pop) cut.

On-the-Ball Screens

The pick-and-roll is a basic two-person play used at all levels of basketball. This play was a staple for one of the best inside–outside combinations in basketball history: Karl Malone and John Stockton of the Utah Jazz. Pick-and-roll occurs when a screen is set on the ball handler. When an effective screen is used and defenders do not switch, the dribbler is open for a shot (dribble-drive layup or set or jump shot). As shown in figure 2.11, the sequence occurs when O_1 V-cuts to get open as O_2 passes and sets the ball screen on defender X_1 (O_2 sprints to set the screen quickly). In this option, X_1 tries to fight through the screen (the defenders do not switch assignments) but is impeded, and O_1 is free for the shot (layup or jump shot).

When a screen (pick) is made on the ball handler and the defenders switch assignments or hedge (help), the screener is open on a roll move to the basket. The pick-and-roll for the screener is shown in figure 2.12. When the ball handler uses the screen, the screener makes a *half* rear turn and shuffle-slides to the basket, staying between the ball handler and the original defender (X_1). The screener should use a proper rear turn

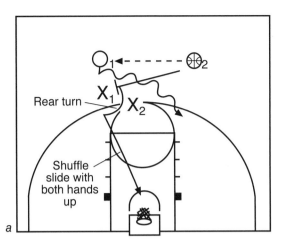

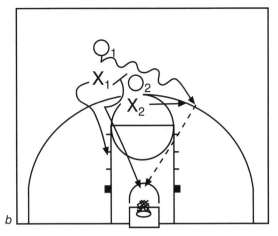

Figure 2.12 Pick-and-roll with defenders switching: *(a)* screen (pick) set and rear turn on the left foot as the dribbler clears the screen on a two-dribble draw; *(b)* roll pass to the screener rolling to the basket.

in order to *maintain vision* on the ball at all times. The ball handler must make at least two dribbles past the screen to draw the switching defender (X_2)—especially when the screener's defender is hedging (helping). This dribble move (usually a hesitation dribble) gives the dribbler time to execute a dribble draw—then make a pass (usually a bounce pass) to the screener on the roll move to the basket. On occasion, the defenders may double-team or trap the ball handler; if so, the screener should "pick and pop"—that is, step back and outside for the return pass and the outside shot.

When an effective screen is made, two scoring options are always possible: The nonscreener is open if the defenders don't switch, and the screener is open if the defenders do switch or hedge. Advanced players should be taught to look for both scoring options.

Another advanced option on all two-person screen plays is for the screener to "slip" the screen, or fake it, and cut to the basket as the defenders choose to switch defensive assignments in early anticipation of the faked screen. This option for on-the-ball screens is shown in figure 2.13. The slip move by the screener is an essential scoring tool to challenge defensive timing and execution of their tactics (especially when helping or switching).

An advanced on-the-ball screening technique that has developed for the middle-of-the-court high ball screen or screen-rescreen is typically used between a larger post player and an exceptional ball handler. It depends on forcing the perimeter defender to fight over a screen, thus falling into a compromised defensive position for following the penetrating dribbler. The dribbler uses the penetrating principle of winning both the battle (of the first step) and the war (of body contact in an advantageous position) by using a hesitation dribble to allow their defender to catch up from behind in a compromised defensive position (basket-ball-defender) (figure 2.14). When this happens,

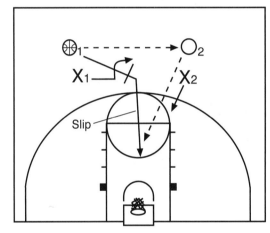

Figure 2.13 Slipping the screen.

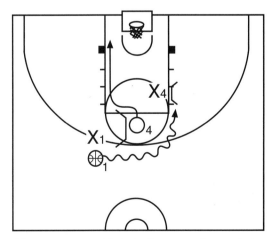

Figure 2.14 High ball screen (no-switch defense).

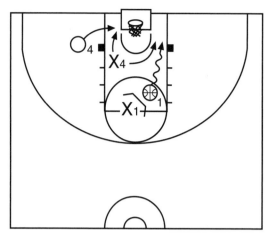

Figure 2.15 High ball screen (2-on-1).

the screener or roller going to the basket forces his or her defender into a 2-on-1 situation (figure 2.15). The defender must switch to the penetrator, which opens up a high pass to the inside player for an easy backboard shot (or dunk shot) or a bounce pass to the player rolling to the basket for the backboard shot. If the inside defender doesn't switch, the offensive perimeter player can use a long-layup technique to score off the backboard with the defender in a disadvantaged position.

Off-the-Ball Screens

This type of screen is set *away from* the ball and occurs as a basic two-player pattern plus the passer. Off-the-ball screens are classified according to the cutter's reaction to the defender's choice for combatting the screen. Possibilities include the pop cut, curl cut, flare (fade) cut, and back cut.

A *pop cut* is used when the defender tries to fight through the screen (figure 2.16). Specifically, O_1 passes to O_2 and screens away from the ball *on the defender* of O_3 (defender X_3). If no defensive switch is made, then O_3 gets an open shot *outside* (figure 2.16a). If X_1 does switch defensive assignments, then the screener (O_1) gets the open shot *inside* by cutting (flashing) to the ball as the switch is made (figure 2.16b). Players should communicate the cut with both hands up while coming past the screen, or at least with the open hand showing where the pass is needed.

In contrast, a *curl cut* is used when the defender trails the cutter around the screen (figure 2.17). In the first option (figure 2.17a), the defense stays and the cutter (O_3) gets the open shot inside (curling to the basket). If the defenders switch (figure 2.17b), the screener (O_1) gets the outside shot cutting to the ball. Larry Bird, former Boston Celtic and hall of fame player, executed this screen cut to perfection. Players should communicate the cut with the inside (lead) hand forward when coming around the screen.

If the defender anticipates the pop cut, then a *flare* or *fade cut* can be used (figure 2.18). When the defenders stay (no switch), the cutter can get open by flaring away from the ball and to the outside (figure 2.18a). As the cutter pushes off the screener on the

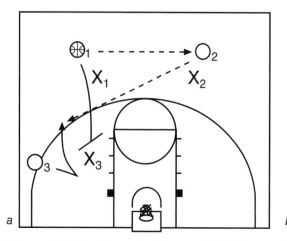

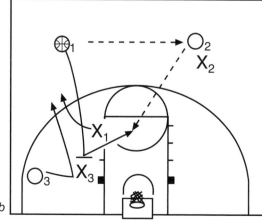

Figure 2.16 Pop cut: *(a)* no-switch defense, *(b)* switching defense.

flare cut, the screener may reset the screen to pin the defender inside. If the defenders do switch, then the screener is open (figure 2.18b) on the inside flash cut (slip) to the ball. The cutter communicates the U-cut (flare cut) by backing out with both hands up.

If the cutter makes a pop cut and the defender fights through the screen, then a *back cut* can be used (figure 2.19). If the defense does not switch (figure 2.19a), the cutter

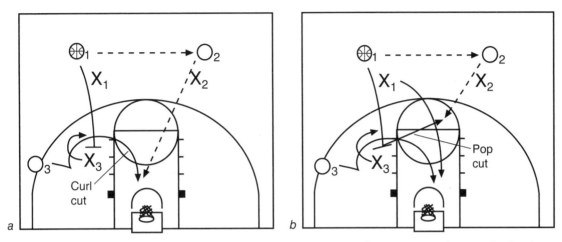

Figure 2.17 Curl cut: *(a)* no-switch defense, which leaves O_3 open to curl-cut to the basket; *(b)* switching defense, which allows a pop cut by the screener, O_1.

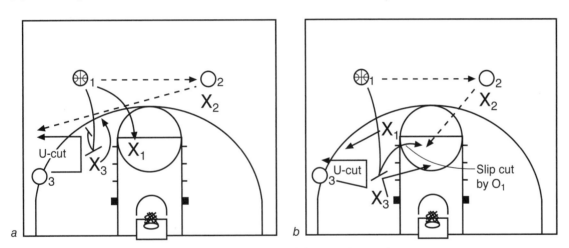

Figure 2.18 Flare cut: *(a)* no-switch defense, *(b)* switching defense.

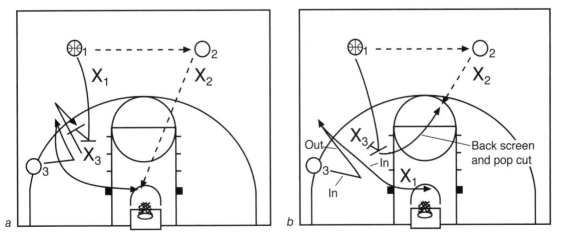

Figure 2.19 Back cut: *(a)* no-switch defense; *(b)* switching defense, which enables O_1 to back-screen and pop-cut.

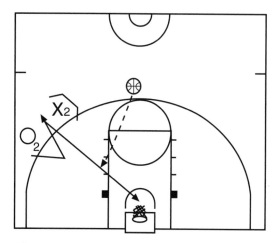

Figure 2.20 Quick back cut.

makes the pop cut, is overplayed, and reacts by making a cut to the basket using the back screen by O_1. The movement sequence for the cutter involves going to the basket (in), making the pop cut (out), and back-cutting (in) to the basket. If, on the other hand, no switch is made, then the cutter gets the shot inside going to the basket. If the defense does switch (figure 2.19*b*), the screener O_1 gets the shot by flashing to the ball from outside as the switch is made. The back cutter communicates the cut using the outside hand with a closed fist down as the out move is made. The back cut can also be done without the use of the pop cut: As the cutter waits while moving toward the screen, the defender anticipates the pop cut and cheats over the screen (figure 2.20). When the screener says *go*, the cutter makes a quick back cut directly to the basket with a front-hand target communication for the layup. On the switch, the screener may slip-cut to the free-throw lane area. An important reminder for players using a back-cut option is to *always* make the back cut—*never* fake the back cut.

Special Screening Situations

Screen–Rescreen

This screening technique is sometimes used against player-to-player defenses that defend screens by fighting over the perimeter screen in order to avoid switching. Specifically, the defender guarding the screener helps (hedges up) to discourage the cutter from using the screen to turn the corner toward the basket (figure 2.21*a*). This

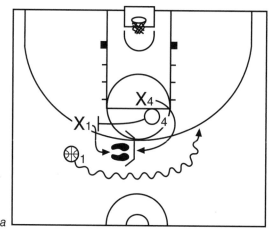

a

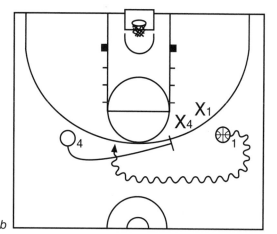

b

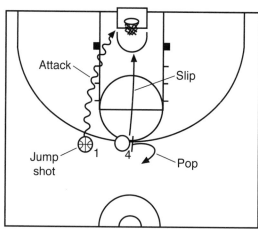

c

Figure 2.21 Screen–rescreen: *(a)* Defense shows and fights over screen; *(b)* O_4 turns and rescreens X_1; *(c)* scoring options are created.

hedge helper recovers to a ball–you–basket position as O_4 then rescreens X_1, who has just fought over the original screen and is not ready to fight over the rescreen (figure 2.21*b*). In this technique, screener O_4 then pivots and steps up to rescreen X_1. O_1 spin-dribbles or goes between the legs with big vision to reverse direction and use the screen from O_4. Both defenders will have difficulty defending the *rescreen* with the same technique (figure 2.21*c*). As a result, O_1 will have scoring options using a jump shot or basket drive as the screener reads the defense and either rolls to the basket or pops back for a jump shot. The screen–rescreen technique is best used in the middle of the floor and against the fight-through-and-hedge defensive technique.

Changing the Screen Angle

Defenses often try to undercut screens by using a technique known as *icing*, in which defenders corral the ball handler to the sideline in order to keep the ball on one side of the floor while also defending against the perimeter screen on the side of the court (figure 2.22*a*). One way for the offense to counter this defensive tactic is to change the screening angle to allow the ball handler an advantage toward the baseline. As shown in figure 2.22*b*, O_2 makes a soft drive or hesitation dribble move to the baseline to create a 2-on-1 situation with screener O_4. When the defense is trying the icing technique, a helping defender will usually be positioned at the basket, so O_2 will have scoring options—taking a pull-up jump shot using the backboard just outside the free-throw lane or passing to O_4 if the safety (X_5) helps up to the ball to defend O_2 (figure 2.22*c*). Thus screeners should always look for the best angle in setting the screen to counter the position of the defender being screened.

Running to the Basket After a High Middle Screen

On most ball screens set in the high middle of the floor, the screener rolls to the basket when the dribbler uses the screen (figure 2.23*a*). This movement is done using a rear turn and a side shuffle in order to maintain vision on the ball. A common alternative to the roll is illustrated in figure 2.23*b*. In this version of the high pick, the screener sets a

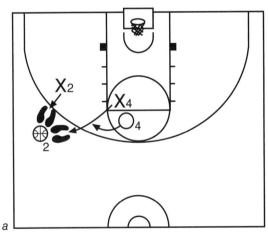

a

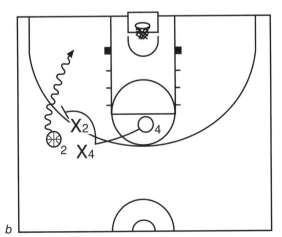

b

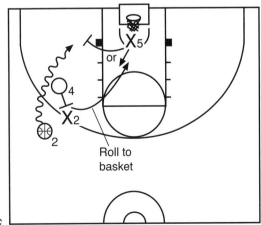

c

Figure 2.22 Screen angles: *(a)* player-to-player icing technique; *(b)* changing the screen angle to combat icing; *(c)* O_2 using an angle screen to drive to the baseline.

high pick (loud, low, and legal) and then, without rolling or pivoting, runs to the opposite side of the basket in preparation for a lob pass over the defense, which can produce an easy shot off the backboard or a dunk shot.

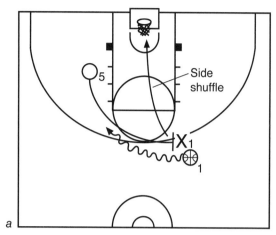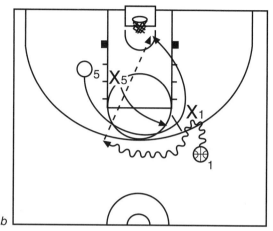

Figure 2.23 High middle screen options: *(a)* high pick and *roll* to the basket, *(b)* high pick and *run* to the basket.

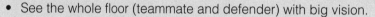

COACHING POINTS FOR MOVING WITHOUT THE BALL

- See the whole floor (teammate and defender) with big vision.
- Use the floor when beginning a move (slow–quick changes with foot-based push off).
- Move with authority.
- Move with purpose.
- Read the defense and the ball with big vision and respond accordingly.
- Get open or get out of the way; don't stand still.
- Know and use the perfect catching position: 15 to 18 feet (4.6 to 5.5 meters) from the ball. Catch the ball, face the basket, and use RPA progression with big vision.
- Be an actor—take the initiative and use believable fakes.
- Lose the defender (by getting away or moving out of his or her field of vision).
- Run through the ball (meet the pass).
- Get close to get open and use V- or L-cuts.
- Alert a teammate with a voice or hand signal when setting a screen.
- Set screens that are loud, low, and legal; sprint to set a screen.
- Set a pick or screen at a right angle to the expected path of the defender.
- When using screens, wait for the *go* signal, use a V-cut or go to the screener, and brush past the screen (with shoulder-to-shoulder contact).
- The two scoring options for on-the-ball screens come from the pick-and-roll.
- Off-the-ball screen cuts include the pop, curl, flare, and back cuts.
- Two scoring options on every screen are the cutter and screener.
- *Make* the back cut; *never fake* the back cut.

TROUBLESHOOTING

Moves made without the ball—where spacing and timing are critical—are considered *big-picture* moves. These advanced team plays are difficult and require patience, attention to detail, and the ability to see the whole floor with big vision. It is usually better to be too late than too early on most screens, so the offensive player has less time to read the defenders and execute the correct response. This especially applies to cutting moves.

Movement mistakes occur when an error is made by a player without the ball. Players need to focus their attention on recovery, call out for help from teammates when needed, and get into position immediately for the next play—especially when an offensive error results in a steal. Players should avoid making two mistakes in a row and should learn to play through their mistakes. Granted, mistakes are necessary for learning, but they should be analyzed and then forgotten. To summarize this mentality, use the acronym NBA: What is the *next best action* after a mistake?

DRILLS FOR MOVING WITHOUT THE BALL

These drills are designed to teach players the most challenging moves—those made without the ball. Players tend to be eager to develop ball skills but reluctant to drill on moves without the ball. These moves require careful team coordination, usually with two or three players working closely together.

LINE DRILL: MOVING WITHOUT THE BALL ◉

Purpose: To teach basic moves without the ball

Equipment: Full court

Procedure: Players form up in a basic four-line drill position on the baseline. The first player in each line moves down the court without the ball, imagining the ball to be in the center of the court (figure 2.24). The coach calls out one of the four moves—V-cut, backdoor cut, front cut, or rear cut—and the players echo (repeat the verbal call) and then

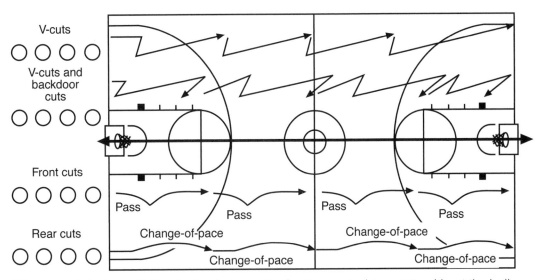

Figure 2.24 Line drill: V-cuts, backdoor cuts, front cuts, and rear cuts without the ball.

execute the cut as they move to the opposite baseline and return to their starting positions (a down-and-back move) in four lines using proper spacing and timing.

Options

- *V-cut to get open (to the basket and to the ball, or to the defender and to the ball):* Players perform repeated V-cuts, followed by quick stops to simulate catching the ball, for the length of the court; they communicate the cut by holding the proper hand up.

- *V-cut to get open, followed by a backdoor cut:* Players should use proper footwork and hand position and communicate with the hands—up when getting open, outside hand down and fist closed for the backdoor cut.

- *Front cut:* A simulated pass to the center of the court is followed by a front cut (V-cut—moving away slowly, then cutting fast to the ball) and quick stops at the free-throw lines and the half-court line. Players communicate with the inside hand across and up.

- *Rear cut:* A simulated pass to the center of the court is followed by a rear cut (change-of-pace, from slow to fast) and quick stops at the free-throw lines and the half-court line. Players communicate with the hands up using the lead hand (forward and up).

Quick stops are used at each free-throw line and at the half-court line. Upon completing each quick stop, players should challenge the imaginary defense by using a catch-and-face move—first a quick stop, then a pivot in order to face the basket and see the whole court.

V-CUT

Purpose: To teach players the basic moves without the ball in a 2-on-0 or 2-on-2 situation

Equipment: One ball per basket per group

Procedure: The basic two-line formation for this drill includes one line of guards or point-position players out front and a line of forwards or wing-position players on the side—in other words, two lines of outside players. Coaches can also develop "positionless" skills by using all players in both lines.

Options

- Use a forward V-cut to get open (fake and break) and, after receiving the pass from the guard, use a catch-and-face RPA move (i.e., facing the basket).

- The guard can make a front or rear cut to the basket (cut to the rim) to catch the forward-to-guard return pass and then go to the end of the forward V-cut line (give-and-go); alternatively, the forward can make a live-ball, dribble-drive move to the basket (figure 2.25a).

- The forward then rebounds the ball, passes to the next guard in line, and goes to the end of the guard line.

- Figure 2.25b shows a forward backdoor move (advanced skill) performed during a guard dribble move (the key is to dribble at an overplayed teammate). The ball handler, dribbling toward (dribble at) the overplaying defender to signal the backdoor cut; alternatively, the receiver, with the outside hand down (closed fist), can key the cut. The forward backdoor cut should be made outside the three-point field-goal line; spread the defense and back-cut.

The forward V-cut may entail a fake to the basket and a break either to get open or to the imaginary defender to get open (L-cut, get close to get open). When players have reached acceptable skill levels, add two defenders and use the drills in a 2-on-2 situation. Players should communicate cuts with the hands (figure 2.26).

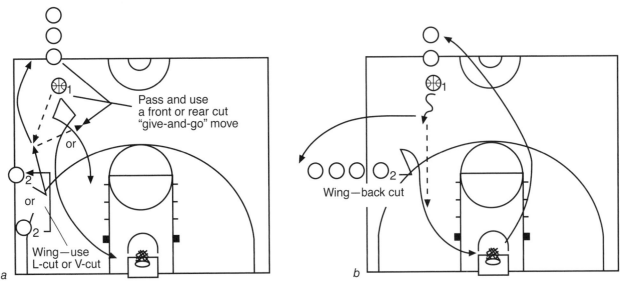

Figure 2.25 (a) V-cut drill and (b) backdoor option (O_2 V-cuts with the outside hand down as the key).

Figure 2.26 Communicate cuts with a hand or both hands: (a) V-cut to get open, and (b) front cut give-and-go (lead hand).

2-ON-2 OFFENSE AND DEFENSE

Purpose: To provide a progression drill for the V-cut

Equipment: One ball per basket per group

Procedure: This is a live offense-and-defense progression that restricts the offense to individual live-ball moves and pass-and-cut options.

Options

- Start with any set: G-G, G-F, both sides, perimeter–post.
- The offense must use only live-ball moves and pass-and-cut moves. Restrict the ball handler to three dribbles with the ball. The offense starts with a live ball.
- The drill can utilize two lines per offensive possession; players rotate from offense to defense to the back of the line. Other options include playing games to 3 or 5, playing make-it-take-it, or having the offense stay on offense until the defense gets a stop.
- Defensive variations can include applying different levels of pressure.

4-ON-4 HALF-COURT OFFENSE AND DEFENSE

Purpose: To teach players to use good timing and spacing while making basic team-offense moves in an unstructured half-court situation

Equipment: One ball per basket per group (eight to twelve players) and a half-court area

Procedure: Players are grouped in fours on the half-court: four on offense, four on defense, and four waiting off the court (if available). They work through the following variations:

- Offense variations: Individual live-ball moves, on-the-ball screens, off-the-ball screens, and live rebounding
- Defense variations: pressure variations, switch and no-switch screen defense, and post defense
- Varied sets: 4-out, 3-out and 1-in, 2-out and 2-in
- Outcome variations: rotation after one possession (offense to defense to waiting), make-it-take-it, rotation when defense gets a stop

4-ON-4 DEFENSE-TO-OFFENSE TRANSITION

Purpose: To teach players to make effective and efficient transitions (from defense to offense)

Equipment: One ball per court with 12 players (4 on offense, 4 on defense, 4 waiting)

Procedure: Four-player teams begin on the half-court using a coach-designated offensive set and fundamental variations. When a shot is taken, the offensive players carry out designated roles.

- Three rebounders go to a gap with hands up to get an offensive rebound. One player serves as a fullback (safety), whose goal is to get to the center circle with big vision before the ball hits the rim or net.

- Two of the offensive rebounding players serve as rebounders, one as a fullback (safety), and one as a halfback who moves to the free-throw area for a long rebound and then picks up the ball handler coming up the court on a made shot or on a defensive rebound and break. The third offensive rebounder transitions with vision (three sprint steps).

When the four defenders get the ball after a basket or on a defensive rebound, they bring the ball up quickly to test the opponent's offense-to-defense transition. If they can score on a fast-break shot or early in a set offense, then they stay on offense. If the four who were originally on offense make a successful transition, then they go back to offense. Players rotate from offense to defense to out on a defensive stop.

ONE-MINUTE CONTINUOUS GAME

Purpose: To teach players to play full-court 3-on-3 offense and defense and use advanced moves without the ball

Equipment: One ball per court with 6 players (3-on-3); two courts for a team of 12, three courts for 18, and so on

Procedure: Minute-long games are played simultaneously, one on each court. Play can start with a jump ball or by other means (e.g., coin flip for possession). Dribbling is not allowed (creates an automatic turnover); all other moves are allowed. Full-court denial defense is required. Otherwise, all regular rules apply. This gamelike drill places a premium on fundamentals: timing and spacing, getting open, catching and facing the basket, and all defensive fundamentals. Play at least three 1-minute games. After each game, winners play winners, and losers play losers. Winners take the ball out first on their next game (coach determines if teams are waiting after a 1-minute game).

PICK-AND-ROLL ▶

Purpose: To teach players the screening and cutting options for on-the-ball screens

Equipment: One ball per basket per group (four or more players per group)

Procedure: Two lines of outside players, positioned 15 to 18 feet (4.6 to 5.5 meters) apart, use the screening pattern of passing the ball and then screening the ball handler's defender. The progression should be as follows:

- 2-on-0: cutter (dribbler) scoring option alternating with screener scoring option (rolling or stepping outside for a shot on a pick-and-pop)
- 2-on-2: defense staying (offense trying to score on the pick) alternating with defense switching (offense trying to score on the roll or stepping outside for a shot or pick-and-pop)
  - Live offense and defense
  - Player rotation: offense to defense to the end of the opposite line
- 3-on-3
  - Live offense and defense
  - Make-it-take-it; rotation when defense stops offense

3-ON-0 MOTION

Purpose: To teach both scoring options on screens away from the ball; two-ball shooting drill

Equipment: Two balls per basket per group (six players preferred) and two passers (coaches or program assistants)

Procedure: At first, the coach determines the cut, and the cutters echo it (repeat coach's verbal call). Then two defenders are added, and the screener or cutters must read the defenders and cut accordingly while calling their cut (see figure 2.27).

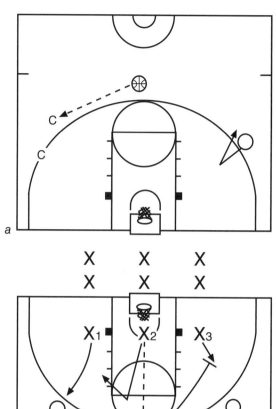

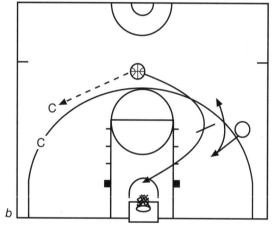

Figure 2.27 3-on-0 motion drill: *(a)* basic setup, *(b)* pass and screen away, *(c)* 3-on-3 motion offense and defense.

3-ON-3 MOTION SCREEN

Purpose: To teach players the screening and cutting options for off-the-ball screens

Equipment: One ball per basket per group (six or more players per group); alternatively, use two balls so coach can pass to both scoring options

Procedure: Three lines of outside players, positioned 15 to 18 feet (4.6 to 5.5 meters) apart, use the following options to pass and screen away from the ball: pop-up, curl cut, flare cut, and back cut. The progression should be as follows:

- 3-on-0

  - Pop cut: Cutter cuts outside, and screener cuts and slips inside.
  - Curl cut: Cutter curls inside, and screener pops outside.
  - Flare cut: Cutter U-cuts outside, and screener slips inside.
  - Back cut: Cutter back-cuts inside, and screener pops outside.

- 3-on-3
  - Defense does not switch (cutter options).
  - Defense switches (screener options).
  - Play uses live offense and defense.
  - Play is make-it-take-it.

Coaching Points

- Sprint to set a screen as you signal.
- Cutter waits for the screen (verbal *go* signal).
- Set screens that are loud, low, and legal.
- Signal all cuts with the hands and use verbal calls on all cuts.
- There are two scoring options on each screen.

Wooden Wisdom

"It's the little details that are vital. Little things make the big things happen."

—John Wooden

CHAPTER 3

BALLHANDLING

"*Passing and catching are offensive team skills, while dribbling is an individual offensive skill; therefore, the pass should be the primary offensive weapon.*"

Ralph Miller, Naismith Hall of Fame coach and former head coach at Wichita State University, University of Iowa, and Oregon State University

Ballhandling encompasses all offensive actions with the basketball—passing, catching, dribbling, shooting, making individual moves, and rebounding. This chapter addresses the first three—passing, catching, and dribbling (the others are covered in separate chapters).

The arm mechanics of passing, dribbling, and shooting are almost identical—the arm and hand motions are the same for each (for one-handed and two-handed techniques). Passing and catching are the most important individual offensive fundamentals with the ball; shooting can be considered as a pass to the basket and passing as a shot to a catching teammate. Dribbling, which can also be considered as a pass to the floor, is a secondary offensive weapon that should not be misused or overused, though it often is. Players should pass first and dribble last.

In order to achieve balanced development of ballhandling skills with the dominant and nondominant hands, players must also apply another ballhandling principle: Work on the weak hand *three times* as much as on the strong hand.

It should become automatic for players to get into triple-threat position (offensive quick stance), from which they can shoot, pass, or dribble (see figure 3.1). In triple-threat position, the player with the ball *pits and protects* the ball—that is, pulls it close to the armpit (or above) in order to protect it from the defender. Players should avoid dangling the ball away from the body; they need to keep their game tight. This protected area is also called the *shooting pocket*.

Players should always use the catch-and-face move with the ball: catching it, moving it to triple-threat position, and then pivoting and facing the basket to see the whole floor with big vision (especially open teammates who may serve as partners for passing and catching). It is possible to catch and face in one motion by catching a pass with the feet in the air and landing facing the basket using the rim–post–action (RPA) rule (see the RPA discussion in the Passing–Catching Principles section a bit later in this chapter). In this position, offensive quick stance is attained with quickness and balance. Players must think quickly, move at top speed under control, and be ready to pass or

CRITICAL CUE

Practice ballhandling skills (passing and dribbling) on the nondominant side three times as much as on the dominant side.

Figure 3.1 Triple-threat position (offensive quick stance with the ball): *(a)* side view, *(b)* front view.

catch first and dribble last. When players become ball handlers, they should first look to pass the ball to a teammate (unless they are open for a scoring opportunity within their range) before choosing to dribble, which is the final option for moving the ball. The primary movement concepts of quickness and balance dictate the preferred order: be prepared (with feet and hands) to shoot in the frontcourt (see the big part of the floor and look with small vision on the shooting target), then prioritize passing before dribbling (pass first, dribble last). The shot is most often the first pass to look for (the first catching priority).

PASSING AND CATCHING

Passing and catching are the most neglected fundamentals in basketball. Players must develop these skills in order to mount a successful team offense. Effective passing and receiving in the form of the scoring assist are measures of offensive teamwork and important tools for controlling game tempo on offense. More specifically, one important measure of offensive team efficiency is the number of scores made from assists (i.e., team scores resulting from passing or catching) as compared with the number of scores made from dribble drives or offensive rebounds (i.e., individual plays). The number of team scores should always exceed the number of individual scores. Another measure of unselfishness is the ratio of assists to turnovers. For unselfish teams, this ratio will generally be greater than 1; in other words, the team will have more assists than turnovers (the number of assists divided by the number of turnovers is greater than 1).

Players who are good passers and catchers, or receivers, have an excellent chance of serving as important team members. From a coaching perspective, good passing tends to take the pressure off of a team's defensive play and break down the opponent's defense. Because passing is the quickest way to move the ball and challenge the defense, it should be the primary weapon of offensive attack, thus applying the priority principle of balance and quickness.

Earvin "Magic" Johnson led his college and NBA teams to championships by becoming one of the greatest passers in the history of the game. John Stockton led the great Utah Jazz teams of the 1990s by doing the same thing. Stephen Curry of the Golden State Warriors does it for his NBA championship team. Sue Bird of the UConn Huskies and the WNBA's Seattle Storm had a career assist-to-turnover ratio of more than 2 to 1.

Coaches should work to convince players that passing and catching are primary offensive team plays. They are, in fact, the most effective ways to achieve the offensive objective—to get a good shot on each possession by moving the ball quickly and getting it to an open player to set up a scoring opportunity.

PRINCIPLES OF PASSING AND CATCHING

The overall goal of passing and catching is for both the passer and the catcher to produce passes that are *on time and on target*. Table 3.1 presents three key passing principles and three related catching principles.

Players need to look for the pass *before* dribbling. When catching, players should follow the rim–post–action (RPA) rule: When they catch the ball within the operating area near the offensive basket, they should catch the ball and face the basket to look for the shot (rim or backboard spot), look to pass to a cutter in or near the post area or an inside post player (post), and then move the ball (action). A player's natural preference, or first instinct, however, is to dribble, which is an individual skill and thus tends to be practiced each time a player touches the ball. Overcoming this instinct requires continual emphasis on the shot and pass options.

Table 3.1 Primary Passing–Catching Principles

Passing	Area	Catching
Pass with the feet on the floor (using a stepping foot for power).	Footwork	Catch with the feet in the air and make a quick stop. Be ready to shoot (pass first to the basket).
Pass to a spot (usually an open hand).	Target	Give a spot target (usually the catching hand).
Pass with a ping.	Speed of pass (sound)	Catch with a click (two eyes and two hands).

Players can make good passes only when coaches teach the fundamental elements of passing, including the three passing rules:

- *Footwork:* Pass with the feet on the floor in most situations. Pass with a quick step for quickness and power (using the stepping foot). When possible, the catcher should catch the ball with the feet in the air. This is critical for avoiding traveling violations; when a player lands with a one-count quick stop, either foot can be used legally as a pivot (turning) foot.

- *Target:* Each pass must be thrown accurately to a spot target. The target is usually provided by the catcher in the form of a raised hand away from the defender. When possible, players should hold both arms up when catching—one to provide a target hand and the other to ward off the defender (figure 3.2). The catcher must give a spot target whenever possible.

- *Speed of pass:* The ball must be passed quickly, before the defender has time to react. The pass should be snappy and crisp—neither too hard nor too easy. A quick step is usually made in the direction of the pass to provide added force. The concept of passing with a *ping* was made popular by Fred "Tex" Winter, hall of fame coach and long-time assistant coach for the Chicago Bulls and Los Angeles Lakers. The most important part of the successful pass and catch is the second part—the catch. Most of the time, the catcher should catch with a *click* (getting two hands on the ball). In contrast, if the ball is thrown too hard, it slaps loudly as it is caught; when thrown too softly, no sound is heard. A proper catch can be made in one of two ways: blocking with the outside spot hand and securing the ball with the other hand, or just getting two hands on the ball as soon as possible when catching it.

Here are three more passing recommendations.

- *Timing:* The ball must be delivered when the receiver is open—not before or after. Pass with a *ping* at the right time. When learning to pass, exaggerate the follow-through.

Figure 3.2 Getting open: Keep both arms up.

- *Deception:* The passer must use deception to confuse the defender, who is reading the passer (especially the eyes) and anticipating the pass. Use ball fakes and use *vision to see the whole floor (big vision)* while focusing on the spot target.

- *Meeting the ball:* Catchers should shorten all passes (i.e., run through the ball) by meeting or coming toward the ball. (This does not apply, of course, on a breakaway, in which the player moves to the basket ahead of the defense.)

Passers should visually locate all teammates and defenders—seeing the rim of the basket when in the frontcourt and the net when in backcourt—while concentrating on the potential receiver without staring. This awareness can best be achieved by surveying the whole floor area (using big vision) with the ball in triple-threat position. When catching a pass, players should always be prepared to shoot (catch the ball and face the basket) if open and within range; if unable to shoot, they should try to pass to an open teammate before dribbling (rim–post–action).

Players must learn to give up the ball unselfishly by passing to an open player. Ball handlers can also dribble-drive and pass (i.e., penetrate and pitch)—that is, create assist opportunities by making dribble moves to the basket that allow them to pass to open teammates who can then score. When players are passing, they should choose to make the easy pass through or by the defender. Coaches should teach players not to gamble on passes; they should be clever but not fancy. Most of the time, a player making a dribble drive should use a quick stop before passing the ball at the end of the penetration or drive, staying under control (maintaining balance) and avoiding the offensive charge. This technique applies the rule of passing and stopping with the feet on the floor. John Stockton, all-star guard for Gonzaga University and the Utah Jazz, became the all-time assist leader in the NBA by making the easy pass (i.e., the simple play). His counterpart at Gonzaga, Courtney Vandersloot, a first team All-American and WNBA all-star was also an unselfish passer known for making the simple play.

> **CRITICAL CUE**
> Make the easy pass.

Choosing the Correct Pass

The quickest passes are air passes. Simple geometry—the shortest distance between two points is a straight line—proves that the air pass is quicker than either the lob pass or the bounce pass, as shown in figure 3.3. Therefore, the air pass is the primary pass to use. Almost all perimeter passes around the defense should be two-handed or one-handed air passes from the chest.

Lob passes are used only when passing to teammates on a breakaway fast break, where the lob allows them to run to catch up with the ball; when teammates are being fronted while playing a low-post position; or when they offer the best way to get the ball past an overplaying defender. The lob is always a slower pass.

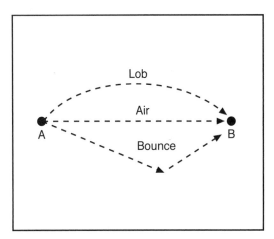

Figure 3.3 Types of passes, their paths, and distances traveled.

Bounce passes are used only when passing out of an emergency situation or to a player who is

- in the post position and smaller than the defender,
- open on the baseline side of a defender, or
- making a backdoor cut.

Defensive basket

Figure 3.4 Danger areas for passing or catching.

Special Passing Situations

Some potential passing situations require special consideration. For instance, the ball should not be passed across the court under the defensive basket because an interception in that area usually results in a score by the opponent. Other danger areas are found along boundary lines and in court corners (figure 3.4). In addition, when a pass comes back out on the perimeter from the baseline, players should reverse the ball quickly to the other side of the court to test the defense and check the defenders' alertness on the help side (test the second side or reverse [swing] the ball to make defenders move out in order to cover more court area).

TYPES OF PASSES

The type of pass used must fit the situation. For example, chest air and one-handed baseball passes are best used in open-court or perimeter situations in which speed is paramount, but the one-handed push pass is the preferred close-quarters or backdoor pass and the preferred perimeter pass.

Chest Pass

The chest pass is the basic air pass for effective, efficient ball movement when an offensive player is guarded loosely or in an open-floor area. It can be used for longer distances because the starting position is reached by using power from both arms to quickly move the ball from triple-threat position to the center of the chest, close to the body, in a thumbs-up position. To throw the pass, a player extends the elbows and pronates the arms (i.e., rotates them inward) to a thumbs-down ending position. The player should push the thumbs through the ball to put backspin on the ball. When there is time, the player should also take a quick step forward to pass, even though passing without stepping is quicker. Most of the time, the player should step quickly and pass. For longer passes, the ball is rolled in a circular move—out, down, and toward the body—to gain momentum before release.

The target of the pass should be either the receiver's throat or neck area if the receiver is stationary and defended from behind (aim for the face or slightly below) or the receiver's outside hand (away from the defender, as with the left hand in figure 3.2) if the receiver is near a defender. Also, during practice drills, the catcher should use two hands as practice targets outside the shoulders to teach passers to choose a hand for the target.

Chest Bounce Pass

This pass is recommended primarily for contested perimeter plays, backdoor moves, and emergencies when the passer must get out of a trap or when the defender is playing in the passing lane. Passing tips include making the pass to a target spot located two-thirds of the way to the receiver and following through (as when making a chest pass) to that spot on the floor. The pass should be thrown hard enough that it bounces up to the receiver at hip level. Starting with the ball in a thumbs-up position, passers should push the thumbs through the ball and follow through to a thumbs-down position (figure 3.5). The backspin produced by this technique is important in this movement because it increases the angle of rebound on the bounce pass, thus making it

Figure 3.5 Bounce pass: *(a)* thumbs-up starting position (targeting a spot on the floor) and *(b)* thumbs-down ending position (freezing the follow-through to the spot) and catcher receiving the pass with the feet in the air.

easier for the catcher to handle. A good bounce pass will bounce higher and "comes up" to the catcher's hands. For power, players may also step forward (using the stepping foot) with the pass.

Overhead Pass

When a player catches the ball, it should always be moved quickly to triple-threat position (*catch and face the basket; follow the RPA rule*). The ball can then be moved quickly overhead to pass over the defense when needed. A pass over the defense to reverse the ball to the second side of the floor (called a *skip pass*) is especially effective against zone defenses. The position of the ball allows the passer to show the ball and make effective pass fakes. Players need to keep the ball up, starting with and keeping the elbows locked or extended, and throw the pass with the wrists and fingers; the ball should be overhead with little or no windup behind the head. Throughout, players should remain in a bent-knee ready position.

The technique involves starting with the thumbs back, pushing the thumbs through the ball, and finishing with the thumbs forward (figure 3.6). The overhead pass tends to drop, so the ball should be thrown to a high target (usually the receiver's head); otherwise, the pass is hard to handle when dropping. For more power, players should step forward with the pass and freeze the follow-through.

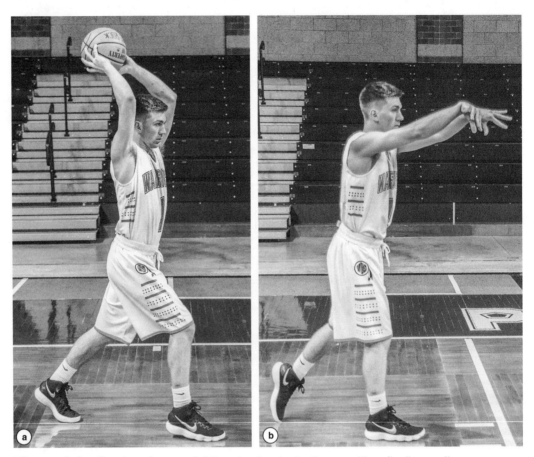

Figure 3.6 Overhead pass: *(a)* thumbs-back starting position (ball up, elbows locked) and *(b)* thumbs-forward and palms-out ending position (using the wrists and fingers, keeping the ball up).

A distinction should be made between overhead passes for longer and shorter distances. Longer overhead passes usually occur on a defensive rebound and outlet, a skip pass from one side of the court to the other (e.g., corner to opposite wing, wing to opposite wing), or in certain other long-pass or over-the-top situations. Shorter overhead passes include high-post to low-post or top-down perimeter-to-post passes and other perimeter-passing situations, most often to the adjacent perimeter receiver. Longer overhead passes necessitate a power step with the pass, as well as full use of both the arms and the thumbs and a complete follow-through (*freeze it*). Overhead passes should be used as air passes, not bounce passes, because of the high starting position of the release.

One-Handed Baseball Pass

A baseball pass is used to throw a long pass (usually more than half-court length) with the dominant throwing arm. Players should keep two hands on the ball as long as possible and use a stance in which the feet are parallel to the baseline (i.e., pointing toward

Figure 3.7 Baseball pass: *(a)* starting position (by the ear, both hands on the ball), *(b)* pulling the string (or fake pass from this position), and *(c)* pronation (thumb down) on release.

the sideline). They should then plant the back foot, point and step with the front foot, and throw the ball from the ear, similar to the way a baseball catcher throws. Proper follow-through includes carrying out a full pronation and extension of the arm, ending with the thumb down (figure 3.7). Players should throw this pass only with the dominant arm; the other hand can be used in the case of a fake pass to catch and stabilize the ball. The turning (pivot) foot for this pass is always the back foot, and the stepping foot is the front foot (an exception when using the PPF concept). Use EPF footwork for proper starting position.

One-Handed Push Pass

The one-handed push pass, or *flick pass*, is the most important pass for interior offense passing. It is a quick pass used to move the ball through or by a closely guarding defender. It is used both near a defender and when a teammate is at the 15- to 18-foot (4.6- to 5.5-meter) distance (perimeter or post). It can be made as either an air or a bounce pass, and it should be used from the triple-threat position; the key is the bent-elbow starting position, which is needed for power. The passer should work one side of the defender's body, especially past the ear, where the biggest gap usually appears, and make the pass above or below the defender's arm after finding an opening. Vertical fakes can be used as the passer reads the defender (figure 3.8). Players should fake low and pass high (air pass) or fake high (maybe with a shot fake) and pass low (bounce pass), reading the defender's arm position and making short, quick fakes. The first look is always past the ear, using an air pass when the defender's arm is down on either side of the defender's body (figure 3.8).

Figure 3.8 Push or flick pass: (a) Use the triple-threat position to work on the side of the defender's body; when the defender's arm is down, pass high, near the hole by the ear (fake low, pass high when needed). (b) Use vertical fakes (fake high, pass low) when the defender's arm is up.

When players move from the preferred side in triple-threat position, the ball is moved quickly (ripped through) from side to side (pit to pit) in order to work the other side of the defender's body: a circle-tight move is preferred to a high or low sweep to move the ball from side to side with quickness and balance.

CATCHING PRINCIPLES

Catching the basketball requires a player to be ready to receive it. To be effective, potential pass receivers should be open, be in quick-stance position with one or both hands up, and give a target away from the defender at the right time.

Another receiving rule calls for catchers to "run through" the basketball by meeting the pass (unless the player is cutting to the basket on a backdoor cut or in a breakaway situation). When defended, the receiver must move toward the ball until contact is made with the ball to ensure possession. Players should make a cut to finish running through the ball, about 15 to 18 feet (4.6 to 5.5 meters) from the ball, thus shortening the passing lane.

Players should catch the ball with the feet slightly in the air whenever possible. Specifically, the receiver should catch the ball with both feet in the air, then come to a quick stop with the ball in either triple-threat position (in normal conditions) or chin-it position (if under duress). This technique enables the player to maintain body control and ball possession and make a quick return to quick stance, where either foot can be used as the pivot foot; this is the quick-stop advantage. Finally, all catchers should catch (the ball) and face (their offensive basket) in order to use big vision to see the whole floor and the rim first for a possible shot (or backboard).

CRITICAL CUE

Catch the ball with the feet in the air.

Two-handed basketball for both passing and catching is a good habit to develop in players. In fact, they should always catch the ball with both hands. Of the three methods for catching the ball, the first is to catch with two hands up (thumbs together); this method should be used when the pass is near the middle of the body and above the waist (figure 3.9*a*). The second method is to catch with two hands down (thumbs apart);

CRITICAL CUE
Catch with a *click*; use both hands and both eyes when catching (look the ball into your hands).

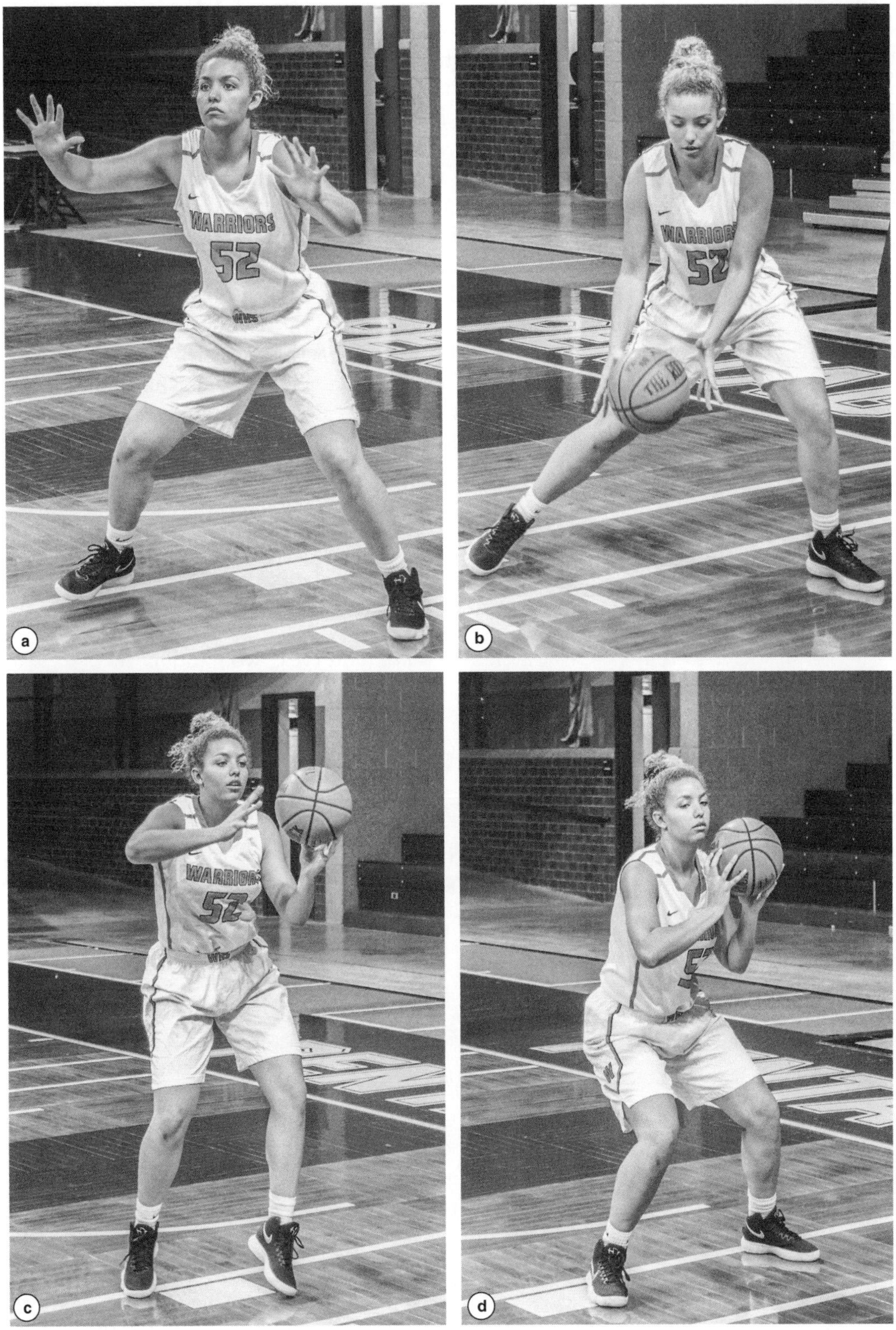

Figure 3.9 Catching the ball: *(a)* above the waist, *(b)* below the waist, *(c)* one-handed block, and *(d)* two-handed tuck.

Figure 3.10 Catch the ball with the wrist back and ball loaded; be ready to shoot (triple-threat position).

it should be used when the pass is near the middle of the body and below the waist (figure 3.9*b*). The third method is the block-and-tuck, which is used when the pass is made to either side of the body. Specifically, the catcher blocks the ball with one hand and tucks it with the other; both hands should immediately be placed on the ball in any way possible (figure 3.9*c* and 3.9*d*). The block-and-tuck technique is more commonly used with a one-handed target catch. The primary objective is to pass and catch simply and safely with two hands when possible.

As the pass is caught, the receiver should let the wrist and elbows give, which is sometimes referred to as using *soft hands*. The receiver should also focus the eyes on the pass until it is in both hands; in this way, the player needs to "catch" the ball with the eyes. The combination of catching with two hands and using both eyes is called *catching with a click*. When possible, the catcher should catch the ball with the wrist back and move the ball to the shooting pocket as quickly as possible (figure 3.10). This "loads" the ball into the shooting pocket for a quick shot. Finally, the pass catcher should meet the pass or shorten the passing lane by coming toward the ball to catch it with the feet in the air (except on a breakaway or backdoor cut to the basket on a defensive overplay).

Here are the three primary rules of pass catching:

- Catch with the *feet in the air*.
- Catch by giving a *spot target*.
- Catch *with a click* (two eyes, two hands).

COACHING POINTS FOR PASSING AND CATCHING

- Use triple-threat position; pit and protect the ball while turning to catch and face up the floor using the RPA progression.
- Help passers develop quickness, the ability to use a spot target, and pass with proper timing.
- Pass with the feet on the floor and with a *ping*.
- Pass and catch with two hands on the ball as long as possible.
- Catch the ball with the feet in the air (*ball in the air, feet in the air*).
- Catch with a *click* (*two eyes, two hands*).
- Protect the ball by moving it to the shooting pocket (load the ball) or chinning position after a catch.
- Catch and immediately scan to see the whole court; catch and face the basket, or catch the ball with the feet facing the basket and follow the RPA rule.
- Be ready for bad passes and stay in a quick stance with the hands up and the feet and body ready to move quickly. Always follow the rule of "possession over position." The priority is always to get possession of the ball on the catch rather than maintain your catching position.

Review table 3.1 earlier in this chapter for a visual reminder of essential passing and catching principles (see the Passing–Catching Principles section at the start of the chapter).

COMMUNICATION IN PASSING AND CATCHING

The passer and the catcher share responsibility for completing the pass; in this endeavor, they should strive for perfection but settle for success. Successful passes depend on communication, especially by the catcher. Every potential pass receiver should always be ready to catch a pass (in quick stance with the hand(s) up), to call the passer's name to show openness, and to communicate with the hands (e.g., both hands up when open, one hand inside for a curl cut, closed fist down by the knee with the outside hand for a back cut, and an open hand up away from the defender when open to catch the ball). Always use one hand to give a target, and the other hand may be used to ward off defenders. The passer, of course, must decide whether to make the pass. Some coaches prefer to have the passer call the catcher's name just before the pass is made, others prefer the catcher to call the passer's name when open, and some prefer both to talk. In any case, passers need to make eye and voice contact with catchers both before and as the pass is made. Players cannot communicate too much in this critical area.

> **CRITICAL CUE**
> Passers should call the catcher's name when open; both passer and catcher should communicate (verbally or nonverbally).

DRIBBLING

Dribbling is not a sight skill but a touch skill. Players should learn to dribble up the court without watching the ball by focusing on the offensive basket (seeing the rim or net) and looking over the whole court (using big vision). Seeing the net in the backcourt allows the dribbler to see the whole court and open teammates. Seeing the rim in the frontcourt establishes the shooting and passing guide to be ready to shoot (when in range) and allows players to see the whole floor (to pass); it gets players in the habit of looking for the shot every time they catch the ball (rim–post–action). The primary objective in the frontcourt is to create a move that allows a player to pass to a teammate for a score. When players are dribbling, this move might entail a live-ball move, a basket-penetration move past an opponent using a dribble drive to the basket, or ball movement in the form of passing to get a teammate open. Dribbling is an acceptable option, preferably for advancing the ball up the court when a pass is not available, maneuvering to get in a better position for a pass to a teammate, executing an offensive play or pattern, or getting out of heavy defensive traffic or a trap situation (two defenders on the dribbler).

> **CRITICAL CUE**
> Dribble with a purpose—*only* to make a live-ball move, penetrate the defense, get a teammate open, advance the ball, execute a play, or get out of trouble.

Dribbling Technique

Players should execute the dribble by first extending the elbow and then flexing the wrist and fingers, thus dribbling with the wrist, hand, and a little forearm motion. The dribble is really a pass to, and catch from, the floor. The fingers and pads of the hand control the ball (the ball should be kept off of the heel of the hand), and the fingers should be spread comfortably and cupped around the ball (figure 3.11). Players should massage the ball, dribble it firmly, and stay low and sit into the game while dribbling. They should make the dribble a short pass for quickness.

Players should maintain maximum contact with the ball. The rules require the hand to stay on top of the ball: The dribble is legal as long as the hand does not leave its

Figure 3.11 Dribbling: *(a)* using the fingers and pads of the hands, *(b)* using elbow extension and wrist and finger flexion to push the ball to the floor.

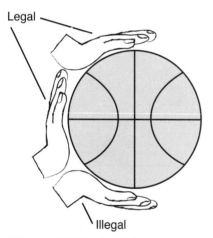

Figure 3.12 Dribbling rules: hand position.

vertical position to get under and carry the ball and as long as the ball is not cupped by a large hand (figure 3.12). When a player starts a dribble on a live-ball move, the ball must leave the hand before the pivot foot leaves the floor (U.S. rules), and the ball must be on the floor before the pivot foot leaves the floor (FIBA international rules).

It is strongly recommended that players use the quick stop to terminate the dribble, especially in traffic (figure 3.13). This is the best way to avoid traveling violations and protect the ball while conserving critical time and space for passing or shooting. In traffic, players should pick up the dribble, use a quick stop, and chin the ball. When chinning the ball, players should get into a quick stance with the ball under the chin, the fingers up, and the elbows out and up (in this way, they make themselves big and protect their territory). On a dribble drive penetrate-and-pitch move, after a quick stop the ball handler can also pivot and pass to a teammate following behind into the driving pathway for an open shot (usually a three-point field goal) on what is often called a "crack-back" move.

Players should learn to use either hand to dribble, developing the weak hand but using the preferred hand whenever possible. They should practice three times more with the nonpreferred hand. When dribbling while closely guarded, they should always dribble with the hand away from the defender and protect the ball with the body and the opposite hand (with an arm bar). They should maintain big vision while keeping the ball low and to the side of the body and staying in a quick stance by sitting into their game (figure 3.14).

Dribbling Strategies

The general dribbling rule is this: When the ball is put on the floor, the dribbler should always be moving purposefully. On drives to the basket, for instance, the dribbler goes past the defender. The primary objective is to use one dribble to score in the frontcourt; however, bouncing the ball once or dribbling while not changing floor position (called

Figure 3.13 Terminate the dribble with a quick stop and chin (or triple-threat position).

Figure 3.14 Closely guarded dribbler: Protect the ball with the body and the opposite hand while keeping tension in the legs and staying in quick stance (for a low or control dribble). Use the body to control the defender.

dropping the ball) should be discouraged. A dribble penetration (*penetrate-and-pitch*) is best accomplished just after the player has received a pass in order to avoid forcing the dribble into defenders who are prepared for the penetration.

One key guideline is for players to stay away from trouble while dribbling. Thus they should avoid dribbling into traffic (between two defenders); they should also keep alert for traps by watching all defenders and avoiding the corners of the court (figure 3.15). Minimize the dribble while attacking the defense to score.

CRITICAL CUE
Dribbling is a touch skill; see the net and the whole court or the rim and the big part of the court.

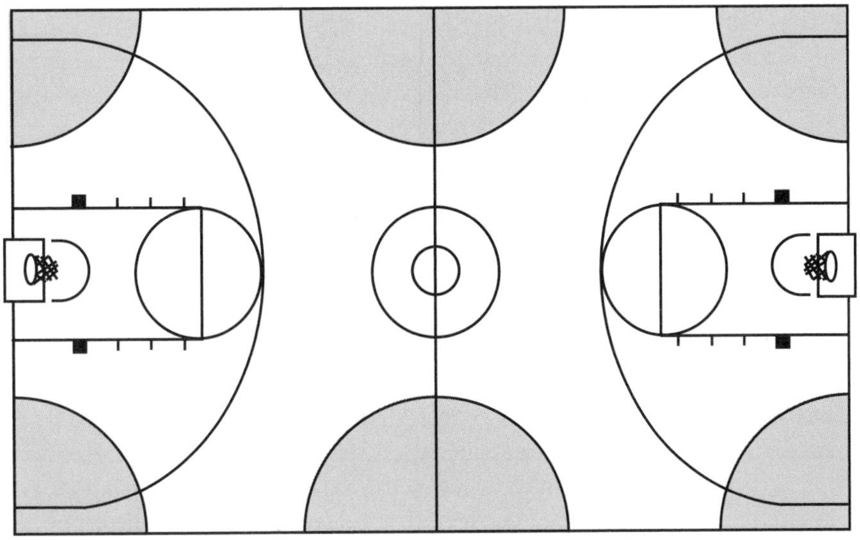

Figure 3.15 To stay out of trouble, avoid the corners of the court when dribbling.

Players should keep the dribble under control and conclude a dribble with a pass or shot, preferably after a quick stop. A dribbler should use the right move at the right time and see the whole court, as well as teammates and defenders, with big vision.

Types of Dribble Moves

The right type of dribble should be used at the right time. A low or control dribble should be used around defenders when the dribbler is closely guarded, whereas a high or speed dribble should be used in the open court when a player is advancing the ball. All dribble moves should change directions at sharp angles using a slow-to-quick motion.

Low Dribble A control or low dribble is the first and easiest dribble to teach players. They should use a staggered stance—bent knees with the ball-side foot back. The opposite hand (as part of an *arm bar*) is used to protect against the defender, but not to push the defender back or hook the defender—only to protect the ball. The basic body motion for dribbling is a sliding movement similar to defensive slides or short steps with a running motion. Players protect the ball by dribbling on the side of the body away from the defender, keeping the ball low, and dribbling hard and fast near the back foot.

Power Dribble An advanced version of the low or control dribble, known as the *power dribble*, is executed by using a sliding foot (step-and-slide or push-step) motion and a low dribble so that the ball is protected by the front leg and hip and the front arm bar. The ball is dribbled below the knee, near the back leg, as far away from the defender as possible. The dribbler advances up the court with push-step moves. As the player goes forward, the ball is near or just in front of the back foot (figure 3.16a); as the player goes backward, the ball is near or just behind the back foot (figure 3.16b). From this position, a player can use advanced dribble moves (described later), such as a pull-back crossover, spin dribble, or fake spin dribble, to create space and attack the basket. Players should maintain big vision up the floor over the lead shoulder—seeing the net when in the backcourt and seeing the rim when in the frontcourt, both of which allow the dribbler to see the whole floor ahead of him or her.

Speed Dribble For a speed or high dribble, players should push the ball out in front and run after it, keeping it ahead of them. The ball can be dribbled higher—near waist level—to attain more speed. The faster the movement is, the farther out in front and the higher the player should dribble the ball.

Change-of-Pace Dribble A change-of-pace dribble, or dribble hesitation, is accomplished by changing speeds from a low or control dribble in a stop-and-start motion. When slowing or stopping, dribblers should straighten up slightly to relax the defender. This technique should be used to move past defenders who take the slow-pace or stop fake. This is another slow-to-fast move that can be used to get dribblers in the clear and to keep them open.

On the change-of-pace or hesitation dribble, players can make it look like they are going to shoot or pass as they hesitate and straighten up the head and trunk. If players are within shooting range, they can fake pulling up for a jump shot; if out of shooting range, they should look to the other side of the court as if they are rising up to pass to that side.

Crossover Dribble A crossover or switch dribble is a basic move used in the open court when sufficient room is available between the dribbler and the defender *and* the dribbler has sufficient momentum to move by the defender (figure 3.17). Players should never cross the ball over in front of the legs (front crossover) on a stationary defender.

Figure 3.16 Power dribble: *(a)* shuffle forward, *(b)* shuffle backward.

Instead, they should attack one side of the defender and use the crossover dribble when the defender has slowed or stopped the initial attack.

In this dribble, the ball is pushed low and quickly across the body. The proper technique is to push the ball from right to left (or vice versa) when a zigzag move or V-cut is

Figure 3.17 Front crossover dribble: *(a)* low dribble, *(b)* low crossover in front of the body, and *(c)* low dribble (opposite hand).

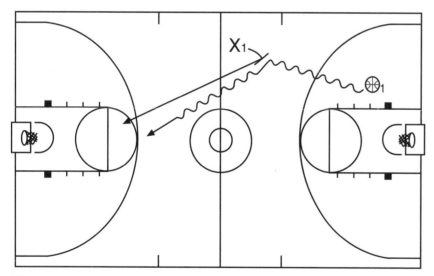

Figure 3.18 Crossover dribble from right to left: offensive zigzag pushing off of the right foot and stepping with the left foot as the ball is crossed over (low and quick) from the right hand to the left hand.

made from right to left (or vice versa) (figure 3.18). This move is used when the defender overplays the path of the dribbler on the ball side. Players should be taught to make the move before a defender gets too close (they need some room to use a front crossover) and to explode past the defender as the move is made.

Head-and-Shoulders Move The head-and-shoulders or in-and-out move is an advanced option for getting around a defender while using the preferred hand (figure 3.19).

Players should dribble the ball with the preferred hand, then continue the move by making a fake opposite to the nonpreferred side with a zigzag move on the opposite foot. At the same time, a head-and-shoulders fake is made to that side, keeping the ball in rhythm with the move. The move past the defender is made with the preferred foot. The rhythm is *right-left-right* to step by for right-handers and *left-right-left* for left-handers. The advantage of this faking move is that the dribbler can face and see the defense while executing a dribble move to get around a defender with the preferred hand. The sequence for a right-handed person, then, is to push from the right foot as the dribble is made; fake left with the left foot, head, and shoulders; extend the right foot with a long step forward and past the defender as the ball is pushed out in front; and step with the

Figure 3.19 Head-and-shoulders (in-and-out) move: *(a)* weight on the right foot while dribbling the ball on the right side, *(b)* zigzag on the left foot with a head-and-shoulders fake to the left (in), and *(c)* moving past the defender with the right foot (out).

left foot and go to the basket and past the defender using hip contact to protect the ball (win the *battle* to get by the defender and win *the war* by using the inside hip to control the defender).

Head-and-Shoulders Crossover Move The head-and-shoulders (in-and-out) crossover, another advanced move, is a dribble move to cross the ball over from the preferred hand to the other hand while moving past the defender on that side and still facing the defense (figure 3.20). This move begins like the head-and-shoulders move. The crossover dribble is kept low and made across the body at the same time that the zigzag move is made from the preferred side to the other side. The footwork is *right-left-right-left*, in order to cross over from right to left (reverse when going from left to right). The dribble rhythm is timed with the footwork movement. The move must be made before the defender is close enough to reach the crossover dribble. The sequence for a right-handed person is to move the foot, head, and shoulders left; come back right (short step); take a short step with the left foot as the ball is crossed over in front of the body from right to left; and bring the right foot across and go to the basket past the defender.

Figure 3.20 Head-and-shoulders (in-and-out) crossover move: *(a)* weight on the right foot while dribbling the ball on the right side, *(b)* zigzag to the left on the left foot, *(c)* weight back to the right foot, *(d)* ball crossover in front of the body from right to left, and *(e)* explosion to the basket using the left-handed dribble.

Spin Dribble A spin or whirl dribble is used for maximum ball protection when the ball handler is closely guarded and the dribbling path is cut off by the defender. During this move, the body is kept between the ball and the defender, as shown in figure 3.21. The disadvantage of this move is that the ball handler briefly loses sight of portions of the court and of defenders and teammates and therefore may be susceptible to blind-side traps or double teams. Spin-dribble footwork uses quick-stop, rear-turn-pivot, and sharp-angled-zigzag moves from right to left (or vice versa). As the 270-degree rear turn is made on the left (or right) foot, the right (or left) hand pulls the ball with the pivot until the turn is completed, and the first step is made with the right (or left) foot. The ball is kept close to the body—the pull is similar to pulling a pistol from a holster. Players should keep the ball tight near the hip and leg to avoid defenders' reach-around or slap-around moves. After the rear turn is completed, the ball is switched to the opposite hand, and full-court big vision is regained. This move changes direction from forward

CRITICAL CUE
Pull the ball to the hip on the spin dribble; keep it tight to the hip or leg on the spin.

Figure 3.21 Spin or whirl dribble: *(a)* low dribble, *(b)* quick stop (rear turn), *(c)* pulling the ball (keeping it in the holster and tight to the hip), and *(d)* changing hands and moving past the defender.

right to forward left (or vice versa) as the ball is changed from the right hand to the left hand (or vice versa).

Back Dribble The back dribble, or rocker dribble, is used to back away from trouble, defensive traffic, or a trap. When dribbling with the right (or left) hand, players should be in a low control or power-dribble position with the left (or right) foot forward into the trouble and then explode back (make an out move) with a sliding power-dribble movement to create space and get away from the defense (out of trouble). After players have reestablished space away from the defense, any dribble move may be used to penetrate or go by the defender. The crossover dribble is especially effective following the rocker or back dribble. The move is into the defender, back out, and then by the defender with a sharp-angled move. When players are crossing over in traffic, it is best to go between the legs or behind the back to protect the ball instead of using the front crossover, especially when facing a closely guarding defender.

CRITICAL CUE
Move in and out on the back dribble and go by low and hard.

Pull-Back Crossover Another important advanced dribble move involves using the power dribble (into trouble, traffic, or a trap) followed by the back dribble (out of trouble or to create a gap) and then the crossover dribble going between the legs and advancing past one defender (figure 3.22). This move allows the dribbler to meet defensive challenges while seeing the whole floor; it also allows a less athletic ball handler to compete well against aggressive, quicker defenders. The dribbler needs to move under control until trapped or in trouble, then back-dribble out hard to create space, and then attack the other (usually outside) defender by crossing over with the ball and going by quickly (thus it is an in-out-by move).

Behind-the-Back Dribble The popular behind-the-back dribble is used to change hands (usually from preferred to nonpreferred) and go past a defender who is overplaying on one side. This goal is achieved by changing direction slightly to the left (or right) and going by on the dribbler's left (or right) side. The dribbler plants the inside foot and steps past the defender with the outside leg. As the left (or right) foot is moved forward, the ball is moved from right to left (or vice versa) behind the back, coming up under the left (or right) hand for a continuation of the dribble. Players can learn to coordinate the dribble and the footwork by doing a stationary side yo-yo V-dribble (figure 3.23), in which they use one hand to dribble back and forth with the opposite foot forward. When the ball is controlled from front to back, it can be moved behind the back as a step is taken with the left or right foot (figure 3.24).

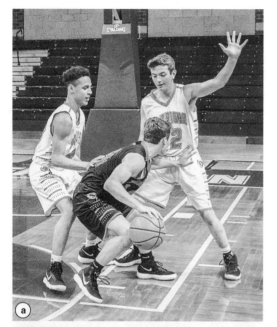

Figure 3.22 Pull-back crossover dribble: *(a)* When in the trap, use a low control dribble. *(b)* To get out of trouble, power-dribble to retreat using backward sliding steps. *(c)* Cross over and go by the defender.

Figure 3.23 Progression for behind-the-back dribble: *(a, b)* front-to-back yo-yo (on the side of the body), *(c)* back yo-yo (from side to side behind the back).

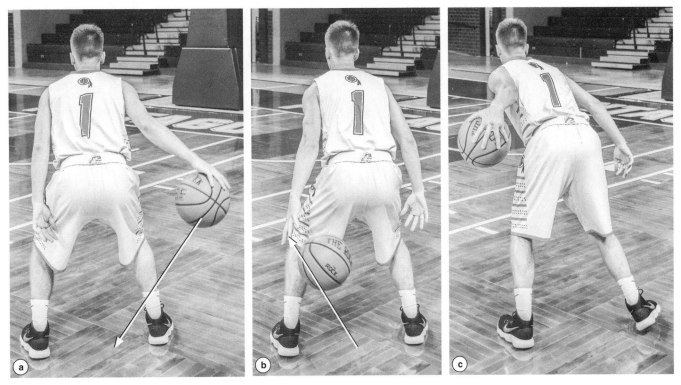

Figure 3.24 Behind-the-back dribble (right to left hand): *(a)* Dribble with the right hand, *(b)* move the ball from right to left behind the back, and *(c)* continue the dribble with the left hand and move past the defender.

Between-the-Legs Dribble The between-the-legs dribble is used to avoid an overplay and to change the ball from one side (i.e., hand) to the other. If the ball is being dribbled with the right hand, it can be changed to the left hand between the legs when the left or right foot is forward (best with the right foot forward); the move is reversed if beginning with a left-handed dribble. The ball is kept low and crossed over between the legs with a quick, hard push across (the ball is snapped between the legs as the player steps with the other foot) (figure 3.25). Players can learn to coordinate the dribble and the footwork by walking forward slowly as the ball is crossed over between the legs during each step.

Figure 3.25 Between-the-legs dribble: *(a)* Dribble with the right hand and *(b)* push between the legs when one foot is forward.

COACHING POINTS FOR DRIBBLING

- Keep the head up to maintain big vision. In the backcourt, see the net and the whole court; in the frontcourt, see the rim and the half court.
- Control the ball with the fingers and the pads of the hands.
- Massage the ball and dribble firmly; pass and catch to the floor.
- When around or close to defenders, stay low and protect the ball (sit into the game, keep tension on the legs, and use an arm bar).
- Use a quick stop and chin the ball when ending the dribble, or pit and protect the ball (triple-threat), and be ready to pass after the quick stop—to the side, to an open post player (especially when the post defender helps up), or behind (when a teammate fills behind where you have driven on a rear turn pivot and crack-back pass).
- Catchers should always be prepared for a shot (hands and feet ready) then pass first; dribble last.

The move is really a one-foot quick stop on the outside foot as the ball is snapped between the legs and a sharp-angled step is made to go by the defender as the ball is switched to the other hand. The planted outside foot is then pulled past the defender to protect the ball. The between-the-legs dribble is the best dribble move to combat pressure, see the whole court, and move past a defender.

BASIC BALLHANDLING DRILLS

These drills for ballhandling skills are usually enjoyed by players. Coaches need to insist on quick and proper execution and timing. Players tend to learn to execute these skills at a slow speed and then progress too quickly to moving at game speed. Instead, they should increase speed *gradually* until they can achieve game moves at game speed.

BALLHANDLING

Purpose: To teach players to control the ball and become familiar with it (see it, hear it, and feel it)

Equipment: One ball per player and a 6-foot (1.8-meter) circle of floor space per player

Procedure: Players spread out in their areas and execute the following drill options, working first for proper execution and then for quickness.

- *Figure-8 speed dribble:* Players start the drill with either the right or left hand. They start dribbling in and out between the legs in a figure-8 pattern. They should start slowly and keep the ball as low as possible at all times. They can gradually pick up speed after they begin to master the drill. There is no time limit, though 20 times around in 1 minute is excellent (or 10 times in 30 seconds).

- *Blur:* Players start the drill with the legs about shoulder-width apart and one hand on the ball in front of the legs. They flip the ball in the air, reverse the position of the hands, and catch the ball in the fingertips. They should try to go as fast as possible for 30 seconds. When the move is executed properly, the ball appears to sit between the legs. Assessment: 81 to 100 is excellent, 61 to 80 good, and 40 to 60 fair.

- *Straddle flip:* Players start with the legs shoulder-width apart, the knees bent, and the hands in front holding the basketball. They let go of the ball or flip it very slightly up in the air between the legs, then bring the hands to the back of the legs and catch the ball before it hits the ground. Next, they flip the ball again in the air and bring the hands back to the front as quickly as possible. They should drill as fast as possible without dropping the ball. Continue the drill for 30 seconds. Assessment: 81 or higher is excellent, 61 to 80 is good, and 40 to 60 is fair.

- *Rhythm:* Players take the ball around the right leg, grab it with the left hand in front and the right hand in back, and then drop it. They quickly reverse hands and catch the ball after one bounce, then move the ball back to the start around the left leg. The drill can also be done starting with the ball in the left hand. Continue the drill for 30 seconds. Assessment: 33 to 40 is excellent, 21 to 32 is good, and 10 to 20 is fair.

- *Double-leg and single-leg:* Players take the ball behind the legs and around the front. When the ball reaches the right hand, they spread the legs and take the ball around the right leg only. Next, they close the legs and take the ball once around both legs, then open the legs and take the ball around the left leg once and back to two legs again. The ball always moves in the same direction. Players then start with the ball in the left hand. Continue for 30 seconds. Assessment: 51 to 70 is excellent, 36 to 50 is good, and 25 to 35 is fair.

- *Around the waist:* Players take the ball in the right hand, move it behind the back, and catch it with the left hand; then, in one continuous motion, they bring the ball around to the front to the right hand. They do the drill continuously for 30 seconds, as fast as possible, then execute it by starting with the ball in the left hand. Assessment: 51 to 70 is excellent, 36 to 50 is good, and 25 to 35 is fair.

- *Around the head:* Players place the ball in the right hand. With the shoulders back, they take the ball behind the head, catch it with the left hand, and bring it around to the front to the right hand in a continuous motion. The opposite drill is to start with the ball in the left hand. Continue the drill for 30 seconds. Assessment: 51 to 75 is excellent, 41 to 50 is good, and 30 to 40 is fair.

- *Figure-8 from the back:* Players start with the ball in the right hand, then take it between the legs to the left hand. Next, with the ball in the left hand, they take it behind the left leg and between the legs to the right hand. The opposite drill is a figure-8 from the front, which takes the ball from the right to the left hand through the front of the legs. Continue the drill for 30 seconds. Assessment: 66 to 85 is excellent, 46 to 65 is good, and 30 to 45 is fair.

- *Figure-8 with one bounce:* Players start with the legs shoulder-width apart and the knees bent. With the ball in the right hand, they bounce it between the legs and catch it with the left hand behind the legs. Then, with the ball in the left hand, they bring it around to the front, bounce it between the legs, and catch it with the right hand. The opposite drill is to take the ball behind the legs and bounce it to the front right and then left hand. Assessment: 41 to 50 is excellent, 31 to 40 is good, and 20 to 30 is fair.

- *Individual ballhandling warm-up sequence (Stephen Curry style):* This individual ballhandling-and-shooting routine is offered as an example of purposeful practice that can be used as an individual drill, a pregame routine, or a warm-up drill for a team of players working at multiple baskets. It exemplifies the "game shots at game speed" practice habits that must be developed by all successful players. It consists of the following elements:

  1. Two-ball stationary dribbling: two balls in front, V out-in (side to side), V up-back, V between the legs

  2. Near-the-basket one-handed touch shooting: one-handed catch and underhand feel shot off the board at a 45-degree angle

  3. Midrange shots to finish at the basket: one-handed set (jump) shots and live-ball attack and finish

  4. Corner shots: three-point field goals

  5. Distance shots: starting inside and moving outside the arc using a hop-back or step-back move for three-point field goals

  6. Back-to-basket from 20-foot (6.1-meter) range: starting with a spin pass to self and simulating soft 1-on-1 defense
     - Catch-and-face choices: drives, one-dribble pull-ups, and dribbles to step-back three-point field goals
     - Spin moves to attack the basket with a one-handed runner shot

  7. Three-point field-goal catch-and-shoot: around the arc, some dribbling variations, and one dribble after a jab fake

  8. Super three-point field goals: moving 6 to 10 feet (1.8 to 3 meters) outside the arc

  9. Free throws

  10. High-elbow attack move from near the free-throw line

  11. Three-point field goals around the arc: baseline corner to baseline corner

LINE DRILL: PASSING AND CATCHING

Purpose: To teach passing and catching techniques and all basic passes

Equipment: Half-court floor space and one ball per line of players

Procedure: Players are positioned in four lines behind the baseline at one end of the court, and the coach is positioned at the top of the key to direct the drill. The first player in each line starts at free-throw line distance facing the baseline as the first catcher (in a ready-to-catch stance). The ball starts with the player on the baseline in each line. Passes are made as the passer moves quickly to replace the catcher. Critical cues are for players to pass with the feet on the floor and catch with the feet (slightly) in the air; for passers to exaggerate the follow-through (*freeze it*), pass with a *ping*, and pass to a spot; and for catchers to give a target, catch the ball with the eyes and both hands (catch with a *click*), and play two-handed basketball. Play should be proper first and quick second. Suggested progressions are as follows (also see figure 3.26):

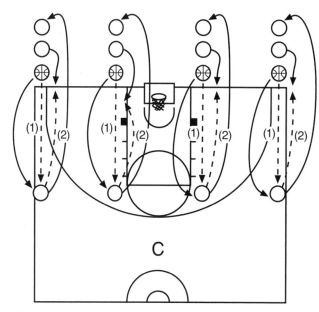

Figure 3.26 Passing and catching.

- Chest pass (air, bounce)
- Push or flick pass
  - Pass to right side (air, bounce) or left side.
  - Pass to left side (air, bounce) or right side; go pit to pit quickly (circle tight).
  - Read the defense; look by the ear first with an air pass (either fake high and pass low or fake low and pass high).
  - Pass and assume a defensive position (with designated hand position).
- Overhead pass
  - Catch, pit, and protect the ball.
  - Put the ball overhead.
- Baseball pass (increased distance)
  - Pass with the dominant hand only.
  - Face the sideline and step with the pass (move to the top of the key or a longer distance).
  - Fake the pass into the nonpassing hand and then pass.

TWO-PLAYER PASSING AND CATCHING ⏵

Purpose: To teach passing and catching with a push pass from either hand after a dribble

Equipment: Full-court floor space and one ball per pair of players

Procedure: Players are positioned in four lines behind the baseline at one end of the court. The players in the middle lines each have a ball and are partnered with the players in the outside lines. Each player with a ball pits it and executes a dribble drive with the hand opposite the partner, who moves parallel to the dribbler. The dribbler makes a quick stop and, if using the EPF approach, makes a push pass to the partner using the closest hand. If using the PPF technique, a right-hander on the right side steps across to use the left-handed pass with the left PPF. On the left side, that player would step with the right foot (left PPF) and pass with the right hand. The partner catches the ball with the feet in air

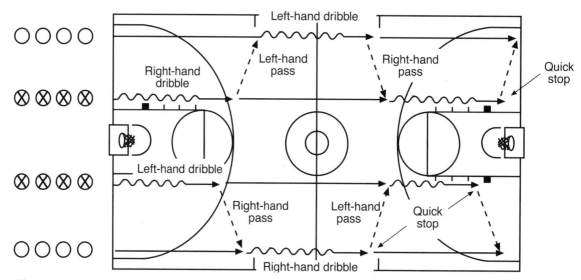

Figure 3.27 Two-player passing and catching.

and repeats the dribble-drive cycle. Each time, the catcher calls the passer's name before the pass is made. The complete sequence is shown in figure 3.27. The next pair begins its passing and catching sequence when the previous pair is 15 to 18 feet (4.6 to 5.5 meters) ahead (near the free-throw line).

This pairs passing drill can be modified using EPF footwork. In that variation, partners dribble-drive and quick-stop, then use the inside pivot foot (toward the partner) to step across and make a two-handed chest pass to the partner. The partner catches the ball with the feet in the air and repeats the dribble-drive sequence with an outside-hand dribble and quick stop. The ball handler pass fakes away, then pivots on the inside foot, steps across, and makes a two-handed pass to partner. Catchers should use proper timing and spacing with the partner.

COACH BEILEIN'S PERFECT PASSING

Purpose: To develop basic passing and catching skills at game speed with high standards of excellence

Equipment: One ball per half court and groups of four offensive players on the court

Procedure: The first four players (two guards and two forwards or four positionless players in those spots) use 4-on-0 offense in the half court. Players must complete 10 passes while running any offensive moves selected by the coach without making any passing or catching mistakes within 30 seconds. Use only pass-and-cut, give-and-go, and dribble-at backdoor moves. All basics must be done correctly:

- Pass with the feet on the floor.
- Catch with the feet in the air (quick stop).
- Give a spot hand target.
- Pass to the target hand.
- Pass with a *ping*; catch with a *click*.
- Catch and face (follow the RPA rule).

When a mistake is made before 30 seconds, four new players rotate in to run perfect passing while the original players run sideline sprints for 30 seconds.

GONZAGA TEAM PASS—CATCH (AROUND THE WORLD)

Purpose: To assess team performance on passing and catching efficiency as well as proper footwork (advanced drill)

Equipment: Two balls per team on a half court

Procedure: Players are divided equally into four groups positioned in a diamond formation (figure 3.28). For a timed 1-minute drill, all passes are made in a counterclockwise direction using a two-handed air pass to the right, after which the passer goes to the back of the line. Players must perform all techniques correctly or face a consequence (e.g., doing push-ups or sit-ups, running circuits, or restarting the drill). The team goal is to make 65 passes (women) or 75 passes (men) in 1 minute.

Coaching Points

- Feet: Pass with the feet *on the floor*; catch with the *feet in the air*.
- Target: Pass to an *open hand*; give a *lead-hand target*.
- Sound: Pass with a *ping*; catch with a *click*.

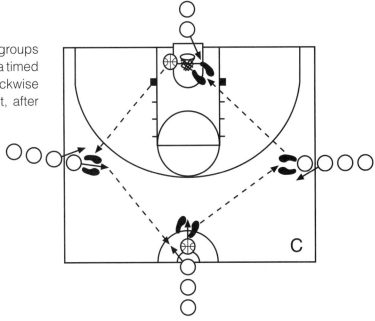

Figure 3.28 Gonzaga team pass–catch drill.

On successful completion of the drill in 1 minute, start over and pass clockwise (i.e., to the left). The goal may be modified based on age, skill, and grade level.

2-ON-1 KEEPAWAY PASSING

Purpose: To teach passing and catching between partners who must pass by a defender

Equipment: One ball per three players and floor space of 15 to 20 feet (4.6 to 6.1 meters)

Procedure: Players are grouped in threes—two offensive players 15 to 18 feet (4.6 to 5.5 meters) apart with a defender between them (figure 3.29). Defensive players rotate out each 30 seconds or after making an interception or defensive ball touch. The following progression is recommended:

- Defender in position and using designated hand position (up, down)
- Defender either close to or away from the passer (thus teaching the passer to take the ball to the defender in order to reduce reaction time)
- Live defense and offense
- Passer using vertical fakes, using quick moves to pass to one side of the defender's body (working one side), and reading the defender's hand position on that side (fake low and pass high or vice versa).

> **CRITICAL CUES**
> Pass with the feet on the floor, take the ball to the defender, use vertical fakes, be quick and accurate, catch with the feet in air, and maintain spacing of 15 to 18 feet (4.6 to 5.5 meters).

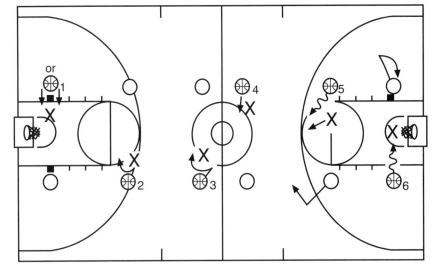

Figure 3.29 2-on-1 passing.

MOVING PAIRS PASSING ▶

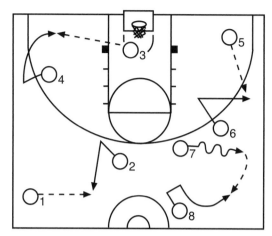

Figure 3.30 Moving pairs—passing and catching.

Purpose: To teach partner passing and catching skills while players are moving and playing against an imaginary defender

Equipment: One ball and floor space of 15 to 18 feet (4.6 to 5.5 meters) in diameter for each pair of players (eight players per half court)

Procedure: Organize players in pairs (one passer and one receiver each) and provide each pair with a ball and sufficient court area (figure 3.30). The receiver gets open against an imaginary defender, receives the pass with the feet in the air, quick-stops, catches the ball, and faces the passer in a triple-threat position. The passer then becomes the next receiver; thus the drill involves continuous passing and catching. All passing and catching rules are practiced. For example, players pass with the feet on the floor and catch with the feet in the air. Another phase can use the following sequence: catch, dribble drive, quick stop, and pass. Catchers need to time their cuts to get open against the imaginary defender just before the passer is ready to pass the ball.

WALL PASSING

Purpose: To teach players passing and catching without a teammate

Equipment: One ball per player and a wall space or toss-back rebounding device

Procedure: All basic passes can be practiced against a wall or target. The toss-back or pass rebounder—a commercial rebound device—is especially helpful for this drill. It rewards a good pass by returning the ball on target, thus effectively informing the athlete when an inaccurate pass is made. The following passes should be practiced: chest, bounce, overhead, baseball, and push. Players should pass the ball with the feet on the floor and catch the ball with the feet in the air. The toss-back device can be used to increase speed and intensity gradually until a mistake is made (thus indicating learning). Players should work toward making game moves at game speed.

LINE DRILL: STANCE, STARTS, AND SKILL BREAKDOWN

Purpose: To teach players to carry out selected footwork skills from a quick stance and a quick start (direct drive, crossover drive)

Equipment: One ball per line (four lines on the baseline)

Procedure:

First Sequence—Without the Ball

- Quick start and quick stops at the free-throw line, centerline, opposite free-throw line, and opposite baseline

- Quick start and quick stop into a 2-and-2 rebound (at the same four locations)

- Quick start and quick stop after two imaginary dribbles, rear turn on PPF, and step and imaginary pass to the next person in line

Second Sequence—With the Ball

- Same variations, with emphasis on a first step that is long and low (direct drive or crossover drive) and using PPF or EPF footwork on live-ball moves

LINE DRILL: STARTS, STOPS, AND TURNS ▶

Purpose: To teach players to combine dribbling, starting, stopping, passing, catching, and turning skills (recommended drill for all levels of play)

Equipment: One ball per line

Procedure: The first player in each of four equally spaced lines on the baseline assumes an offensive quick-stance position with the ball (triple-threat position). On command, the player takes two or three dribbles forward, past the free-throw line distance, does a quick stop, uses a rear turn on the PPF (nondominant foot), faces the catcher on the baseline (the next person in line), steps and makes a push pass, and then goes to the back of the line. The coach can designate any pass to be used and either direct drive or crossover drive when starting the play. PPF or EPF footwork may be used.

MASS DRIBBLING ▶

Purpose: To teach the basic ballhandling skills of dribbling

Equipment: One ball per player (or one per pair of players—one dribbler and a buddy coach) with players spread out on a half court

Procedure: All players have their own dribbling space and face the center circle. Players start with an overhead toss and trap the ball as it comes off the floor to begin the low dribble. Each player follows the coach's commands to execute the following dribble moves:

1. Stationary control and low dribble

   - Right-hand control and low (command: *right low*)
   - Change from right to left (command: *change*)
   - Left-hand control and low (command: *left low*)

2. Moving low with power dribble

   - Right-hand low (command: *right low*)
   - Change from left to right (command: *change*)
   - Left-hand low (command: *left low*)
   - Shuffle-slide forward (command: *forward*)
   - Shuffle-slide backward (command: *back*)

3. Rhythm push-and-pull (yo-yo)

   - On the sides of the body (command: *side yo-yo*)
   - In front of the body (command: *front yo-yo*)
   - Between the legs laterally (command: *side to side*)

Coach commands should be given slowly at first to ensure proper technique at a slower speed and with a higher dribble. Commands can then favor increasing speed and lower dribbling until mistakes are made. Players should use the nonpreferred dribbling hand two or three times more often than the preferred hand. Coaching emphasis is for players to sit into the game (*stay low*) with the head up (*see the net*) and dribble hard and low (*pound the ball*); to perform correctly first and then go faster until mistakes are made; and then to continue progressing toward making game moves at game speed.

FULL-COURT DRIBBLING

Purpose: To teach the ballhandling skills of dribbling

Equipment: One ball per line (minimum) on a half court (minimum)

Procedure: Using the line-drill formation, players should form four lines on the baseline. The dribble moves of the drill are then practiced for one circuit. Players concentrate on maintaining eye contact with the net on the opposite end of the court. Coaches can also use two lines (the sidelines) to give players feedback on ball location, going by the position of the defender and by player location on the court. Cones can be spaced on the court to simulate defenders.

Options

- *High or speed dribble:* Players dribble down the court with one hand and then return while dribbling with the other hand.

- *Change-of-pace dribble:* Players move down the court while alternating high dribbles for speed with low dribbles for control; they use the opposite hand on the return.

- *Between-the-legs dribble:* Players use this move to travel down the length of the court.

- *Back dribble and crossover (pull-back crossover):* Players dribble into and out of imaginary traps at the free-throw line, the half-line, and the opposite free-throw line, then finish with a quick stop and a ball chin.

- *Pull-back crossover repeated, three forward dribbles, two back dribbles, crossover, and go:* Players repeat the sequence over the whole floor.

- *Coach's signal:* Players use a specified dribble and quick-stop under control.

- *Zigzag or crossover dribble or spin dribble:* Players start in triple-threat position and then dribble down the court in a zigzag pattern while using V-cuts and a crossover or spin dribble.

- *Two-ball dribbling (advanced):* Players dribble two balls while executing these selected dribble moves: low rhythm (both hands), low nonrhythm (both hands), high rhythm (both hands), high nonrhythm (both hands), and high to low (right high and left low and vice versa). Players should start dribbling hard and low, then dribble high, then alternate rhythm (one high, one low), then add changes of direction and speed, and, finally, use various combinations. The two-ball dribbling progression should include the following:
  - Stationary: low rhythm, low nonrhythm, high rhythm, high nonrhythm, high to low and reverse, windshield wipers (side yo-yo), front-to-back yo-yo.
  - Dribbling on the move to half-court (using all dribble move combinations).
  - Dribbling from the centerline to the baseline (using all five combinations as well as changing sides or hands with the balls).

- *Dribble drills*
  - Offense–defense zag (1-on-1 offensive dribbler with defender).
  - 1-on-1 attack to score: Dummy defender at top of key, add defensive hoop

player near basket; line defense at top of key, add defensive hoop player near basket.

- 1-on-1 full-court (offensive player with one or two balls): Goal is to get past the free-throw lane line (live offense and live defense).

WALL DRIBBLING

Purpose: To teach ballhandling skills in a challenging format

Equipment: Flat wall surface and two balls per player

Procedure: In a line at each wall location (where wall space is available), players perform the following options using both preferred- and nonpreferred-hand dribbling against the wall.

Options

- One hand and one ball (left and right)
  - Pound
  - Around the world (circle pattern)
  - High to low and low to high
- Two hands or two balls (one ball dribbling with each hand)
  - Pound
  - Around the world
  - High to low; low to high
  - Two-ball stutter (nonrhythm)
  - Two balls (one pounding, one moving)
  - Two balls (both circling)

BASIC BALLHANDLING DRILL ▶

Purpose: To develop basic dribbling, passing, and catching skills

Equipment: Basketballs, tennis balls, floor space

Procedure

1. *Taking infield:* This is a favorite ballhandling drill from baseball hall of famer Ozzie Smith. To adapt it to basketball, players find a wall space and get into a low, wide quick stance with the toes pointed slightly outward and positioned about 20 feet (6.1 meters) from the wall. Players then throw a tennis ball hard against the wall 6 inches (15 centimeters) above the floor and catch it with a *click* (*two hands, two eyes*) when it caroms off the floor. Players gradually move toward the wall to increase the difficulty. They should always throw sidearm during this exercise, not overhand, to protect the rotator cuff muscles.

2. *Dribble and juggle:* This drill works on nonpreferred-hand dribbling and requires players to avoid watching the ball while dribbling. The player dribbles a basketball with the nonpreferred hand while tossing and catching a tennis ball. Players can increase the difficulty by tossing the tennis ball higher and catching it in different ways and by adding various dribble moves while the tennis ball is in the air. Teaching tips are to get low and wide and pound the dribble hard. Players should keep control of the dribble at all costs, even when they lose control of the tennis ball; they should never give up their dribble.

3. *Partner dribble and toss:* Pairs of players talk to each other while dribbling with the nonpreferred hand and playing underhand toss. Players should never give up the dribble.

4. *Partner dribble and throw:* Pairs of players throw the ball overhand to each other while dribbling with the nonpreferred hand. To increase the difficulty, they should move away from each other in a random fashion.

5. *Partner three-ball passing:* Players can use two basketballs and one tennis ball, or two tennis balls and one basketball. They pass to each other with a one-handed push or flick pass, using the preferred hand to begin with and then switching together to the nonpreferred hand in order to increase the difficulty. Talking is critical. The ball is in the air (no bounce passes), the feet are in the air on the catch, and the pass should be made to the nonpassing shoulder of the catcher. The player who starts with two (of the three) balls starts the drill with the first pass.

6. *Partner bad-pass reaction:* Pairs of players (each pair with its own ball) are positioned 15 to 20 feet (4.6 to 6.1 meters) apart from each other. The partners make sharp, crisp, *inaccurate* passes to each other. The catcher catches with a *click*, then captures and chins the ball. To test the catcher, the coach or partner may also throw underhand (softball-style) bullet passes. The catcher should be in a quick-stance catching position. Players should move the feet, get the body in front of the pass, and catch the ball with the feet in the air.

7. *Partner back to the passer:* Pairs of players (each pair with its own ball) are positioned 15 to 20 feet (4.6 to 6.1 meters) apart from each other. The player without the ball has his or her back to the passer and assumes a quick-stance catching position. The passer makes a crisp pass while calling the catcher's name. The catcher makes a quick jump turn to face the passer and catches the ball with both hands. The players then exchange roles and repeat the sequence. They should pass as fast as needed to test their teammates. Each catch should be made with a *click*.

8. *Pull-back crossover progression:* With one ball each, players start in a stationary position with the foot opposite the dribbled ball forward. They implement the following sequence (pointing the lead foot in the direction of travel):

   - Push-pull on the right side; get a rhythm.
   - Cross over to the left side; repeat.
   - Push-pull two or three times, cross over, and repeat.
   - Perform the same sequence as in preceding moves but with a baby step, then do a lunge step forward.
   - Dribble forward two or three times, dribble back two or three times, cross over, and repeat.

GONZAGA FULL-COURT FOOTWORK AND LAYUP (PEER-PRESSURE DRILL) ▶

Purpose: To teach and review EPF inside pivot footwork and two-handed passing and catching in pairs with 15-to-20-foot (4.6-to-6.1-meter) spacing and timing

Equipment: One ball for each pair of players and a full-court space

Procedure: Players form two lines starting on the baseline at one end of the court. They run the drill in pairs (one player from each line). The player with the ball passes diagonally ahead to the partner and moves up the floor with two-lane fast-break spacing. The catcher makes a two-handed catch with a quick stop. This process is repeated until the pair completes a two-lane fast break from the top-of-key area. The remaining pairs follow in the same manner, and the sequence is then repeated to move back to the starting basket. After catching with a quick stop, players should establish an inside pivot foot and step across diagonally to make the next pass; see figure 3.31. Players should use proper spacing and timing and run the drill in circuits (down and back) according to the following progression:

- *Circuit 1 (pass-and-catch only):* Catch with the feet in the air, quick-stop, establish EPF inside pivot foot to step across, and make the next pass. (*Note:* This is the circuit shown in the online video.)

- *Circuit 2:* Some coaches may prefer to use this PPF version. Catch with a quick stop, make a two-dribble move to the outside and quick-stop, then use PPF pivot-foot technique to step across and use a one-handed pass to the teammate, who repeats the sequence.

- *Circuit 3:* Use the same technique as in circuit 2 but finish with a dribble-at backdoor layin.

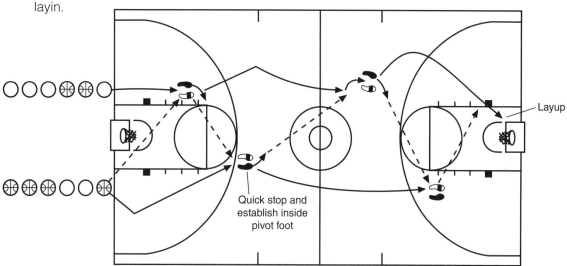

Figure 3.31 Full-court layup drill.

Wooden Wisdom

"Do not let what you cannot do interfere with what you can do."

—John Wooden

CHAPTER 4

SHOOTING

"The main thing on offense is that we get a good shot every time down the floor."

Pete Carril, former Princeton University men's basketball coach, Naismith Hall of Famer (from *Pete's Principles*)

Shooting is probably the best-known fundamental skill in basketball—every player is interested in scoring. If given a basket and a ball, even a novice invariably dribbles and shoots.

Shooting, the fundamental skill that players enjoy and practice most, can be practiced alone because it produces immediate feedback. Most coaches contend that all players can become good shooters through long hours, days, and years of practice. Of course, *great* shooters must also possess special physical talents. Any player, however, can become a good shooter, and an excellent free-throw shooter, with enough purposeful practice.

One of the two basic objectives of basketball is to get a good shot in order to score a basket (the other objective, of course, is to prevent the opponent from doing the same). This chapter presents guidelines for teaching players how to get a good shot on every attempt and how to become better scorers (making a high percentage of shots taken) through physical practice (with proper technique) combined with mental practice to build confidence.

FIELD-GOAL SHOOTING

Players and coaches should realize that field-goal and free-throw scoring percentages are the most important statistical factors related to winning, both on offense and on defense (for more on defense, see chapters 7 and 10). Therefore, it is critical for players to build shooting confidence over time through careful preparation and by shooting with proper mechanics at game speed while using proper mental techniques. Players literally cannot overpractice shooting (physically or mentally) as long as they are taking game shots at game spots at game speed in order to prepare properly for competition. Because coaches cannot provide enough shooting time during team practices, players need to understand the necessity of individual shooting practice in order to reach their shooting-percentage goals. The key to building confidence for becoming a better scorer is proper preparation—that is, purposeful practice. In his book *Outliers: The Story of Success,* Malcolm Gladwell (2011) states that *full potential* in any skill depends on purposeful practice for at least 10,000 hours. This can be accomplished in *ten* years of practice for four hours per day and five days per week. This is a tough task that few players will accomplish (unless they become professionals). Remember, though, it's not where you are but which direction you are going and how fast you are getting there!

CRITICAL CUE

The ultimate practice goal is to take game shots at game spots at game speed.

General Concepts

Coaches should teach players to become scorers, not just shooters. Anyone can shoot, but considerable skill is required to score consistently in game situations. To maximize scoring-to-shooting ratio, players must learn when to shoot, when to pass, what their shooting range is, and from which spots on the court they can consistently make field goals. The recommended minimal-percentage guidelines for all players are shown in table 4.1. Practice goals should be set at least 5 percent higher than game goals to allow for expected "game slippage" in shooting percentages due to competition. Even-higher goals need to be set by elite players who want to become great scorers.

Practice and game shooting percentages provide a bottom-line feedback measure for shooting effectiveness, and players need to pay attention to both. In particular, beginners and any other players who shoot below the desired percentages for their age group should adopt the guidelines completely. Players who shoot near or above the percentage goals should adopt one new goal to add to their game. Players should always use percentages as self-feedback on their practice and game shooting habits in order to

Table 4.1 Desired Baseline Field-Goal Percentages

Ages	U.S. grade levels	Comments	Practice 2FG% (inside arc)	3FG%	Game 2FG% (inside arc)	3FG%
4-7	K-2	Parent assisted	N/A	N/A	N/A	N/A
Formal basketball begins						
8-10	3 and 4 (lower elementary)	**Equipment modifications** #5 ball, lower basket height, half-court play	30-35	N/A	25-30	N/A
10-14	5-8 (upper elementary)	**Equipment modifications** #6 women's ball or #7 regular ball	40	N/A	35	N/A
14-20	9-12 (secondary school)	**Equipment modifications** #6 women's ball or #7 regular ball	45	35	40	30
18-25	College or university (postsecondary school)	N/A	50	40	45	35
Professional						
N/A	N/A	N/A	55	45	50	40

2FG% = two-point field-goal percentage
3FG% = three-point field-goal percentage

assess status and progress. They must learn to play "against the game" by setting scoring percentage goals and practicing game shots at game spots at game speed. Shooting percentages ensure that players can't fool themselves when developing scoring skills; thus they provide a basis for purposeful practice.

Proper shooting technique can be developed only with sufficient basic skills and strength. With this reality in mind, coaches can use a smaller ball and a lower basket when teaching shooting skills to players who are younger than age 10 (generally grades 5 and below in the United States). In this way, proper mechanics can be learned early (at ages 8 to 10, or in U.S. grades 3 and 4) and later applied readily to a regulation ball and basket; young players should learn proper mechanics that can be easily carried out. This adjustment of equipment—modifying the ball (smaller), the basket (lower), and the court size (half)—allows young players to learn to shoot sequentially and progressively and build confidence more quickly.

Complete guidelines for modifying the game for younger players (including equipment recommendations) are available in a companion coaching book, *NABC's Handbook for Teaching: Basketball Skill Progressions* (2003) by Jerry Krause, Curtis Janz, and James Conn (or the most current revision). It also details what basketball skills to teach and when to teach them; in other words, it provides a sequential, progressive approach to shooting. Even though some youngsters want to play with the big ball and the higher basket, they must be sold on solid progressions and correct mechanics at an early age. Using the big ball and the 10-foot (3-meter) basket too early in their learning can be harmful to their skill development and result in improper shooting habits that are difficult to correct later.

The most important shooting fundamentals are passing, catching, and quick stops. Players should learn to get a shot by first moving to get open while using proper footwork. Then they must catch the ball and face the basket in triple-threat position and be prepared to shoot (hands and feet ready)—also while using proper footwork. Thus both footwork and handwork are essential for proper shooting. In addition, players need good vision habits to go from big vision (to get their shot) to small vision (with a specific target) before the shot is taken (in order to hit the shot).

Coaches should teach players to attack and get shots as close to the basket as possible on a dribble drive. Players should challenge the defense by probing for the basket; after all, the ultimate shot is the layup (or layin). Coaches can help players learn key concepts of shooting by teaching them certain acronyms. For instance, younger players can learn proper shooting mechanics using the BEEF principle.

B for balance: Balance is the most important foundation of every shot. The shot starts on the floor, before the player catches the ball, with proper footwork—knees bent and feet ready. Kevin Eastman, longtime college and professional coach, conveys this importance through a simple phrase: "The feet make Js" (jump shots). The shot really does begin on the floor with proper footwork.

E for eyes: To shoot accurately, players must pick up the target early (giving it full focus for at least 1 second) and narrow the focus to the spot target (i.e., the center of the back of the rim [shooting for net] or the upper corner of the backboard rectangle when using the backboard). Remember: "The eyes make layups."

E for elbow: Generally, players should limit all shooting-arm motion to a vertical plane—especially keeping the elbow up, in, and under the ball (except for pedestal-pocket shooting). This approach ensures that the ball will *go straight* to the target.

F for follow-through: Players should use full extension of the arm (with a locked elbow), held for one count on a field goal or until the ball goes through the net on a free throw. This essential reminder can be expressed in the phrase *freeze the follow-through* to help produce the same finish on each shot. The wrist is fully flexed, with the fingers pointed down (as in making a gooseneck shape, putting a hand in the cookie jar, or making the shape of a firm but floating parachute with one hand). The follow-through must be firm but relaxed. The proper release angle is 60 degrees above horizontal for most shots. Shooters should finish high (*release it high and let it fly*); the critical guideline for proper arc is to *shoot up, not out.* Shooting high and soft is especially important on backboard shots. A 55- to 60-degree release angle on the shot produces an optimal entry angle into the basket of 45 degrees (a range of 43 to 47 degrees). See the following discussion about data collected using the Noah Basketball shooting system.

CRITICAL CUE
Shoot up, not out.

CRITICAL CUE
Freeze the follow-through.

The release angle of 60 degrees was advocated as optimal by John Bunn, a Naismith Hall of Fame coach and an educated mechanical engineer, in his 1955 book *Scientific Principles of Coaching.* Bunn held that the shooter should get as much arc as possible, given his or her strength. He also found that more missed shots were short rather than long, which can occur with a shot arc that is either too low or too high.

Arc and basket-entry angle can now be measured accurately by means of a new technology, the Noah Basketball shooting system, which provides instantaneous feedback. Each shot or arc is filmed, logged into a digital database, and analyzed, after which the shooter is provided with precise feedback about entry angle. Thus, in addition to heeding the coach's reminder to *shoot up, not out,* shooters can also use modern technology to assess their muscle memory. The optimal *release* angle of 55 to 60 degrees translates into an optimal basket-*entry* angle of 45 degrees (a range of 43 degrees to 47 degrees). Data collected using the Noah Basketball shooting system confirms the theory that successful shots are shot steep (target release angle of 60 degrees) in order to produce a deep entry into the back half of the basket (2 inches past center or 11 inches from the front with a desired entry angle of 45 degrees).

This information is relevant because studies have shown that many players shoot with a release angle—and therefore a basket-entry angle—that is too low. In fact, a basket-entry angle of less than 35 degrees produces only a 9-inch (23-centimeter) window for the ball to go in, provided that it is exactly on line. This common problem can now be addressed both through coaching emphasis on a high (60-degree) release angle and through practice using digital data about muscle memory.

Thus shooters generally need higher arc (consistent with their strength) in order to produce accurate shots. Great shooters release consistent shots in terms of start, finish, and release angle. Each shooter must find an optimal arc (neither too low nor too high) by balancing accuracy and strength in order to maximize the chance for scoring.

Of course, players also need to develop the skill of shooting the ball *straight*. Here again, the Noah system can help. In this case, it provides the shooter with verbal feedback derived from the video information about shot accuracy in two forms: distance to the right or left when the ball arrives at the basket and angle of deviation to the right or left. This verbal feedback on shooting the ball with proper mechanics (shoot it *straight* and shoot it *deep* in the basket) can then be used to develop muscle memory which results in consistent shooting.

Overall, then, in all shooting practice and drills, research by Marty and Lucey (2018) has proven that proper shot mechanics must focus on two critical outcomes: shooting the ball straight and shooting it deep into the basket (i.e., when the center of gravity of the ball is 11 inches from the front or in the back half of the hoop). These two simple outcomes can be addressed through the following keys to learning:

- *Shoot it straight.* This outcome must be the focus for all motion involved in preparing and executing the shot. Generally, the shooting foot must point at the target: for rim shots, the middle of the back of the rim; for backboard shots, near the upper corner of the rectangle for a 45-degree shooting angle. In addition, the shooting foot, shoulder, elbow, and hand need to be aligned in a vertical plane that extends through the target. All shooting motion should occur in the vertical plane, including freezing the follow-through. The *essential* progression drill for this technique is the shoot-the-line drill option presented later in this chapter.

- *Shoot it deep (into the back half of the basket).* To accomplish this, the start of the shot (shooting pocket close to body with wrist fully loaded back or extended) and the finish of the shot (full wrist flexion and relaxed) are critical steps. The best shots into the back half of the basket are, of course, the swish (net only) and what is sometimes referred to acronymically as the BRAD (*back rim and down* into the net). The ball's necessarily parabolic path (shaped like half of an egg) requires players to shoot it high enough to get it above the basket and go into the basket from above while minimizing the muscle force required to get it there. Again, research has shown that the best way to achieve this goal is to shoot with a departure angle (when the ball leaves the hand) of 55 to 60 degrees and an entry angle (when the ball comes into the basket) of 45 degrees (or a range of 43-47 degrees). These are *optimal* angles for making shots; when the angles are too high or (more common) too low, the ball is less likely to go into the basket.

You can find more in-depth information about the shooting research that has proven these principles from the scientific-based company that conducted much of this research, Noah Basketball (see the Resources list at the back of this book). Another helpful learning device for shooters is a memory aid based on the acronym ROBOT, which stands for range, open, balance, one-count, and team. Players can use this aid to help themselves become shooting robots—that is, scoring machines!

R: The player is in effective scoring *range* and shooting in rhythm ("feeling" the shot). For instance, in secondary school (ages 14 to 20), effective scoring range means the area within which the player makes at least 45 percent of two-point shots and 35 percent of three-point shots in practice. (For a full set of appropriate goals based on age and skill level, refer back to table 4.1.)

O: A good shot requires the shooter to be *open*—that is, not guarded by a defender with a hand in the face.

B: A good shot is always taken on *balance*. According to John Wooden, Naismith Hall of Fame player and coach, balance depends largely on footwork (as well as head position). In other words, the shot starts from the floor; therefore, players should get their feet ready. Moreover, shooting can be evaluated by the position of the feet before and after the shot. After the set or jump shot, the feet should land slightly forward (about 6 inches, or 15 centimeters)—never back, right, or left. The head should remain slightly forward, especially before the shot.

O: Good shots are *one-count* shots, meaning that the player's feet and hands are ready and the ball is shot in a single positive motion from the shooting pocket—no two-count ball dip (down and up) or swinging a leg to get the feet adjusted unless needed for rhythm.

T: No teammate has a better shot. Players should leave their feet and go up to shoot, and pass only when a teammate really has a better shot. Players should be reminded to get the best *team* shot. A final shooting reminder is to develop consistency: consistent arc, consistent alignment, and consistent depth in the basket.

Building Field-Goal Confidence

After mastering the physical technique, players can concentrate on the mental aspects of shooting. Players can gain a mental edge by developing confidence built on careful preparation, which produces consistent success in both practice and game competition. Mental-edge techniques include shot preparation, shot execution, and after-shot skills.

1. *Shot preparation:* Players should pick up the spot target early and focus on it with narrow concentration for 1 second. Players must learn to ignore distractions and see only the ball and the net in their minds. This full focus is learned using the verbal prompt *focus*.

2. *Shot execution:* Motor learning studies have shown that players can improve their skills by becoming more aware of the feel of a shot, from the start (the shooting pocket) to the finish (the full follow-through). During each shot, the verbal prompt *feel* reminds players to increase their awareness of the shot from start (pocket) to finish (release).

3. *After-shot skills:* Psychocybernetics research points to the importance of controlling self-talk after each shot in order to build confidence. When players are shooting, the proper feedback is *remember the makes and forget the mistakes*. This process requires a shooter to emphasize and celebrate made shots and play down (with little emotion)—that is, *analyze and forget*—missed shots. Players should never be too hard on themselves over a missed shot. On a miss, a player is asked only to note the shot location and then continue with play. Here are the verbal prompts:

Made shot: *yes, net, swish, money*

Missed shot: shot location (*short, long, right, left,* or something more specific for great shooters) and a short memory

4. Summary: During practice, players need to use the verbal prompts for each shot: *focus, feel,* and *feedback* (*yes* on makes, shot location on misses). Confidence is built daily and requires many successes at high percentages over long periods of time.

COACHING POINTS FOR SHOOTING

- The shot starts on the floor—feet ready (*the feet make jump shots*), hands ready (*ball to loaded shooting pocket with full wrist extension*).
- Offensive quick stance: Put weight on the whole foot for quickness and balance, point the shooting foot at the basket, and finish on the balls of the feet with weight forward.
- Full focus: Pick up the target early (rim or backboard) for 1 second (*laser focus on the target*).
- Shooting hand: Hold the ball in the whole hand; lock and load it into the shooting pocket.
- Bookend hand: Place it on side of ball; move it out and up on the shot (it is used only to balance the ball).
- *Release it high and let it fly*: Shoot up, not out, with a 60-degree angle of release above horizontal; thrust the fingers through the ball to get backspin (*feel*).
- Follow through fully—firm but relaxed. *Freeze* the follow-through in full wrist flexion (for a field goal, 1 second; for a free throw, until the ball enters the net or contacts the backboard).
- To build confidence, remember the makes and forget the mistakes.
- Use confident self-talk; focus (before the shot), feel (during the shot), and feedback after each shot (*yes, swish,* or *board* on a made shot; shot location on a missed shot).
- Use quickness without hurrying. Be quick in preparing for the shot but don't hurry the shot.
- Maintain vertical alignment; keep the ball in the plane with the elbow in, up, and under the ball (unless using the pedestal shooting pocket). To get the ball up and into the shooting pocket quickly, use a two-handed bookend hand pickup from under the ball.
- Use physical and mental practice: see, hear, and feel the perfect shot.
- Use the BEEF principle.
- Become a shooting machine by applying the ROBOT concepts.
- Take game shots at game spots at game speed to accomplish purposeful practice.
- Practice shooting progression daily and end with shots from the pass and the dribble.
- Become a consistent shooter (alignment, arc, and depth).

Proper practice can make a shooter into a scorer; this is the secret of good shooting. To that end, players should spend ample time shooting with proper form. Practice makes permanent (not perfect); therefore, players must learn to practice correctly, both physically and mentally—game shots at game spots at game speed. Players can also use mental practice alone by spending 3 to 5 minutes visualizing successful shooting situations and specific shots and imagining the look, sound, and feel of a perfect shot: *See it, hear it, and feel it*. As they visualize the perfect shot, players should repeat the cues *focus, feel, yes,* or *net* at least 25 times per day. The greatest progress can be made by combining physical practice with mental practice.

CRITICAL CUES FOR SHOOTING

- Early: Laser-focus on the target.
- During: Take a smooth, "one-count" shot.
- After: Remember makes; forget mistakes.

Figure 4.1 Vertical-plane shooting.

SHOOTING MECHANICS

The specific physical techniques of shooting, or shooting mechanics, include movements of the torso, feet, and hands. The movements are the same for the one-handed set shot and the jump shot. The essential difference is that the jump shot is executed by shooting the set shot just before the peak of a jump.

The best compromise between the optimal arc for shooting (an almost-vertical trajectory) and the player's available strength for accurate shooting is generally found in a medium-arc shot released at an angle of about 60 degrees. In contrast, most beginners shoot with a release angle lower than 60 degrees. When using the regular side shooting pocket, the shooting foot, elbow, wrist, and hand are aligned in the same vertical plane with the basket when the ball is brought up past the face (figure 4.1). The hand and arm motions are the same on all set and jump shots—the power differential comes from the legs. Putting backspin on the ball increases the angle of rebound off the rim—that is, produces a more vertical bounce—thereby giving the shot a better chance of going into the basket. Backspin also stabilizes the flight of the ball. Players can produce backspin by thrusting the fingers through the ball on the release, thus creating a softer shot.

In addition to these general points of shooting mechanics, players should be taught specific fundamentals, such as maintaining proper body position, holding the ball correctly, and executing the basic steps of the shot in the proper sequence.

Balance With Feet Ready

A good shot starts with the feet ready, the knees bent, and the dominant foot slightly forward and *pointed toward the basket* in a quick stance or offensive triple-threat position (figure 4.2). The player's head is balanced and slightly forward, and the body is generally facing the basket (the shoulders are not exactly square to the basket—the dominant shoulder is slightly forward). The player should point the shooting foot at the basket and sit into the shot (*the feet make Js*). For pedestal-pocket shooting (explained later), the feet are square to the basket.

Footwork is the foundation that provides balance for the shot. Dan Hays, Hall of Fame coach (Oklahoma Christian University men's basketball), uses a unique way to teach proper footwork for set and jump shots. Players stand with the feet together and touching (figure 4.3*a*). The shooting foot is moved slightly forward so that the nonshooting toe aligns with the middle of the shooting foot (figure 4.3*b*). Then the shooting foot is moved laterally to a balanced, feet-ready position for shooting (figure 4.3*c*). Of course, when shooting a shot from a pass, proper footwork is best facilitated when catching with "feet in the air" and then landing in the described position with the "feet ready" to shoot.

Target

When the ring (rim) is the target, players could focus either on its imaginary center (the perfect target) or the best practical substitute, which is the middle eyelet loop on the back of the ring as viewed through the net. The back of the rim is the preferred spot target because accuracy tasks require a spot target, most misses are short, and most made shots are near the back half of the basket. Some coaches prefer the front of the rim, but the authors prefer the back of the rim for the previously stated reasons.

CRITICAL CUE
Get the feet ready (balanced) and the hands ready (ball in the shooting pocket with wrist fully extended and ball loaded).

CRITICAL CUE
Full focus—early target (rim or backboard).

Figure 4.2 Shooting balance: *(a)* triple-threat position with the feet ready (front view), *(b)* triple-threat position with the feet ready (side view), and *(c)* pedestal pocket (square stance) with the feet ready.

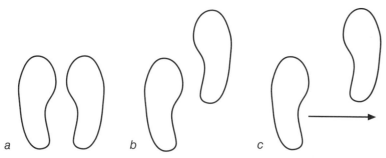

Figure 4.3 Developing balance: *(a)* Start with feet together, *(b)* move the dominant foot slightly forward, and *(c)* end with the feet in a widened stance.

For angled shots (45 degrees with the backboard), players can use the upper corner of the backboard rectangle as the spot target. The best court areas from which to shoot the board shot are shown in figure 4.4. Coaches should remind shooters to hit the backboard target with the ball on the way down in order to have the same arc on ring and backboard shots (which tend to be too low or flat). Both types of shots should have the same arc; generally, the top of the ball on a medium-range shot is at the same height as the top of the backboard to attain the optimal release angle of 60 degrees.

On both rim and backboard shots, players should pick up the target early with a full focus of one count. Key guidelines are as follows: *Release it high and let it fly*; shoot *high and soft* with backspin (especially on backboard shots); and *shoot*

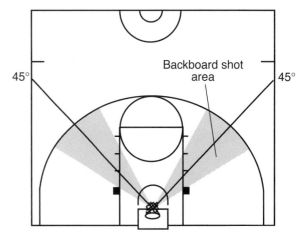

Figure 4.4 Use the backboard target when shooting near a 45-degree angle with the backboard.

up, not out. The eyes should be kept on the target at all times (except in the weekly drill, described later, of following the flight of the ball after release to check proper backspin).

Shooting Hand

The next step is for the shooter to grip the ball properly. The fingers of the shooting hand should be spread comfortably, and the ball should touch the whole hand except the heel (figure 4.5). The angle between the thumb and first finger is about 70 degrees (not 90 degrees); in other words, players should form a V, not an L, between the thumb and index finger. To get the feel of this configuration, players (facing the coach) can hold up the shooting hand, spread the fingers as much as possible (for a 90-degree angle), relax the hand slightly (so that the thumb and first finger form a V), and place the ball onto the whole shooting hand while holding that palm up in front of the body (figure 4.6). When handling the ball, players can move it to shooting position by grasping it with both hands (on the sides) and then rotating it so that the shooting hand is behind and under the ball. This technique is called *locking and loading* the ball into the shooting pocket with full wrist extension.

The lock-and-load technique enables consistency by placing the shooting hand in the same position at the start of each shot. Thus the shooting pocket is always in the same starting position.

To lock and load the ball into the triple-threat shooting pocket (the same starting position for each shot), players should first place the ball on the whole hand in front of and to the side of the body (figure 4.6a). Then the nonshooting hand grasps the shooting hand's wrist in order to lock it into the starting position (4.6b). The nonshooting hand is

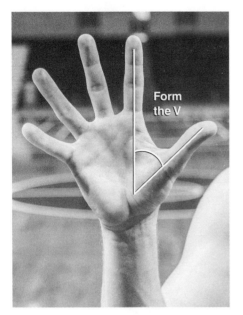

Figure 4.5 Proper hand grip for shooting: Use the whole hand, except for the heel; the finger and thumb form a V at 70 degrees.

Figure 4.6 Lock and load: *(a) Hold* the ball in the whole hand (palm up); *(b) load* the ball to the shooting pocket, *locking* the wrist in; and *(c) load* the ball close to the body into the shooting pocket with full wrist extension.

then placed on top of the ball or the hand in order to load the ball into the shooting pocket with full wrist extension (figure 4.6*c*). This technique puts the shooting hand into a position that produces wrinkles on the wrist.

After moving the ball into shooting position, the shooter should bend the wrist back in full extension and load the ball in, forming an L at the wrist and at the elbow (see wrinkles on the back of the wrist). The player sets the ball on the hand as if holding a tray with the shooting hand. This position for the side shooting pocket is shown in figure 4.7. The locking-and-loading technique ensures that the starting position is the same on each shot for consistency.

The elbow (the L) is kept up, in, and in front of the wrist (figure 4.7). Beginners may have a lower starting elbow position, but the elbow should still be in front of the wrist and above the shooting foot. Younger players tend to drop the ball too low to gain momentum, pull the wrist in front of the elbow, and, in the process, develop inefficient shooting mechanics. Shooting power comes properly from the legs; the

Figure 4.7 Regular side view of pocket—elbow up, in, and in front of the wrist to balance the ball.

CRITICAL CUE
Hands ready—get the ball to the shooting pocket.

arm shooting mechanics should stay the same. The most common error that players make with the shooting hand or arm is having the elbow out when the shooting foot is pointed at the basket and when they are using the regular armpit or shoulder shooting pocket. Elite players can modify the pocket by moving it higher. The *pedestal pocket*, as a middle shooting position, is described later and is best suited for inside players facing the basket at closer distances.

Balance or Bookend Hand

The balance, or bookend, hand is used only to steady the ball, not to shoot it. The term *bookend*, which more aptly describes the position and function of the nonshooting hand, was first applied by Dan Hays of Oklahoma Christian University. The bookend hand is kept on the side of the ball to avoid thumb drag; it does *not* guide the ball. As the shot is released, the bookend hand is moved *slightly* up and out of the way, and it finishes in a vertical position off the ball, with the fingertips at the level of the wrist of the shooting hand. The elbow of the same arm remains slightly flexed.

Common errors related to the bookend hand include the thumb push (to help shoot the ball), the heel pull (to hold over and drag the ball), and rotation of the off hand with the shot (it should serve as a stationary vertical guide). These errors can be caused by extending the nonshooting elbow during the shot. Figure 4.6*c* shows the correct shooting-pocket position and the position of the bookend hand, which can also be described as pointing the bookend thumb at a right angle to the shooting thumb. The most important role of the balance or bookend hand is to lift and drive the ball from the dribble into the shooting pocket on the dribble pickup. The last dribble uses a hard bounce to get the ball quickly into the shooting pocket, and this move is assisted by

CRITICAL CUE
Bookend hand: Move it off the ball and up slightly before release. Keep the same-arm elbow bent. Point the thumb back with the fingers up in a vertical position.

the balance (bookend) hand lifting the ball from underneath quickly to the shooting pocket.

Coaches can illustrate the concept of the whole hand and that of locking and loading without the ball by asking players to place the shooting hand in front of the body (palm up) and spread it to the whole-hand position (figure 4.8a). Players should imag-

Figure 4.8 Locking and loading (without the ball): *(a)* ball grip with whole hand (palm up), *(b)* locking in the wrist, *(c)* loading the shooting hand, and *(d)* start of the process of shooting the ball and freezing the follow-through (holding it for at least one count).

ine that a ball is sitting on the hand. Next, they should grasp the shooting hand's wrist with the nonshooting hand and rotate it inward until it won't rotate further, thus establishing a locked-in position (figure 4.8*b*). Finally, they should place the balance hand on the shooting hand (palm to palm) and load the imaginary ball with full wrist extension into the final shooting pocket (figure 4.8*c*). All of these motions can be performed without a ball in order to ensure that players understand the feel of establishing the same starting position (the shooting pocket) for each shot. The shot can be simulated by pushing the elbow to extend it and propel the imaginary ball to the basket, freezing the follow-through in full but relaxed wrist flexion.

Release

In order to shoot up and over by pushing the elbow button to cause full elbow extension (figure 4.8*d*), players must thrust the fingers up and forward through the ball or snap the wrist to produce a soft shot with backspin. Players should visualize shooting over a 7-foot (2.1-meter) defender. Backspin is produced when players use the fingers to firmly *thrust* the ball up and over (pushing through the ball and snapping the wrist) (figure 4.9). The ball comes off the index and middle fingers last.

Figure 4.9 High release and follow-through: Freeze it for at least one count with full but relaxed wrist flexion.

Backspin produces a soft shot that can hit the rim, slow down, and bounce in; thus it keeps the ball around the shooting target. Players can check their backspin weekly by shooting a vertical shot without a target or following the flight of the ball after the release of a regular shot (shoot the line for five repetitions). Players should not, however, develop the habit of watching the ball normally; they should focus on the target instead and check their backspin only on occasion.

As discussed earlier, the proper release angle for a shot is about 60 degrees above horizontal. For most players, however, the release angle is too low, which decreases the size of the available target as the ball approaches from above, thus lowering their shooting percentage. Therefore, coaches should guide players to *release it high and let it fly* (*shoot up, not out*).

Although many players would benefit from shooting with a higher arc, they may struggle to attain it. The higher the arc is, the greater is the muscle force needed to propel the ball, and more force tends to produce less accuracy. Thus players and coaches must be aware of the need to attain an *optimal* release angle and shot arc. This goal can be achieved through a smooth, rhythmic release that uses minimal force to produce a 55- to 60-degree release angle and, in turn, an optimal basket-entry angle of 43 to 47 degrees (45 degrees optimal).

The Importance of Arc in Shooting

Here is how the ball sees (so to speak) the hoop as it approaches the basket on its entry angle:

1. Coming from an angle of 90 degrees above horizontal, the target area is 100 percent of actual size.

2. Coming from an angle of 51 degrees above horizontal, the target area is effectively 56 percent of actual size (i.e., much smaller than on the 90-degree approach angle).

3. Coming from an angle of 31 degrees above horizontal, the effective target area is only 33 percent of actual size. (For a clean shot, the *minimum entry angle* is about 35 degrees.)

4. Coming from an angle of 20 degrees above horizontal, the target area is 22 percent (too small).

5. Coming from an angle of 9 degrees above horizontal, the target area is 12 percent (no chance).

Figure 4.10 Pedestal-pocket shooting: Shoot up.

Studies at the University of Calgary (Harle & Vickers 2006) have shown that the ideal release angle for free throws is 52 to 55 degrees. To shoot at an angle higher than 55 degrees requires extra velocity or ball speed (i.e., extra muscle force from the shooter), which reduces accuracy. Even so, because of learning slippage, the best compromise between force on the ball and accuracy for most shots and most players is an optimal release angle of 55 to 60 degrees, which produces the optimal basket-entry angle of 45 to 50 degrees. This compromise, based on applied research, balances available muscle force with optimizing the size of the target as the ball comes toward the basket.

This principle applies more easily to pedestal-pocket shooting from an overhead or middle starting spot. As the ball is pushed up (not out) from the pedestal pocket, it is thrust up and over with the fingers touching it last to produce backspin (figure 4.10).

Follow-Through

The final step in shooting is full follow-through with complete elbow extension (locking the elbow), arm pronation (turnout), and wrist flexion (controlled relaxation). Players should visualize making a gooseneck, putting their fingers in a cookie jar, putting a hand in the basket, or making a parachute shape with a firm floating hand and holding that position for at least one count (figure 4.9). The hand and fingers are firm but relaxed. A consistent, full follow-through (*freeze it*) ensures that the ending position is the same for each shot.

As described earlier, shooting skill is built first on proper mechanics and technique. Players must develop correct technique as a physical foundation for the shot:

- Feet ready for balance

- Ball into shooting pocket (same starting point) using whole-hand grip (forming the V), locking and loading the ball with full extension (two-handed pickup), and using a bookend (balance) hand

- Release and full follow-through (same ending point)—shooting up (not out) near 60 degrees and holding the full wrist flexion follow-through (freezing it for one count)

- Balance at the end of a shot (head forward)

OTHER TYPES OF SHOTS

The basic mechanics of shooting that are found in the set and jump shots are also applied in closer shots (including layups) and longer shots (three-pointers). The same mechanics are also used in post-player shots.

Layup

All players should learn to shoot both left- and right-handed layups while jumping from one foot. The best starting technique is to jump from the left leg when shooting right-handed and from the right leg when shooting left-handed. A high jump is made by stamping on the last step to minimize the forward long jump and maximize the high jump. Coaches should have players use the backboard for layups whenever possible; exceptions include the baseline dribble-drive reverse layin and, of course, the dunk shot. The dunk shot should be used only when a player can dunk the ball without strain and defensive traffic is minimal.

Approach Attacking or accelerating to the basket is a positive approach that players can use readily. When shooting a layup, the attack move is made by taking the ball up in a two-handed pickup motion. Players should bring the free hand to the ball when dribbling, chin the ball near the shooting shoulder in the power position—usually opposite the jumping foot—and keep the ball chest high on the side away from the defender (see figure 4.11a). They should keep the ball away from the hip and avoid dangling it away from the power position (near the upper chest or shoulders). The two-handed high pickup and the chin move are used to prevent players from "rocking the cradle" (figure 4.11, b and c), which exposes the ball to the defender as it is brought across the body.

Figure 4.11 Shooting the layup: *(a)* Perform a two-handed pickup; *(b, c)* avoid rocking the cradle.

The last dribble is timed with the last jumping step on the inside foot when the player is using a dribble-drive move; this approach is often called an *opposition move* when a player shoots a right-handed layup with a jump from the opposite (left) foot (figure 4.12). On a left-foot jump, the opposite (right) knee drives up toward the basket, as if the knee were on a string lifting it up with the same-side (shooting) elbow. Coaches should teach beginners to use a gallop move with a layup. For a right-handed dribbler and shooter, the last one-two gallop move is with the right foot first and then with the left foot, which serves as the jumping foot.

Another layup-shooting reminder is for players to pick up the target (usually the backboard) early and focus on it for at least 1 full second: *eyes make layups*. Players should then finish the layup with one hand. Thus they should take the ball up with two hands to the power position but finish with one hand; the shooting hand should be behind the ball for overhand layups and under the ball for underhand layups.

When facing shot-blocking defenders, offensive players can use an advanced layup move in which the footwork is the opposite of what is normally done for a one-foot-jump opposition layup. For example, an offensive player on the right side of the basket would jump with the right-foot, use a two-hand high pickup, and finish with a one-hand layup. This unusual same-side-foot-and-hand technique can be used to throw off the timing of a shot-blocking defender.

Jump When the player is jumping for a layup, the knee opposite to the jumping foot is raised high (figure 4.13) and straightened just before the peak of the jump. Other tips include using the backboard for a higher percentage shot to one's advantage, shooting softly with a feather touch (*shoot high and soft*), and focusing on the target. For one-foot-jump layups, coaches can teach both the primary overhand or push layup (with the palm of the shooting hand facing the target, as in figure 4.13) and the underhand or scoop

Figure 4.12 Layup—opposition move.

Figure 4.13 Overhand, or push, layup.

Figure 4.14 Underhand, or scoop, layup.

layup, which produces a softer shot and is executed with the palm of the shooting hand facing up (figure 4.14) as the elbow and wrist are flexed to shoot the ball.

CRITICAL CUE
One-foot layups: opposition, two-handed pickup, high and soft shot on the backboard.

Power Layup This layup is really a quick stop with the player facing the baseline and continuing into a one-handed, two-foot layup. The quick stop is made for power and balance and is used in traffic or under defensive pressure when control and power are required. Thus the power layup is a slower but stronger move than the one-foot-jump layup. On approaching the basket, the shooter lands in a quick stop (with a one-count landing on both feet) facing the baseline or backboard with the feet pointed toward the baseline (figure 4.15). The player then scoops the ball up after a hard dribble, chins the ball on the outside shoulder, away from the defense, and explodes vertically from both feet to the basket in order to shoot a one-handed layup off the backboard (with the shooting hand either facing the target or under the ball).

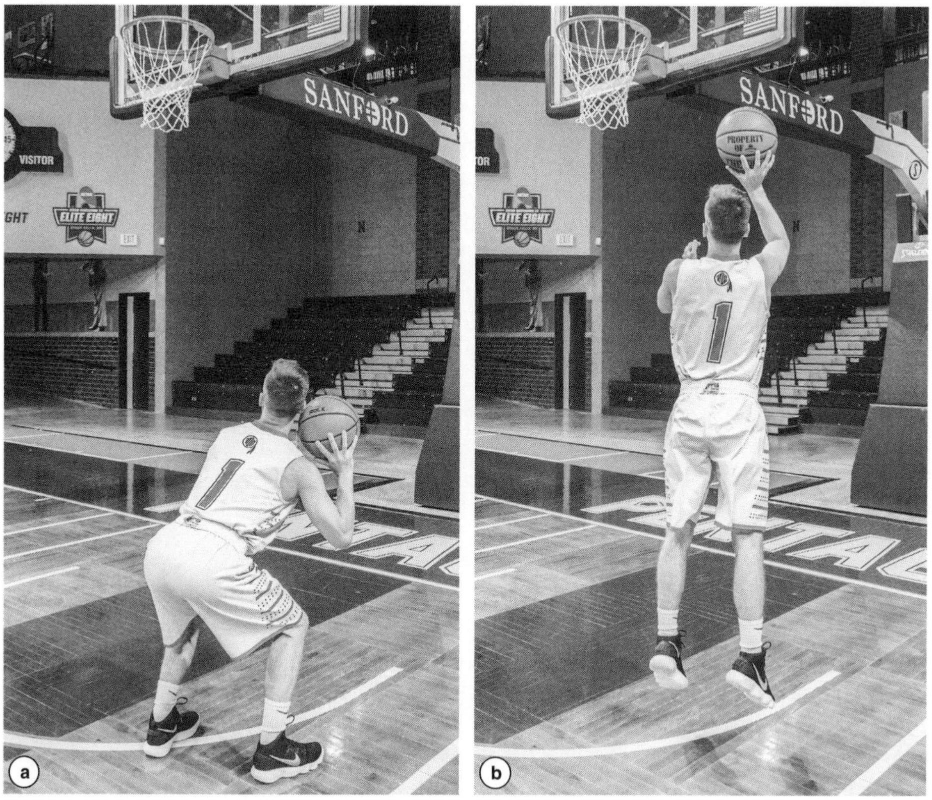

Figure 4.15 Power layup: *(a)* quick stop, *(b)* power shot (outside hand).

Long Layup This layup is an advanced skill used when finishing shots at the basket near or around shot blockers. As shown in figure 4.16, this skill involves attacking the basket from the top of the key (wide free-throw lane) down the wide free-throw lane alleys (as labeled in figure 4.16) or just outside the free-throw lane (to avoid shot blockers). The offensive player uses a one-hand runner shot or baby hook off the backboard with the ball located on the outside shoulder (power position). The player should also be aware that if a shot-blocking defender comes out on the edge of the free-throw lane (to help up and out), the backside layup area will open up for a cutting teammate. This move can be especially useful when a shot-blocking defender has limited mobility or range, as may be the case in women's basketball.

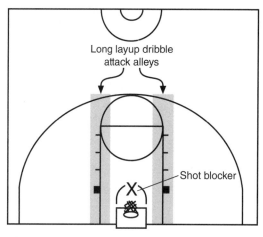

Figure 4.16 Attacking the basket with the long layup.

Three-Point Shot

Shooting the three-point shot, or trey, requires some adjustment. For one thing, three-point shooters must develop a sense of where the line is without looking down (*respect and know the line*). In addition, long shots produce long rebounds, and rebounding teammates must adjust accordingly. Also, though all shooters should know the time and score in a game, this is especially true for three-point shooters, given the greater potential to affect the score.

The three-point shot should be attempted only after a plant and pivot (figure 4.17) or as the player is moving toward the line with a quick stop (for stronger players). These movements provide the greater force needed for this shot and allow beginning players to take it without straining. Emphasis should be placed on gaining momentum by bending the knees more for extra power from the legs, using the elbow L, and releasing the shot on the way up with a full follow-through. For many players, the three-point shot is more of a set shot than a jump shot.

Coach Homer Drew, formerly of Valparaiso University, taught his players to get the three-point field-goal from the pass in the following six ways:

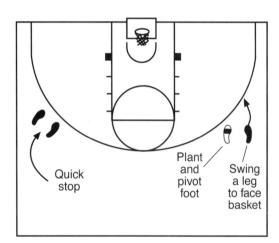

Figure 4.17 Footwork for the three-point field goal.

- Inside-out pass
- Offensive rebound and pass-out
- Penetrate-and-pass (pitchout or on a crack-back pass behind)
- Fast break to the trey (dribbler and fast-break lanes)
- Skip pass (with or without a screen)
- Screen and fade (flare)

Hop-Back Jump Shot

The step-back or hop-back jump shot requires shooters to alter their jump-shot footwork, especially against excellent defenders, from a basket penetration move to set up the shot. The basket penetration move clears space for a jump shot, such as a three-pointer. In order to create space from the defender and take a balanced shot, the shooter needs to develop advanced footwork and ballhandling skills. As shown in figure 4.18, the ball handler must aggressively penetrate the arc, thus forcing the defender to defend the basket (ball–defender–basket). This penetration move requires a weight shift to the inside penetration foot, which the dribbler uses to push off in order to produce a hop-back motion and move back behind the arc. The ball handler then lands facing the basket at an angle opposite to the defender's momentum (offensive move against defensive momentum). Thus the ball handler

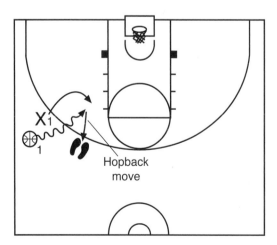

Figure 4.18 Step-back or hop-back jump shot: Penetrate, then hop back from the left foot to set up a jump shot.

can either drive right and hop back to the left from the right foot, or drive left and hop back to the right from the left foot.

Pedestal-Pocket Shot

Modifications can be made for players with greater strength (especially in the core and upper body) and for inside players who shoot most of their set and jump shots closer to the basket. For an in-depth treatment of these techniques, see *The Perfect Jump Shot* by Scott Jaimet (2006). These recommendations depart from the usual shooting techniques (described previously in this chapter) and may not be suitable for most players, but they offer the advantages of high arc, added balance, symmetry, and increased relaxation during shooting. Thus the technique is useful for elite players who possess high levels of upper-body strength and for post players on close-in shots.

Jaimet advocates focusing on four important factors: balance, rhythm, extension, and symmetry. The one-handed set or jump shot described in the previous section depends heavily on shooting rhythm, full extension, and balance. In turn, balance depends primarily on footwork but is more challenging when using the shooting pocket on one side of the player's body. In contrast, shifting the ball to a position directly overhead and near the middle of the body facilitates balance. This overhead or forehead shooting pocket is known as the *pedestal-pocket position*. To use it, players should grip the ball, form a V with the shooting hand, and then lock and load the ball to the pedestal pocket with a two-handed pickup, as shown in figure 4.19. The whole shooting hand is always placed under the ball in the shooting pocket, whether using the traditional side pocket

Figure 4.19 Pedestal-pocket shooting: *(a)* Grip the ball and form the V, *(b)* lock and load to form the tent (full focus—see under the tent), and *(c)* fold the tent and hold the follow-through.

or the more centered pedestal pocket. Players should always lock and load the ball into the shooting pocket with a two-handed pickup.

The pedestal pocket is a balanced trigger point for initiating the shot. From there, players shoot the ball up (not out) toward the basket by "pulling the trigger" or "folding the tent" (figure 4.19c). The middle or pedestal-pocket position has the distinct advantage of encouraging the player to shoot up, not out, thus preventing the most common error in shooting—putting less arc on the shot and thereby reducing the available entry area into the basket.

When players use the pedestal pocket, the position of the arms and feet must also be modified. The shooting hand (under the ball) and the bookend hand (on the side) are placed on the ball in similar fashion to using the side pocket. The feet, however, are positioned in a more parallel stance, and both elbows are pointed outward in a balanced, relaxed position to form a sort of tent (with the elbows at the base and the ball at the peak in the pedestal pocket; see figure 4.19b). The forearm and upper arm form a right angle (90 degrees) at the elbow.

Another advantage of the pedestal pocket is that the shooter can more readily pick up the shooting target early and achieve full focus on the target without visual obstructions from the arms or the ball. Players should form the shooting tent and put the ball in the pedestal pocket above the head and between the eye and ear (toward the shooting-hand side).

Coaches should emphasize that the elbows should be at eye level and the arms at right angles at the elbows. Putting the ball in the pedestal pocket with the elbows high makes it easier for players to shoot the ball up rather than out. When players shoot from this trigger spot, they should fully extend the arms (shooting arm at the elbow and wrist). They should also use a full follow-through that is firm but relaxed for *pulling the trigger* and *folding the tent* as the ball is thrust upward and released at the peak of the jump (or on the toes for the set shot).

Note the symmetry of the feet and arms when using the pedestal-pocket shooting technique (figure 4.19). The body faces the basket directly in a balanced, symmetrical position before, during, and after the shot.

COACHING POINTS FOR PEDESTAL-POCKET SHOOTING

- Face the basket with the shoulders square to the basket and the feet parallel in quick stance. Sit into the shot and use the legs for power.
- Lock and load the ball in a tight arc into the pedestal pocket. Use a quick two-handed pickup with wrinkled wrists.
- Form the tent with the elbows out and the ball at the trigger point. The arms, elbows, and thumbs should be at right angles. Establish early and full focus on the target (back of the rim or upper corner of the backboard rectangle).
- Jump with full extension—straight up or slightly forward.
- Pull the trigger to shoot up (not out) with full follow-through; fold the tent.
- Land in a balanced quick stance.

As shown in figure 4.19, here is the complete sequence of the pedestal-pocket shot:

1. Use a quick stop (or plant and turn) into a balanced quick-and-square stance facing the basket. Sit into the shot and square to (face) the basket; grip the ball properly so that wrist wrinkles are visible (figure 4.19a).

2. Use a two-handed pickup in a tight arc to move the ball quickly to the pedestal pocket—form the tent (figure 4.19b). Lock and load the ball into the pedestal pocket; put the ball in the trigger spot with the thumbs forming a right angle.

3. Establish full focus on the target for one full count (see the target through the V under the tent) while jumping with full extension.

4. Release the ball at the peak of the jump and use full follow-through (*freeze it*; figure 4.19c). Pull the trigger and fold the tent (make a parachute and hold it for one count).

5. Land, with balance, slightly in front of the takeoff spot.

Post Power Shot

The power shot, an adaptation of the power layup for post players, is the most basic scoring move for players with their backs to the basket. It is used when the defender plays on the side (side-fronting with hand across denial) position; see figure 4.20. The offensive post player gets into a position on the post line, as shown in the figure, and, in this case, the pass is made to the baseline hand (and leads to a score). After catching the ball (capturing and chinning it, as shown in figure 4.21a), the offensive player maintains contact with the defender's lower body and seals the defender with a half rear turn or leg whip (figure 4.21b), immediately followed by a two-handed, two-foot bounce-and-hop move (power dribble) with the ball and to the basket. Figure 4.22 shows this move with the one dribble taken from a two-handed chin-it position inside the lead foot as a two-foot

Figure 4.20 Low post: high side-front defense.

Figure 4.21   Post power shot: *(a)* Catch and chin the ball, then *(b)* make a half rear turn to seal the defender.

Stepping foot

Figure 4.22   Power shot: *(a)* bounce and hop (inside lead foot), *(b)* quick stop and chin, *(c)* shoot a power shot.

jump is made with a quick-stop landing. The post player lands facing the baseline and shoots a power shot by exploding up to the basket or backboard from the chin-it ball position (figure 4.23).

The post power shot can be used in two ways: without the dribble (with only a leg whip) when the player catches the ball in the lane and with the dribble, bounce, and hop (two-feet to two-feet move) when the player catches the ball outside the lane. Both shots, called *angle baskets*, allow the offensive player to use a body-position advantage to make a post-player angle move to the basket. The move can be made in either direction—always opposite to the side defender.

The power move can be used for basket penetration when posting up with the post player's back to the basket. It can also be used in the low-, medium-, or high-post position as a penetrating move to the basket on the side opposite to where the defender is playing. It is a powerful but safe move that uses the body to protect the ball for one-dribble basket penetration.

Post Hook Shot

The preeminent player who used the post hook shot was Lew Alcindor (now Kareem Abdul-Jabbar), who played at Power Memorial High School (New York City), at UCLA, and in the NBA, where he developed and mastered the *skyhook*. His Los Angeles Lakers coach, Pat Riley, described his post hook shot as "the most awesome weapon in the history of any sport" (Nielsen 1988).

Players in the United States used to dominate the world by learning to play with the back to the basket and using size and position. The skyhook fit Kareem perfectly because it is an act of faith by a willful, driven person. As Jabbar stated, "Everybody wants to see the ball as they let it go, to have it on-line from the start." But the post hook shot won't allow players to see the ball as they release it from behind and then over the head. As Jabbar described it, "It requires triangulation and rhythm, touch and repetition." The lesson is that the post hook shot requires faith, willpower (a strong mistake mentality), and considerable practice (Wolff 2002).

Sometimes called the baby hook or modern hook shot, the post shot is used by players who receive the ball in a low-post position with their back to the basket. The best location for a post shot is just outside the free-throw lane near the block (near the first and second free-throw lane spaces; figure 4.24). The post player generally sets up on or near the post line—an imaginary straight line between the passer and the basket.

Figure 4.23 Power shot: Explode to the basket.

CRITICAL CUE
Power move—seal, two-handed power dribble (bounce), and hop; quick stop and score.

CRITICAL CUE
Power dribble—two-handed power dribble (bounce) near the lead foot.

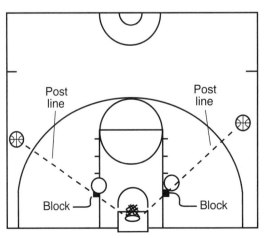

Figure 4.24 Posting up on the block.

On receiving a pass with the back to the basket in the post, the player should capture and chin the ball with two hands. In the low-post area, the player should put the ball in the two-handed power position under the chin (chin-it). Any player receiving a pass should be in quick-stance position and chinning the ball. The footwork for the post shot involves making a partial rear-turn pivot into the lane, using the baseline foot as the pivot foot. The other foot is used to step into the lane as far as possible in a balanced position facing away from the basket. Ideally, this foot is parallel to the baseline. When the nonpivot foot hits the floor, the pivot foot is raised as the knee is lifted high and rotated to face the basket, as in a normal layup. The ball is then moved from the chinning position past the side of the head, pushed overhead, and released with full arm extension (with the elbow locked) and pronation. This move is led by the inside elbow. The complete sequence is shown in figure 4.25 and includes these essential steps:

1. Post up with a two-handed target; sit into the stance (figure 4.25a).

2. Catch the ball and chin it to the power position—possession is more important than position (figure 4.25b).

3. Make a partial rear turn using the baseline foot as the pivot foot and step into the lane with the stepping foot parallel to the baseline (figure 4.25c).

4. Move the ball up and over the head with full extension and pronation of the arm; keep the ball close to the body until the release (figure 4.25d).

5. Rotate and shoot the post shot (figure 4.25e).

6. Land in quick-stance position and assume that the shot will be missed; put both hands up and assume a quick stance for a possible offensive rebound (figure 4.25f).

Figure 4.25 The post shot: *(a)* Post up with a two-handed target ready to receive the pass (in this case, the pass is to the left hand because the pass leads the post player to a scoring move toward the middle); *(b)* meet and chin the ball—use the quick stop when possible. *(continued)*

Figure 4.25 *(continued)* The post shot: *(c)* Step into the lane, with the stepping foot parallel to the baseline; *(d)* protect the ball on the outside shoulder; *(e)* take the ball up and over the head; *(f)* follow through, face the basket (hands should be up), and assume that the shot will miss.

Post Jump-Hook Shot

A variation of the post-player hook shot, the jump hook is simpler, requires less skill, is easier to teach, and has a quicker release. All players can be taught this shot, which can be used close to the basket and over taller defenders.

The teaching progression for the shot is as follows:

1. *Shot mechanics:* Practice with both the preferred hand and the nonpreferred hand in front of the basket while facing the sideline (home base). As shown in figure 4.26, shoot from a deep crouch or wide-stance position, with the ball on the outside shoulder-chin location, to a shot directly overhead. Emphasize the overhead release with full arm extension and wrist snap; the inside elbow or shoulder is pointed at the basket. Repetitions should be taken with the nonpreferred hand two or three times more than with the preferred hand; in both cases, shots are taken with the feet pointed to the sideline.

Figure 4.26 Jump hook: *(a)* starting position and *(b)* ending position (without jump).

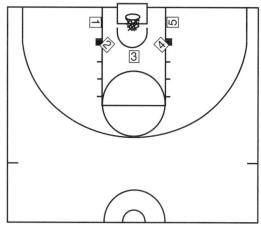

Figure 4.27 Jump hook—five spots.

2. *Jump hook from home base:* Start while facing a sideline; release the ball on the way up, near the peak of the jump, and come down in a ready position with the arms up (assume the shot will miss).

3. *Jump hook:* Shoot with the right hand and the left hand from five spots—baseline, 45 degrees, home base, 45 degrees, baseline (figure 4.27).

4. *Dummy defenders:* Shoot with each hand at five spots over dummy defenders or shooting pads (both hands up).

5. *Power move to the middle:* Make a one-dribble power move to home base (in front of the basket or in the lane), then shoot a jump hook (figure 4.28); alternatively, make the move to home base, give a shot fake, and then shoot a jump hook (figure 4.28).

CRITICAL CUE
Post power move to the middle—get to home base (face the sideline) for the jump hook.

Figure 4.28 Power move to the middle: *(a)* Catch with the defender on the baseline side, *(b)* power move to the middle (rear-turn seal), *(c)* power move to the middle (bounce and hop to home base, facing the sideline), and *(d)* jump hook from home base in front of the basket.

6. *Jump hook after pass catch:* As a pass is made into the free-throw lane, the post player moves to catch it with both feet in the air. The player turns to see the basket, points the nonshooting shoulder at the basket, and lands in the lane. The ball is chinned near the shooting shoulder. The jump hook is shot from a two-foot power jump and released directly up from the shooting shoulder with a locked elbow and flexed-wrist follow-through. Thus the sequence is catch and turn, jump hook up and over, land from the shot in quick stance, and assume that the shot will be missed.

Shot Fakes

When players prepare to shoot by getting the feet and hands ready (triple-threat position and shooting pocket), they can be quicker and more aggressive. They also enable themselves to use the complement of the shot—the shot fake.

Proper technique for the shot fake involves moving the ball quickly and vertically from the pit or triple-threat position or pedestal pocket. The body stays in quick-stance position as the player makes a quick, short (1-inch, or 2.5-centimeter), vertical fake upward with the ball while the eyes remain focused on the target. Next, the player should give the fake time to work rather than rushing into the move. The shot fake can be used when facing the basket, when the back is toward the basket, or when executing a jump hook. In an effective shot fake, the offensive player's heels stay down on the floor and the legs stay locked in a crouched or explosive position. In other words, the player needs to stay in proper stance when using a shot fake (figure 4.29).

Figure 4.29 Shot fake—lock the legs, give a 1-inch (2.5-centimeter) shot fake, and keep the heels down.

FREE-THROW SHOOTING

Top statistical factors related to winning include not only field-goal percentage (on both offense and defense) but also free-throw percentage. Players and coaches need to know correct shooting techniques and practice them properly. Free-throw shooting is especially critical for the following reasons: It is a mental as well as a physical technique (confidence is crucial), the game stops during performance of the skill, and little improvement has been seen in free-throw percentages for more than 40 years (National Collegiate Athletic Association 2016). Free-throw shooting is truly a team skill in that every player should develop and master the skill, at least up to the level of national average, regardless of age or gender.

Teams should practice free throws in proportion to their importance in games, which is reflected in the fact that they account for 20 to 25 percent of scoring, shots taken, and games decided. Therefore, when practices are evenly divided between offense and defense, 10 to 12 percent of total practice time should be spent on free throws. Given that 10 percent of 60 minutes is 6 minutes, at least 5 minutes per hour of practice or game time should be spent on free throws both during the season and in the off-season. This is the 5-minute free-throw rule.

CRITICAL CUE
Put in the time to master free throws—a minimum of 5 minutes per hour of individual game and practice time.

In-game percentage goals should be set in relation to age (see table 4.2). These measures indicate whether players should adopt the goals completely or adapt them partially to improve free-throw shooting. Practice standards should be 5 percent higher than game goals due to typical slippage in game performance as compared with practice.

Table 4.2   Free-Throw Percentage Goals

Ages	U.S. grade level	Game modifications	% in practice	% in game
8-10	3 and 4 (lower elementary)	#5 ball Lower basket height Half-court play	50	N/A
10-14	5-8 (upper elementary)	N/A	55	50
14-20	9-10 (secondary) 10-11 11-12	N/A	65 70 75	60 65 70
18-25	College or university (postsecondary)	N/A	80	75
N/A	Professional	N/A	85	80

COACHING POINTS FOR FREE-THROW SHOOTING

- Keep the shot simple and the same; simplify the motion and do it the same way each time (from foot position to follow-through).

- Groove the shot daily (e.g., take 20 shots and record the number of makes).

- Compete in all free-throw situations (e.g., one shot, bonus, two shots, three shots)—make every shot a game shot in the player's mind and set competitive shooting goals.

- Keep written records, set game goals, and practice at 5 percent higher than game goal.

- Put in the time; spend at least 5 minutes on free throws for every hour of practice or game play (purposeful free throw practice).

Free-Throw Technique

The key differences between free-throw technique and field-goal shooting involve aligning the foot position on the dot or spot (middle of the free-throw line), establishing a set ritual, pausing at the bottom of the shot, and exaggerating the follow-through. Players should keep the free throw simple and do it exactly the same way each time. The complete free-throw technique is shown in figure 4.30.

Figure 4.30 The free throw: *(a)* Align and get down on the spot with body weight forward, *(b)* focus for 1 full second, *(c)* be certain the ball is in the same *start* position and *finish* position each shot, and *(d)* use a full follow-through (freeze it and hold until net).

Players should know how a good shot looks, sounds, and feels and eventually be able to shoot free throws with their eyes closed. The shot should be executed with controlled tension—neither too relaxed nor too tight. The important physical mechanics are as follows:

• *Find the spot (dot).* Align on the center of the free-throw line each time; specifically, the shooting foot, shooting elbow, shooting hand, ball, and shooting-side eye are aligned in a vertical plane with the basket. The shooting foot should be in the same spot every time and pointed toward the basket or slightly to the left of a line perpendicular to the free-throw line. Place the toe of the dominant or lead (shooting) foot (the right foot for right-handers and the left foot for left-handers) in the exact center of the free-throw line. Hardwood courts have a nail hole at the center for measuring purposes. On other courts, mark that spot. Put the lead foot near the center and point it at the corner of the backboard on the opposite side (right foot to left backboard edge and vice versa) in a *slightly* open stance. Place the other foot in a comfortable position and position the feet shoulder-width apart to establish a balanced, staggered stance. This slightly open stance is preferred to the parallel or square stance because it relaxes the shooting arm and shoulder muscles and puts the shooting arm directly in the vertical plane leading to the center of the basket. For a pedestal-pocket shooter, however, the eyes and the ball should be centered on the dot or spot and the feet should be in a closed, square stance (figure 4.31).

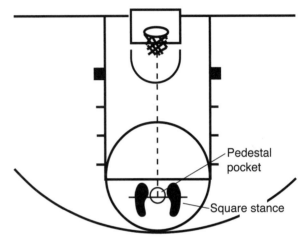

Figure 4.31 Pedestal-pocket free-throw position.

• *Focus fully.* The focus should be on the center of the back of the rim or the center eyelet at the back of the rim. Players should focus on the target and think *nothing but net* or *make the defense pay for fouling*. The focus on the target should begin early and be held for 1 full second (using the *focus, feel, feedback* mental approach).

• *Bounce at the bottom.* At the bottom of the shot, the player should pause for an instant of physical and mental calm and focus, then bounce (dip the ball slightly) for rhythm. After the pause and the dip, all motion should be up and over and toward the basket after the starting dip to activate the shooting muscle reflex. This technique is referred to as taking a *one-piece* or *one-count* shot with all positive motion toward the basket. Players should keep the shot simple and eliminate down and up motions, which should be replaced with simpler positive motion in the last phase of the shot.

• *Establish a ritual.* A ritual should be developed for the complete shot. Coaches should help each player do the same thing the same way every time—it is much easier to groove a pattern that is always the same. Every ritual should include a deep breath (in through the nose and out through the mouth) just before the shot (preliminary phase). Players should also use the same grip on the ball each time. Most players put their fingertips across the seams of the ball. Players should be slow and deliberate with the ritual while keeping it simple; in fact, it is sometimes best to eliminate dribbling from the ritual to simplify it and eliminate nonpurposeful motion. Finally, a verbal prompt such as *nothing but net* is used to clear the mind.

CRITICAL CUE
Get on the spot or dot with an open stance (*same spot, same way*).

CRITICAL CUE
Laser focus: Pick up the spot target early and hold it for 1 second (the preferred target is the back of the rim).

COACHING POINTS FOR PHYSICAL TECHNIQUE OF FREE-THROW SHOOTING

- *Find the spot.* Get on the dot in the same way each time and use the same alignment with the lead foot on the nail hole and preferably pointing at the opposite backboard edge.
- *Perform a ritual.* Make it simple and the same each time: Early in the ritual, take a deep breath (in through the nose and out through the mouth for relaxation), use the same grip on the ball, and use a verbal prompt to clear the mind and get a mental picture of the expected outcome.
- *Bounce at the bottom.* Use a positive motion to the basket (one-piece shot) with rhythm after a slight ball dip or bounce one or two times to begin the free throw.
- *Use a full follow-through (freeze it).* The follow-through should be firm but relaxed. Hold it until the ball hits the net (keep body weight forward up on balls of feet; stay in the shot until the ball goes through the net).

CRITICAL CUE

Freeze the follow-through until the ball goes through the net.

- *Follow through fully (freeze it).* The keys to the follow-through are full extension and pronation. The shooter should come up on the toes to get power from the legs (hold this position), and the upper arm should be near 60 degrees above horizontal on the follow-through. Players should release high and hold the follow-through (*freeze it*) until the ball hits the net—put the shooting hand in the basket. They should also finish on the balls of their feet with the weight slightly forward. Thus they should stay in the shot and keep body weight forward with the hand in the basket.

Free-Throw Confidence Building

Players can develop confidence in free-throw shooting through a gradual, long-term approach using specific mental techniques and proper preparation. In addition to the previously described ritual, players need to groove their techniques early in practice and during the season by shooting consecutive free throws properly, picking up the spot target early, and using full focus (verbal prompt *focus*) for 1 second early in the shot. Coaches can teach players to concentrate on every shot using positive thoughts, such as making the opponents pay for every foul, thinking *net* or *swish* (shots that hit only *net*) or BRAD (*back rim and down* into the net) shots, and seeing the net ripple as the ball goes through (swish shots). Shooters can develop shot awareness by using the verbal prompt *feel* during each shot.

CRITICAL CUE

Before the shot—see and say *net* or *nothing but net* during the ritual.

A positive shooting attitude can also be developed by celebrating successful shots and evaluating missed shots using proper feedback (verbal prompts: *yes* on makes and *short, long, right,* or *left* on misses). Thus the shooter blocks all negative thoughts and uses only the positive. Overall, confidence is developed through careful preparation and demonstrations of skill in competition. Players need to shoot free throws in competitive situations and make every shot a game shot.

Younger players (ages 8 through 12) should use a smaller ball, lower baskets (8 feet or 2.4 meters high), and a shorter free-throw line (9 feet [2.7 meters]). Older players (ages 12 through 14) should shoot from 12 feet (3.7 meters) at a basket set at a height of 9 feet (Krause, Janz, and Conn 2003).

CRITICAL CUES FOR MENTAL TRIGGERS

- Focus
- Feel
- Feedback

TROUBLESHOOTING FOR SHOOTING

- **Problem:** Off-balance shots, with side drift or backward movement

  Correction: The antidote is to use proper footwork—balanced quick stops or stride stops (plant and turn or pivot) and feet shoulder-width apart while sitting into the shot.

- **Problem:** Low-arc shots

  Correction: The shooting pocket is too low or too far in front of the body (dangling the ball). Raise the side shooting pocket or use the centered pedestal pocket for inside players. Shoot up, not out, in order to shoot over the basket rather than at it.

- **Problem:** Late target pickups

  Correction: Use full focus and early target sighting. Sight the target while dribbling or right after catching the ball (*laser focus with small vision*).

- **Problem:** Poor alignment, or direction problems (shooting foot too open and not pointed, which prevents getting power from the legs)

  Correction: Face the basket with either a slightly staggered stance (if using the side shooting pocket) or a parallel stance (if using the pedestal pocket). With the regular side pocket, check the vertical alignment of the ball and the shooting hand, shooting elbow and shoulder, and shooting foot and knee. Close the stance to ensure that the feet are pointed at the target in order to obtain shooting power from the legs. With the pedestal pocket, center the trigger spot overhead and ensure that the arms and the body are symmetrical.

- **Problem**: Lack of momentum on release and short or flat shots caused by a too-open foot stance

  Correction: Square the stance.

- **Problem:** Slow shot release

  Correction: This problem is often caused by players using a slow ball pickup to the shooting pocket (side pocket), dangling the ball low, locking and loading to the pocket too slowly (or not completely in full wrist extension), or making a down-and-up motion in shooting (i.e., shooting a two-count shot). To address the problem, quicken the movement, tighten the arc to the shooting pocket, and make the shot a completely positive motion toward the basket. Eliminate the dip, bend the knees more, and sit into the shot. Get the feet and hands completely ready.

- **Problem:** Rushing the shot

  Correction: This problem usually derives from not focusing on the rhythm of the shot and shooting too quickly. Although players should take game shots at game spots at game speed, they should—as advocated by Naismith Hall of Fame player and coach John Wooden—be quick but not hurried.

- **Problem:** Inconsistency

  Correction: This problem often results from shot-to-shot changes in technique or insufficient practice. Every shot should use the same starting or trigger point and ending point with a full follow-through. Players should groove the shot with many repetitions so that it becomes automatic.

- **Problem:** Slowness in building confidence

  Correction: Coaches should reteach the self-talk shooting technique (*focus, feel, feedback*). Insist on game shots at game spots at game speed. Apply the BEEF and ROBOT shooting principles.

COACHING POINTS FOR A MENTAL EDGE IN FREE-THROW SHOOTING

- *Ritual:* For comfort and confidence, use the verbal prompt *nothing but net* to clear the mind, take a deep breath, and use the same ball grip every time. See and say *net* to form the proper mental picture.
- *Full focus:* Use early target pickup and laser focus on the preferred middle spot on the back of the rim for 1 second for field goals and free throws. Say *focus.*
- *Feel:* Say *feel* during the shot and become aware of the shot from start to finish.
- *Feedback:* After every shot, remember the makes (celebrate with *yes*) and forget the mistakes (analyze them using verbal prompt for shot location—*short, long, right,* or *left*—then forget them).

SHOOTING DRILLS

Coaches should be creative in developing shooting drills that are sequential and progressive and include all of the basics of shooting: footwork and balance without the ball, spot shots, shots from a pass, and shots from the dribble. Emphasize correct execution first, then progress to shooting game shots at game spots at game speed.

LINE DRILL: SHOOTING ADDITION (WITHOUT BALL, WITH BALL) ▶

Purpose: To teach shooting in a simulated game situation

Equipment: Half-court (minimum), four basketballs (added later)

Procedure: This is a form shooting exercise with no ball and no defender (the ball is added later). Players are positioned in four lines in the baseline formation. In the drill, they execute a quick stop in shooting position after jumping from the foot closest to the basket. Later, the drill may be done using a ball and an underhand spin pass or a dribble.

Options

- *Straight line:* Imaginary shots (i.e., shooting motions performed without a ball) are taken without a target at the free-throw line, half-court line, opposite free-throw line, and opposite baseline. Players focus on the basket at the opposite end of the floor and hop into a quick stop at each of the four shooting locations.

- *Offensive zigzag:* An imaginary shot is taken at the location of each change-of-direction spot just before the adjacent free-throw line, the half-court line, opposite free-throw line, and opposite baseline. Most movement should be lateral to make it easier for players to select the proper inside foot adjacent to the basket, the foot ahead of the far basket).

- *Straight line with shots called by the coach:* With players in four lines at the baseline, the first four players (one from each line) begin on the coach's *go* command; the next four players begin when the preceding group has moved 15 to 18 feet (4.6 to 5.5 meters) down the floor. The coach designates an imaginary basket at the side of the court (use the intersection of the sideline and the half-court line). Players move forward under control in the basic position until the coach gives the *shot* command. Then each player on the court simulates catching a pass with a quick stop or shooting off the dribble and takes a shot to an imaginary basket. On the *go* command, all players continue up the court until the coach throws another imaginary pass. Players must be ready to shoot with balance and control at any time; they should shoot to the right going down the court and to the left coming back (or to the basket straight ahead).

- *Line shots with the ball:* The first four players start together and use proper technique to shoot four imaginary shots with the ball (at the free-throw line, half-court line, opposite free-throw line, and opposite baseline). At each shooting spot, players shoot at the opposite basket and then shoot as though the basket were to either side. To shoot to the side, they hop from the basket-side foot and land facing the imaginary basket, catching the ball and turning in the air to face the side and shoot. Players can shoot from a pass to themselves—a two-handed underhand spin pass with backspin thrown at the location of the intended shot. They can then dribble instead of passing in another round to shoot from a dribble. The shot is taken with a 60-degree arc slightly in front of the shot location—the follow-through is exaggerated and held until the ball hits the floor. No target is used; coaches should simply emphasize shooting up and holding the follow-through until the ball returns to the floor. Players can mix in shots after a shot fake to check balance and footwork technique.

LAYUP SHOOTING PROGRESSION ▶

Purpose: To teach players progressively to shoot game-type layups properly and quickly

Equipment: One ball per player (when possible; or one ball per two players when paired for buddy coaching) and one basket per 12 players

Procedure: The coach should use as many stages of the progression as are appropriate to the age and skill level of the players.

Layup Progression

Note: One possible progression before doing regular layups from a pass is to carry the ball in a shoulder-and-chin position near the shooting shoulder while galloping to the basket.

- Do a line drill down and back with the following versions: no ball layup simulation, carrying the ball, and dribbling the ball. Shoot a simulated layup at the free-throw line, half-court line, opposite free-throw line, and opposite baseline. Exaggerate the follow-through (*freeze it*).

- Carry the ball in pickup position, using the high pickup (outside chin spot) for the ball; shoot a one-handed layup in each of the four locations.

- One-line dribble-in layups: Players each have a ball (six per basket). They start in live-ball quick stance and use an appropriate direct or crossover drive-and-dribble from the wing position. Emphasize early focus on the target, opposition leg action, two-handed pickup with one-handed finish, and high jump (rebounding one's own shot before the ball hits the floor). Consider adding a dummy defender or cone at start, halfway to the basket, or at the layup finish.

- Two-line layups (12 players and three balls per basket):
  - One line dribbles in, and the opposite line rebounds.
  - Shoot a layup after receiving a pass from the opposite line.
  - Shoot a dribble-drive layup after receiving an early pass near the half-court line (catch pass with feet in the air).
- Dribble-chase layups: Players form pairs, and each pair has a ball. The player with the ball stands behind the baseline and outside of the free-throw lane. The partner (the catcher) serves as the outlet between the free-throw line and the half-court line. The passer makes a baseball pass to the outlet catcher, who receives the ball, faces up the floor, and speed-dribbles to the other end for a layup as the original passer chases the dribbler down from behind (cannot foul but can go for the ball). This sequence occurs simultaneously in pairs at opposite ends of the court; half of the groups are located at each end. Rotate clockwise for left-hand layups and then change to counterclockwise for right-hand layups to ensure ample practice with the nonpreferred-hand dribble and layup.

Team Peer-Pressure Drills

The origins of peer-pressure drills can be traced back to the heartland at the University of Kansas. More specifically, peer-pressure drills were emphasized as part of a focus on fundamentals by basketball pioneers, Kansas graduates, and direct descendants of basketball inventor James Naismith, such as Forrest "Phog" Allen, John Bunn, and Ralph Miller. In fact, the Ralph Miller version of such drills provided the basis for the original edition of this book, titled *Better Basketball Basics*.

This is a special category of team drills focused on combination offensive drills that can help players develop essential offensive skills—especially footwork, passing and catching, and timing and spacing—that result in made field goals (whether layups or set [jump] shots). This drill technique greatly enhances the ability of coaches and players to help each other practice game moves at game speed. Specifically, it allows coaches to do the following:

- Set team scoring goals.
- Focus on related offensive skills.
- Focus on related spacing and timing moves.
- Develop team cohesion by challenging players to meet rigorous goals as a team (all team members must accomplish the goals).
- Focus on process and outcomes related to essential scoring goals.
- Reset the drill scoring goal if it is not met (it may also be reset due to lack of execution of selected essential related skills).

GONZAGA FULL-COURT TEAM LAYUP

Purpose: To provide a competitive peer-pressure drill for team passing, catching, and layup shooting that requires the use of all ballhandling moves at game speed

Equipment: Full court, two to four balls, and four coach or manager passers (two at the top of the key on the outside of each free-throw lane)

Procedure: Players are positioned in two lines—one behind the baseline under each basket on a full court (figure 4.32). Start with one ball at each basket (may add two per

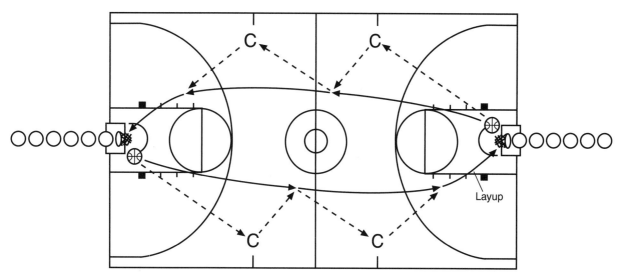

Figure 4.32 Gonzaga full-court team layup drill.

basket later). The first player in each line gets a two-handed rebound from a made or missed layup and outlets to the coach on the same side while fast-break-sprinting to the other basket in the sideline lane. The player receives the ball back near the half-court line from the first coach, passes on the move to the second coach, receives a return pass for a layup, and goes to the back of the line at the opposite end of the court (where the layup is shot). The player who started from the other end does the same actions simultaneously (thus two balls are going at the same time). The coach may add two more balls for the higher skill levels.

Coaching Points

- *One-foot layups:* Use proper opposition (jumping foot and shooting hand).
- *Two-foot layups:* Power up from a one-count, two-foot quick stop.
- *Two-handed pickup and chin on shoulder away from the defender:* The balance hand drives or picks the ball up to the shoulder (prevents rocking the cradle). Go up with two hands and finish with one.
- *High jump, not long jump:* Stamp hard on the last step.
- *Early target:* Hit it high and soft; use the board almost all of the time.
- *Team goals:* Set goals for number of shots made based on age and skill level.

FIELD-GOAL PROGRESSION ▶

Purpose: To self-teach and progressively practice the skill of shooting in a warm-up drill that provides needed feedback for improving shooting in all situations. Some form of field-goal progression needs to be used *daily* by all players to relearn or review physical and mental techniques. You may select drills for variety and emphasis to create a customized shooting progression package or simply use the following field-goal progression options that are marked as "essential."

Equipment: One ball per player (when possible) or per two players (for buddy coaching), one basket, full-court space (preferable)

Procedure: Each player reviews shooting by performing five repetitions of each drill in the selected progression.

Options

- Two-handed ball slams develop the feel of having the ball in the whole hand. Players hold the ball in the nonshooting hand (palm up) and *slam* the hands against the ball five times. They should do so each time they pick up a basketball and enter the court. The fingers should be spread comfortably so that the ball hits the whole shooting hand (*feel it*).

- Players perform a one-handed arm swing to the shooting pocket, shoot the ball, and retraces the motion (without the ball). Players may also use the bookend hand. Repeat five times.

- TV shooting without the ball: Players lie on their back with the shooting elbow on the floor and an imaginary ball on the horizontal hand (as if holding a TV tray). They perform the shooting motion vertically and hold the follow-through. Repeat five times.

- TV shooting with the ball: This option is performed as in the preceding one but with the ball, which must be shot into the air at least 6 feet high (1.8 meters) with full follow-through. Players should hold the follow-through for 1 second, then catch the ball coming down. Repeat five times.

- Wall or backboard shooting without a basket target: Players start with the ball in the shooting hand and the open hand facing up (forming the V). Then they lock and load into the shooting pocket, place the bookend hand up but not touching the ball, and shoot up and high on the wall or the backboard (one-hand shooting with the bookend hand up but not touching the ball).

Essential Field-Goal Progression

Use the field-goal progression options marked as "essential" *daily*:
- Shoot-the-line (shoot the ball straight and deep)
- Soft-touch (one or two close shots at each of five spots)
- Hays footwork drill
- Pass and dribble pickups (with proper footwork)
- Shots from a pass and shots from a dribble

These options should be included in all field-goal progressions.

- **(Essential)** Shoot-the-line form shots, or shoot-it-straight shots: These are one-handed vertical shots without a target that start with the ball in the shooting hand in a palm-up position. Players align the shooting foot on any line on the floor, rotate the ball into the shooting pocket (lock and load) with the balance hand off the ball and slightly to the side in a vertical position, shoot with good thrust (for backspin), snap the wrist, hold the follow-through in full extension (freeze it) until the ball hits the floor, and check where the ball bounces. It should bounce on or near the line to indicate that the shot is straight and 6 to 8 feet [1.8 to 2.4 meters] in front of the player to indicate that the player is shooting up rather than out. Repeat five times (minimal goal is five shots taken; hitting the line is better). This drill can also be done with regular two-handed shooting (using the balance hand).

- **(Essential)** Soft-touch, close-to-the-basket shots are taken with a target (rim and backboard). Remind players to practice from the inside out, starting close to the basket and gradually moving out. *All* shots should be taken *inside* the free-throw lane (6 feet, or 1.8 meters, from the basket). At least five shots are taken per spot (set higher goals such as at least four makes per basket for intermediate and advanced players). Alternate sessions using one-handed and two-handed shooting techniques.

- The circle-shots drill emphasizes footwork. Each player moves in a circle, carrying the ball chest high with two hands (*pit and protect*) and using proper quick-stop footwork: Hop from the basket-side foot, land with the feet aimed at the basket ready to shoot, and shoot a short shot. Players move clockwise to shoot from five spots inside the free-throw lane (figure 4.33), then take five shots moving counterclockwise. Shots taken at 45 degrees—from spots 2 and 4—are board shots, whereas shots taken at spots 1, 3, and 5 are rim shots. No dribbling is allowed—this drill focuses on getting the feet in position and the hands ready to handle the ball. Rotate the circle after every shot. When players are moving clockwise, the proper footwork is to hop from the basket-side (right) foot in order to land with the

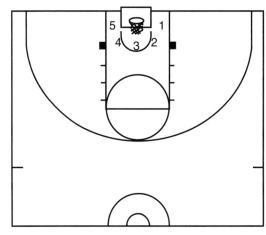

Figure 4.33 Soft-touch or circle-spot shots.

feet ready to shoot from a quick stop—that is, facing the basket with the dominant foot forward and the hands ready (with the ball in the shooting pocket). Clockwise movement uses hopping from the right foot to end facing the shooting target with a quick step; counterclockwise movement uses hopping from the left foot into the quick stop, facing the basket.

- **(Essential)** Another version of the shooting footwork drill that can be used as a warm-up progression is the Hays footwork drill, developed by Dan Hays at Oklahoma Christian University. It is simple and quick and encompasses pass pickups and footwork for shots from a pass as well as footwork from a dribble. It is carried out from elbow to elbow at the free-throw lane (or from side to side anywhere near the free-throw lane, 15 to 18 feet [4.6 to 5.5 meters] between shooting spots). The footwork for shooting from a pass begins at the left elbow. The player faces the opposite sideline and, using a two-handed underhand pass to herself with backspin, tosses the ball near the opposite elbow and moves toward the pass while performing proper footwork (hopping from the basket-side foot and landing with a quick stop facing the basket). The player then snaps the ball to the shooting pocket with a two-handed pickup move. The player picks up the spot target early (verbal prompt: *focus*) and tests body balance by using a short, quick shot fake (with the legs bent and locked and the heels staying down) but does not shoot the ball. Next, the player faces the opposite sideline, uses a bounce pass to herself at the height of the chest or the shooting pocket, and repeats the pass footwork, going from right to left. This time, the hopping foot is the right foot. This process is repeated 10 times—5 to the right and 5 to the left. This sequence simulates, in the form of a warm-up, the action of catching the ball and being ready to shoot from a pass with balance (shot fake check) and quickness while moving to the right or to the left. See figure 4.34.

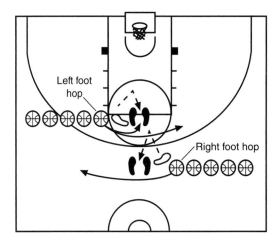

Figure 4.34 Hays footwork (elbow-to-elbow) drill.

Follow with 10 repetitions of shooting from an outside-hand dribble; in other words, the right hand is used if dribbling from left to right, and the left hand is used if dribbling from right to left. Players should focus on making a good self-pass (the last hard dribble) as they hop from the basket-side foot. The last dribble is a hard dribble that gets the ball to the shooting pocket accurately and quickly (by means of a two-handed dribble pickup) at the same time

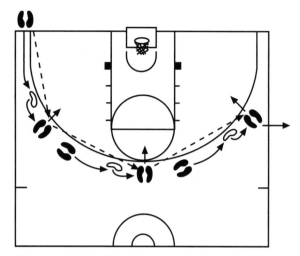

Figure 4.35 Work the arc: Perform pass and dribble pickups around the three-point line (no shots are taken; focus on footwork and shot fakes).

that the basket-side foot is used to hop into a quick stop. Initially, no shot is taken, but a shot fake is made as a balance check (phase 1); then a shot is taken after a self-pass or dribble (phase 2).

- **(Essential)** In the work-the-arc drill for shooting *from a pass*, players toss a high, two-handed underhand pass to themselves in a desired spot and use proper footwork to land in triple-threat position, facing the basket and ready to shoot. This drill should be preceded by the pass-pickups footwork drill around the three-point field-goal line (clockwise and counterclockwise). No shots are taken—the focus is on footwork and using a shot fake to check balance (figure 4.35). On pickups, the ball is snapped quickly into the shooting pocket from a two-handed pickup or grab. Whether receiving a pass or completing a dribble, players must get the ball quickly into shooting position. In this drill, players should make a pass to themselves, hop from the basket-side foot, land facing the basket with the feet ready, use a shot fake to test balance, and then repeat the sequence (clockwise and counterclockwise).

- **(Essential)** In the work-the-arc drill for shooting *from the dribble*, players make a dribble-drive move to the left or right, perform a quick stop facing the basket, and shoot from triple-threat position from a spot 15 to 20 feet (4.6 to 6.1 meters) from the basket. Preliminary work should be done on pickup technique. The footwork is identical to that used for shots from the pass. With a dribble, the last *hard* dribble occurs as the basket-side foot is used to hop into a quick stop facing the basket (with the lead [shooting] foot forward). Coaches can have players take the last dribble with either hand while hopping from the opposite foot with a quick stop and landing in the triple-threat position. *Before* taking shots from the dribble, players go from baseline corner to baseline corner, tracing the three-point arc while using proper footwork and practicing the *dribble pickup* technique (snapping the ball into shooting position). Players should practice the technique with both clockwise and counterclockwise motion. They should dribble with the outside hand, hop from the basket-side foot as the last hard dribble drives the ball into the shooting pocket (two-handed pickup), land facing the basket with a quick stop (with the feet ready), use a shot fake to test balance, and then repeat the sequence. Work the arc counterclockwise and clockwise for one circuit.

SHOOT-THE-LINE AND SOFT-TOUCH SHOOTING

Purpose: To review shooting mechanics and build confidence by shooting on a regular basis (recommended warm-up for each practice); see the previous Field-Goal Progression drill for a description of shoot-the-line form shots.

Equipment: Ideally, one ball and one basket per player (no more than four players per basket)

Procedure: Five soft-touch shots are taken at each of five spots (five shots at five spots) with specific goals appropriate to players' skill level. For example, beginners might shoot or make one shot at each spot (two backboard shots at 45 degrees and three rim shots—corner, middle, corner); see figure 4.36. The mental goal is to develop the habit of full focus (pick up the target early and see or hold for one count). Intermediate players, in contrast, might be able to make two or three shots at each spot, and advanced players might set a goal of making only swish shots at the five spots (make three or make up to five in a row). Of the two soft-touch options—one-handed and two-handed—either or both can be used, but especially the one-handed version, in which the player goes to the spot, places the ball in the whole shooting hand (palm up), locks and loads the ball into the shooting pocket, places the balance or bookend hand to the side of the ball (not touching it), and shoots the shot to freeze the follow-through.

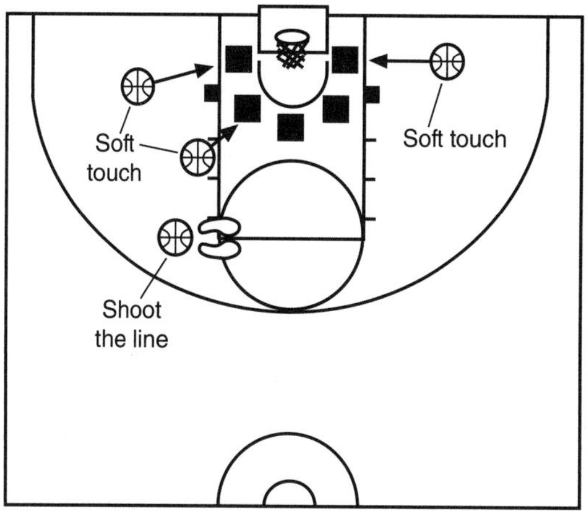

Coaches can emphasize getting the feet ready, sitting into the shot, putting the ball in the shooting pocket, using full focus (verbal prompt *focus*), and executing a full follow-through. Each player goes through the checklist to review the basics on each shot. The same drill of five shots in five spots can also be done with the use of the balance hand (touching the ball) added. The essential two steps of field-goal progression should be performed each time a player steps onto the floor to practice. Every time a player picks up a basketball, it's an opportunity to relearn shooting and self-teach shooting basics; the essential shoot-the-line form shots and soft-touch shots should be taken every time.

Players can also use soft-touch shooting to apply mental practice and use verbal prompts: *focus, feel* (during the shot), *feedback* (after the shot—*yes* or *net* on makes; shot location on misses).

Figure 4.36 Soft-touch or shoot-the-line shooting drill.

GROOVE-IT SPOT SHOOTING

Purpose: To evaluate shooting effectiveness and range

Equipment: Ball, basket, and court area

Procedure: At any spot or shot, make at least 5 of 10 shots (preferably 7 of 10). The preferred spots or shots are shown in figure 4.37. Select the distance and spot for each location, and set practice goals, based on the desired game goal.

Options: To groove the shot at each spot, start at five locations inside the arc with a live ball.

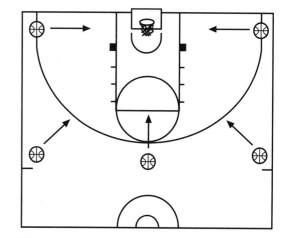

Figure 4.37 Groove-it shooting spots.

- Pass right and left. Repeat sets of 10 shots until reaching the goal for made shots. Start close and work your way out.

- Use a shot fake and dribble right and left with proper footwork. Shoot sets of 10 shots until the goal is met. Start close and work your way out.

- Face away from the basket in front of the five spots at 10 feet (3 meters) from the basket. Toss a two-handed, underhand self-pass at 12 feet (3.7 meters), use a two-handed pickup and a PPF rear turn (or EPF footwork) to face the basket, and shoot using mental-edge technique (*focus, feel, feedback*). Players should keep track of their personal records for consecutive makes at each spot.

PAIRS IN-AND-OUT SHOOTING ▶

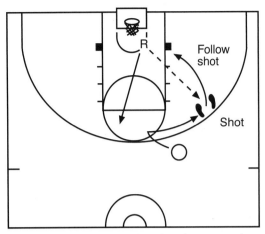

Figure 4.38 Pairs shooting (one pass).

Purpose: To teach shooting in a 2-on-0 game-simulation drill that covers all shooting situations

Equipment: Basket and one ball per pair of players (or per group of three or four)

Procedure: This continuous, competitive shooting drill, shown in figure 4.38, incorporates multiple principles of movement: passing and catching, shooting, and offensive rebounding. Players are grouped in pairs (one or two pairs per basket). The basic rules are as follows:

- All pairs begin on the coach's command, starting with the passer under the basket with a ball.
- A teammate gets open for a shot, calls the passer's name, and receives a pass for the shot (catch ball with feet in the air, catch and face basket when necessary).
- Shooters rebound their own shots until a basket is made (always assuming that the shot will be missed), then gain possession after the make to pass to a teammate for a shot.
- The receiver must always get open and call the passer's name.
- Passers make a quick, on-target pass at the right time to a teammate for a good shot and go quickly to another location near the edge of their shooting range, ready to move only when a teammate has scored and has possession of the ball.

Options

- Groove: Each player gets open and shoots (catch with feet in the air and repeat sequence) for 30 seconds while a teammate rebounds; players take turns shooting and rebounding, changing roles every 30 seconds.
- The shooter makes five baskets, then switches positions with a teammate.
- The 10-scores game: This game, played to 10 made baskets (or 5), involves players moving and taking shots from a pass and from a dribble.
- The coach designates the type of pass (push, overhead, air, bounce) and the type of shot (regular; shot fake and shot). This drill is excellent for practicing passes with the nonpreferred hand (passers can be required to use only the nonpreferred hand in order to increase repetitions with it).
- Pressuring the shooter: This option involves the rebounder passing to the shooter and then making a poor defensive closeout while applying some type of false pressure (going by, shouting, putting a hand in the shooter's face, making contact). The defender cannot block or alter the shot or foul the shooter. At least once per week, use the variation of having defenders pressure shooters with the hands up in order to help shooters develop the greater arc needed for shooting over defenders.
- Three-pass shooting with a post-up involves shooting from an outlet pass (passer posts up), a pass to the post (passer cuts), and a return pass for a shot (figure 4.39).

- The beat-the-star variation places shooters in competition with a designated star shooter; a partner acts as a rebounder. The game begins with one free throw and continues with players shooting set or jump shots. Scoring rules for free throws give challengers 1 point for a successful shot and give 3 points to the star on misses; similarly, challengers score 1 point for successful field goals, whereas the star gets 2 points for misses. The game can be played to 11 or 21 points.

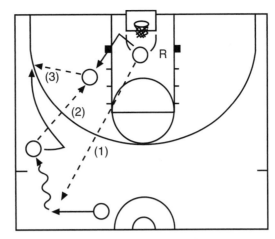

Figure 4.39 Pairs shooting (three passes with post-up).

MAKE-IT-TAKE-IT ROW SHOOTING

Purpose: To teach the skill of shooting in a self-testing format adjusted to standards set by the coach or player. One example would be a field-goal shooting goal of three made shots in a row followed by a made free throw before going to another spot or doing a different move.

Equipment: Basket and one ball per player

Procedure: All tasks in this drill are self-testing and require the player to meet effective scoring standards (a selected number of made field goals in a row to earn the right to shoot the free-throw challenge). All moves are to be carried out consecutively without rest to practice shooting in game situations.

Players make dribble-drive layup moves from the left and right corners (with a foot on the sideline), from each hash mark, and from the top of the key. Players are allowed only one dribble and must make three baskets in a row from each spot. Frontcourt players who can dunk the ball must do so by dribbling only once. The objective is to cover the greatest distance possible with a layup scoring move. After each row of three shots is made, the player earns the right to shoot free throws. The percentage goal must be met on free throws or the player repeats the move and the free throws (four of five free throws for college players; three of four for older (secondary-school level) players; two of three, or one of two, for younger players).

Advanced Options

- *Consecutive miss:* Shoot from a spot with a selected move until two shots in a row are missed.

- *Consecutive swish:* Shoot from a spot with a selected move until a swish shot (net only) is made twice in a row.

- *40-point scoring:* Use three different scoring moves from each of five spots along the three-point line: on the baseline on both sides, on the wing on both sides, and from the top of the key. The first shot is a three-pointer from a spin pass. If the player makes it, 3 points are scored. The second shot is a quick one-dribble pull-up jump shot worth 2 points. The third shot is a drive after a shot fake and a power layup at the basket for 2 points. Players finish with five free throws for 1 point each. Thus a perfect score is 40 points—7 points per spot plus 5 points for the free throws.

- *Three-pointer contest:* Shoot five three-point shots from the same five spots used in the 40-point scoring drill. Players get 1 point for every shot made, except for the fifth shot, which is worth 2 points. Thus a perfect score is 30 points.

INDIVIDUAL GROOVING THE SHOT

Purpose: To teach players to self-assess the mechanics of the shooting hand and the balance hand while increasing shot range

Equipment: Ball, basket, and teammate or coach to rebound and provide feedback

Procedure: Players "one-hand form-shoot" along a straight line directly in front of the basket moving toward the free-throw line and the half-court line. Players start in close in the free-throw lane, about 6 feet (1.8 meters) in front of the basket. They place the ball on the whole shooting hand (held horizontally facing up). Then, using only the shooting hand, they rotate the ball and move it to the shooting pocket (locking the wrist in, bending it back, and placing the ball on the shooting tray or forming an L). With the bookend hand directly to the side of the ball (but not touching it), players shoot a high-arcing shot and hold the follow-through for one full count. They move progressively away from the basket while using correct form, which allows them to quickly find their effective range (where they can hit more than 50 percent of their shots).

This drill also provides a good check of vertical-plane alignment of the shooting hand, elbow, and shoulder (keeping the ball straight) and of using the legs for power. Players should keep the shot the same with the arms while getting lower for added leg power. The shooter's partner can help check position and mechanics. The balance hand should finish high. As the shooting elbow is locked and the wrist is extended and loaded for the shot, the fingers of the balance hand should be vertical at the end of the shooting wrist on the follow-through. Players can also use the pedestal-pocket shot with both hands, usually at close distances.

FIELD-GOAL CORRECTION

Purpose: To focus on specific problem areas for shooters

Equipment: Ball, basket, and coach

Procedure: Focus on one problem at a time: footwork, balance, shooting hand, balance hand, starting shooting pocket, or follow-through. Practice from the inside out: 3, 6, 9, and 15 feet (0.9, 1.8, 2.7, and 4.6 meters) from the basket. The coach should view the shooter from the side and from behind.

Options

- *Footwork and handwork:* Players move right and left while carrying the ball in the shooting pocket, then use a quick stop after a basket-side foot hop to shoot, and then dribble right and left to shoot with proper footwork.

- *Balance:* Check head and foot position before and after the shot (head straight or toward the basket—not left, right, or away).

- *Shooting hand and balance hand:* Check the shooting hand at the start (elbow in an L position, wrist fully loaded and extended at the start) and at the finish (55- to 60-degree release, follow-through held firm but relaxed). Similarly, check the balance hand at the start (at the side of the ball, vertical or at a right angle to the backboard and the floor) and at the finish (balance hand slightly off the ball, elbow still flexed, shooting hand above balance hand and wrist fully flexed on the follow-through, or fingertips of balance hand at the level of the shooting wrist).

- *Swish game (plus 3, minus 2):* Count a swish shot as 1 point, a make that hits the rim as 0, and a miss as –1. A score of +3 wins the game, and a score of –2 loses (the winning and losing scores can be modified according to skill level).

- *Consecutive swish:* Players shoot until they fail to swish two shots in a row; keep track of swishes made in a row.
- *Consecutive misses:* Players shoot until two or three shots in a row are missed; record the number of field goals made.

COACH HUTTER'S COMPETITIVE SHOOTING

Adapted by permission from D. Hutter, "Practice Drills and Ideas," accessed February 23, 2018, http://www.coachhutter.com/team-drills.

Purpose: To provide players and coaches with a set of competitive shooting drills from a highly successful basketball program. These drills were developed by Dennis Hutter, head coach of the women's basketball team at Mayville State University. Hutter is an excellent coach who has adapted ideas from the Krause–Meyer coaching tree to develop a successful basketball system, including a variety of competitive shooting drills. His shooting guidelines are as follows:

- Make workouts like a game so that your games can be like your workouts.
- The best way to improve the team is to improve individual players' skills; when each player gets better, the team gets better.
- Compete "against the game."
- Take game shots at game spots at game speed.

Equipment: One ball per player (or per player and partner), court area with basket (at least half court)

Procedure: Each shooting drill is competitive—against self, time, or a standard—and can be done either individually or with a partner.

1. 10 Shots Without Missing 2 in a Row
   - Work at game pace.
   - If 2 shots are missed in a row, a swish on the next shot restores the string of makes.
   - All shots are taken from a self-pass for rhythm shooting; the drill can also be done with stop-and-pop shots from a dribble as well as jump shots from the self-pass.

2. 10 Shots in 75 Seconds
   - All shots are shots taken from a self-pass for rhythm shooting.
   - Work at a pace that allows a chance to make 10 shots.
   - Get your own rebound on all shots.
   - This is a great drill for warming up players before a workout begins.

3. 25-Point Shooting Drill
   - Alternate between three-point field goals and "stop-and-pop" two-point jump shots taken after a drive and pull-up.
   - Shooter attempts to get 25 points within 2 minutes.
   - Do not catch the ball in the same spot twice in a row; use the entire half court.
   - Alternate between the right hand and the left hand when attacking the rim.
   - Use a teammate rebounder for this drill.

4. 10 Spots in 2 Minutes

- Shoot from 5 spots—corner, wing, top, opposite wing, and opposite corner—then go back the other way for a total of 10 spots.

- Shoot from a spot until you make two in a row, then advance to the next spot.

- Shots 5 and 6 are taken in the same corner.

- Use a rebounder for this drill and an extra ball if there are long rebounds.

5. 21-Point Conditioning Challenge

- Use a coach or partner passer.

- Starting at the half-court line, sprint toward the three-point arc, receive a pass at the arc, and begin shooting continuously in the following order:

    a. Drive in, shoot a layup, and then sprint back to the half-court line.

    b. Attack the rim, shoot a stop-and-pop, and then sprint back to the half-court line.

    c. Shoot a three-pointer from the top of the key, then sprint back to the half-court line.

- Layups are worth 1 point, stop-and-pops 2 points, and of course three-pointers 3 points.

- Continue the indicated shot order until 21 points have been scored.

6. 30-Point Shooting (Pairs)

- Use a rebounder/passer for this drill.

- Shoot from four spots: wing, pro spot (elbow), pro spot (elbow), and wing.

- Set up a chair or cone at each spot, just outside of the three-point line.

- Receive a pass and attack the chair or cone.

- Shoot three shots from each spot: a stop-and-pop three-pointer, a right-to-left crossover to a stop-and-pop, and a left-to-right crossover to a stop-and-pop.

- Shoot the ball and then sprint back behind the chair or cone to receive the ball and make the next move.

- Stop-and-pops are worth 2 points, and three-pointers are worth 3 points.

- Thus the top possible scores for the spot shooting are 7 points for each spot and 28 points in total. Finish the drill with two free-throws (each worth 1 point) for a grand total of 30 possible points.

- The scoring goal is 23 points or higher.

7. 44-Point Shooting

- The goal is to complete the drill within 90 seconds. Use a rebounder.

- Receive the ball at the top of the key and attack for a layup—two with the right hand and two with the left hand (alternating hands).

- Receive the ball at the top of the key, attack the rim, and shoot a stop-and-pop—attacking twice with the right hand and twice with the left hand.

- Shoot eight three-pointers (at the wing, pro spot, wing, and pro spot) on the left side and eight on the right side.

- Finish with four free throws.

- Layups and stop-and-pops are worth 2 points each, three-pointers are worth 3 points each, and free throws are worth 1 point each—for a total of 44 possible points.

8. 6-Minute Free-Throw Game
   - Make 16 free throws in 6 minutes.
   - Free throws are shot in one-and-one fashion: If both are made, sprint to the half-court line and back; if the first is made and the second missed, perform one full-court sprint; if the first is missed, perform a double sprint (down and back twice).
   - For all sprints, dribble the ball with the weak hand.
   - Continue the drill until either 16 free throws have been made or the 6 minutes have expired.

DON MEYER'S COMPETITIVE SHOOTING

Used with permission of Don Meyer.

Purpose: To provide players and coaches with competitive shooting drills developed by legendary coach and master teacher Don Meyer

Equipment: One ball per player (or per line, as needed) and a half-court space

Procedure: Set up the drill with three lines per basket and one ball for each line. Keep the lines small by using more baskets when possible.

1. *Three-line warm-up:* Start in close to the basket (10 to 12 feet, or 3 to 3.7 meters, away), as shown in figure 4.40. Shoot a perfect shot—shoot straight, get the shot up, hold a high one-count follow-through, and land 6 inches (15 centimeters) closer for balance. Players rebound their own shots and pass to the next player in line. Rotate right or left but do not go under the basket. After a line hits three in a row, the first player in that line moves back progressively one step. The coach sets the duration for this warm-up (5 minutes or more).

2. *Three lines with a closeout:* One shooter is out on the court and three lines are formed under the basket (one ball per line). First player in line will pass and close out low with high hands to pressure the shot. The closeout player becomes the next shooter.

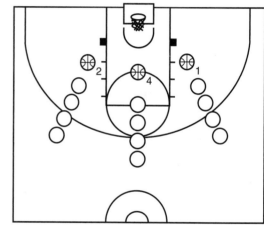

Figure 4.40 Three-line field-goal warm-up.

3. *Contest to 10 shots made:* Take game shots at game spots and game speed. On the second miss in a row, younger players take a layup and older players take a regular redemption shot (must get a swish or BRAD).

4. *Five in a row:* Inside players flash to the high post and shoot a jump shot. Players rebound their own shot, and put-backs count as makes if the ball never hits the floor.

5. *25-shot drill:* If solo, start with a spin pass to self; if paired, one player rebound-passes to the shooter and pressures the move or shot.
   - First 5 shots (pairs or three lines): Shoot guarded layins off of one foot or two feet. Use the glass whenever possible. Try to make it clean (swish or BRAD).
   - Second 5 shots: Call for the ball and shoot jump shots inside the arc.
   - Third 5 shots: Use a one-inch (2.5-centimeter) shot fake (no foot fake outside the arc). Get to the basket on one dribble or use two dribbles on a hesitation move. Use one long layin when attacking outside the free-throw lane.
   - Fourth 5 shots: Shoot outside the arc. Use a shot fake, drive, and pull-up jump shot. Use at least one step-back or hop-back move.

- Fifth 5 shots: Shoot three-pointers. The partner passes to the shooter, then closes out to apply simulated pressure and attempt a block (no fouls). Each pair takes 6 minutes total.

  - If using as a team drill, shoot free throws when done (modify shot choices for inside players).

6. *Free-throw swish drill:* A swish or BRAD is worth 1 point, a make that hits the rim is worth 0 points, and a miss is worth −1. Play to 2 (win) or −2 (lose). Great shooters can play to 6 (win) or −2 (lose). This is an excellent competitive-pressure drill for developing concentration.

7. *Team free-throw drill (end of practice):* Each player shoots a one-and-one. The coach sets the goal for made free throws and the team penalty if the goal is not met (e.g., full team of 12 must make 20 free throws). Players can be divided into two teams of six to eight each at two baskets.

TROUBLESHOOTING COMMON SHOOTING FAULTS

- **Problem:** Improper footwork and stance

  Correction: Reteach footwork and stance; begin shooting close to basket.

- **Problem:** Negative arm–ball motion (two-count shot)

  Correction: Pass to shooting pocket; shooter uses only one-count shot.

- **Problem:** Vertical misalignment (e.g., elbow out when viewed from behind)

  Correction: Shoot the line, then shoot soft-touch shots.

- **Problem:** Hang on shot, shoot on way up

  Correction: Start with close shots and ensure shot is taken just before peak of jump.

- **Problem:** Balance- or bookend-hand drag

  Correction: Use one-handed form shots, then progress to close in two-handed shots.

- **Problem:** Watching the ball rather than the target

  Correction: Start with soft-touch shots and laser focus on target each shot; use "focus" verbal reminder.

GONZAGA COMPETITIVE SHOOTING

Purpose: To provide players and coaches with a set of competitive shooting drills

Equipment: Two or three players per basket with designated number of balls

Procedure: Players catch passes with the feet in the air and land in triple-threat position facing the basket. The coach designates the type of pass (regularly including a one-hand, off-hand pass). Passes must be made on time and on target; every pass is a shot to a teammate. Players should get open to shoot game shots at game spots and game speed.

1. *Pairs with a ball:* Players do one-pass shooting (rebound own shot or partner rebounds), two-pass shooting (partner rebounds), and three-pass shooting (rebound own shot).

2. *Timed shooting:* Pairs try to make 50 three-pointers within 4 minutes.

3. *In and out:* This drill is run with three players and two balls. Players shoot in two spots (corner-wing and wing-top) on both sides. They shoot for 1 minute, then rotate—3 minutes per side for three players.

4. *Three in a row plus a free throw:* This drill can be done in pairs or alone with a spin pass. The coach designates a game move and a goal, such as making three elbow shots in a row. Players must meet the goal, then either make a free throw or repeat the drill. Use all of half-court and a variety of moves.

5. *100-point shooting:* Players shoot from five spots: baseline, wing, top of key, opposite wing, and opposite baseline. At each spot, they shoot three shots: three-pointer, midrange shot, and layup. They finish with one dribble layup from the arc. Players shoot at each spot as long as they make baskets. Each made shot scores 3 points, and a 1-point bonus is added for a swish or BRAD. The goal is to score 100 points before going through all three shots (three-point field goal, drive pull-up, layup) at all five spots (corners, wings, top of key). The drill can be timed, so each shooter scores max points for all spots.

FREE-THROW PROGRESSION ▶

Purpose: To provide players with a daily drill that reteaches and reviews free-throw fundamentals during each practice period

Equipment: Ball, court area, and basket

Procedure: This drill consists of four parts and associated learning reminders.

1. Five slams: Players each grab a ball and slap or slam it hard on the sides with both hands simultaneously to check proper grip.

    Learning reminder: Shoot the ball with the whole hand—spread the fingers and form a V with the thumb and first finger. *Feel it.*

2. Players shoot five form shots from any spot without a shooting target. The shooting foot is placed perpendicular to any line on the court (e.g., sideline) and at any spot. Players shoot five free throws using perfect technique and holding the follow-through until the ball hits the floor.

    Learning reminders:
    - Find the spot.
    - Establish a ritual.
    - Bounce at the bottom to one-count shot.
    - Use a full follow-through (exaggerated).
    - Shoot up, not out.
    - Use the legs for power (up on the toes).
    - Keep body weight forward on the finish and freeze the follow-through.

3. Players shoot at least 10 soft-touch free throws from a position 6 feet (1.8 meters) in front of the basket with complete physical technique. When the coach or the player is satisfied with proper physical technique, add the mental-edge technique for confidence building. Set appropriate goals for free throws made (from 5 makes to 8 or 9 makes to 10 swishes) depending on skill level.

    Learning reminders:
    - Apply the four physical technique essentials: find the spot, establish a ritual, start the same, and finish the same.
    - Add mental-edge technique: focus, feel, feedback.

4. Players go to the regular free-throw line and shoot free throws with perfect technique. They use all of the correct physical and mental techniques to groove the free throw. Use these techniques in competitive situations. Set goals and keep written records.

Learning reminders:

- Use all physical techniques.
- Use all mental techniques.

FOUL-SHOT GOLF

Purpose: To teach players to shoot free throws with competition against self or others

Equipment: Ball and basket

Procedure: Players start at the foul line and play 18 "holes." A birdie is assigned for each swish (–1 point), par for each nonswish make (0 points), and a bogie for each miss (1 point). Players get three shots at a time, or a round of three holes, until all players have taken a round. The game is over after six rounds, and the player with the lowest score wins.

KNOCKOUT SHOOTING

Purpose: To practice shooting in a competitive situation

Equipment: Two balls and three to eight players per basket

Procedure: Players form lines at the selected spot (at least two lines at each basket). The first player shoots and rebounds his or her own shot. If the shot is made, the player passes back to the next open teammate in front of the line and goes to the back of the line. The next shooter must make the shot before the next player in line with a ball makes a shot to attempt to knock out the player ahead. If the shot is missed, the player follows and re- bounds the shot to make the rebound shot before the next outside shooter makes an out- side shot. If the next shooter makes the shot first, the layup player is knocked out—to run a lap, sprint to the opposite wall and back, or perform some other penalty action before returning to the game (temporary knockout). Play for 1- to 3-minute periods. The coach can also set up the game with permanent knockouts until a final winner is determined.

ROW-PLUS FREE-THROW SHOOTING

Purpose: To provide competitive shooting practice

Equipment: Ball and basket

Procedure: Any player can compete against the game by selecting a move, shot, or situ- ation and practicing it until a certain number of field goals are made in a row and a free throw is made. This approach to shooting practice is modified from an approach used by many great offensive players, notably Bill Bradley, who used it in high school (Crystal City, Missouri), college (Princeton University), and the professional ranks (New York Knicks) to become one of the best scorers in the history of the game.

For example, a player might start at the top of the key and select a move consisting of a shot fake or a dribble drive with a pull-up jump shot at 15 to 18 feet (4.6 to 5.5 meters). The goal might be to make two in a row plus a free throw. That is, the player would replicate the move and the shot at game speed until two field goals are made in a row, then follow with a made free throw before going on to another move or shot. If the free throw is missed, the player must start over and repeat until the goal has been met (two made field goals in a row plus a free throw). Elite players might use goals as challenging as five in a row (or more) plus a free throw in order to compete against the game.

FOOTWORK AND FIELD GOALS (OR FREE THROWS) ▶

Purpose: To provide competitive shooting practice

Equipment: Ball, basket, and half-court playing area

Procedure: Possible goals for this game include making a certain number of shots in a row (field goals or free throws) and avoiding consecutive misses either for a certain period of time (e.g., 3 minutes) or for a given number of attempts (e.g., 10, 15, or 20). The player with the ball may select any field-goal situation (e.g., shot from a pass or from a dribble) and any move (e.g., pull-up jumper, layup, runner). A free-throw situation can also be selected.

The competing player begins the drill facing away from the baseline while positioned directly under the basket in the triple-threat position. Using a shot fake, the player executes either a direct drive or a crossover drive (any live-ball move) for two or three dribbles in order to get as far past the three-point line as possible, then terminates the move with a controlled quick stop. On landing in a triple-threat quick stance, the player executes a PPF rear turn to face the basket in triple-threat position. The player then either tosses a two-handed underhand pass to a shooting spot (in order to shoot from the pass) or uses a shot fake and a dribble-drive or live-ball move (shot from a dribble) into a competitive move (e.g., layup or pull-up jumper). The player assumes that every shot is missed and either retrieves the made shot out of the net or follows the missed shot until it is made. After capturing the ball with two hands from the net and chinning it, the player, now facing the baseline, executes a PPF rear turn to face away from the basket in a new direction and repeats the cycle. Here is the sequence in a nutshell: Capture and chin the ball, use a live-ball move away from the basket for two dribbles, use a quick stop, execute a PPF rear turn to face the basket, shoot from a pass or dribble, do a completion move, be ready for a possible rebound, and repeat.

During the drill, the player needs to use all live-ball moves and the entire half court—drive to the corner, the wings, and the out-front position. A goal may be set for number of repetitions (10 to 20) or field goals made in a row. If the player is doing footwork and free throws, the drill terminates each time the player quick-stops and executes the PPF rear turn to face the basket. At that time, the player goes to the free-throw line. The drill continues again after a free throw is either made or missed. This drill allows players to practice a considerable amount of footwork with the ball in a short time. As many as four players can do the drill at once on each basket.

MENTAL PRACTICE FOR FIELD-GOAL AND FREE-THROW SHOOTING

Purpose: To teach players to use automatic verbal prompts, shooting rituals, and self-evaluation to build shooting confidence

Equipment: Ball and basket

Procedure

1. Mental-practice shooting: Carry out at least 25 perfect shots daily in a quiet, focused place.

   - Field goals: Use verbal prompts—*focus* (on the back-of-the-rim target), *feel* (feel the shot from successful start to finish, from shooting pocket to held follow-through), and *feedback* (*yes, net, swish,* and *money* on made shots). Note: There are no misses in the mind to analyze and forget.

   - Backboard shots: *Focus* (high), *feel* (soft), and verbalize *feedback* on a make. Visualize every shot perfectly in the mind: see it, hear it, and feel it. Players should paint the perfect picture in their minds.

   - Free throws: Use verbal prompts—see and say *net* or *swish* (or *nothing but net*) during the preshot ritual (e.g., bouncing ball; focus, feel, feedback [*yes* or *net*]).

2. Soft-touch: On each soft-touch or close shot, use verbal mental-practice prompts.

   - Rim shots: focus, feel, feedback (*yes* or *net*)
   - Backboard shots: focus high, soft, feedback

3. Mental-practice personal-record test: Chart status and progress weekly. From a 12-to-15-foot (3.7-to-4.6-meter) distance, shoot as many shots as possible in 5 minutes to attain the greatest number of consecutive makes in that time.

   - Rim shots: Move from the baseline around the court to the opposite side of the free-throw lane on the baseline. Keep track of consecutive makes in 5-minute periods in two situations:

     – Use a two-handed underhand toss to the 12-foot (3.7-meter) spot; *catch facing away from basket.* Using the PPF, face and focus, shoot (*feel*), and use feedback. Time and record results for a 5-minute period (personal record for doing catch-and-face).

     – Use a two-handed underhand toss to the shooting spot; after the catch, land *facing the basket* and then use verbal prompts (*focus, feel, feedback*) while shooting. Record the number of consecutive makes in 5 minutes (personal record for facing the basket).

   - Backboard shots: From a 12-to-15-foot (3.7-to-4.6-meter) distance on the 45-degree angle with the backboard, players should go from side to side (between two spots) while shooting backboard shots in two situations: (a) catch-and-face and then (b) face-and-shoot. Use verbal prompts on each backboard shot: *high* (focus), *soft* (feel), and *yes* or *net* (feedback). Record the number of consecutive makes in a 5-minute period.

     – Catch-and-face (personal record for the backboard): Land facing away from the basket, turn and face, and then shoot (personal record for facing the backboard). Record the 5-minute personal record.

     – Land facing the basket and shoot (catch and shoot) or use an EPF drive (personal record for 5-minute period).

LONG LAYUP ATTACK ▶

Purpose: To provide perimeter players with a long layup attack-the-basket drill from the middle of the court (free-throw lane extended)

Equipment: Perimeter players at the top of the key with a ball (option for later: basket defender under the basket)

Procedure: A perimeter player starts with a live-ball or dribble move from top of the key on the free-throw-lane alley to draw the shot blocker (big defender) away from the basket (up or out) for a pass down (behind) or to take a long-layup, one-hand "runner" shot off the backboard (see figure 4.41). After the long-layup skill is achieved on the move without a defender, a shot blocker (big defender) may be added for a 2-on-1 situation. The shot blocker can fake-help or help to block the long layup, thus forcing the attacker to use a dump-down pass to a cutting or posting teammate.

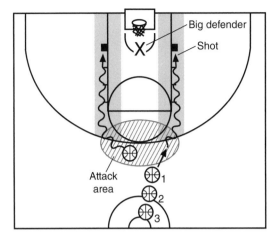

Figure 4.41 Long layup attack drill.

HOP-BACK (STEP-BACK) SHOOTING

Purpose: To work with perimeter players on the hop-back (step-back) shooting skill

Equipment: One ball for each of three to five perimeter players and one basket (option for later: defender)

Procedure: An offensive player on each wing penetrates on a dribble drive to the middle or to the baseline, then pushes off the inside (basket-side) foot using a hop-back move for a three-point jump shot. A defender may be added later in two stages: first a soft dummy defender, then a live defender. The offensive player must attack the basket in order to get the defender to commit to defending the drive, then use the hop-back move opposite and away from the defender (figure 4.42) to shoot a three-point field goal. The drill may be modified to utilize a hop-back move sideways along the three-point arc after a defensive "fly-by" closeout and a hop back for a three-point field goal.

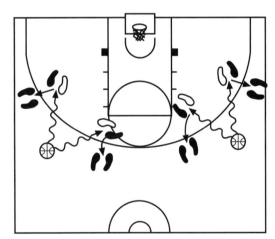

Figure 4.42 Hop-back (step-back) shooting drill.

GONZAGA FULL-COURT LAY-AND-J (PEER-PRESSURE DRILL)

Purpose: To practice shooting jump shots and layups as well as passing and catching skills (peer-pressure team-scoring drill)

Equipment: Full basketball team, five basketballs, and a full court (both game baskets)

Procedure: Setup for this 5-minute drill begins with the players forming three lines on one baseline (A in figure 4.43a) and one ball provided to the player at the head of the middle line (under the basket). At the opposite end of the court (B in figure 4.43a), two players stand on the baseline—one on either side of the basket and each with a ball. Another player waits under the basket to rebound the layup and then to return down the court in the middle lane for a layup at the other end of the court (see figure 4.43b).

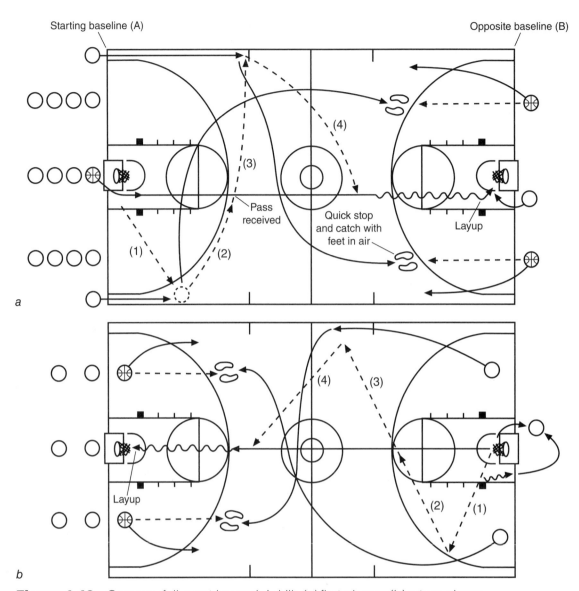

Figure 4.43 Gonzaga full-court lay-and-J drill: *(a)* first phase, *(b)* return phase.

The drill starts at baseline A in the middle line under the basket. The middle player with the ball passes once to the wide lane player on either side (to the right in figure 4.43*a*), then gets a return pass and ends with a layup in the middle lane. The two wide lane players then shoot finish jump shots at the opposite end of the court. Three players return to start and repeat the drill (see figure 4.43*b*).

Shooting goal: The team tries to make 50 to 100 shots (total layups and jump shots) within 5 minutes, depending on the coach's goal for shooting jump shots (inside the three-point arc; beyond the arc; shot fake beyond the arc and one-dribble pull-up; drive inside the arc and hop-back beyond the arc). This drill is for taking game shots at game spots at game speed. Coaches may choose to implement a consequence according to the number of missed layups.

Pass–catch area shooting options are as follows:

1. Midrange jump shot

2. Three-point field goal

3. Three-point shot fake and one dribble to jump shot

4. Drive and step-back or hop-back to three-point field goal

GONZAGA SCRAMBLE PASS-AND-CATCH LAYUP (PEER-PRESSURE DRILL) ▶

Purpose: To perform game moves at game speed in the half court while working on footwork, passing and catching, and layup shooting (team peer-pressure drill)

Equipment: Half court and one basketball (can add a second ball to increase difficulty)

Procedure: Players form three lines under the basket on the baseline with one or two balls in the first line (by spot 1) as shown in figure 4.44. The drill begins with the first player passing accurately (on time and on target) to the first player in the adjacent line (spot 2) and then moving in that direction by skipping two spots (e.g., in figure 4.44, 1 passes to 2 and moves to spot 4). The drill may be run counterclockwise and then clockwise as a team peer-pressure drill with a goal of making 10 to 15 layups in a row in a given amount of time (or repeat the drill).

Drill Rules

- Pass to the adjacent line, cut hard to the next line (two spots away), and prepare for a return pass on time and on target.

- The catcher gives a one-handed target and uses a two-handed catch with the feet in the air.

- Catch the pass and continue the circuit with another two-handed pass to the adjacent spot.

- When the player reaches spot 6, he or she pauses to make a fake-and-break front cut for the layup (giving a hand target).

- Rotation goes from spot 3 to 2 to 1 when passing counterclockwise and in reverse order when passing clockwise.

- When the layup goal is met, reverse direction and restart the rotation.

- Note the pass numbers in figure 4.44 (eight passes per circuit).

- Reset (start over) on a missed layup or when the coach observes an error in passing, catching, or footwork.

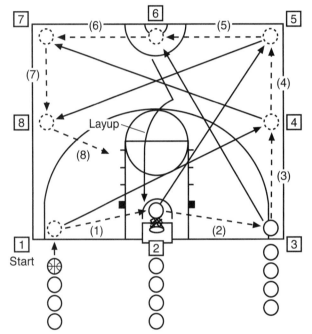

Figure 4.44 Gonzaga scramble pass-and-catch layup drill.

Wooden Wisdom

"Success comes from knowing that you did your best to become the best you are capable of becoming."

—John Wooden

CHAPTER 5

OUTSIDE OFFENSIVE MOVES
— PLAYING THE PERIMETER —

"Drive and dish (penetrate and pitch), pass and catch, and create scoring chances for teammates should be the job description of a perimeter player. Scoring is important but a lower priority than passing to a teammate."

Jerry V. Krause

Any discussion of individual offensive moves should begin with the reminder that basketball is first and foremost a team sport. Although every game situation provides opportunities for individuals to use offensive moves, the player with the ball must coordinate offensive moves closely with four other players. Therefore, coaches need to place limitations on individual offensive moves in order to ensure that players use their strengths to benefit the team and get the best team shots.

Outside moves are offensive moves made around the perimeter of the court while players are facing the basket. The four types of individual outside moves are as follows:

- Live-ball moves (made when the player with the ball still has a dribble available)
- Dribbling moves (made when the player is in the process of dribbling)
- Dead-ball moves (made when the player has used the dribble and stopped while still in possession of the ball)
- Completion shots (taken after a dribble)

Proficiency in live-ball moves should be coupled with the development of quick, controlled dribble moves that are used with purpose. All live-ball moves and dribble moves should result in a pass, a dead-ball move, or a completion shot. This chapter describes both live-ball and dead-ball moves (dribble moves and completion shots are described in chapters 3 and 4, which address ballhandling and shooting, respectively).

FUNDAMENTALS OF LIVE-BALL MOVES

CRITICAL CUE
Start live-ball moves from the triple-threat position facing the basket; use the rim–post–action (RPA) vision progression.

All live-ball moves begin with the player facing the basket in offensive quick-stance or triple-threat position, from which the player can shoot, pass, or dribble. When making moves, players should be in their effective shooting range. They should get into position by catching the ball with their feet in the air and landing with a quick stop facing the basket (i.e., catching and turning in the air). The alternative is to catch and face, in which the player catches the ball with both hands, uses a quick stop facing away from the basket, and makes a pivot (turn) into triple-threat position to face the basket (using the nondominant foot as the permanent pivot foot [PPF] whenever possible and resorting to either-pivot-foot [EPF] moves when necessary). Players should especially explore live-ball moves as they catch the ball (i.e., on the catch).

Players should always protect the ball and keep it close to the body in a power position (i.e., pit and protect the ball) while using the body as a shield. They provide this protection in various ways: by keeping the ball near and under the shoulder with the dominant hand behind the ball (wrinkle-wrist position and bent elbow) in triple-threat position (figure 5.1), by dribbling the ball on the side opposite the defender during a live-ball move, by using a catch-and-face RPA technique (chin-it and pivot to triple-threat position) in defensive traffic (figure 5.2), and by not dangling the ball with the elbows locked or extended. Dangling the ball in extended elbow position means danger; specifically, it causes players to lose arm quickness with the ball, lose power to protect the ball, and possibly lose the ball to a quick-handed defender.

One basic guideline for making outside moves with the ball is to conserve time and space through balance and quickness. Whenever possible, all moves should be quick and made in a straight line toward the basket. For instance, when moving past a defender on a dribble drive, the offensive player should make slight shoulder contact with the defender (figure 5.3), then use quick shot fakes and pass fakes while maintaining a quick stance. The live-ball move (using the dribble drive past the defender) should be made with a quick first step that is long and low and goes past the defender in a straight line toward the basket. During dribble drives past a defender on a live-ball move, players

Figure 5.1 Triple-threat position: *(a)* side view and *(b)* front view.

Figure 5.2 Catch and face—protect the ball: *(a)* Catch facing away from the basket; *(b)* pivot (turn) to face the basket using the PPF or EPF footwork.

can remember the phrase *shoulder to knees, feel the breeze*. The driver must get the head and shoulders past the defender's trunk; at that point, contact will result in a foul on the defender. This technique, referred to as *winning the battle* of the first step, can be used to drive against the defender's momentum or front foot.

CRITICAL CUE
Dribble drive—
shoulder to knees,
feel the breeze.

The rule of attacking the front foot or hand is applied when the defender is in a staggered stance (see figure 5.3a). The most vulnerable part of the defender is the front-foot or front-hand side because the defender must pivot before angling back to cut off the dribble penetration. Therefore, the offensive player should be aware of the defender's front foot and hand and use a live-ball move to that side of the body whenever possible. The *war is won* on the dribble drive when inside hip contact is made with the defender to prevent defender recovery on the drive.

The offensive player should attack the basket on the dribble drive by accelerating to the basket under control. *Now or never* means that the live-ball move is best made immediately after the player receives a pass, before the defense can adjust, and while the defense

Figure 5.3 PPF direct drive: *(a)* attacking the front foot, *(b)* defender in staggered stance (left foot forward), and *(c)* defender forced to pivot to cut off the move, thus leading to hip contact with defender (*winning the war*) on the second step.

is moving. Drive against momentum, or in the opposite direction of the defender. If in doubt about whether the dribble drive is open, the driver should pass the ball (*pass first, dribble last*).

The primary objective of any live-ball move in the power zone is to score a layup with one dribble (two or more dribbles are seldom needed). Players should read the defense to anticipate chances to use a controlled dribble drive as a reaction to a defensive adjustment. Players can challenge the defense even more if they learn to get by the defender and control the dribble drive well enough to permit a last-second pass to an open teammate or a pull-up for a shot. The penetrate-and-pitch is an excellent perimeter move that is needed by all perimeter players. When using the dribble drive, players should be looking for the following options: layup, pass (using a quick stop first) if a help defender appears, and pull-up jumper or completion move if another defender is waiting at the basket.

Permanent Pivot Foot Moves

These moves should be used when a permanent pivot foot (PPF) is used for all live-ball moves. The left foot should be used by right-handed players and vice versa. The following moves for getting by the first defender should be taught as basics: direct drive, hesitation move, rocker step, and crossover drive.

PPF footwork is preferred for perimeter moves by younger players because it is simpler and easier to learn than the either-pivot-foot (EPF) approach. Players can attain greater skill levels with a PPF approach because it involves fewer choices and moves to be learned. On the two primary live-ball moves—the direct drive and the crossover drive—success occurs on the second step with the more comfortable and quicker preferred side and on the first step to the slower, less comfortable nonpreferred side. With the direct drive, the battle is won on the first step (getting the head and shoulders past the defender), whereas the war is won on the second step when hip contact is made on the defender (i.e., locking in the defender with inside hip contact). For the crossover drive (to the nonpreferred side, which is normally slower), both the battle and the war are won on the first step as the driver gets the head and shoulders by the defender at the same time that inside hip contact is made on the defender. The key to live-ball moves is the long and low first step (*shoulder to knees, feel the breeze*).

> **CRITICAL CUE FOR PPF MOVES**
> - Direct drive: Second step wins the war.
> - Crossover drive: First step wins the battle and the war.

Direct Drive This is a drive past the defender with the dominant foot. A right-handed player should drive past the defender's left side, taking the first step with the right foot (vice versa for a left-handed player) by establishing triple-threat position in a staggered stance and pushing off of the pivot foot without a negative step. The move is quick, long, and low and is made with the stepping foot straight to the basket as the ball is pushed to the floor and in front of the lead foot before the pivot foot is lifted. Finally, a step is taken past the defender with the PPF to attack the basket. The breakdown count consists of the explosion step with the dominant stepping foot (one) and the player pushing the ball ahead to the floor on the dribble drive (figure 5.3) while the second step is taken (two). U.S. rules require the ball to be out of the hand before the pivot foot is lifted; for international play (FIBA rules), the ball must hit the floor on the first dribble before the foot is lifted, which requires a longer and lower first step.

Hesitation or Step-Step Move This secondary dominant-side move is executed by establishing the triple-threat position and making a short jab step at the defender and basket with the dominant foot. If the defender doesn't react to the jab step, then a second long and low explosion step can be made as a direct-drive step past the defender. The breakdown count consists of a jab step (slightly forward and down) with a short pause, a long and low explosion step (go move), and a dribble drive initiated by pushing the ball ahead to the floor as inside hip contact is made on the third step with the foot next to the defender (figure 5.4).

Figure 5.4 PPF hesitation or step-step move: *(a)* short first step, *(b)* long and low second step past the defender, and *(c)* near hip contact with the defender (third step).

Rocker Step Another dominant- or preferred-side move is the rocker step, which involves a direct-drive jab fake and return to triple-threat position, followed by a direct-drive move. The sequence is to establish triple-threat position, make a direct-drive short jab step, and then return to triple-threat position where a short shot fake may be used to lure the defender forward. When the defender moves toward the offensive player in reaction to the return to the triple-threat position (and a possible shot fake), the offensive player should make a direct-drive move. The rule is to drive against the defender's momentum. The breakdown count consists of a jab step (down), a move rocking back to triple-threat position (up), a long and low explosion step against the defender's momentum (down), and a dribble drive (go) started by pushing the ball ahead to the floor (figure 5.5).

Figure 5.5 PPF rocker step: *(a)* Jab-fake (down), *(b)* return to triple-threat position (up), and *(c)* take a long and low first step past the defender reacting to the shot fake (down).

Crossover Drive When the defender overplays the dominant side, the basic PPF countermove to the opposite side consists of establishing the triple-threat position and then crossing the dominant stepping foot over to the other side of and past the defender while keeping the ball close to the body and swinging it across the chest area (circle tight). The ball is then taken from the nonpreferred triple-threat position and pushed ahead to the floor with the player's nonpreferred hand to begin the crossover dribble drive. The dominant foot is pointed toward the basket. Players should keep the pivot foot stationary while the crossover step is made with the same stepping foot as in the direct drive but on the nonpreferred side. The breakdown count consists of assuming triple-threat position, then swinging the dominant foot over to the other side (long step) as the ball is snapped over from pit to pit while placing the nonpreferred hand behind the ball (circle tight) and pushing the ball ahead to the floor on the dribble drive (figure 5.6). The ball should be moved across the body (pit to pit) high in the chest area. Some coaches prefer the high sweep and low sweep, but this is too slow and takes the ball too far from shooting or driving position. Some coaches also teach a jab step to the preferred side to set up the crossover, but this move is slower and tends to make the reaction crossover move more lateral than toward the basket.

The direct-drive and crossover moves are the basic PPF live-ball moves and are sufficient to enable most players to handle most defenders. Beginners can usually depend on one basic go-to move (direct drive) and one countermove (crossover), with the secondary moves being the rocker and hesitation to the preferred side (the side that each player is more comfortable using).

Figure 5.6 PPF crossover drive for a right-hander: *(a)* Assume triple-threat position (jab), *(b)* bring the ball to the nonpreferred side (circle tight), and *(c)* move with a long and low step past the defender and toward the basket.

Moves With Either Pivot Foot (Advanced)

These moves can be taught when either foot is used as the pivot foot (EPF) in live-ball moves. Both right-handed and left-handed players should be able to use this method to establish either foot as a pivot foot.

EPF Direct Drive With the Direction Foot (Right Foot, Drive Right; Left Foot, Drive Left) This move, used to dribble-drive past a defender, consists of making the explosion step with the foot on the side to which the player is driving. The sequence is to make a quick stop facing the basket and, when driving right, use the left foot for a pivot foot and take an explosion step past the defender with the right foot; when driving left, step with the left foot and use the right foot as the pivot foot. The ball is pushed ahead on the floor on the dribble drive. The breakdown count consists of taking a long and low explosion step with the foot on the same side as the dribble drive (right foot to the right side, left foot to the left side) and pushing the ball ahead to the floor to start the dribble drive. The ball must be out of the hand before the pivot foot leaves the floor. The *disadvantage* of this direction-foot move is that hip contact on the defender (with the goal of winning the war of hip contact) occurs on the second step; in other words, the first step of the drive wins only the battle—not the war.

EPF Direct Drive With the Opposite Foot This move is used to drive past a defender on either side by using the opposite foot to step across and shield the ball as a long and low direct drive is made. The opposite-foot drive is executed by making a quick stop facing the basket and, when driving right, stepping past the defender with a left-foot explosion step and pushing the ball ahead on the dribble drive. The breakdown count consists of taking an explosion step past the defender with the foot opposite the side of the dribble drive and pushing the ball ahead on the floor for the dribble drive (figure 5.7). This move offers the advantage of getting the head and shoulders by and making hip contact on the defender—thus winning both the battle and the war—with the first step.

> **CRITICAL CUES FOR EPF MOVES**
> - Direct drive: Use the direction foot or the opposite foot.
> - Crossover drive: Use the opposite foot.

Figure 5.7 Live-ball move for either pivot foot (EPF)—direct-drive move with the opposite foot: *(a)* to the right with the left foot, *(b)* to the left with the right foot.

EPF Crossover Drive Players can also learn a countermove using either foot as the pivot foot: Either fake right and then cross over left with the left pivot foot or fake left and then cross over right with the right pivot foot. This move is carried out by making a quick stop facing the basket, making a jab step and crossover with the same foot to the opposite side (swinging the ball across and close to the body), and, finally, pushing the ball ahead to the floor and starting a dribble drive. The breakdown count consists of a jab step, then a crossover step with the same foot while bringing the ball across the body, and a dribble drive started by pushing the ball ahead to the floor (figure 5.8). This is the preferred EPF move as it allows the offensive player to win the battle (get by defender's front foot) and win the war (inside hip contact) with one crossover step (or by a jab and crossover).

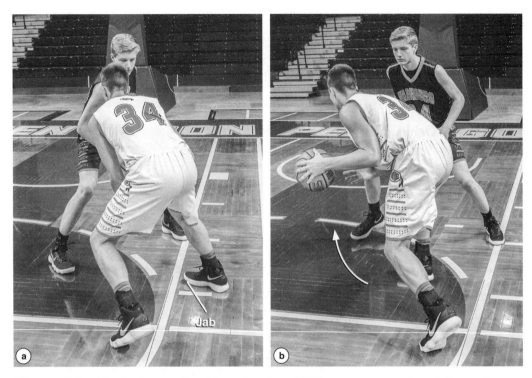

Figure 5.8 Live-ball move for either pivot foot (EPF)—crossover drive: *(a)* crossing over from right to left (jabbing right), *(b)* crossover drive to the left past the defender.

COACHING POINTS FOR OUTSIDE MOVES

- Visualize and learn to read and react to the defender.
- Attack the front foot and drive against the defender's momentum.
- Develop a go-to move and a countermove.
- Use game moves at game speed.
- Develop balance and quickness during all moves.
- Go at top speed under control.
- Make legal moves (know the footwork rules).
- Execute moves correctly first, then correctly and quickly: Do them right first, then speed up until mistakes are made, and then strive for game moves at game speed.

FUNDAMENTALS OF DEAD-BALL MOVES

These maneuvers are used at the completion of a dribble move when the quick stop is made within 10 to 12 feet (3 to 3.7 meters) of the basket. Players can use dead-ball moves when moving either left or right, but they must be within close shooting range for the moves to be maximally effective. Players in possession of the ball should avoid dead-ball situations whenever possible unless a pass or shot is anticipated. In other words, they should maintain the preferred live dribble.

Dead-ball moves using either pivot foot should be made after a quick stop, either from a pass or (more commonly) at the termination of a dribble. Remind players to see the whole court with big vision as the quick stop is made in order to read the defense and quickly make a proper decision (pass or shoot). The dead-ball move requires calmness as the offensive player may use a move and counter-move while reading the defense in order to be most effective.

Jump Shot Players should execute a quick stop and take the jump shot with balance and control (see chapter 4). The quick stop allows the shooter to slow momentum, go straight up, and land slightly forward of the takeoff position. Stopping with a closed (square) stance helps the shooter transfer forward momentum into the upward momentum of the shot.

Shot Fake and Jump Shot Players should make a quick stop and follow with a believable shot fake—eyes on the basket while making a small, quick vertical fake. More specifically, with vision on the basket (RPA), the player moves the ball up slightly (1 inch, or 2.5 centimeters) while maintaining a quick stance with the legs locked and the heels down, then quickly follows with a jump shot.

Step-Through Move Into One-Foot Layup (Advanced) Another attacking option is the advanced EPF move past either side of the defender to shoot a layup after a quick stop (with or without a shot fake). Players should make a quick stop facing the basket, followed by a shot fake to get the defender out of quick stance (unless the defender is already overcommitted). When going to the right, players take a step past the defender with the left foot (use the right foot when going left) and shoot a right-handed (or left-handed) running layup or a post shot. The breakdown count consists of a shot fake, a step past the defender with the opposite foot, and a layup shot (one-foot or power).

Crossover Step-Through Move (Advanced) This advanced EPF countermove is used to step toward a defender by faking one way and going the opposite way for a layup or post shot. It is performed by making a quick stop facing the basket, taking a jab step with either foot followed by a crossover step with the same foot to move past the defender for a layup or post shot. The breakdown count consists of jab step, crossover move, and layup or post shot (figure 5.9).

Step-Through Move Into Power Shot or Layup (Advanced) Even though the step-through and jab-step moves can be legally used to get layups, they are sometimes called as traveling by officials. To prevent this call, players can use a step-through completion move and finish the move with a two-foot power shot so that the pivot (turning) foot leaves the floor at the same time as the stepping foot. This move is shown for right-handed players in figure 5.10. Coaches should take every opportunity to educate officials about this move before their players use it.

Figure 5.9 Dead-ball crossover step-through move: *(a)* quick stop, *(b)* jab step toward the defender with the left foot, *(c)* crossover move (with left foot as pivot foot), and *(d)* layup or post shot.

Figure 5.10 Dead-ball crossover step-through move to a power shot: *(a)* quick stop, *(b)* jab step with the left foot, *(c)* crossover move with left foot while using right pivot foot and *(d)* power shot or jump hook from two feet.

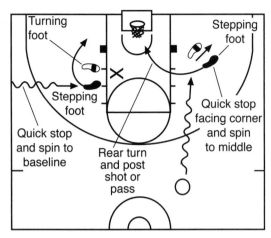

Figure 5.11 Dead-ball EPF spinner steps—from wing-middle or guard-side dribble drive.

Spinner (Advanced) When the player is stopped by a defender in the direct path or on the ball side of the dribbler on a middle drive, a pivoting rear turn into a layup or post shot is most effective from a dead-ball quick stop at a right angle to the baseline. Coaches can teach this advanced move by having players penetrate drive to the middle, make a quick stop facing the opposite sideline near the free-throw lane while chinning the ball, make a rear turn on the pivot or turning foot closest to the basket, and shoot a layup (one-handed runner, two-handed scoop, or power layup) or a post shot. The breakdown count consists of a using a quick stop, making a rear turn, stepping past the defender to the basket with the opposite foot, and shooting the layup or post shot (figure 5.11). Post players may use a spinner move when using a Zak-attack middle-post drive from the short corner (as described in chapter 6).

TROUBLESHOOTING

Here are some common problems with perimeter play, along with coaching corrections.

- **Problem:** Poor execution when learning

  Correction: Do it right first, then do it fast. Demonstrate again and slow down to get proper execution first.

- **Problem:** Trouble executing moves with the nonpreferred side

  Correction: Practice the moves two or three times more often on the nonpreferred side than on the preferred side.

- **Problem:** Traveling violations

  Correction: Coaches should reteach the rules of movement and footwork at a slow pace done correctly as boundaries of performance, then increase speed gradually.

- **Problem:** Ballhandling difficulties

  Correction: Coaches should prescribe added practice on passing, catching, dribbling, and basic ballhandling.

- **Problem:** Challenges when defenders are present

  Correction: Coaches should develop sequential, progressive practices. Players should use slow but correct moves first, get a rhythm, gradually increase speed until mistakes are made (acknowledge, understand, and learn from them), and then execute game moves at game speed. Coaches can add dummy defenders for all situations and, finally, add live defenders with all variations. Ultimately, players must learn to read the defender.

PERIMETER-PLAY DRILLS

These drills should be adapted to a coach's style of play and to situations encountered by perimeter players when using that style. As always, drills should be used in a manner that is sequential and progressive.

Guidelines for Perimeter Drills

1. When working alone, use a two-handed, underhand, spin self-pass before moves; always face the basket in triple-threat position with a live ball and use RPA (big vision).

2. Respect the three-point arc: Keep the feet behind the arc or penetrate for a pull-up shot or finish at the basket.

3. On all layups, go for swish or BRAD (back-rim-and-down) shots; mix up power and one-foot layup completions with opposite and same foot finishes.

4. When learning attack skills for perimeter play, precede all drives by giving a shot fake.

5. Tighten your game: Increase balance and quickness for making game moves at game speed.

6. Remember: Proper preparation develops confidence.

WARM-UP FOR PERIMETER PLAYERS

Purpose: To provide perimeter players with a warm-up for fundamental skills

Equipment: Two basketballs per player, tennis balls, half court with basket

Procedure: Spend 1 minute on each of the following exercises.

1. *Dribbling sequence:* one ball, two balls, dribbling and juggling, pull-back cross-over sequence

2. *Imaginary defense with talk:* on-the-ball, off-the-ball, off-the-ball to on-the-ball, post defense and blockout, transition

3. *Moving without the ball (offense):* pass-and-cut, screen-and-slip, screen cut, offensive rebounding, transition moves

4. *Fast-break package sprints:* without the ball

5. *Shooting progression:* field goals and free throws (using drills in chapter 4)

6. *Fingertip push-ups and stretching:* especially a long-and-low-drive stretch for the groin and hyperextension of the wrist for shooting

7. *Ballhandling sequence:* around the body, the arms, and the legs

Coaching Points

- Use imagination to simulate game moves.
- Do things right, then do them quickly at game speed.
- Become a detail player by focusing on the little things.

LINE DRILL: LIVE-BALL, DEAD-BALL, AND COMPLETION MOVES ADDITION

Purpose: To teach players live-ball and dead-ball moves and review dribble moves

Equipment: Full court and one ball for each of four lines of players

Procedure: Form four lines of players on the baseline. No defenders are placed on the court. Each circuit should include a beginning live-ball move, a dribble move in the middle

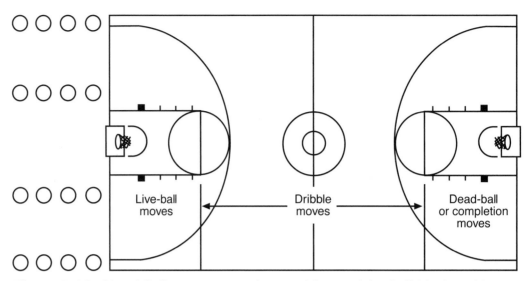

Figure 5.12 Line drill: Starts, stops, and turns while practicing individual outside moves.

of the court, and a dead-ball or completion move at the far baseline basket (quick-stop ending) (figure 5.12). The coach starts drill with all four lines at the same time. The first player in each line continues the drill until all players have completed the circuit or as many rounds as the coach designates.

Variations: There are two other line drill options.

- The first option is to put the first player in each line at the free-throw line extended. The next player in line assumes a triple-threat position with a ball. The ball handler passes to the opposite player at the free-throw line and then closes out to play defense; the catcher makes a 1-on-1 move past the defender. The defender first uses a dummy closeout (overplaying left, then overplaying right); the next progression is to a live closeout and a two-dribble live ball move to penetrate past the defender. The penetrator moves past the defender; the defender goes to the free-throw line and then rotates to the closeout defender line on the baseline.

- The second option is for the first player in line to use a live-ball move, make a quick stop at the free-throw line, and catch and face (using a rear turn). That player then makes a crisp, one-handed push pass (can use the nonpreferred hand) to the next player in the line. Finally, the passer becomes a closeout defender to the catcher, who makes a live-ball move around the defender. Repeat the action.

OUTSIDE MOVES USING A SPIN PASS ▶

Purpose: To develop skill in using outside moves

Equipment: Half-court area with basket and one ball per player

Procedure: Players practice live-ball moves and completion or dead-ball moves from a simulated passing-and-catching situation. Players use the two-handed, underhand spin self-pass to begin the drill in all primary offensive locations and situations. The sequence is to first spin a self-pass in spot locations near the edge of the three-point field-goal line, then catch the ball on the first bounce with the feet in the air and land facing the basket. Apply RPA technique. Every time players handle the ball, they should catch and face the basket by using the quick stop and the pivot and then attack the basket. Set goals, such as making two or three baskets in a row with a designated move or making three to five baskets with a specified move. Coaches should evaluate moves—only perfect practice makes perfect. Use PPF (basic) moves or EPF (advanced) moves for developing footwork. This self-monitored drill makes it possible to practice appropriate live-ball, dribble, and dead-ball or completion moves using the basic principles. A toss-back training device, partner, or coach passer may be used in conjunction with the spin-pass technique in order to simulate passing-and-catching situations used with the outside moves.

Options

- Catch and shoot: Make a spin pass to self and take a shot that is quick but unhurried and balanced.

- Catch and quick drive: Make a spin pass to self, V-cut away, catch and face from the self-pass, give a shot fake, dribble-drive, and finish.

- Catch and dribble: Make a one-dribble, pull-up jump shot.

- Catch, shot fake, and dribble: Make a quick, short shot fake (1 inch [2.5 centimeters]) with quick stance (legs locked and heels down), followed by one dribble and a pull-up jump shot.

- Catch, pass fake, and shot: Move only the arms and the head on the pass fake. Keep the fake short and quick—stay balanced.

- Catch, pass fake, drive, and shot: Coach may designate a completion move (e.g., Zak attack or long layin).

- Catch, jab step, and shot: Create space for the shot; stay balanced and use a short jab step.

- Catch, jab step (hesitation or rocker), drive, and shot: Drive to the left or to the right.

- Catch, one dribble, direction change, and shot: Attack the basket on the initial dribble, change direction (with a crossover, spin, or behind-the-back move) to continue penetration, and finish.

- Catch, two dribbles, step-back (hop-back) move to change direction, and shot behind the arc.

- General note: Perform extra (three times total) repetitions of moves to the nonpreferred side.

CLOSEOUT: 1-ON-1, 2-ON-2, 3-ON-3, 4-ON-4 ▶

Purpose: To practice all outside moves by perimeter players

Equipment: One ball and one basket per group

Procedure: Form a line of defensive players off the court at each basket. Position a line of offensive players 15 to 18 feet (4.6 to 5.5 meters) away, facing the basket. The first defensive player steps under the basket with the ball and makes a crisp air pass (with the feet on the floor) to the first player in the offensive line and then closes out to defend that player. The drill begins as soon as the pass is made. The perimeter offensive player should catch the ball with the feet in the air and facing the basket, read and react to the defender's actions, and apply fundamentals to shoot or make an outside move.

Players play make-it-take-it or any arrangement of their choice and rotate to the back of the opposite line each time. The drill may also be run as a 2-on-2, 3-on-3, or 4-on-4 option (figure 5.13) and then becomes a teamwork competition with on-the-ball and

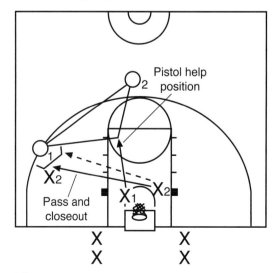

Figure 5.13 2-on-2 closeout: on-the-ball and off-the-ball defense.

off-the-ball play. The passer guards the ball handler on the first pass, or the coach may call either defender's name to close out on the ball with the other defender sprinting to the help position.

1-ON-1

Purpose: To provide varied 1-on-1 competition for perimeter players

Equipment: One ball and one basket per group

Procedure: 1-on-1 competition allows each offensive player the chance to evaluate the effectiveness of perimeter play in all situations: live-ball, dribble, and completion moves.

1-on-1 Starting 15 to 20 Feet (4.6 to 6.1 Meters) From the Basket

- Begin with a move to get open—V-cut or L-cut—then use catch-and-face and RPA techniques. Coach or teammates can make the entry pass.
- Play make-it-take-it or rotate after a certain number of possessions (two or three).
- Play games to five made baskets.
- Allow 5 seconds or two dribbles to make a move.

1-on-1 Starting Near the Half-Court Line

- Use a teammate or coach for a passer.
- Use a cut to get open and then use catch-and-face and RPA techniques.
- Use dribble moves to go by the defender.
- Use a completion move to score, usually on a layup or a jump shot.
- Option: Add a second hoop defender in the lane (first defender goes only to the extended free-throw line).

1-on-1 Completion Moves in the Lane

- The defender allows an entry pass or a self-pass. Alternatively, use the manager or program assistant with a dummy defender.
- The offensive player makes a move from the perimeter, catches the ball, and faces the basket in the free-throw lane.
- The offensive player scores with a completion move made without a dribble (jump shot, step-through layup, crossover layup, or spinner move).
- Alternate possessions for games to five or play make-it-take-it.

1-on-1 From Offensive Positions

- Players receive the ball at the locations of the fast-break or set offense and then go 1-on-1.
- A secondary defender can be added at the basket.

PARTNER PENETRATE-AND-PITCH ⊙

Purpose: To practice live-ball moves and passing to a teammate for a score at the completion of a dribble drive

Equipment: Two players, ball, and basket (up to three pairs per basket)

Procedure: Partners start 20 to 25 feet (6.1 to 7.6 meters) from the basket and are spaced 15 to 18 feet (4.6 to 5.5 meters) apart in point–wing or guard–forward and forward–forward combinations (figure 5.14). The ball handler makes a spin self-pass and starts with a live-ball move into a dribble drive. The partner (potential catcher) times a cut to be open at a spot when the passer is ready to pass and with proper spacing. The guard–forward partners use the cutting options of sliding away (drifting) or filling behind (crack-back move) the driving path. The cutter looks for completion shots to the basket or outside shots—medium-range shots or three-pointers. The penetrator or passer passes (pitches) to the partner or fakes the pass and shoots the shot. The forward–forward partners are on opposite sides of the floor. The penetrator drives the baseline and, using the baseline hand, executes a push pass to the partner catcher, who slides (by means of a drift or baseline release) to an open position toward the baseline on the opposite side of the floor. Except for the baseline release pass, which is a bounce pass, all other perimeter passes are air passes. The partner catcher may also make an overplay basket cut on occasion.

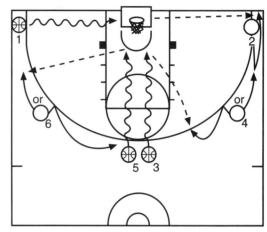

Figure 5.14 Penetrate-and-pitch drill (pairs).

PARTNER PASSING AND SHOOTING

See chapter 4 for descriptions of a variety of shooting drills for shots after individual outside moves—for example, using one, two, or three passes. Here is one selected practice combination: Make six field goals after one pass, six field goals after two passes, and six field goals after three passes.

TIMED LAYUPS

Purpose: To practice ballhandling and layup shooting in a competitive situation

Equipment: Ball, free-throw lane, basket, timing device

Procedure

- *V-layup:* Starting on the right elbow at the free-throw line in triple-threat position, dribble-drive to the basket and shoot a layup. Use two hands to grab the ball out of the net. Do a right-handed dribble past the free-throw line to the left elbow and a left-handed dribble continuously for the left-handed layup. Make a two-handed grab and do a left-handed dribble past the free-throw line to the right elbow. Repeat as many times as possible in 30 or 60 seconds. Record the number of layups made for each player as their personal record.

- *Reverse V-layup:* Generally perform the same drill but cross the rim to shoot a layup on the other side of the basket with the appropriate dribbling hand. For example, start at the right elbow, use a left-handed dribble to cross in front of the basket, and shoot a left-handed hook layup or reverse layback move. Then use a right-handed dribble past the free-throw line to the left elbow and reverse back to the other side. Time for 30 or 60 seconds; record the layups made as a personal record. This drill is a good way to finish a perimeter workout.

PERIMETER GAME

Purpose: To practice all of the perimeter moves with the ball in competition against one's own personal record for the drill

Equipment: Ball, half court, two or three players per basket

Procedure: This drill can be done from three spots (wing, top of the key, and opposite wing) or five spots (add both baseline corners). See the sequence of moves in the following list. For layups, mix power layups, and one-foot layups, all layups must be clean (swish) to be worth 2 points (0 points if not a swish). Jump shots are worth 2 points. For making a swish, BRAD, or set of jump shots, the player gets a bonus point. The coach can designate any combination of jump shots at various locations to create a set. Call out the score on *every* shot attempt and the cumulative score, regardless of whether it is made or missed. Put back all misses, even though they don't count. For the free throws, use swish rules (a swish or BRAD = 1 point, a make that hits the rim = 0, and a miss = –1).

The moves are as follows:

1. Three field-goal attempts on each set
2. Middle drive to cross rim
3. Baseline drive to rim (toes pointed to baseline on power layup)
4. Middle drive to pull-up jump shot
5. Baseline drive to pull-up jump shot
6. Middle drive to quick stop, step-through move, and power shot (or runner)
7. Baseline drive to quick stop and spinner or power shot
8. Middle drive and three-point hop-back shot
9. Baseline drive and three-point hop-back shot
10. Middle drive, hesitation or rocker off hop-back, to the rim
11. Baseline drive, hesitation or rocker off hop-back, to the rim
12. Jab step to field-goal attempt (three)
13. Free throws (four)

Coaching Points

- On power layups, point the toes to the baseline.
- Execute game fundamentals properly and quickly for the good of the team.
- Be a practice player first.
- Make game moves at game speed; practice and play with the intensity and poise of a championship team player.

FIVE-SPOT DRIBBLE AND FINISH

Purpose: To practice dribbling moves and finishing at the basket (appropriate for a warm-up)

Equipment: One ball per player, five cones, four players per half court with basket

Procedure: Place five cones on the arc (corner, wing, point, opposite wing, and opposite corner). To start the drill, the player with the ball is under the basket.

One-Ball Series

1. Make a live-ball direct drive to the corner cone, circle the cone, dribble with right hand to the basket, and finish with a power layup.
2. Make a direct drive to the wing cone, circle with a right-hand dribble, and finish off the glass.
3. Make a crossover drive with the left hand to the middle cone around the cone and to the basket and finish with the left hand.
4. Make a crossover drive left to the wing and around the cone and finish with the left hand.
5. Make a crossover drive with the left hand to the corner cone, dribble around the cone, and finish with a power layin.

The next player starts after the player ahead finishes the third cone. The coach can contest finishes with soft contact. All five of these moves are timed for player personal record.

Two-Ball Series

Perform the same moves but omit the shot finishes. The dribbler uses opposite-hand non-rhythm dribbling technique.

DIAMOND DRIBBLE MOVES (FULL-COURT)

Purpose: To practice rebounds and full-court perimeter skills (dribble moves at the free-throw line, half-court line, and opposite free-throw line to finish at the basket)

Equipment: Full court, four cones or chairs (dummy defenders), two balls, eight players (two or three under each basket)

Procedure: Set up the court with four obstacles arranged in a diamond shape as shown in figure 5.15. Two players (O_1 and O_2) start the drill with a rebound toss high off the backboard. They rebound and face up the court with big vision to attack the first defender (at the free-throw line), then attack the second defender using big vision at the half-court (on the opposite side of court as the player is coming up the court), and finally attack at the opposite free-throw line to create a game-shot finish at the basket. New players come in at each basket and repeat the drill. Waiting players can replace the dummy defenders.

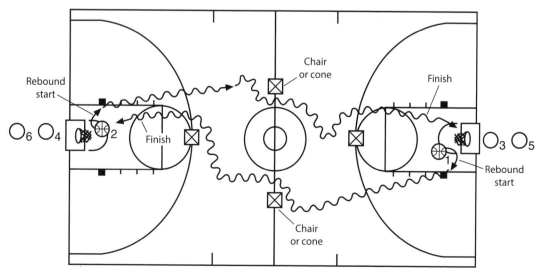

Figure 5.15 Diamond dribble-moves drill.

CONTINUOUS PASS-AND-TRAP

Purpose: To practice passing and catching in a continuous 2-on-2 trapping drill that sequences into a continuous 4-on-4 defensive trapping drill

Equipment: Two balls and a 12- to 15-foot (3.7- to 4.6-meter) rectangular space in each of two opposite corners of a half-court area with eight players split into two groups of four each—two on offense and two on defense (figure 5.16a)

Procedure: Phase A of the drill is a teaching-and-learning activity in which defensive and offensive players switch positions after 2 minutes, thus each spending 2 minutes on offense and 2 minutes on defense. During each 2-minute period, if the defenders steal the ball, they hand it back to the offense and continue on defense. Dribbling is discouraged— only a step-through move to split the trap is allowed, and the ball handler can jump in the air to pass over the trap as a last resort.

At the end of phase A (4 minutes total), the groups in opposite small-side rectangle spaces form groups of eight (four on offense and four on defense with different-colored jerseys); see figure 5.16b. A coach begins the 4-on-4 drill (phase B) with a pass to one team in one rectangle court space. The catcher is trapped by adjacent players with different-colored jerseys, and two teammates who are positioned deeper become interceptors, as shown in figure 5.16b. Play continues until the defense gets the ball. The coach then restarts the drill by passing to a defender from the new offensive team.

- Passer rules: Focus on the trap. Pass around or over or step through; dribble only as a last resort (on a four-count of being closely guarded in a trap).

- Trapper rules: Use active feet to prevent a step-through move. Maintain a high inside hand and trace the ball with the outside hand. Make chest contact only—no ball reaching. On a pass, move to interceptor position.

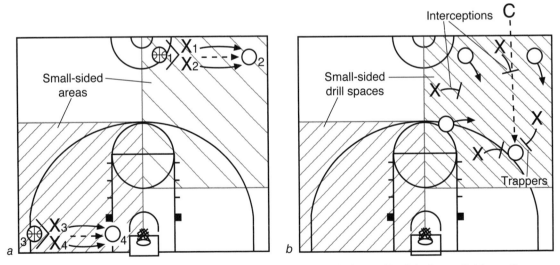

Figure 5.16 Continuous pass-and-trap drill: *(a)* phase A (2-on-2), *(b)* phase B (4-on-4).

FINISH THE PLAY ▶

Purpose: To progressively practice in a variety of basket-attack-and-finish situations from varied positions

Equipment: One ball for every pair of players (three pairs per half court); at least two half-court areas

Procedure: Player pairs alternate offense and defense; two player pairs wait to rotate in (figure 5.17). The coach picks three driving spots per round. Apply defense in the following sequence:

1. No defense anywhere (1-on-0)
2. No outside defense (soft D on the finish)
3. No inside finish defense (only perimeter defense)
4. Live defense everywhere

Move and Finish Options

1. Right corner
   - Middle drive, dead-ball finish
   - Baseline drive, under-basket finish
2. Left corner
   - Middle drive, dead-ball finish
   - Baseline drive, under-basket or power-move finish on same side
3. Right wing
   - Middle drive, hop-back finish
   - Baseline drive, layup on opposite side of lane
4. Left wing
   - Middle drive, spinner finish
   - Baseline drive, layin choice
5. Top of key
   - Drive to the right, inside finish
   - Drive to the left, outside finish

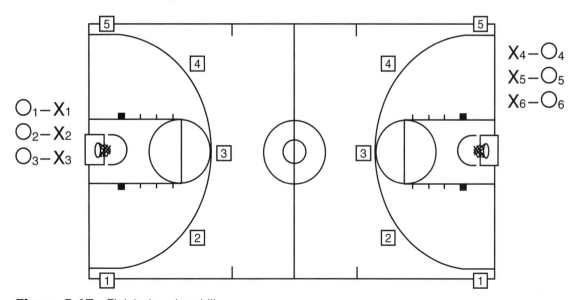

Figure 5.17 Finish-the-play drill.

THREE-LANE-RUSH PASS—CATCH (PEER-PRESSURE DRILL)

Purpose: To provide a full-court layup drill that develops the skill of pushing the ball up the floor on the pass (no dribble allowed)

Equipment: One ball and a full court

Procedure: Players form three lines under one end basket on a full court. The ball starts with the middle player, who passes to a wing player coming to the middle lane. The passer should pass and go behind to sprint the floor. O_1 scores with a layup in three passes. O_5 gets the rebound, makes the return-trip first outlet pass to O_3, and goes behind to sprint for a layup at other end. O_5 gets the second pass and passes to O_3 to make a layup at the original basket (figure 5.18). The coach can begin with a 1-2-3 down-and-back circuit or a time goal. Later, the goal may be advanced (in terms of repetitions or time) until the team reaches the level of all groups of three doing a perfect passing circuit and all layins are made with no dribble. All passes are air passes, and no dribbling is allowed.

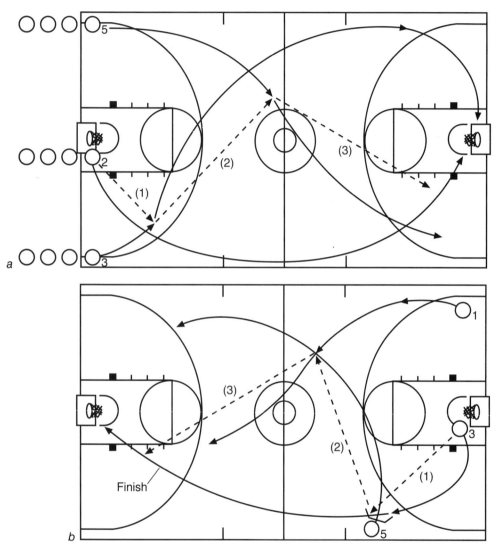

Figure 5.18 Three-lane-rush pass—catch drill: *(a)* start and *(b)* retrieve to start.

Wooden Wisdom

"You can't live a perfect day without doing something for someone who can never repay you."

—John Wooden

CHAPTER 6

INSIDE OFFENSIVE MOVES

—— PLAYING THE POST——

*"Get the ball inside first—take the ball inside or to the baseline.
Place pressure on the defense to foul. Post play is a key to success."*

Dean Smith, Naismith Hall of Fame coach and former head coach at University of North Carolina

Most coaches and players recognize the importance of establishing an inside game by having a post player receive a pass near or inside the free-throw lane area or cutting an offensive player from outside into the post area (low or high). This inside game can serve several purposes. First, it can produce a high-percentage shot—a scoring opportunity close to the basket. It can also increase opportunities for the original three-point play (inside score plus a foul shot), because post players in a congested inside area are difficult to defend and are often fouled when attempting a shot. In addition, when the ball is passed to inside post players (via pass penetration), the defense is forced to collapse in order to contain them; if they pass the ball back outside to teammates, they can create opportunities for outside shots, including three-pointers. In summary, this chapter emphasizes another key element of the general scoring objective—getting the ball inside for a high-percentage shot and forcing the defensive team to respect the inside game in order to open up outside shooting opportunities, especially the three-point field goal.

POST-PLAY FUNDAMENTALS

Post play is the key to building the offense from the inside out. Playing the post is a skill that requires minimal ballhandling and can be learned readily by players of all sizes with sufficient practice time and patience. All players should learn post-up skills because advantageous matchups do occur in game play and should be a key component of "positionless basketball." Good post players get open for high-percentage shots by developing a variety of inside moves known as *back-to-the-basket* scoring moves, which are usually made from a low- or medium-post position (figure 6.1). Post players need to learn how to get open, stay open, catch the ball safely, and score simply. This also applies to facing-the-basket moves that post players must develop outside and around the free-throw lane when attacking the basket in this manner.

Penetrating To be successful, the offensive team must penetrate the perimeter of the defense on a regular basis by taking the ball inside through a dribble drive (penetrate-and-pitch, drive-and-dish) or a penetration pass to a post player. In short, the defense can be penetrated with either a dribble or a pass. The objective of offensive penetration is to create the opportunity for a shot taken as close to the basket as possible—usually inside or near the free-throw lane—or to force the defense to collapse and thus open up an outside shot. This principle can dramatically increase efficiency in team offense, partly by drawing more fouls and creating balance between inside and outside offense.

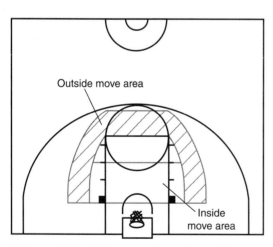

Outside move area

Inside move area

Figure 6.1 Prime inside and outside move areas: The inside move area is the low- to medium-post area and is used for back-to-the-basket moves, whereas the outside move area is used for facing-the-basket moves.

Backboard Shots Offensive players should use the backboard when shooting after most back-to-the-basket inside moves, especially when shooting from a 45-degree angle, using a power move, or in an offensive rebounding situation. Backboard shots are higher-percentage shots than rim shots for inside play, where contact and congestion are common. The rule is as follows: When going to the glass, use the glass (unless dunking the ball). The margin of error is greater when the backboard is used as a shooting target (shoot it high and soft near the rectangle's upper corner); for more on using the backboard as a target, see chapter 4.

Assuming the Miss Since inside players are stationed close to the basket, they can serve as primary rebounders. Because the shooter can best gauge the exact location and timing of the shot, a post player using an inside move always assumes that the shot will be missed and prepares to rebound from a quick stance with the elbows out and the arms and hands extended above the shoulders (2-and-2 rebounding with the hands up). An inside player can also block out a defensive opponent, when fronted, or at least make a rebounding move to the middle of the lane to secure a primary rebounding spot (look for the middle gap).

Everyone as a Post All players are post players. Although some of the best inside players have been medium or large people, technique is more important than size. A more critical factor is *relative* size—each player should develop basic post moves and be able to post up a defender of similar or smaller size. For example, Cliff Hagan was a 6-foot, 4-inch (1.9-meter) college center at Kentucky who was inducted into the Naismith Hall of Fame. In addition, many undersized post players enjoy the physical play in the post area and are effective playing there. The recent emphasis on facing-the-basket post play also creates more opportunities for all offensive players who prefer attacking moves and contact.

Creating Contact The inside area, which is frequently congested, offers considerable physical contact. In fact, inside offensive players should *create* contact (post up on defenders to create open space for passes) and use their bodies to control defenders. Players must learn to initiate contact with the hips and upper thighs while maintaining balance and stance: Stay low with a wide base and keep the feet active in a quick stance. Generally, defensive players are allowed by the rules to take one defensive position on the offensive post with contact limits by the defensive player, which allows post players to create contact to keep defenders in their original position.

Hands Up Passing to inside players is difficult and challenging, and the margin for error is small because of congestion and time constraints. Thus, inside players should always be prepared to receive a quick pass from a teammate by using the post stance: both hands up as contact is created (figure 6.2). Players should sit into the stance, create contact with the defender, use the legs and the lower trunk, and then provide *two-handed* targets for the passer with both hands up (upper arms horizontal with the shoulder, forearms nearly vertical, and hands slightly forward of the elbows so that the offensive post player can see the backs of their hands). The feet should be kept active in order to maintain contact with the defender.

CRITICAL CUE Assume a miss on every shot and go to a defender's gap with hands up (unless already inside the defender).

CRITICAL CUE Get low and wide. *Create* contact when on offense in the post area; *maintain* contact with active feet.

Figure 6.2 Post player's basic stance: *(a)* front view, *(b)* side view.

Patience Many large post players are late developers and may have poor self-images as a result of their size and relative lack of coordination. The prescription is coaching time, patience, and regular practice (repetition, repetition, repetition). George Mikan, selected as the best NBA post player of the league's first 50 years, spent hundreds of hours with his coach, Ray Meyer, during his college years at DePaul University. His workouts focused on footwork, ballhandling (passing and catching), shooting, and coordination drills.

POST SKILLS

Coaches should train players to get into a post-player stance and remain there. The inside or post player must develop the ability to assume an exaggerated basic position, with a wider than normal base, a low center of gravity, the elbows out, the forearms vertical, the upper arms parallel to the floor as extensions of the shoulders ("arms of steel"), and the hands up and slightly forward with the fingers spread and pointing to the ceiling (figure 6.2). The post player's hands provide two possible targets for passers; the hands are kept up and ready.

Posting up should take place on or near the post line, which is the imaginary straight line through the ball or the passer and the basket (figure 6.3). The inside player should try to get open on or near the post line and either inside or just outside of the free-throw lane. Establishing position on the post line shortens the distance that the pass must travel from the post feeder. Ideally, the post player should be posted up with the shoulders square (at right angles) to the post line, "showing numbers" to the passer; that is, the passer should be able to read the post player's jersey number when making the pass. The post player should keep the passing lane open by showing numbers to the passer and moving the feet (using active feet, or footfire) while creating lower-body contact on the defender (using the posterior as a radar bumper). This rule applies in all situations except when defenders are fronting—that is, playing between the passer and the offensive post player.

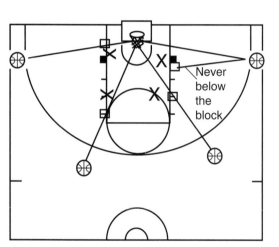

Figure 6.3 The post line (posting in the low or medium post).

The post line should be used whenever possible to shorten the passing lane, except when the passer is in the corner; in that case, the lowest foot of the post player should be on or above the block in order to leave space for a baseline scoring move. Low-post players sometimes start on one side of the post line to force defenders to defend them on one side or the other.

Getting Open in the Low or Medium Post

The post player needs to get open on the post line between the passer and the defender whenever possible by using a V-cut and swim move; stepping into the defender; using a rear turn to seal the defender (place the turning foot between the defender's legs); or stepping across the near leg of the defender (sitting on the defender's leg or fighting the front foot) as contact is created (figure 6.4). The offensive post player uses proper footwork to post up, then

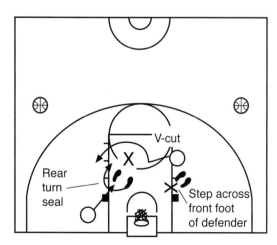

Figure 6.4 Getting open in the post (three ways).

maintains contact and takes the post defender further in the set direction of defense. In other words, the post player moves a high defender higher, a low defender lower, a defender who is behind farther toward the basket, a defender who is in front farther away from the basket, and a side defender farther to that side.

Primary tasks of the inside player include getting open at the right time and staying open. Because post play is a constant 1-on-1 battle between offense and defense, offensive players must learn to *create contact* and stay open. Once the defender has taken a position, the inside player should make contact to keep the defender in place. The post player should also keep the *feet active* and use the whole body to work in a half-circle move (figure 6.5). The hips and buttocks (i.e., the lower trunk) are used to sit on the defender's legs or body and maintain contact.

When posting up inside the free-throw lane close to the basket, post players need to be aware of the time restriction (3 seconds). Thus they should post up in that location for 2 seconds (silently count *one thousand one, one thousand two*), then quickly move out of the time-restricted area.

Catching the Ball Inside

Post players must want the basketball. They need to build confidence in their teammates that they will get open, catch the ball safely when it is passed to them, and score simply inside when open or pass outside when they draw two defenders.

To do so, they should maintain contact in order to feel and seal the defender (use radar bumpers, not the arms or hands). They should also be able to locate the defender by reading the pass. The passer feeding the post player should pass to the hand target away from the closest defender; in this way, the placement of the pass helps the post player locate the defender, and the pass leads to the desired score. One of the toughest tasks for post players is that of keeping the passing lane open. They must keep their feet active, maintain contact until the ball hits the receiving hand, and show numbers to the passer (face the passer).

Post players must also step into the pass and meet the ball while still holding their position by catching the ball with two hands and with both feet slightly in the air (when possible). They must then execute a quick stop (except when fronted). Possession always takes precedence over position, even though position is necessary to get open. Therefore, coaches should train players to focus on the ball until it hits their hands. After catching the pass, players must protect the ball by using the chin-it technique—elbows out and up, fingers up, ball under the chin (or from shoulder to shoulder)—which keeps them from dangling the ball and allows good ball protection.

If the defender establishes a ball–defender–post (fronting) position, two techniques are recommended: the lob and the ball reversal. In the over-the-top lob pass (figure 6.6), the passer shows the ball (going from triple-threat position to ball-overhead position), uses a check (fake) pass to read the help-side defensive coverage, and then quickly throws a pass over the defender to the junction of the backboard and the rim. The post player, maintaining quick stance and keeping both hands up (with the palms facing the passer), faces the baseline and establishes contact with the defender by using the hips and buttocks (radar bumpers). The post player waits until the ball is overhead before releasing to catch the ball with two hands with the palms facing the ball. Care must be taken for the fronted post player to maintain contact with the lower body and not push off with the arms (especially the forearms) to catch the lob pass.

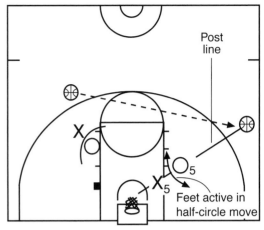

Figure 6.5 Half-circle move: Stay open by saddling up on the defender and showing numbers to the passer.

CRITICAL CUE
Use active feet (footfire) to stay open.

CRITICAL CUE
Post catches: Catch with two hands (catch with a *click*) and chin it.

CRITICAL CUE
Post catches: Possession over position.

Figure 6.6 Lob pass over the defender: *(a)* both hands up—contact with the rear end and hip, *(b)* check pass (*pulling the string*) to test the help-side defender's reaction to the pass fake, and *(c)* two-handed capture-and-chin catch with a power scoring move.

The second technique to get the ball to a fronted (denied) post player is to use ball reversal to the high post or help side. If a defender is fronting on one side of the court, the ball can be reversed (to the second side) as the defender is sealed off and the post player steps to the ball (figure 6.7).

Taking Out the Defender

Inside players must learn to take the defender out of the play automatically. If post players are defended on the low side, they should take defenders lower; if defended on the high side, take them higher. Similarly, if fronted, post players should make lower-body contact while facing the baseline and take defenders away from the basket; if played from behind, they

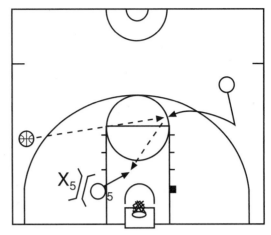

Figure 6.7 Post play: Reverse the ball (to the second side) and pin and seal the fronting post defender (use radar bumpers).

should step into the lane before posting up with a V-cut or a rear turn and seal to take the defender closer to the basket. The idea is to allow defenders to take a position of choice and then take them further in that direction and pin or seal them in that position by creating contact with the legs or the lower trunk (use radar bumpers) in a post stance with active feet.

Reading the Defense

When the defender is fronting—playing between the passer and the post player—coaches should have their players either use a lob pass over the defender or reverse the ball and then pin or seal the defender and feed the post from the opposite side. On the lob play, offensive players should use a power move or reverse layup to score. With the defender playing directly behind the post player, the passer delivers the ball to the head target (or middle of the body), and the post player then catches and faces using post facing moves. The middle pass indicates to the offensive post player that the post defender is playing directly behind and between him or her and the basket. The post shot is also a possibility in this situation.

A defender positioned on the low side (baseline side) effectively tells the post player to use the post or wheel move or the power move to a jump hook. The wheel move and power move are also indicated when the defender is positioned on the high side. The guideline for the perimeter passer and the post catcher is that the pass should lead the post player to the score.

For the post player, the process of reading and reacting means learning to feel contact, reading the pass, looking to the middle (for helping defenders and open teammates), seeing the whole court, and challenging the defense. Excellent post players with the ball attract two defenders and create open teammates.

POST OR INSIDE MOVES

Finally, coaches should teach post players to move aggressively and be alert for open teammates. Their objective when using inside moves is to either gain position for a close-in shot or free a teammate to receive a pass in scoring position. This second option develops when the post player attacks and must be guarded by two defenders, which can be achieved best by mastering a few basic inside post moves to score simply.

Post Shot

This move to the middle and into the free-throw lane is a basic back-to-the-basket tool for the post player and an essential scoring option. The move is normally made without dribbling; the footwork and the mechanics of the post shot and the jump hook shot are explained in chapter 4. One advantage of the post shot is that it is a quick move to the middle of the defense and into the high-scoring area (the free-throw lane). Alternatives are the power move and the jump hook, which are slower and require a dribble.

Power Move

The power move is typically used to the baseline side when the defender is on the high side (away from the baseline). It may also be used toward the middle when the defender is on the baseline side. The sequence for the baseline power move is to pivot with a half rear turn on the foot closest to the defender and seal off the defensive player with the hips and buttocks. Then the post player takes a one- or two-handed power crab dribble between the legs (near the foot closest to the basket), makes a two-footed power jump moving to the basket at the same time, and executes a quick stop with the feet at right angles to the baseline (belly to baseline). This dribble can sometimes be eliminated when the post player is in the lane and close to the basket. Finally, the power shot or jump hook is used to protect the ball with the body and to score with the shooting hand away from the defender; the backboard is used whenever possible (figure 6.8). This move is fully described in chapter 4 as a strong move from two feet to two feet.

The power move to the middle (figure 6.9) is executed in the same way: Catch the ball and chin it (with the defender on the baseline side), pivot on the baseline foot and use a rear-turn seal, use a power crab dribble between the legs near the lead foot as a two-footed power jump to the basket and into the free-throw lane is made, and finish with a two-footed power layup or jump hook (may need a shot fake). The best finishing position for this power move is to complete the power move with a quick stop facing the sideline. This is the best position to finish the post move with a dead ball move like the jump hook. The most common error is to dribble or drop the ball outside the base (feet position) as the rear turn or drop step is made; doing so exposes the ball to defenders in the congested post area. Make the two-handed bounce between the legs and inside the front leg as a two-footed (two feet to two feet) hop move is made toward the basket.

Jump Hook

The jump hook is a two-footed shot with the hand away from the defender; it is used close to the basket. The technique is to chin the ball and move it to the shoulder away from the defender, then make a power jump (from two feet) and use an arm bar to keep the defender from the shot as the ball is taken up over the head and above the defender. The nonshooting shoulder points at the basket. The jump hook can be used with either hand; it is a safe, powerful scoring move that many players prefer to use in heavy traffic close to the basket.

Wheel Move (Advanced)

This advanced move combines a power move to a quick stop, followed immediately by a rear-turn post shot. It is used when the defender begins by playing high-side (or low-side) defense as the power move is made but then anticipates effectively and cuts off the offensive player's first move. The post player then immediately executes a countermove (figure 6.10). The sequence is to initiate a power move, do a quick stop and chin the ball when the defender overreacts, and then carry out a post shot countermove.

Figure 6.8 Power move to the baseline: *(a)* catch and chin-it, *(b)* half rear turn and seal, *(c)* crab dribble—both hands between the legs with the ball inside the front foot (bounce and hop), and *(d)* power shot (facing the baseline).

Figure 6.9 Power move to the middle: *(a)* catch and chin-it, *(b)* rear-turn seal, *(c)* two-handed bounce and hop, and *(d)* jump hook, facing the sideline.

Figure 6.10 The wheel move: *(a)* power move to the middle (cut off by the defender), *(b)* post move back to the baseline, and *(c)* post shot.

Facing Moves

These basic perimeter moves are used when the defender is playing behind the post player, especially with a defensive gap. The offensive player pivots with a front turn or a rear turn on either foot to face the basket and the defender. The front-turn options are the jump shot, the shot fake followed by a jump shot, and the crossover post shot (figure 6.11). All live-ball moves can be used in this situation—for instance, the rear turn on either pivot foot followed by a jump shot. This rear-turn move, first popularized by

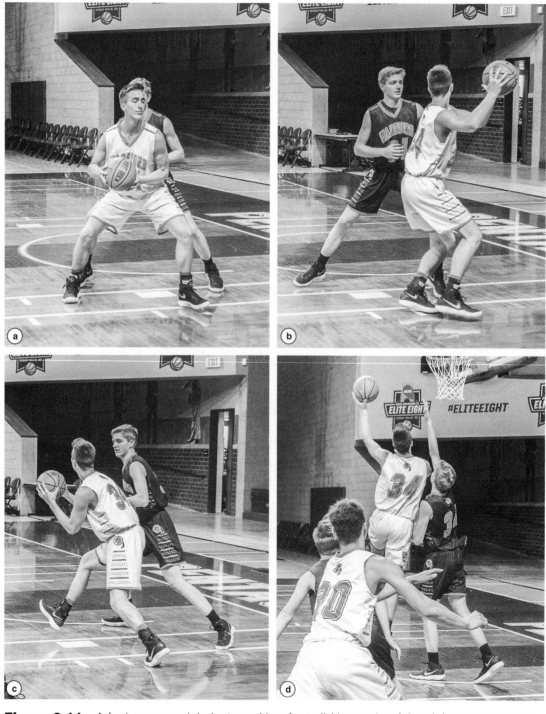

Figure 6.11 A facing move: *(a)* pivot on either foot, *(b)* jump shot fake, *(c)* crossover, and *(d)* post shot.

Jack Sikma of the Seattle Supersonics, tends to clear the defender and create a gap for the quick jump shot (figure 6.12).

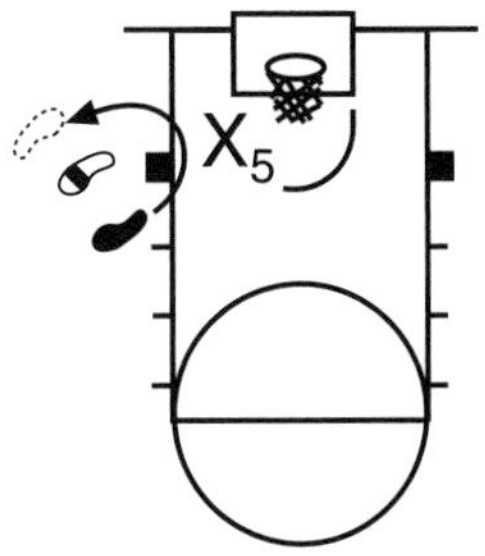

Passing to the Post

For most post players, the preferred pass into the post is the bounce pass, when passed to the baseline side. The bounce pass is hard for the defender to deflect or steal. However, the air pass is quicker and should be used more often to the more congested middle or on the reverse (second-side) pass and of course on the lob pass (when the defender fronts the low post). On the direct air pass to the post, players should either make an overhead pass from above the shoulders and hit the hand target away from the defender above the shoulders or use a one-handed push or flick pass past the defender's ear from the triple-threat position (*fake low, pass high*). To confirm that the passing lane is open, perimeter players should be sure that they can see the numbers on the post player's jersey before making the inside pass. The perimeter player needs to pass to the hand on the open side (opposite the defender) because the pass should lead to a score. The post player needs to keep the passing lane open using the post stance ("arms of steel"), footfire, and lower-body contact. The location of the pass tells the post player which move to make (plus reading the defender). When the defender plays directly behind the post player, the pass is made to the head target (or middle of the trunk) of the post player.

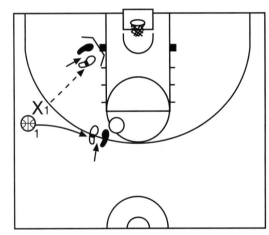

Figure 6.12 Sikma post move: rear turn (right pivot foot in illustration).

Facing-the-Basket Post Play

The technique used for high-post play or short-corner play (from the low-post position) combines back-to-the-basket and facing-the-basket techniques. Often, the defender in the high-post area defends with a hand in denial position on the ball side. Offensive high-post players may get open by initiating contact with the lower body and providing a target hand away from the defender (figure 6.13). This contact method of getting open has the disadvantage of establishing *one foot* as the pivot foot when the high-post player catches and faces the basket using RPA. Using either-pivot-foot (EPF) footwork, the post player may give up his or her position in order to catch the ball with both feet in the air facing the basket.

When cutting into the post area as a trailer on the fast break or cutting from below, players should cut into the high post and catch the ball with a quick stop facing the basket (ball in the air, feet in the air), as shown in figure 6.14.

However, when high-post players catch the ball, they need to catch and face using RPA with a determined pivot foot (established). If the post player catches the ball facing the basket with the feet in the air, attacking options to either side are readily available. If permanent-pivot-foot (PPF) footwork is used, the high-post player can attack the preferred side with a direct drive or the nonpreferred side with the recommended crossover drive plus shooting options. When EPF footwork is chosen, players should use the following facing options (Zak attack) in the congested area of the high post (15 to 20 feet, or 4.6 to 6.1 meters, from the basket). These facing-the-basket attack moves are designed to penetrate to the basket using *only one or two dribbles* that result in a layin; a pass to a teammate; or a jump shot, floater, or dead-ball move closer to the basket.

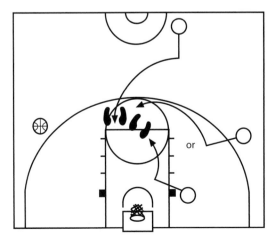

Figure 6.13 Getting open in the high-post or the short-corner (low-post) area.

Figure 6.14 High-post cuts from low post, wing, or trailer position.

▶ Zak-Attack Post-Play Techniques

The Zak attack is a perimeter (facing-the-basket) move that is best used in the free-throw lane extended plus 3 feet (1 meter) on each side of the lane and when attacking defenders from near the free-throw-line distance with a *one- or two-dribble* approach. The preferred footwork for the individual move involves a quick stop with either pivot foot (EPF) available. The attacking moves are somewhat limited if PPF footwork is used or when a pivot foot is chosen during a catch-and-face action. The *prime* attacking moves shown in the illustrations and video are those made from a quick stop with EPF available and when an *inside* pivot foot is used.

The Zak attack is best used with EPF footwork that establishes the inside pivot foot in the high-post elbow area or the pivot foot away from the baseline (inside pivot foot) in the short-corner area (figure 6.15). The idea is to allow the post player using the Zak attack to drive to the basket toward the middle of the court with the optimum protected-ball position using only one or two dribbles for a close shot (layin, runner, post shot, jump hook, or dead-ball completion move). Zak-attack moves best attack the middle of the court.

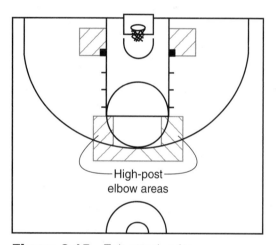

Figure 6.15 Zak-attack prime areas.

This approach allows the post player facing the basket to attack the defense by choosing the best move to the middle of the defense. When overplayed to the middle, the post player can test the defender with a jab step to the outside of the defense. If the defender tries to close off the middle drive, the post player can attack the defender outside at the baseline or outside the free-throw lane in the high-post area with a quick stop by using the jabbing (stepping) foot to dribble-drive by the over-playing defender. The test is to use a stepping-foot jab fake toward the basket. From the high-post elbow areas, the post player can use EPF footwork, choosing the *inside* pivot foot and the primary-crossover-drive footwork to attack the middle of the defense (figure 6.16).

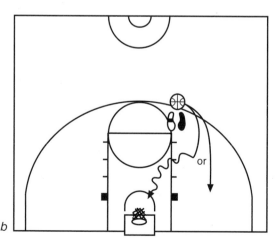

Figure 6.16 Zak-attack prime move from high-post area: *(a)* From the right-elbow area, establish the inside pivot foot (left) and use the right-foot crossover (jab right, crossover left) to attack the middle; (b) from the left elbow, establish the inside pivot foot (right) and use the left (stepping) foot to jab-step left and crossover-drive right to attack the middle.

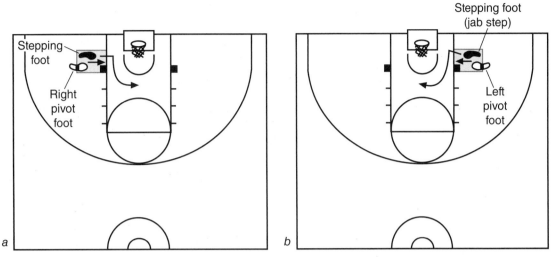

Figure 6.17 Zak-attack prime moves from the low- or medium-post position: *(a)* On the left side (facing the basket), use the right-foot pivot; *(b)* on the right side (facing the basket), use the left-foot pivot.

From the low- or medium-post position, the post player can use EPF footwork to choose the pivot foot away from the baseline (figure 6.17). This technique allows the baseline-foot jab step to test the defender and make the baseline-foot crossover step, thus attacking the middle of the defense. If the defense overplays the primary inside attack move, the post player can attack the baseline side with a direct-drive stepping-foot move.

Alternative outside-pivot-foot moves can be used in the high-post and short-corner areas facing the basket as shown in the following illustrations:

1. Arc drive outside with outside-foot pivot foot (figure 6.18)

2. Arc drive to baseline from right side to baseline-side with right pivot foot (figure 6.19*a*)

3. Arc drive to baseline from left side to baseline-side with left pivot foot (figure 6.19*b*)

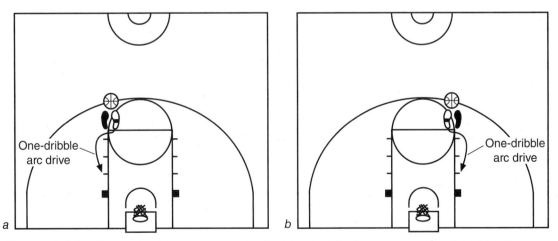

Figure 6.18 Alternative high-post attack—inside-pivot-foot moves: *(a)* arc right-foot direct drive from the right elbow, then drive to the left; *(b)* EPF-footwork left-foot direct-step arc drive to drive left.

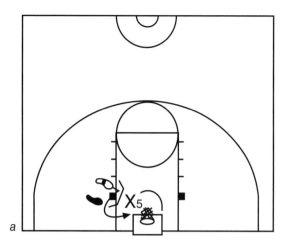
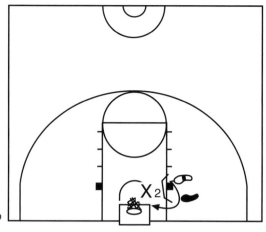

Figure 6.19 Alternative inside-pivot-foot attack moves (left corner) from short-corner areas: *(a)* right-foot arc drive to baseline; *(b)* left-foot crossover to middle (from right corner), or arc drive to baseline.

COACHING POINTS FOR ZAK-ATTACK POST-PLAY TECHNIQUES

- Establish pivot foot away from baseline or sideline to use the Zak-attack crossover move to the middle.
- Preferred moves are as follows: *left*-foot crossover step, then drive to the *right*; *right*-foot crossover step, then drive to the *left*.
- Protect the ball with the stepping foot and leg.
- Use big vision with the eyes up as the attack move is made. Pick up the backboard rectangle-upper-corner target early when possible.
- Use a hard dribble to a two-handed high pickup.
- Preferred finish is an underhand *layup* or an overhead *layin* off the glass.
  - The shoulders are square to the path (closed position), and the ball is protected by the nonshooting arm.
  - Use flip-wrist soft-release action to soften the shot against the backboard (up or forward).
  - Release from two fingers to keep it straight.
  - Layup: Use an underhand (palm-up) release to the backboard.
  - Layin: Use a palm-forward soft release forward and up to the backboard; use the elbow as an aiming device with the shooting arm in the vertical plane.
- The upper body should lead the turn on all spin moves.
- Other completion moves include the jump shot, the one-handed runner, and quick-stop dead-ball completion moves.

Note: All Zak-attack prime moves and alternative moves are shown in the video library. The Zak-attack principles are modified from Coach Holger Geschwindner's FIBA clinic from January 8, 2015 (available on YouTube: "Are you sure we teach the shooting?").

TROUBLESHOOTING

Here are some of the common post-play errors, as well as coaching responses and corrections.

- **Problem:** Not consistently creating contact

  Correction: Sit into the game, stay in a post stance, and then progressively make contact on pads or managers, dummy defenders, and then live defenders. Keep the feet active to maintain contact.

- **Problem:** Trouble staying in post stance

  Correction: Do more practice with the post-player line drill, develop added core strength, and stay in stance for progressively longer periods.

- **Problem:** Difficulty staying open

  Correction: Coaches should reteach players how to create contact in all situations, use progressive contact drills, and check for active feet (footfire) and proper arm position to maintain contact.

- **Problem:** Inconsistent catching of the ball

  Correction: Increase partner passing and catching with a *click* (*two hands, two eyes*) and emphasize possession over position.

- **Problem:** Losing the ball (after the catch)

  Correction: Check capture-and-chin technique: fingers up, elbows up and out, squeezing the ball, and using turns to shield the ball and escape defenders.

- **Problem:** Not scoring quickly and simply

  Correction: Work harder before the catch for a deep post position, sit into a lower stance to maintain quickness, practice the same scoring moves over and over until they're automatic, read and respond quickly, always assume a miss, and score on an angle whenever possible.

- **Problem:** Using more than one dribble on facing-the-basket moves

  Correction: Develop Zak-attack moves with crossover attack moves to the middle that use one protected dribble to attack the basket when facing (first with no defender, then with a soft defender, and then with a live defender). After one dribble (or two, at most), finish the play with a proper scoring move: live ball (jumper or runner); dead ball (jump hook, regular hook shot from a step through crossover, or a wheel move).

COACHING POINTS FOR POST PLAY

- Use the slogan *want the ball, call for the ball*.
- Coaches should teach post players inside moves (one go-to move and one countermove) that they can perform with confidence, then have the team take the ball inside (*in the paint*) regularly so that post players can use these moves. Teams should play from the inside out.
- Use the backboard on most inside shots; doing so enables higher-percentage shots.
- Coaches should view all players who are competitive and who like contact as potential post players. Develop positionless post players.
- Keep the hands up inside.
- Get in post stance with two hand targets on or near the post line; always catch with two hands to capture and chin the ball.
- Remember that getting open usually requires contact with radar bumpers (the lower body and thighs) using quick, strong moves.
- Create contact on offense with radar bumpers to pin and seal the defender in order to get open.
- Prioritize possession of the ball over position when the pass is made inside (go after passes when necessary).
- Take defenders further in the direction in which they position themselves.
- Capture and chin every pass to the post (catch safely).
- Read the pass, your contact with the defender, and the position of other defenders. See and prime attack the middle and into the free-throw lane when possible.
- Develop the post shot or power move and jump hook as the basic shot to the middle of the free-throw lane from the chin-it position in order to score simply.
- Understand that keeping the body between the defender and the ball during the power move is essential to its effectiveness.
- Use the wheel move as a power move, a quick stop, and a post countermove in sequence.
- In some post situations, catch and face to use perimeter moves, especially in the free-throw lane or the high-post area, the short corner (low-post) area or when the defender plays directly behind in the low- or medium-post areas.
- Use only one or two dribbles on Zak-attack moves when possible.

POST DRILLS

These drills should be developed progressively with no defense, with dummy defense in different positions, with managers using handheld air dummies for contact, and finally with live defense. Note: Post players should also do general skill drills, such as those presented in chapters 3 and 4.

POST WARM-UP ▶

Purpose: To teach inside players basic skills while preparing for practice

Equipment: Basketballs, tennis balls, half-court area, basket

Procedure: Select at least six of the following options daily and spend 1 minute per item.

- Two-ball dribbling sequences
- Dribbling and juggling
- Tennis-ball infield (*low and wide, toes to the outside, sit into the game*): Use tennis balls thrown against a wall to improve catching. Use a side-arm wall toss to create the tennis ball rebound and catch the tennis ball rebound with two hands.
- Defensive slides or moves against an imaginary offensive player while talking through the defensive move
- Moving without the ball on offense (alone or in pairs)
- Rim-to-rim fast-break sprints
- Crab dribbles with bounce and hop moves down a line (two-handed ball bounce between the legs near the lead leg followed by a ball chin and two-footed hops down the line)
- Capturing and chinning the ball from an overhead toss or a spin pass to self from the floor
- Round-the-world jump hooks (left-handed and right-handed) from 4 to 6 feet (1.2 to 1.8 meters) from the basket (five spots)
- Soft-touch shots—five spots and five shots (any goal) or with jump hooks
- Mikan series (regular, reverse, power, shot fake and power, freelance)
- Post stance with weight plate in each hand (thumb in weight plate hole) as post player moves in half circle from block to block using active feet or footfire in a hands-up position

LINE DRILL: POST-PLAYER STARTS, TURNS, AND STOPS

Purpose: To teach inside players proper footwork using the fundamental four-line format

Equipment: Half-court area (minimum)

Procedure: Position four lines of post players on the baseline: at the sideline, outside the free-throw lane (both sides), and on the opposite sideline. The movement options are begun with a post stance and a sequence of starts, stops, and turns:

- Post stance into post start (no negative steps)
- Post stance with active feet after quick stop at the free-throw line, quick rear turn, and return to the baseline (quick stop into post stance [active feet]); repeat with front turns
- Full-court option: post stance stops at the free-throw line, half-court line, opposite free-throw line, and opposite baseline (using two quick turns at each location, restarting together, and verbalizing each move)

Coaching Points

- Post stance and starts
  - Feet more than shoulder-width apart
  - Sitting into the game
  - 90-degree elbows and hands held high (arms of steel)
  - Positive step forward (no negative or backward starting step)
- Stops
  - Quick stop (heel to toe or landing lightly)
  - Whole-footed stop with active feet (footfire)
- Turns
  - Executing front turns with right and left turning foot
  - Executing rear turns with right and left turning foot
  - Lifting the heel and pivot on the ball of the turning foot
  - Staying low and level (head)
  - Leading with the elbow on the rear turn; throwing a forearm punch on the front turn

POST PAIRS

Purpose: To teach and practice basic skills for post players, including post stance, passing and catching, and chinning the basketball

Equipment: One basketball and player pairs spaced at least 15 to 18 feet (4.6 to 5.5 meters) apart (optional: one player positioned in the post)

Procedure: Both players in a pair assume a post stance without the ball and a perimeter quick stance (triple-threat position) with the ball as they pass and catch and then capture and chin the ball on each pass. Whoever has the ball is the perimeter player, and whoever is catching is the post player (then switch roles with each pass). The pairs pass and catch repeatedly for 1-minute segments.

Options

- Use regular posting and passing and catching (in and out).
- Bad-pass variation: The catcher must give up position in order to gain possession of the ball by doing a two-handed capture and chin of the ball.
- Floor pass (bowling pass), capture, chin, and pass out: The feeder bowls the ball to one side of the post catcher, who captures, chins, and passes back. Do 10 passes, then reverse roles. The feeder then bowls the ball to the other side. The post player should have to step-slide to the right and then to the left in order to capture the ball with two hands, chin it, and return it to the feeder.

- Back to the feeder or passer: The post player assumes a post stance facing away from the passer. The feeder passes to the post player and calls the player's name, whereupon the post player turns to face the passer, captures and chins the ball, and then returns the pass to the feeder (10 passes and reverse roles).

- Feeder and rebounder: The post player assumes the post stance as the feeder shoots the ball or tosses it in the air near the post player, who performs a 2-and-2 pursuit and capture of the imaginary rebound. Coaches should teach players to post up, go to the gap with hands up on the shot, to pursue the ball, rebound out of their area, and capture and chin the ball with two hands.

Coaching Points

- Post players get in and stay in a post stance.

- Capture and chin the ball on every catch.

- Get possession over position.

- Catch every pass.

- Do everything from two feet and with two hands.

- Catch the ball with a *click* (two eyes and two hands).

SPIN-PASS POST MOVES ▶

Purpose: To teach individual offensive post moves

Equipment: Ball, basket, and optional toss-back rebound device

Procedure: At a desired post location with their backs to the basket, post players use either a two-handed overhead toss and a chin-it catch or an underhand back spin pass to the floor and a chin-it catch, or a pass and a rebound from a toss-back device to feed themselves. Players execute 3 to 5 repetitions of each post move on each side of the free-throw lane. The sequence for inside or low-post moves includes the following elements:

- Post shot—to the middle

- Jump hook shot—around the lane (catch and turn; catch, crab dribble, and shot)

- Power move—to the baseline (power shot on the glass); to the middle (jump hook)

- Wheel—to the baseline and wheel to the middle; or to the middle and wheel to the baseline (use glass)

- Face—jump shot, shot fake and jump shot, and crossover post move (front-turn option) or live-ball move (rear-turn option)

Coaching Points

- No defender is used for this drill.

- The coach may pass to the post to check post stance, post line, footwork, hand target, catching technique, chinning of the ball, and post moves.

- Another option is to make three to five consecutive baskets before going to the next move.

- Players should assume a miss on all shot attempts and rebound until a shot is made.

POST PROGRESSION

Purpose: To provide players with a self-teaching progressive drill for offensive post moves

Equipment: Ball, basket, and optional toss-back device or other method of receiving passes

Procedure: Post players begin with an underhand spin pass to themselves (or a pass and rebound from a toss-back device) and make post moves in sequence. Five baskets are made for each move in the sequence:

- Power move to baseline—left side, low post
- Power move and jump-hook move to middle—left side, low post
- Post move—left side, low post
- Wheel move—left side to middle or baseline first
- Facing move—left side, low post
- Facing move—high post, left elbow
- Same moves on the right side

After players make the fifth basket for each move, they must make two consecutive free throws (*row five plus two free throws*) in order to advance to the next move (or repeat the post move and free throws).

Options

- For advanced players, require three to five post-move baskets in a row and two or three free throws in a row.
- Use the following defensive progression: no defense, position defense, air-dummy defense, and live defense.

Coaching Points

- First do things right, then go toward game speed.
- Assume that all shots are missed; rebound and score on misses.

BIG SPACING AND POST FEEDING ▶

Purpose: To teach big spacing by perimeter players at one basket from four perimeter spots (figure 6.20a) and to teach triangle spacing with six players at one basket (post feeding; figure 6.20b)

Equipment: Ball and basket on one half-court area with four players at a time (big spacing drill); two balls and a basket on the other half-court area with two groups of three (one post and two perimeter players) on each side

Procedure for Big Spacing

Four perimeter players fill the four perimeter spots on the half court. Using either a regular ball or a weighted ball, players swing or reverse the ball around the perimeter as quickly as possible (reversals can be timed).

Coaching Points for Big Spacing

- Players should step and pass (*pass with the legs*).
- Players cannot space too high or too wide to reverse the ball. Locate near the sideline and the half-court line.

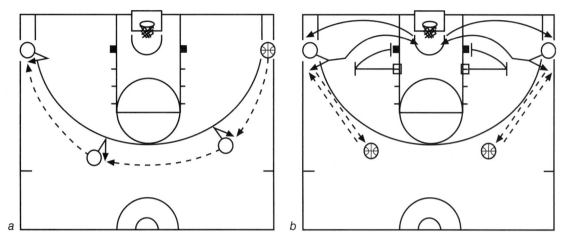

Figure 6.20 Big-spacing and post-feeding drill: *(a)* big spacing—perimeter, *(b)* post feeding.

- Players should work the ball around the perimeter.

- Catchers should use a V-cut and shorten the passing lane.

- If defenders are used, passers should pass away from the defenders as catchers present an outside-hand target with both hands up (one as the target and one to ward off the defender).

- Coaches should emphasize rip pivots or turns for players to step across the body in order to protect the pass and increase pass power from the legs; players should use two-handed air passes.

- Players should call for every pass (use the passer's name).

Options: Add four defenders, basket cuts, or dribble drives.

Procedure for Post Feeding

A post player is positioned on each side of the lane. Two perimeter players are spaced at least 15 to 18 feet (4.6 to 5.5 meters) apart to work with the post player on their side of the floor (six players are working at once). The guard on top passes to the wing on that side, who catches facing the basket or pivots or turns to face the basket and calls out *rim–post–action* to remind teammates of the priorities with the ball: look for the shot, feed the post, and take an action (pass or dribble drive). The perimeter wing then passes back to the guard and uses a back screen from the post to cut to the basket. The post player then immediately down-screens for the perimeter player and slips or posts up again. On the second catch from the top guard, the wing player feeds the post.

Coaching Points for Post Feeding

- An air-dummy defender can be used on the post to teach passing away from the defender (pass leads to a score).

- Insist on verbal calls for passes, cuts, screens, and rim–post–action with the ball or on the perimeter.

- Emphasize all passing and catching principles as well as moving and pivoting (turning) concepts.

- Focus on back-screen, down-screen, and cutter techniques. Post players must always screen and slip to get two scoring options on each screen.

Options: Add defenders later; allow players to change courts to get work in both drills.

ALL-AMERICAN POST WORKOUT

Purpose: To teach or practice all offensive post moves (for advanced players)

Equipment: Ball, half court, basket

Procedure: Players should make all shots before going to the next move in this 30-minute workout. The drill should be performed daily at game speed with proper and quick repetitions. Players can work from their favorite side of the lane. Here is the sequence:

- Four baseline power moves
- Four power moves to the middle and jump hook as a completion shot
- Four turnaround jump shots, pivoting on the turning foot away from the baseline
- Four turnaround jump shots with a shot fake
- Free-throw swish game (+2 for swish/0 if made shot, not a swish/–2 if missed)
  - If lose (–2), do push-ups or sprints.
  - If win (+2), shoot a string until a miss; when a miss occurs, the shooter gets another shot and the swish gives the player a reprieve to keep going.
- Four moves starting low, making a V-cut, and flashing to the free-throw line elbows for a jump shot
- Four moves stepping out to the short corner for a jump shot on the baseline
- Free-throw swish game
- Four moves making a V-cut and flashing to the free-throw line elbow for a shot fake to a jump shot
- Four short-corner shot fakes to jump shots on the baseline
- Free-throw swish game
- Four moves making a V-cut and flashing to the free-throw line for a shot fake and a drive to a power shot or a dunk in the free-throw lane
- Four short-corner shot fakes to a power shot or a dunk
- Free-throw swish game

2-ON-2 FEEDING THE POST

Purpose: To teach offensive and defensive post-play skills, passing to post players, and movement after the pass for a possible return pass

Equipment: Ball, basket, groups of four players (two offense and two defense)

Procedure: Two offensive and two defensive players work on perimeter and post play from various locations around the free-throw lane while applying all offensive and defensive principles of post play. Two players are needed on offense (one perimeter and one post). When defenders gain possession, they make the first outlet pass or dribble for transition. Outside offensive players make a V-cut move for a possible return pass when they pass to post players and call the post's name as they cut.

Options

- Designate two offensive perimeter players (undefended), plus one defensive and one offensive post player (rotate after each score); see figure 6.21.

- Designate two perimeter players and two post players (one on offense, one on defense). Start the ball on the perimeter at the top of the key. The perimeter player dribbles to either wing as the offensive post player gets open on that side; the post player may cut to the high post or come outside and screen for a teammate (pick-and-roll or back pick).
- Players engage in a 2-on-2 game of make-it-take-it.

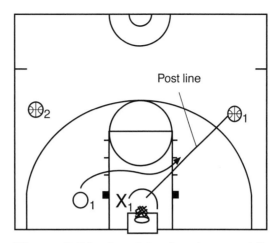

Figure 6.21   2-on-2 feeding-the-post drill.

MIKAN

This drill, named after George Mikan, the first dominant post player in basketball history, can be used for all players (perimeter and post).

Purpose: To teach players footwork, ballhandling, and layup shooting close to the basket

Equipment: Ball and basket per player

Procedure: Players shoot alternating layups (with the left hand on the left side and with the right hand on the right side). They should move their feet quickly and be in a position to shoot as soon as they rebound and chin the ball. Players should catch and chin the ball with two hands, try to backboard each shot, and follow through each time. The ball should never hit the floor. Players should develop and maintain a rhythm and go at game speed as they alternate backboard shots on the left and right sides of the basket.

Options

- 1 minute or three, four, or five made baskets in a row
- Regular Mikans
- Reverse-layup Mikans
- Power Mikans: jumping under the basket on the shot, catching and chinning while jumping to the other side, and repeating the move while going from two feet to two feet (side to side in front of the backboard)
- Power Mikans with shot fake: staying in stance, giving a 1-inch (2.5-centimeter) fake, and keeping the heels down on the shot fake
- Freelance: 1 minute of consecutive shots or making 10 scores using any move around the basket continuously. Catch the ball coming through the net and go to the next move.

5-ON-5 POST PASSING

Purpose: To teach post players to get open, catch the ball, make post moves, and pass from the post position as they read and react to defenders (especially traps); to teach defensive players to double-team (trap) a post player and rotate to the ball on passes from the post

Equipment: Ball, half-court space, and 10 players (5 on offense, 5 on defense)

Procedure: Position three perimeter players and two post players as shown in figure 6.22. In figure 6.22a, the defense allows the first pass (always), and the post player goes 1-on-1 (no traps). In figure 6.22b, a trap is made. Post player must pass out of the trap, and play is continued. After the first pass, all play is live.

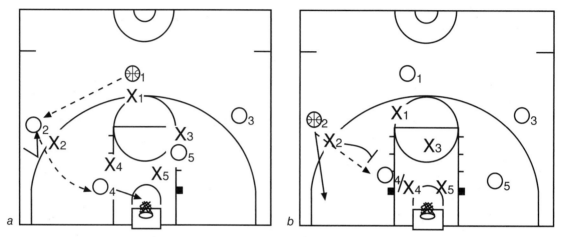

Figure 6.22 5-on-5 post passing: After each possession, the defensive team has a quick huddle, decides on a trap, and sprints to play defense. In (a), the pass happens with no traps; in (b) the defense employs a trap.

POST SCORE THROUGH DEFENSE

Purpose: To teach post players to capture and chin the ball and score repeatedly from two feet through a defender or blocking pad (getting fouled and scoring)

Equipment: Five basketballs, one basket, and one defender with a blocking pad

Procedure: Five players, each with a ball, form a half circle around the basket (at five spots) at a distance of 6 feet (1.8 meters) from the basket. One defender is positioned in front of the basket, preferably with a blocking pad. One player on offense starts on the baseline without a ball, receives a shovel pass or floor pass (good or bad) from a player with the ball, captures and chins the ball, and, without dribbling, turns and scores through contact with a two-footed power move. This move is repeated 5 times (one from each player without a ball). Rotate and repeat for all five players to make 5 scores each while finishing through contact.

1-ON-1 POST CUTTHROAT

Purpose: To practice post offense and defense in a 1-on-1 live format (playing to 2 or 3 baskets or for 1 minute)

Equipment: Ball, basket, three perimeter feeders (point, wing, wing), and two post players (one on offense, one on defense)

Procedure: Offensive and defensive post players are positioned in the lane, and three players are designated as perimeter players. The ball starts with the defensive post player, who passes it to a perimeter player of choice; live play begins with 1-on-1 post play in the lane. The ball can be passed anywhere on the perimeter before being passed to the offensive post player.

Coaching Points

- Offense: Post players establish good post stance on the post line, create contact and seal the defender, point to where they want the ball on the three perimeter spots. Get open and stay open, catch safely, and score simply.

- Defense: Defenders avoid contact unless a position or advantage is offered; keep the ball from the post. Then defend the post with the ball until a score or rebound (one dribble limit for offense).

PERIMETER–POST PROGRESSION

Purpose: To allow perimeter and post players to practice working together as outside–inside units in 1-on-1, 2-on-1, and 3-on-1 ratios, first without defense and then progressing to playing against additional defensive players in 2-on-2, 3-on-2, 3-on-3, 4-on-2, 4-on-3, and 4-on-4 formats

Equipment: Four perimeter feeders, two post players, and one ball per basket

Procedure: Begin the drill with one perimeter player and one post player, then progress to 2-on-1, 3-on-1, and so on. Defenders may be added until the drill becomes 4-on-4 with selected offensive and defensive options and using repetitions with variety (see figures 6.23 and 6.24).

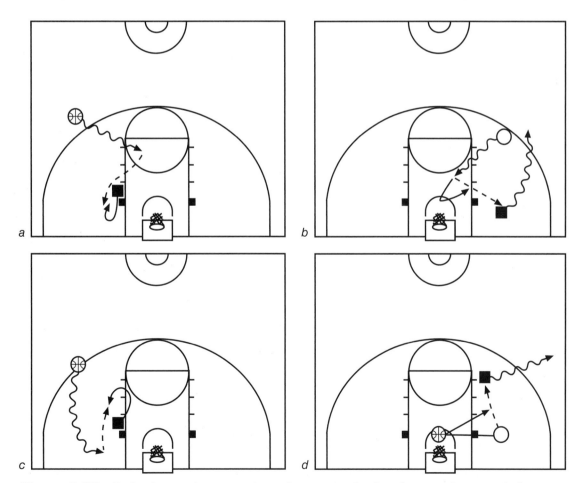

Figure 6.23 Perimeter–post progression using one perimeter player and one post player: *(a)* Middle drive—post player steps out; *(b)* post player dribbles out, and perimeter player posts; *(c)* baseline drive—post player cuts up-lane facing the ball; *(d)* post player dribbles out, and perimeter player posts.

- Middle drive: Post player steps out.

- Post player dribbles out, and perimeter player posts.

- Baseline drive: Post player cuts up the lane facing the ball.

- Post player dribbles out, and perimeter player posts up.

- Perimeter feeds post and cuts to corner (slides low), to wing area (slides high), or to basket.

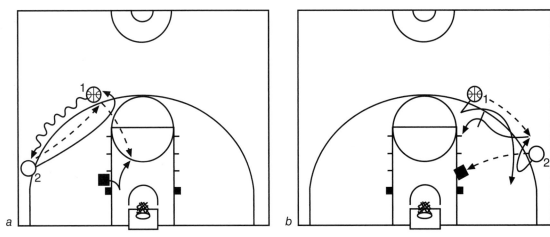

Figure 6.24 Perimeter–post progression using two perimeter players and one post player: *(a)* Point dribbles at wing, wing loops to top; wing to point pass and feed post player from the top; *(b)* perimeter players cut off post after perimeter pass to post player.

Wooden Wisdom

"Learn as if you were going to live forever, and live as if you were going to die tomorrow."

—John Wooden

INDIVIDUAL DEFENSE

*"My teams are built around tough defense,
stingy shot selection, and being hard-nosed."*

Don "Bear" Haskins, Naismith Hall of Fame coach, former head coach at University of Texas at El Paso,
coach of first NCAA Division I Championship team with black players (1965-1966)

Individual defense poses a great challenge for both coaches and players because it depends on developing fundamental skills that rely less on ability than on determination. For the same reason, however, defense can become a consistent part of each player's game. The effectiveness of this phase of the game depends especially on what is taught, emphasized, evaluated, and *demanded*. Players who seek to develop defensive skills will face both mental and physical challenges. To meet them, they will need both determination and courage—the two most important ingredients for success in individual defense.

Basic skills of individual defense are needed in all defensive systems, whether player-to-player, zone, or combination. These essential skills are as follows:

- Defensive stance and steps
- On-the-ball, off-the-ball, off-the-ball to on-the-ball, and on-the-ball to off-the-ball defense
- Defense for special situations—screens, traps (double-teaming), and the defensive charge

Individual defensive skills need to be blended into a consistent defensive system that addresses level of coverage (full-court, three-quarter-court, half-court), pressure (lane, sagging style), and assignments (player-to-player, zone, combination), as well as the influence of the dribbler. This chapter discusses individual skills geared to an aggressive style of man-to-man defensive play, but coaches can adapt them to other situations or to a specific philosophy of team defense.

Defense is critical to winning, more consistent than offense, and more controllable. Naismith Hall of Fame coach Ralph Miller (Oregon State University) stated that losses are rooted in breakdowns on defense—specifically, individual or team defense, defensive rebounding, or turnovers caused by the opponent's defense. Defense also generates fast-break offense, easy baskets, and offensive confidence.

FUNDAMENTALS OF DEFENSE

Defense is as much mental as it is physical. Players should be encouraged to be proactive, rather than reactive. Generally, defenders are at a disadvantage, and one way to offset this initial deficit is to use the rule that action is usually quicker than reaction. Coaches can emphasize the active elements of defense by using the acronym ATTACK.

A for attitude: All defense starts with the determination to become an aggressive, intelligent defensive player. Players must develop and maintain control of their playing attitude, especially on defense. Coaches cannot coach unless players decide to *play hard* during each defensive possession. Excellent defense requires that players give maximum physical, mental, and emotional effort.

T for teamwork: The collective effort of five defensive players is greater than five individual efforts. The synergy found in defensive team chemistry can offset the natural advantage held by offensive players; defenders must play together to survive and thrive with *team* defense. Coaches should tell players, "Don't let your teammates down on defense!"

T for tools of defense: The four basic tools of defense are the mind, the body, the feet, and the eyes. The hands can be either a help or a hindrance; however, when the other tools are used first, especially body position, the hands can be a defensive plus.

A for anticipation: Players must use good basketball sense and judgment (mind) triggered by vision. They must see the opponent and guard the ball—the ball is the only thing that scores. Players should see the ball at all times and use their eyes to anticipate. For example, they should see a careless pass instantly and decide to act quickly. Quickness is based on both physical readiness and mental anticipation.

C for concentration: Players should be alert and ready to play defense at all times. They must assess the situation and be able to take away the opponent's strength. Players must avoid resting, physically or mentally, when playing defense. Concentration can be aided through communication, and everyone can improve their communication.

K for keeping in stance: Defenders must maintain defensive quick stance at all times. They should seldom gamble by making moves that take them out of stance or position, and all players must be constantly ready to take advantage of an opponent's mistakes. Therefore, keeping in stance is the most important physical readiness concept for defenders. Coaches need to remind players constantly to get in stance, stay in stance, and be ready for the opponent's best move. Coaches and players can use this concept as a subjective measure of defense. Great defensive players and teams can stay in a quick stance (on and off the ball) during the entire defensive possession. Each defensive player also needs to stay in an alert defensive *mental* stance—that is, be physically and mentally alert and ready for the opponent's best move during the entire defensive possession.

ESSENTIALS OF DEFENSE

In addition to being proactive defenders, players must know nine essentials of defense: transition, purpose, pressure, position, prevention of penetration, moving, line of the ball, blocking out, and communication.

Transition The first task is to anticipate shifting from offense to defense, which requires an organized transition facilitated by communication among all five players and includes rebounding balance: Assume that every shot will miss—either get back on defense or go to the offensive board. Sprint to protect the defensive basket, pick up the ball, find shooters, and recover to all open offensive players. More specifically, players going to defense should *sprint* toward the defensive end of the floor while seeing the ball (look over the inside shoulder—red-light situation [i.e., extreme danger]) but may run or slide backward (yellow-light situation [i.e., cautionary danger]) once the offense is contained. Thus defense starts when a shot is taken on offense and ends only with a defensive rebound, steal, caused turnover, or opponent's basket. Transition to the defensive basket should be made in straight lines parallel to the sideline, which helps the team cover all outside shooters. When the opponent gains possession of the ball, transition to defense according to the following rules:

- Sprint with vision for at least three quick steps.
- See the ball during the whole transition (look over the inside shoulder) and assess the situation.
- Communicate to ensure all opponents are covered.

Purpose The purpose of defense is to prevent easy scores and gain possession of the ball through a rebound or steal. Defenders must learn to prevent situations that lead to easy baskets for the opponent; for instance, they should prevent *all* layups. The defense

CRITICAL CUE
Defense: Allow *no* layups; allow *only* one contested shot.

must make the offense work to get shots and then only under pressure (i.e., give the opponent one pressured shot). Of course, the overall goal of defense is to prevent the opponent from scoring. However, since doing so all the time is impossible, the best defensive purpose is to allow the opponent only one contested shot.

Pressure Offensive play has a basic rhythm that can be disrupted by pressure. Therefore, defensive play must maintain continuous physical and mental pressure on ball handlers. More specifically, every shot must be pressured both physically and verbally. Defenders should bother players who have the ball (whether a live ball or dribbling), swarm players who have a dead ball (i.e., who have used their dribble), and, when defending off the ball, be ready to protect the basket and support the defender who is on the ball. The defense should pressure *all* shots by making the shooter adjust the shot. The defender's hand should go up vertically through the face area to disrupt the shot. This ball pressure must be combined with off-the-ball positioning and readiness.

Position Coaches should train players to stay in a stance and be in proper court position when on defense. Defenders should also sprint to the next proper position as the ball moves on offense. Most fouls occur when defenders are out of position or have not maintained individual defensive stance. Players should get in and stay in a defensive quick stance (physically and mentally) as they maintain proper defensive positioning relative to the ball and the basket. Whenever the opponent passes or dribbles the ball, defenders should change positions and sprint to help the defender guarding the ball.

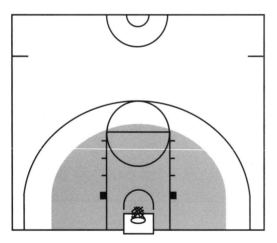

Figure 7.1 Power zone—extends this far out from the basket area, about 15 to 18 feet (4.6 to 5.5 meters) from the basket.

Prevention of Penetration Offensive players try to take the ball toward the basket by passing or dribbling, and defenders must prevent this penetration whenever possible. One defender always pressures the ball while the four other defenders play zone areas toward the basket to protect it and support the defender playing on the ball, while guarding an assigned opponent away from the ball. Defensive helpers assume a *pistol* help position—one hand pointed to the player they are guarding and one hand pointed at the ball. When playing on-the-ball defense (especially in the power zone shown in figure 7.1), defenders should prevent middle-of-the-floor penetration toward the goal by offensive players using the dribble or direct air passes to that area. Off-the-ball defense, in contrast, means keeping passes and dribble drives out of the middle of the floor (especially in the power zone) by defending zone areas toward the basket area. In short, defenders should prevent the ball and the offensive players (with and without the ball) from entering the power zone.

Moving Players must learn to move every time the ball is passed or dribbled. All five players should adjust their floor positions with every pass. On the ball, after the ball handler passes the ball, the defender moves instantly toward the ball and the basket—jumping or exploding to the ball. Off the ball, defensive players adjust their positions toward the ball with every pass to maintain their pistol positions to see the ball and their assigned offensive players.

CRITICAL CUE
Defenders move when the ball moves (*sprint to help*).

Line of the Ball The line-of-the-ball principle states that players should defend the opponent only after the opponent has taken a position ahead of the ball and toward the defensive basket. This position is past the line of the ball, which is an imaginary straight side-to-side line parallel to the court end lines and passing through the ball handler's location. For example, in figure 7.2, X_1 and X_2 need to get ahead of the ball at O_1 (ball–defender–basket) before getting in proper defensive position to defend against the opponent with the ball, as well as other opponents who do not have the ball (pistol position).

Blocking Out Successful coaches recognize that defensive rebounding is an important part of team defense and devote appropriate time to teaching it (see chapter 8). Each defensive player is responsible for blocking (checking) offensive players from the basket area and obtaining the defensive rebound when a shot is taken. This rule applies to any style of defense played. When an opponent shoots, get in an assigned opponent–you–basket position.

Communication Communication is always necessary for group success. All players must react to each other both verbally and physically in order to produce an effective team defense. Essentially, the five players should act as one. Men's basketball coach Mike Krzyzewski of Duke University says that the relationship between individual players and a team is similar to that between fingers and a fist. Fingers cannot accomplish nearly as much alone as they can when gathered into a fist. Communication links all five fingers into a fist, just as it links all five players into a defensive team. Therefore, especially on defense, players cannot talk too much.

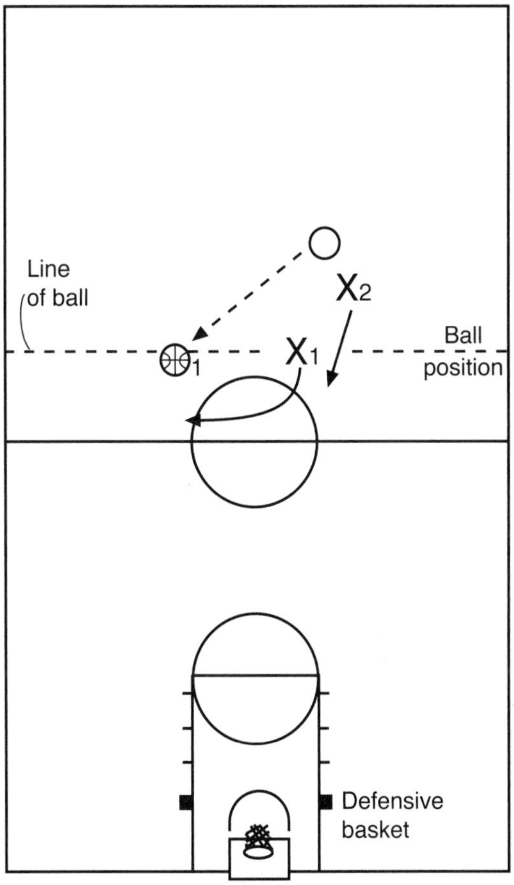

Figure 7.2 Line of the ball.

ON-THE-BALL DEFENSE

On-the-ball defense can be considered the spearhead of the defense; all good defense starts by defending the ball. In this defensive location, the concepts of *seeing the assigned offensive player* and *guarding the ball* merge and can both be accomplished at once. Even so, on-the-ball defense is also one of the most challenging defensive tasks, and it requires both good technique and determination to stay between the player with the ball and the basket. Prevent dribble penetration by staying in the ball–you–basket position.

The skills, principles, and defensive concepts covered in this section are based on the experiences of a lifetime of coaching on defensive stance and steps—the footwork needed in order to be a successful defender when guarding the ball handler. As players become more skilled ball handlers, and bigger and better athletes, the advantage for offensive players increases. As a result, it becomes virtually impossible to defend 1-on-1 on the ball without proper and highly skilled defensive techniques and team help. Nonetheless, it remains critical to stop the ball and keep the ball handler in front of the defender (ball–defender–basket).

These recommended techniques for on-the-ball defense have evolved to meet the increasing challenges of the modern game and the growing advantages enjoyed by offensive players. The concepts have been developed through collective playing and coaching experience—especially through discussions with Mike Nilson, strength and conditioning coach at Gonzaga University. Nilson has incorporated the concepts of balance and quickness into the recommended on-the-ball defensive skills. These recommendations allow all players to become significantly better on-the-ball defenders.

Defending the Live Ball

When guarding a player with a live ball (i.e., who still has the dribble available), the defender needs to be in a defensive quick stance with active feet (footfire). Communicate *ball* when the defender's assigned offensive player catches the ball and then say *ready, ready.* Defenders should be taught to maintain their position between the ball handler and the basket (ball–defender–basket), as shown in figure 7.3, to prevent dribble penetration as they recognize and take away the ball handler's strengths (on the preferred or dominant side) and keep a gap between them and the offensive player to prevent the dribble drive to the basket.

It is also important to distract and disrupt the player with the ball while preventing pass and dribble penetration. Defenders should force and encourage slow bounce or lob passes by using active feet or footfire (patter steps) and active hands from a stance with the arms and the legs bent for quickness and balance. They should match the offensive player toe to toe in a squared-up ball–defender–basket position (not shading or opening the defensive stance, which would open the dribbling lane to the basket). The feet are in a staggered stance with the inside foot slightly forward and the back foot toed slightly outward. The back or butt should be pointed toward the basket to facilitate lateral movement (figure 7.4). This stance is low and wide, with the hips down, the knees spread, and the head lower than the offensive player's head (level with that player's chest).

Dropping the back foot too much is an error that opens the door for the dribble drive. It is sometimes called *matador defense* on the ball because it allows the offensive player easier access to the dribble drive on the side of the dropped foot, thus leaving the defender in the position of a matador—that is, waving to the dribble driver as he or she passes by. This foot position also makes it more difficult for the defender to move laterally with quickness in order to maintain the ball–player–basket relationship. In addition, it allows a dribble move to the side of the front foot (figure 7.5) that is difficult to defend. Therefore, players guarding the ball handler should position themselves with their butt to the basket in order to flatten out or arc the offensive player dribbling laterally—to prevent dribble penetration by forcing the dribble to go wide. Defenders seldom need to swing-step or

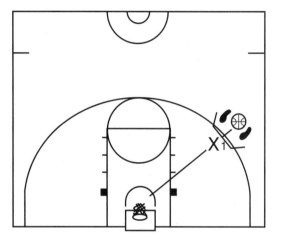

Figure 7.3 Ball–defender–basket position when guarding the ball handler.

Figure 7.4 Defensive stance with the butt to the basket while guarding the ball (active feet).

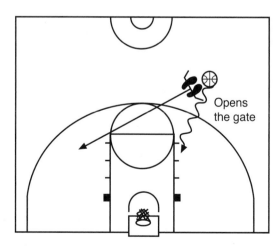

Figure 7.5 On-the-ball defensive error: The matador defense gives the offensive player an opening. Correction: Keep the butt to the basket with active feet.

drop-step on a live-ball move if their stance and hand position are properly maintained. This positioning allows defenders to keep the trunk and chest in front of the ball handler in a ball–defender–basket alignment without grabbing or holding. Stop the dribble drive with the body or trunk.

The recommended hand position on the live ball is for the ball-side hand (usually the front hand) above the front foot to mirror the position of the ball. To mirror the ball, do the following:

• **If the ball is overhead,** the front hand should be overhead as the arm is extended to deflect the pass when the defender moves closer. This technique can be accomplished with a quick two-foot hop forward. With the ball overhead, the offensive player suffers reduced ability to make a quick drive or take a quick shot so the defender gets closer (*ball overhead, hand up, move closer*). Stay in a quick stance with the front arm extended and vertical and the back hand either near the front hand or near the waist in a horizontal arm-bar position and ready for contact (figure 7.6*a*).

• **If the ball is in the shooting pocket,** keep the hand in front and near the ball with palm facing the ball (if possible), where it is ready to challenge and change a shot attempt while preventing a quick air pass by the ear with the other hand (the thumb-in ear position) (figure 7.6*b*).

• **If the ball is low,** keep the hand horizontal and above the ball to prevent the ball handler from taking a quick shot or bringing the ball up or across the body (in a high or low rip or circle-tight move); see figure 7.6*c*. If the offensive player has the ball low, the defender should play even lower because of the increased threat of the dribble drive. The defender must keep the trunk in the ball–player–basket position in order to prevent the driver from lowering the shoulder and getting the head and shoulders by the defender's trunk on the dribble drive.

Figure 7.6 Defensive hands and feet when guarding the ball: *(a)* ball overhead, *(b)* ball in triple-threat position, and *(c)* ball low.

The other hand is in front of the body, with its arm flexed at the elbow, and therefore ready to become the disrupter if the ball is moved to the opposite side by the offensive player. This back hand is also ready to chase the ball following a pass to this side; the defender should try to get a touch on any pass to that side.

Taking a stand on the ball is a phrase that coaches can use to remind players to establish and maintain a ball-defender-basket position on ball handlers as they attempt to distract and disrupt the player with the ball. The defender should be close enough—about an arm's length away—to get a touch on the ball. This technique applies to defending the live ball and the dribbler.

Note: On an offensive jab step, defenders should use a 6-inch (15-centimeter) retreat step to that side. Specifically, they should use a power push-step slide to prevent the possible dribble drive.

Defending the Dribbler The dribbler, or point position, should be defended with a gap that is small enough to allow the defender to get a touch on the ball yet adjusted as necessary according to the relative quickness of the offensive and defensive players involved. On determining the direction of the offensive player who is using the dribble drive, the defender uses push steps to prevent the intended drive and maintain or regain the ball-defender-basket position. A slight rear turn is made in the direction of the dribble drive as the defender uses repeated explosive push steps (usually three steps) from the power leg to prevent dribble penetration. Defenders should be reminded to use their mind, feet, and body to stop the dribbler: Anticipate the drive direction (mind), use explosive push steps (lead with and point the foot in the direction of movement) to maintain the ball-player-basket position, and take contact on the chest or trunk (body) in a legal guarding position to prevent dribble penetration. If the dribbler gets by the defender (head and shoulders past), then the defender turns and sprints to regain the ball-defender-basket position (*run to recover*).

Push-Step Technique From a balanced defensive quick stance, players should thrust the lead foot (in the direction of movement) laterally as the head and body weight are shifted in that direction. That foot is toed outward slightly as the foot position of the quick stance is maintained. Although some coaches prefer pointing the lead foot, it is preferable to keep the feet parallel. The power for the push step comes from a forceful push from the power or trail foot. The movement of the lead and trail foot is 6 to 18 inches (about 15 to 45 centimeters) laterally as the feet are kept apart at shoulder width or wider. The trail foot then returns to quick-stance position. Usually, three explosive push steps are sufficient to prevent dribble penetration in one direction. At this point in the sequence, the dribbler either has gotten past the defender (who must run to recover) or reverses direction on the dribble (in which case the defender must use three push steps in the opposite direction). In that event, pointing the lead foot is preferable, as it gives more leverage to change direction and prevent penetration on the reversal counter move. Partial rear turns may be needed to maintain proper defensive position prior to the push steps.

The teaching segments for the lateral push-step movement are as follows:

- Use a partial rear turn when needed to stay ahead of the dribbler and to maintain the ball-defender-basket position (figure 7.7a). Point the lead (stepping) foot in the direction of movement.

- Explosively push from the trail (pushing) foot while the lead (stepping) foot is pointed and moves laterally 6 to 18 inches (about 15 to 45 centimeters) and the head and body weight shift in the direction of movement (figure 7.7b).

- Focus on the lead foot landing with balanced weight distribution (toe and heel hit at once, with 60 percent of the weight on the ball of the foot) while keeping the feet in a parallel stance (or with the toes pointed slightly outward), unless leading with and pointing the foot in the direction of movement.

- The trail foot also moves 6 to 18 inches (15 to 45 centimeters) as the feet maintain a shoulder-width relationship (figure 7.7c).

- The start and end of the movement are always made from and to a balanced quick-stance position (with the feet toed out only slightly).

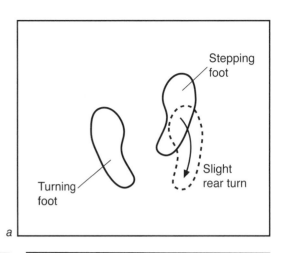

Push-step technique is sometimes referred to as *step-and-slide* motion. For a good learning reminder, use the verbal prompt *push step and slide, low and wide: can't get too low, can't get too wide*.

In the point stance, the defender's nose is on the ball to get ahead of the dribbler. The near (dig) hand is pointing to the ball with the palm up, and the elbow of that arm is bent. When step-sliding to the right, the defender's near (dig) hand is the left hand. The lead (back) hand is in the "thumb-in-ear" position, with the elbow of that arm at a right angle and the forearm acting like a windshield wiper, in order to take away or prevent the quick air pass by the ear. When the dribbler puts the ball on the floor,

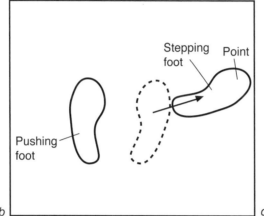

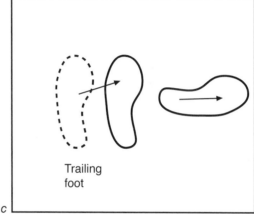

Figure 7.7 Lateral movement footwork sequence: *(a)* partial rear turn (only when needed), *(b)* push step, and *(c)* return to quick stance.

the defender communicates *point, point*. The defender should turn the dribbler in the backcourt and adjust to the ball–defender–basket position in the frontcourt. On a spin dribble, defenders should jump back one step away from the dribbler to prevent the dribbler from hooking them with the protection arm bar to get by more readily.

Traditional Method of Defending the Live Ball

Live-ball defenders must be ready in a defensive quick stance and in a ball–defender–basket position. The forward foot may be placed opposite the dominant hand of the offensive player. If the offensive player is right-handed, defenders can position the left leg and arm forward to force the offensive player to pass or dribble with the weak hand. Another option is to place the inside foot slightly forward in the ball–player–basket position. Coaches should have players defend with the palm of the lead hand facing the ball (see figure 7.8), which allows them to move easily and flick at and pressure

Figure 7.8 Live-ball defense: Palm of the lead hand faces forward; palm of the trail hand faces up. Left foot is forward against the right-handed offensive player influencing the dribble to go left.

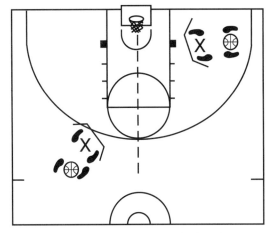

Figure 7.9 Foot position—inside foot forward (guarding the ball).

the ball. This hand position is more common when players are guarding the live ball.

Players should distract and disrupt with the hands as they keep the inside foot slightly forward. Most coaches prefer to have the inside foot forward, as shown in figure 7.9. In addition, many coaches prefer to point the lead foot during step-slide defensive movement to cut off lateral movement. When a dribbler gets the head and shoulders past, the defender runs to recover the ball–defender–basket position.

Defending the Dead Ball

When a ball handler has used the dribble, two defensive techniques are recommended: swarming and sagging (i.e., pressuring and dropping back). When swarming the ball, defenders trace the ball with both hands and attack the ball handler's senses while staying in stance (figure 7.10). When sagging, defenders drop back toward the basket while staying in the ball–defender–basket relationship to anticipate the next pass and aid team defense. This latter option can be used especially when the ball handler is out of shooting range. The pressure option is also referred to as the *stick* position, and defenders can communicate with *stick, stick* to alert teammates to deny other passing lanes.

OFF-THE-BALL DEFENSE

Figure 7.10 Dead-ball defense.

This most challenging individual defensive skill makes a crucial contribution to team defense. Despite a natural tendency for players to relax away from the ball, they must learn the importance of playing off-the-ball defense. Coaches should teach them that protecting the basket and supporting the defender who is playing on the ball is just as important as attending to the assigned player away from the ball. Thus, when defending away from the ball, players should see the person but guard the ball. These multiple tasks require greater attention than is needed for on-the-ball defense.

The two types of off-the-ball stances are as follows:

- Open (*pistols*) stance, used when the defender is relatively far from the ball (two passes away)
- Closed (denial) stance, used when relatively close to the ball (one pass away)

These stances are shown in figure 7.11, where X_2, X_3, and X_5 use a closed stance but X_4 uses an open stance to support defender X_1, who is guarding the ball handler. The common concept is that off-the-ball defenders should be in a ball–defender–player position in either an open or closed stance, depending on proximity to the ball.

The farther the offensive player is from the ball, the farther the defender should be from the assigned opponent, while always maintaining a ball–defender–player position. The defender needs to keep a gap (a distance cushion) to provide extra response time, as shown in figures 7.11 and 7.12. The closer the ball is to the offensive player, the closer the defender should be to the assigned opponent away from the ball.

What the defender does before the offensive player gets the ball determines what the offensive player can do with the ball. Defenders should keep the ball away from the assigned opponent in the opponent's favorite spots on the floor. Always take away an opponent's strength, whether on the ball or off the ball.

Defenders should also prevent player cuts to the ball (ball–defender–player position) in the middle and power zone areas. Coaches must teach defenders to force offensive players to go around or away from a desired position. If contact must be made, the defender should beat the offensive player to a desired spot, make contact using an arm bar and a closed stance, force the cutter high or out of the power zone, and then reestablish a gap.

Seeing the ball at all times helps players defend the ball handler and support the defender who is playing on the ball. Players should follow the ball visually to anticipate offensive cuts and careless passes. They should guard the ball and see the offensive player being guarded—the ball always scores, not the player.

Defenders who are two passes away from the ball should assume an open *pistols* stance, which allows them to see the ball and their assigned opponent. In this position, one hand points at the ball and the other points at the opponent (*pointing pistols*), thus forming a flat triangle: ball–defender–player (figure 7.12).

Defenders who are near the ball need to deny the pass to the player they are guarding. In a ball–defender–player position and a closed stance, defenders should place the back partially to the ball in order to see both the ball (over their shoulders) and the player they are guarding. They should also put the lead foot (the one closest to the ball) and the lead hand in the passing lane; the hand should be positioned with the thumb down, the fingers spread, and the palm facing the ball. The defender's ear should be at the level of the offensive player's chest. Denial pressure can vary from putting the hand in the passing lane (moderate pressure) to putting the elbow in the lane and even the shoulder and head in the lane (high pressure).

The back hand near the opponent is the brush hand; the back of this hand feels the opponent and is ready for use as an arm bar if the opponent cuts to the ball. The

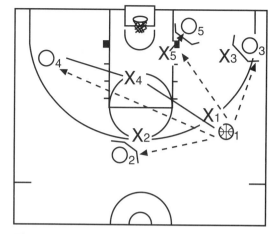

Figure 7.11 Closed stance (X_2, X_3, X_5) and open *pistols* stance (X_4).

Flat triangle

Figure 7.12 Open stance: The off-the-ball defender forms the flat triangle and *points pistols* at defensive responsibilities—that is, at the ball (as a helper) and at the offensive player being guarded (primary assignment).

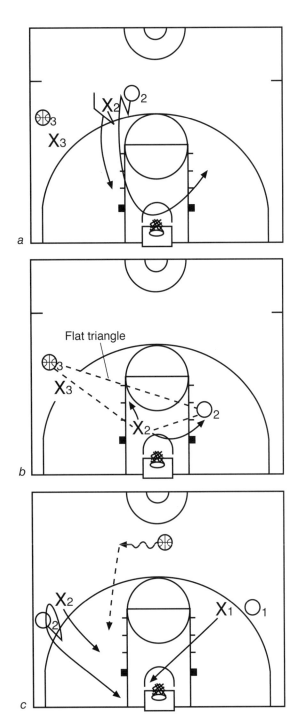

Figure 7.13 Defending the backdoor cut:
(a) moving with the cutter, *(b)* opening up
away from the ball (forming the flat triangle),
and *(c)* backdoor-cut defense (X₁ helping).

defender makes a fist with the brush hand to prevent grabbing or holding fouls. The defender's vision is *down the gun barrel* of the extended near arm.

With the defender in a closed stance (denying the pass to the player guarded), the offensive player needs to V-cut to get open; therefore, the defender must stay in a closed stance and move continually to maintain the desired ball–defender–player position. Also, when overplayed, the player being guarded may cut behind the defender in a backdoor move. The proper response to the backdoor cut is to go with and stay in the ball–defender–player closed-stance position (snap the head and change the denial hand) until the cutter reaches the lane, then open up and assume the open stance to see the ball. The defender should *not* follow the cutter away from the ball. See figure 7.13. In all off-the-ball situations (open or closed stance), the communication is *help right, help right* or *help left, help left*. A defender in the key with an open stance calls *hoop, hoop* to communicate to teammates that they have support help in the basket area.

POST DEFENSE

Techniques for guarding an offensive post player in or around the free-throw lane include the ball–defender–player closed stance (with the hand across the passing lane in a ball–defender–player arrangement; figure 7.14*a*) and the fronting stance (figure 7.14*b*). As a rule, one of these two stances should be used to keep the ball out of the power zone (post area). In a closed stance, the hand is in the passing lane (ball–defender–player) with the thumb down and the palm facing the ball.

The most common post-defense technique is the closed stance, in which players avoid contact with the offensive post player (unless they have a position advantage), keep a hand in the passing lane, and defend in a position on the side of the defender. This technique is used most often in the high post (free-throw line area) or medium post. This half-front position serves as a compromise between keeping the ball out of the post area (full front) and being ready to check or block out the post player (from behind the post) if a perimeter shot is taken. One added positioning rule is needed: When the offensive post is in the low or medium post, defenders should take a position above the post player when the perimeter passer with the ball is above the free-throw line extended but take a closed-stance position below or on the baseline side when the ball is below the free-throw line extended (figure 7.15). When the ball changes positions on the perimeter relative to the free-throw line, the defender can choose to go behind the post (easier but more susceptible to a deep repost) or go in front of the post (more difficult but better prevents entry passes to the post) to regain the closed stance with the ball–defender–player position.

When in a full fronting stance, the defender should see the ball and stay in defensive stance, with radar bumper contact (the butt front), feet active, and hands up. This technique allows the defender to anticipate and move for the pass to the post as long as the feet are active from a balanced position. The fronting stance offers the advantage

Figure 7.14 Post defense: *(a)* closed stance (high side) and *(b)* fronting stance (full front).

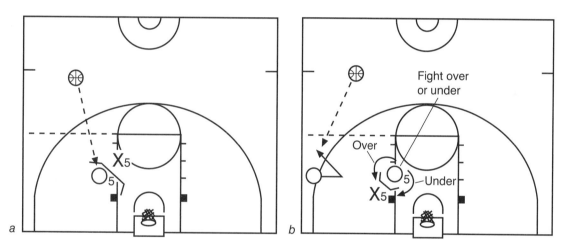

Figure 7.15 Defending the post—closed stance: *(a)* ball above the free-throw line and *(b)* ball below the free-throw line.

of better keeping the ball from post players but suffers from the disadvantage of giving the offensive post player a definite edge for rebounding if a perimeter shot is taken.

Offensive post players control defenders by establishing and maintaining contact. Therefore, post defenders should avoid contact (unless they have an advantage in position), maintain a safe distance from the ball handler, and continue to move in order to keep the offensive post player (and the passer) guessing about their defensive location.

The fundamentals also apply to defending a post player with the ball: Defenders should stay in a defensive quick stance with both hands ready. When an offensive post player receives the ball in the low or medium post, the defender should be taught to take a step back and reestablish a ball–defender–basket position to prevent angle baskets with direct access to the basket. Maintaining distance gives the defender reaction time to defend against an offensive post move, prevents the offensive post player from using contact to control the defender, and allows a teammate time to help from the perimeter.

CRITICAL CUE

Fronting post: Stay in stance with the hands up, butt in contact, and feet active; be ready to move for the pass.

ON-THE-BALL TO OFF-THE-BALL DEFENSE

When a player is guarding the ball handler as a pass is made, the defender can achieve the necessary and immediate transition from on-the-ball status (ball–defender–basket position) to off-the-ball status (ball–defender–player position) by jumping (or exploding) to the ball (primarily) and to the basket (secondarily) and assuming a closed *or* open stance (figure 7.16). This technique, also called *chasing the ball*, involves attempting to touch the pass with the hand nearest the direction of the pass. Jumping to the ball prevents the passer from using a pass-and-cut move to make a front cut and catch a return pass going toward the basket.

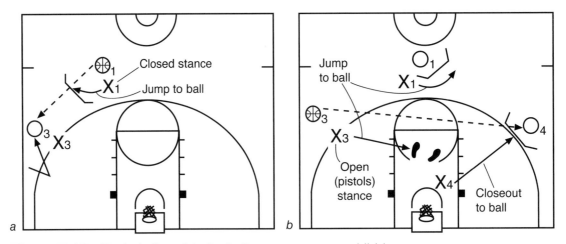

Figure 7.16 Explode (jump) to the ball on every pass or dribble move.

OFF-THE-BALL TO ON-THE-BALL DEFENSE

When the ball is passed to the player being guarded, another defensive change, called *closing out to the ball*, occurs as players change status from off-the-ball (open stance) to on-the-ball coverage from a help defensive position (protecting the basket and supporting the defender on the ball). Correct technique for closing out to the ball includes the following steps (see figure 7.17):

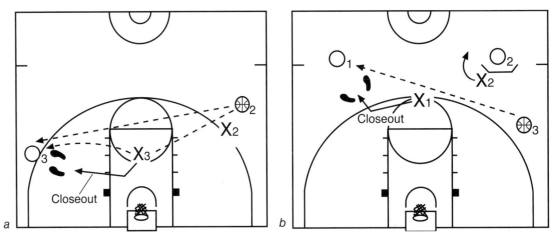

Figure 7.17 Closeout to the ball—going from off-ball to on-ball defense: *(a)* wing-to-wing pass, *(b)* wing-to-point pass.

- Sprint halfway to the guarded player with the ball near the ball-to-basket line (close out short).

- Break down into a regular defensive stance using active feet (stutter steps) with both hands above the shoulders and above head level. Approach the ball handler with caution on the line between the ball and the basket to prevent the drive, but be aggressive and prepared to contest a shot or pass.

- Recommended foot position is with the inside foot up (belly open to the sideline or baseline).

- Close out in a ball–defender–basket path with the butt to the basket to prevent the drive.

- Close out short (keep a gap) with the body weight back; throw the hands up and back to prevent the quick air pass and prevent the drive.

The objectives on a closeout are to prevent penetration first (dribble or quick air pass past the head) and then pressure the ball handler, especially on the shot, secondly.

CRITICAL CUE
Close out short to prevent the drive.

CRITICAL CUE
Defensive on-ball closeout:
- Put hands up.
- Close out short; use active feet.
- Keep butt (back) to basket.

COACHING POINTS FOR DEFENSE

General

- Get in a stance and stay in a stance (mentally and physically).
- Use the mind, body, feet, and eyes as the first tools of defense.
- Use the hands only as secondary defensive weapons.
- Prevent easy scores; allow no layups.
- Keep pressure on the ball.
- Prevent penetration by the pass or dribble.
- Move toward the ball on every pass or dribble.
- Take away the opponent's strength.
- Upset the opponent's offensive rhythm.
- Allow only one contested shot and block out all offensive rebounders to capture and protect the rebound.

On-the-Ball

- Get low and stay low. Be lower than the offensive player (*nose in the chest*).
- Maintain the ball–defender–basket position.
- Guard players in a live-ball situation with front foot to front foot, with hands and feet active, and within touching distance (lead or front hand up). Take away the favored driving path with foot position.
- Keep space between self and the dribbler (*keep a gap but get a touch*).
- Guard the dribbler, keep the head and chest in front, jab with the lead hand, and run to recover when necessary.
- Guarding a dead-ball situation: Either swarm the ball handler, tracing the ball without fouling, or sag away from the ball handler while reading the passer's eyes for a possible interception.
- Jump (explode) to the ball when a pass is made (chase the ball); always move toward the ball on a pass or dribble—sprint to help.

(continued)

Coaching Points for Defense *(continued)*

Off-the-Ball

- Close out to the ball on the ball-to-basket line, when it is passed to an assigned offensive player; sprint, break down, and prevent the drive (always close out short). Close out on the driving line to the basket.
- Maintain the ball–defender–basket position.
- Get in an open (*pistols*) stance when far from the ball or a closed stance (hand across and thumb down) when close to the ball.
- Keep the ball from offensive post players unless they pose no offensive threat (use a closed or fronting stance).
- Be able to help and make the decision to bluff or switch on screens, penetrations, and closeouts.

SPECIAL DEFENSIVE SITUATIONS

CRITICAL CUE

Capture and chin a loose ball; never dribble a loose ball.

In addition to the basic skills of on-the-ball and off-the-ball defense, several other tactics can help the team defend against special offensive threats. A situation that occurs mostly on defense but can occur on offense is a *loose ball* from a bad pass, errant dribble, or other loss of ball control by an offensive player. The best rule for this situation is to get both hands on the ball (capture and chin it). If the ball is in the air, use a two-handed pickup and snap it to the chin-it position after a quick-stop. If the ball is on the floor, dive on the loose ball with both hands. Rules require players to pass to an open teammate before getting up from the floor with the ball. The reminder for this situation is "*never* dribble a loose ball, *always* capture and chin a loose ball."

Help-and-Decide

On clearouts, or any penetration situation, off-the-ball defenders are critical to the success of the defense, whether they help and rotate (protect the basket and cover the penetrating dribbler) or decide to switch defensive assignments, trap with the defender on the ball, or bluff to buy recovery time for the teammate guarding the dribbler. Communication is the key—defenders must be ready to help and communicate the decision. Two options are shown in figure 7.18. The critical help situation in this case, called *help on the help* by X_1 in figure 7.18*a*, occurs when X_3 helps on dribble penetration by O_2 outside the free-throw lane.

Defenders should use the help-and-decide defensive technique to combat the offensive tactic of dribble penetration, which clears out one side of the court for the ball handler to dribble-drive in order to beat the defender. The off-the-ball defender should be ready to help and decide (to help, switch, or trap) if the defender on the ball is beaten, or if the assigned offensive player vacates the area.

Screens

When an offensive player screens or shields a defender to help a teammate get an open shot, the defense must use special tactics, including avoiding screens whenever possible—defenders should be in motion when offensive players approach them to set a screen. Screens generally can be defeated by fighting through (going over or under) the screen, in which case a teammate may help out the screened defender by using a hedge-and-go (or show-and-go) move (figure 7.19); by switching assigned opponents, espe-

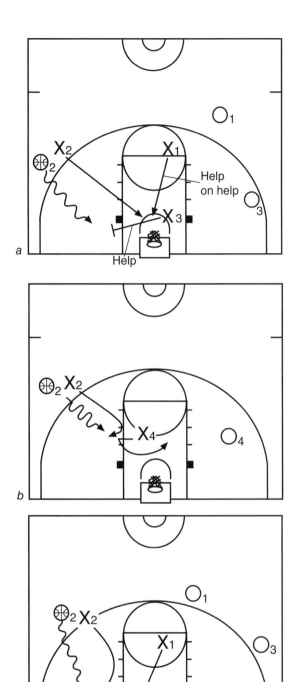

Figure 7.18 Help and decide (help, switch, or trap) on dribble penetration: *(a)* Help and switch, *(b)* help and recover, or *(c)* help and trap.

Figure 7.19 Fighting through screens: *(a)* Defender goes over the top, *(b)* helper hedges, and *(c)* teammate recovers when the offensive player leaves.

Figure 7.20 Switch screen: (a) Helper calls the switch; (b) helper *steps up* to switch on the ball handler; and (c) teammates exchange the assigned players to defend.

cially when a defender is unable to get through the screen (figure 7.20); or by trapping the dribbler on a screen. The defender guarding the screener calls the switch, switches (hedges) forward (up), and contains the ball handler.

On screens away from the ball, players should avoid or slide through the screens, usually on the ball side. Defenders should be moving targets (*don't be screened*). Defensive players should stay sideways and use their arms as shock absorbers to prevent the screener from getting to their body. The player guarding the screener should jump to the ball, stay on the ball side, and help a teammate through the screen; give help when needed.

Traps

Coaches may also want to develop defensive techniques to handle an exceptional offensive player or to function as a surprise tactic. One such technique, trapping, occurs when two defenders double-team an offensive ball handler (2-on-1) in certain court areas or on ball screens. Coaches should emphasize that both players must stop the ball handler from escaping the trap by being in good basic defensive position, keeping the feet active, positioning themselves knee-to-knee with each other, and keeping the inside hands up to prevent a quick air pass. The objective is to force a lob or bounce pass, and players should learn not to reach for the ball or commit a foul. All other off-the-ball teammates should close off the nearest passing lanes to prevent any passes from the trap into their zones; in other words, they should play a three-player zone. As shown in figure 7.21, the best places to set traps are in the corners of the court. The figure also shows an example of a frontcourt trap; specifically, the trap is made in a frontcourt corner, and the other defenders deny the near passing lanes and force the offense to play on half of the court (frontcourt in this case). Coaches may also want to trap or double-team a larger effective post player in the low or medium post.

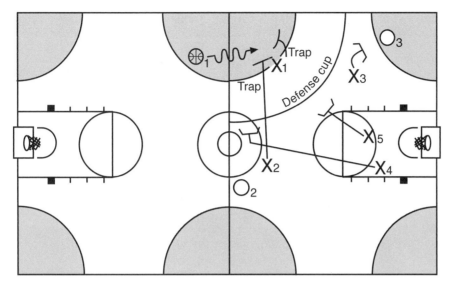

Figure 7.21 Optimal trapping locations.

Defensive Charge

The defensive charge—one of the fundamental defensive plays—is used when a defender has beaten an offensive cutter to a desired position on the floor and is in a legal guarding position. It must be learned properly, not only for its great potential as a team play (it can prevent an opponent's three-point play and result in two free throws for the defender) but also because it involves a contact skill that must be developed progressively in order to avoid injury. The rules that apply to this situation are that the defender is entitled to any spot on the floor that is taken in a legal guarding position. The defender doesn't have to give the dribbler any certain amount of space, but the defender must be in a legal position before the offensive player's head and shoulders pass the defender's body. Away from the ball, offensive cutters must be given the chance to change direction (never more than two steps), and defenders must always be in a legal guarding position before an offensive player becomes airborne; defenders can move their feet and protect their bodies. Near the basket, the defender's feet must be outside the protected area under the basket where taking a charge is prohibited.

Players should be taught the following techniques for taking the charge:

1. Get in and stay in a good basic defensive stance and keep the feet active (footfire) to adjust position slightly; the defender must be knocked down from a legal guarding position and should not flop on contact.

2. Take the blow in the chest area without letting the offensive player get head and shoulder past the defender's torso.

3. Resist giving up an established position but keep most of the weight on the heels (must be knocked down).

4. Keep the arms out of the action and use them for protection without grabbing the offensive player (as in screen-setting technique). Protect vital areas (men cross hands over the groin, women cross arms over the chest). Position the shooting hand close to the body and grasp the shooting wrist with the other hand.

5. Fall properly with the arms up and in front. The buttocks should hit the floor first, followed by the lower and upper back as the palms either slap the floor or stay crossed. Keep the head in a curled chin-tuck position (figure 7.22).

6. Assume that the officials will not call an offensive foul and scramble up to regain basic position to help the team defense in the event of a "no call."

7. Know when to take the charge. Disrupt the offensive player's movement but pick a situation in which the offensive player has poor body control and is not alert.

Figure 7.22 Defensive charge—falling properly: *(a)* The defender must be knocked down (protect the vital parts with the arms—women cross the chest, men cover the groin area). *(b)* Land on the rear end first, roll onto the back with the neck curled (head tucked), and either slap the floor or keep the arms crossed. *(c)* Scramble to regain basic position in the event of a "no call."

PRESSURING THE SHOT

A special skill is needed if defending the player with the ball when a set or jump shot is taken. The general rule is to pressure every shot as follows:

- Stay in the stance and keep the ball-side hand up with palm facing the shooter when the ball is in the shooting pocket (triple-threat position); don't leave the feet until the shooter does.

- Use the lead hand to force the shooter to alter the shot. Don't try to block it—make the shooter change the shot. The lead hand goes up vertically past the face on the shot.

- Keep the lead hand up in a vertical position with the wrist back (don't slap down and cause a foul).

- Also apply verbal pressure (shout, make noise, scream, call the player's name). Yell *shot* to alert teammates of a rebound situation (help them see and hear the shot).

TROUBLESHOOTING

Here are some common defensive errors, along with coaching responses.

- **Problem:** Failure to get in and stay in a stance

  Correction: Coaches should review or reteach stance and gradually increase the time spent in defensive stance in drills (increase emphasis and reminders). During team play, they should develop team consequences when a player comes out of a stance (mentally or physically).

- **Problem:** Lack of motivation to play defense

  Correction: Coaches should provide players with concrete reasons for the need to play good defense—both a qualitative rationale (e.g., "don't let your teammates down") and quantitative analysis for sound defense (lower opponents' shooting percentages). They should also emphasize and demand high levels of defense.

- **Problem:** Slow reaction to ball movement

  Correction: Coaches should emphasize *sprinting* to the next assignment.

- **Problem:** Failure to talk on defense

  Correction: Coaches should emphasize communication, require and practice talking on every ball movement during drills (use incentives and consequences), and recognize the best defensive communicator each day. They should also teach and use echo calls to communicate with team members on defense.

- **Problem:** Fear of taking defensive charges or diving on the floor for loose balls

  Correction: Coaches should do *sequential, progressive* teaching and physical practicing of the skill to ensure safety and provide experience. They should also recognize great taking-the-charge team plays (and use incentives).

- **Problem:** Failure to play hard on defense

  Correction: Coaches must convince players that getting coached depends on giving their best effort. Coaches should establish playing hard as a tradition and substitute for players who do not play hard on defense in competitive practice and game situations.

- **Problem:** Lack of confidence on defense

  Correction: Coaches should provide progressive success situations in practice, demand effectiveness and execution that produce success, and define success in terms of proper technique and effort instead of the ultimate result (made or missed shot).

DEFENSIVE DRILLS

Insist on execution first but also demand intensity on defense. Players must learn to play hard individually in order to develop a cohesive team defense with skilled techniques.

STANCE-AND-STEPS PROGRESSION ▶

Purpose: To provide a sequential method of developing defensive stance and power push-step (step-slide) technique

Equipment: Half-court floor space for movement

Procedure: Players are spaced facing the coach and perform the sequences on command or at their own pace. Five repetitions of each move are recommended.

1. One-foot balance, defensive stance, with the chest up, the butt muscles on stretch, and the trunk slightly forward (alternating hops with right foot and left foot)

2. Lateral jumps (one foot to one foot—right to left and left to right)—i.e., side jumps from a one-foot stance to a one-foot stance on the opposite foot

3. Lateral jumps with step-slide recovery steps (placing the other foot down to gain balance in the push-step slide)

4. Consecutive lateral jumps with recovery steps—three repetitions in each direction (left and right)

5. Lateral continuous seamless push steps—three repetitions in each direction

6. Piggyback seamless push steps in groups of three (three right, three left, three right or three left, three right, three left)

7. Free-throw lateral lane slides—push steps from outside the lane to the opposite side and then returning (right to left, left to right)

8. Baseline closeouts and lateral push steps (three right, three left)—four lines or line drill with one offensive player 15 to 18 feet (4.6 to 5.5 meters) from the baseline defensive players

   - Pass is made to offensive player (O), and defender (D) closes out.
   - D closes out and defends with push steps, then O goes for two dribbles to the right.
   - D closes out and defends with push steps, O goes for two dribbles to the left.
   - D closes out and defends, O goes for two dribbles to the right, then reverses for two dribbles to the left.
   - D closes out and defends, O goes for two dribbles to the left, then reverses for two dribbles to the right.
   - D closes out and defends, O goes for two dribbles to the right or left.
   - D closes out and defends, O goes for two dribbles to the right or left, then one spin-dribble reverse to opposite direction.

Coaching Points

- Stay in defensive quick stance.
- Emphasize quickness with balance.

- Take a stand on the ball—maintain the ball–defender–basket relationship with the defender's trunk.
- Use explosive push steps.
- Step and slide, low and wide.
- Defend with the mind, the feet, and the body (in balance).
- Do it properly first, then quickly.

MOVING STANCE AND STEPS

Purpose: To develop individual defensive stance and steps

Equipment: One ball for the coach, half-court space (minimum)

Procedure: All players are spaced about the court and facing the coach with a clear view. Players assume a basic defensive stance on the coach's signal (*palm down*), then respond to the coach's signals and commands with continuous defensive stance and step moves. The coach uses the ball for most signals. The direction moves used are shown in figure 7.23.

Signal	Meaning and Movement
Palm down for live ball	Assume basic stance (active feet).
Ball in stomach or back dribble	Slide forward.
Ball in right front or dribble drive right	Angle-slide retreat left.
Ball in left front or dribble drive left	Angle-slide retreat right.
Finger point left or right (or side dribble)	Push-step (three).
Ball in triple-threat position, then toss	Close out and dive on floor for loose ball (on floor or passed from coach to floor).
Ball overhead or dead ball	Stay in stance and get hands tracing ball.
Ball shot in place	Call *shot*, block out, and rebound simulation.

Note: This drill can be done with three steps and active feet for any step-slide signals and then later continuously until the next signal is given.

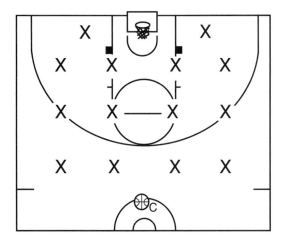
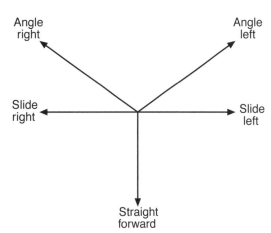

Figure 7.23 Moving stance and steps—direction of movement.

LINE DRILL: INDIVIDUAL DEFENSE ▶

Purpose: To develop individual defensive skills in a progressive manner

Equipment: Ideally, one ball for every two players (at least four balls, or one per line)

Procedure: Players form four lines on the baseline and execute offensive and defensive zigzags in pairs. The first player in each line assumes a defensive stance, and the next player assumes an offensive stance. The offensive player zigzags down the floor while the defender maintains defensive distance and ball–defender–basket position. The players switch positions for the return trip.

Options: These moves should be done in the following sequence as a learning progression:

- Offensive zigzag—90-degree change of direction. Perform without the ball and then with the ball (dribbling).

- Defensive zigzag—three push steps or 45-degree backward defensive slides (lead-hand palm up, flicking at imaginary ball, and trail hand near shoulder or with thumb in the air). On change of direction, players lead with the elbow as they rear-turn and continue slides at a 90-degree change of direction, going from baseline to baseline using swing steps and push-step sliding technique.

- Defensive zigzag—90-degree change of direction with running steps (to simulate getting beaten by the dribbler). The move always starts and ends with push-step sliding steps; slide diagonally left (dribbler gets past), sprint to reestablish position, break down and slide again. Change direction and repeat (slide, run, slide). Continue from baseline to baseline.

- Offensive–defensive zigzag—offensive and defensive pairs. The dribbler first coaches the zigzag defender while moving zigzag and carrying the ball under the armpit to simulate the dribble. The defender starts with three push-step slides, then continuously zigzags. The offensive player then dribbles down the floor (using pull-back-crossover, regular-dribble-crossover, spin-dribble, or behind-the-back moves). The focus is still to make the defender perfect.

- Offensive–defensive zigzag in pairs—live offense and defense. Use two side alleys (free-throw lane line to sideline) down the court.

- 1-on-1 full-court—live offense and defense to score. The defender slides, runs when needed, turns the dribbler in the backcourt, pushes the dribbler to the weak hand or the sideline in the frontcourt, maintains the ball–defender–basket relationship, and prevents layups. Mix all player pairs.

ON-THE-BALL AND OFF-THE-BALL: 2-ON-2 ▶

Purpose: To teach defenders to adjust quickly to on-the-ball and off-the-ball positions while defending against penetration (help-and-decide situations)

Equipment: Two lines of players at wing positions, one ball, and a half court

Procedure: The coach starts with the ball in the middle (both defenders are in a closed stance) and then dribbles to one side as the defenders adjust to positions of closed and open stance. The coach may pass, and offensive players go live or penetrate at any time. The drill rotation is from offense to defense to the back of the opposite line (figure 7.24).

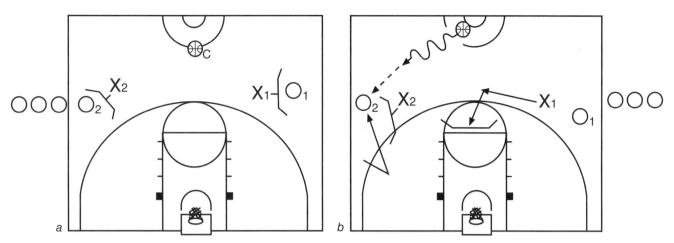

Figure 7.24 On-the-ball and off-the-ball (2-on-2): *(a)* starting positions and *(b)* coach dribbling and passing.

1-ON-1 CLOSEOUT PROGRESSION

Purpose: To develop the individual defensive skill of closing out on an off-the-ball offensive player who has just received a pass

Equipment: One ball and basket per group (ideally per pair)

Procedure: When practicing the closeout technique, the defensive player starts under the basket with a ball (figure 7.25). The offensive player is in basic position, facing the basket within a range of 15 to 18 feet (4.6 to 5.5 meters). The defender passes the ball to the offensive player with a crisp air pass and closes out to defend. The coach can select a pass, preferably a nonpreferred-hand pass. The rule is to first prevent the drive by breaking down in the stance halfway to the ball handler (with the feet active, the inside foot forward, and both hands up with the palms facing the ball). The defender then pressures the ball and the shooter and blocks out when a shot is taken. From that point, live competition between offense and defense ends when a basket is made or when the defense gains possession of the ball. The dribbler is limited to two dribbles.

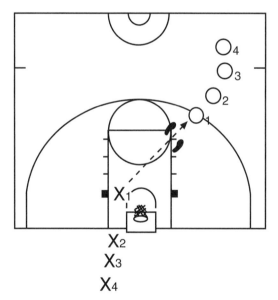

Figure 7.25 1-on-1 closeout drill.

Options

- Closeout—shot only
- Closeout—shot fake, drive only (right, left)
- Closeout—live offense (rotating lines each time)
- Closeout—live offense and defense (rotating)
- Closeout—live make-it-take-it (rotation when defense stops offense)

CLOSEOUT: 1-ON-1, 2-ON-2, 3-ON-3, 4-ON-4

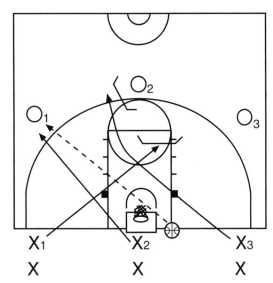

Figure 7.26 3-on-3 closeout: Coach passes; closeout defenders cannot cover players in their line and must communicate.

Purpose: To practice all outside moves by perimeter players

Equipment: One ball and one basket per group

Procedure: Form a line of players under each basket (off the court). The first player steps under the basket with the ball and serves as the defender. A line of offensive players is positioned 15 to 18 feet (4.6 to 5.5 meters) away, facing the basket from the corner, wing, or point position. The defender makes a crisp air pass with the nonpreferred hand (and with the feet on the floor) to the first player in the offensive line, then closes out to defend that player. The drill begins as soon as the pass is made for both offense and defense. The perimeter offensive player should catch the ball with the feet in the air and facing the basket, read and react to the defender's actions, and apply fundamentals to shoot or make an outside move. Players may rotate to the back of the opposite line each time, play make-it-take-it, or use any other arrangement of their choice. The drill may be run as a 3-on-3 option (figure 7.26) that then becomes a teamwork competition with on-the-ball and off-the-ball play.

DEFENSIVE SLIDE: MOVING STANCE AND STEPS

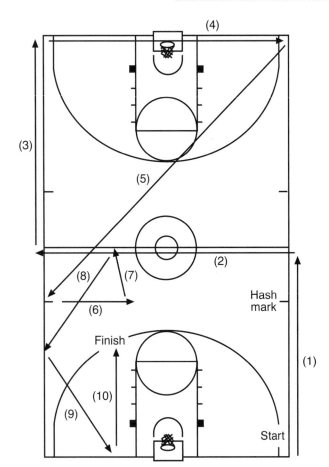

Figure 7.27 Moving stance and steps (may be started from right or left side).

Purpose: To develop individual defensive steps

Equipment: Full-court boundary lines

Procedure: All players begin the drill in the court corner on the right side and use defensive steps as described in the following list; they follow the path noted in figure 7.27. Players should allow the preceding player to reach the adjacent free-throw line before starting. The drill includes the following 10 movements and combinations:

1. Forward slide
2. Slide to the left
3. Closeout to the baseline
4. Slide to the right
5. Angle slide, run, slide
6. Slide to the right
7. Closeout to the half-court line
8. Facing belly to the sideline with an angled left side
9. Facing belly to the sideline or to the baseline with an angled right side
10. Closeout to the free-throw line

Players then repeat the circuit starting from the left side of the court; thus they complete one circuit starting at each corner of one end line. Coaches may want to record the time taken to complete the circuit after using the drill several times and after emphasizing proper technique.

HALF-COURT: 2-ON-2, 3-ON-3, 4-ON-4

Purpose: To develop individual defensive skills in a team setting

Equipment: One ball, half court

Procedure: Three (or four) offensive and three (or four) defensive players play a half-court game centered on various offensive moves and situations to be played by the defender. Start with various sets and situations. The coach may rotate players after one defensive stop (successful team defense) or set challenging group goals, such as two or three consecutive defensive stops.

Options

- Screens (on and off the ball)
- Post play
- Penetration
- Closeouts
- Traps
- Charges

HALF-COURT PLUS TRANSITION: 4-ON-4

Purpose: To develop individual defensive skills in a team setting and make the transition from defense to offense after defensive rebounding

Equipment: One ball, full court

Procedure: Begin play as 4-on-4 half-court action with the defensive players defending against any offensive situation desired. When the defenders gain the ball on a steal or defensive rebound (i.e., make a defensive stop), they may fast-break to score at the other end of the court. Four new defenders then take their positions, and the successful defenders come to the original half court as offensive players.

TEAM TRANSITION: OFFENSE-TO-DEFENSE AND DEFENSE-TO-OFFENSE

Purpose: To practice adjusting quickly as a team to critical transition situations

Equipment: One ball, full court

Procedure: The coach initiates play with one team on offense and one on defense (5-on-5) playing on the full court. A transition coach (usually the head coach) can interrupt play at any time by loudly using the word *floor*. On this signal, the player with the ball instantly places it on the floor and makes the transition from offense to defense with teammates. The closest opponent picks up the ball (two-hand capture and chin) and transitions from defense to offense with teammates. Both transitions are repeated each time the transition coach makes the *floor* call. The drill continues for 5 to 7 minutes. Offensive players can run primary and then secondary fast breaks into an attacking set offense in a controlled 5-on-5 team transition situation (offense to defense and defense to offense).

3-ON-3 GET-BACK TRANSITION

Purpose: To practice offense-to-defense and defense-to-offense transitions in a breakdown of 3-on-3 situations

Equipment: Full court, one ball, 10 players at a time (5-on-5 with opposite-color jerseys), and a third team of 5 rotating into the drill if available

Procedure: Three offensive players are positioned at one end of the court near a starting basket, and three defenders are positioned inside the three-point arc (figure 7.28). Two offensive teammates are positioned near the hash marks (called the "heat line" in this drill). Coach (C) starts the drill by passing to O_1, O_2, or O_3 (O_1 in figure 7.28a), who passes ahead to O_4 or O_5 to create a transition challenge for X_1, X_2, and X_3. These defenders must respond quickly, both physically and verbally, to cover the basket (X_2), pick up the ball handler (O_4) to slow or stop the ball, and pick up the remaining open offensive player (O_2 or O_3). After passing the ball ahead, O_1 replaces O_4 at the sideline near the heat line. The offense tries to score by the following means (in order): primary fast break (numbers), finding an open teammate, or passing and cutting to get a good shot. The defenders try to protect the basket, stop the ball, and pick up open offensive players.

Figure 7.28b illustrates the second transition with the drill running in the opposite direction. When the defense gets the ball from a rebound, the ball handler (X_1 in figure 7.28b) passes ahead to a teammate waiting at the heat line (X_4), then replaces that player. The 3-on-3 transition drill continues until it is stopped by a coach's whistle to make corrections or to rotate in a new team and start the drill again with a pass from the coach to an offensive player.

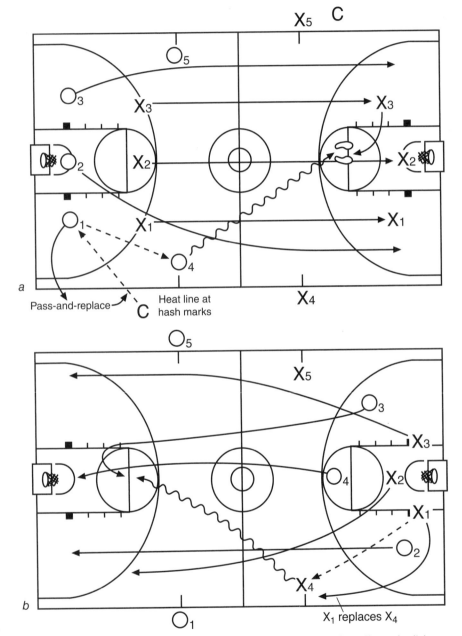

Figure 7.28 3-on-3 get-back drill: *(a)* first transition (to offense), *(b)* second transition (defense to offense).

Wooden Wisdom

"Success is never final; failure is never fatal. It's courage that counts."

—John Wooden

CHAPTER 8

REBOUNDING

"Offense sells tickets, defense wins games, [and] rebounding wins championships."

Pat Summitt, Naismith Hall of Fame coach, former head coach at University of Tennessee,
seven-time national championship coach

In basketball, rebounding can be defined as gaining possession of the ball after a missed shot. Players need to learn both offensive and defensive rebounding skills. The objective of offensive rebounding is to regain possession of the ball after your team attempts a shot, whereas defensive rebounders try to gain possession of the ball after the other team has attempted a shot. Rebounding is a major part of the game at all levels. It may even be more important in a game played by younger players because of the higher percentage of missed shots at beginning levels.

REBOUNDING TOOLS

Although height and jumping ability provide advantages, the keys to rebounding are determination, discipline, and technique. Statistics on the leading rebounders in professional and college basketball are not merely a list of the tallest players or the ones with the highest vertical jumps. Most rebounding, even in the college and professional ranks, is done below the rim. The most essential factor in rebounding, then, may *not* be leaping ability, or vertical movement, but positioning and quickness to the ball—that is, horizontal movement or angle jumps to the ball (more horizontal than vertical). Thus rebounding requires more than physical tools; it also requires considerable effort and proper execution of skills.

Examples abound. Joan Crawford was a center who stood 5 feet 11 inches (1.8 meters) tall and became an AAU star in the 1950s and 1960s as she led her team and the competition in rebounding. She took the U.S. national team to the 1957 World Championship and was inducted into the Naismith Hall of Fame in 1997. Denise Curry, at 6 feet 1 inch (1.9 meters) tall, was also a 1997 Hall of Fame inductee. She holds the UCLA rebounding record, was the 1981 USA Player of the Year, won an Olympic gold medal, and was named French Player of the Decade for the 1980s. Dennis Rodman came from a small NAIA school in Oklahoma to lead the NBA in rebounding for many years despite standing only 6 feet 8 inches (2 meters) tall, which is short for an NBA frontcourt rebounder.

Notwithstanding these keys to rebounding, it is of course also true that certain physical attributes are advantageous to rebounders. Players who are tall and have long arms, large hips, and well-developed leg and upper-body musculature hold an advantage over other players. In addition, vertical jumping ability and skill is an asset for a rebounder. Therefore, although coaches should ensure that all players learn rebounding skills—not just jumping skills—players should also develop their jumping ability and skill to their full potential. Coaches can use strength and power programs and other conditioning programs to enhance players' vertical jumps in practices. In addition to helping them jump their highest, coaches must make sure that they are jumping correctly and skillfully. Proper jumping technique involves bending the knees, jumping from both feet, and using the thrust of both arms to reach full extension (2-and-2 rebounding). Teaching players to jump in this manner not only develops their leaping abilities to the maximum but also helps them maintain their balance in contact jumping situations and reduces the number of over-the-back fouls when rebounding.

MOTIVATING PLAYERS TO REBOUND

The first step in teaching rebounding is to convince players that it is a relevant and important skill to learn and perform in game situations. Explain that the entire team—not just those who are tallest, play post positions, or have exceptional jumping ability—must master rebounding skills. Every player can become a good rebounder. If coaches bypass this initial step, they will probably be disappointed by the rebounding performance of certain players during the season, especially the smaller players. In fact, smaller guards are essential defensive rebounders for many teams.

Reasons for Rebounding

Coaches should give players solid reasons to develop the crucial skill of rebounding. They must see the importance of rebounding in getting and maintaining control of the ball and its key role in team offensive and defensive production. Rebounding at both ends of the floor can improve efficiency by providing extra possessions when on offense and ending possessions when on defense; indeed, as the final phase of defense, rebounding is a critical finish for team defensive possessions.

Ball Possession Rare is the player who does not like to shoot the basketball. But players can't shoot if they don't have the ball, and rebounding is the primary way of gaining or maintaining possession of the ball. At the offensive end of the court, rebounds maintain possession and frequently lead to quick and easy baskets. Getting an offensive rebound is like causing a turnover by the opponent—it takes the ball away from the other team. At the defensive end, rebounding gains possession, which is the final part of defense. One of the best confidence boosters for a team is to complete the defense with a defensive rebound (or a steal).

Fast Break A team's ability to begin a fast break depends on defensive rebounding and forcing turnovers by the opponent, which is why teams with a well-developed fast break implement effective defensive rebounding. Whether a team's offensive style is fast or slow, the basic strategy should emphasize getting the ball up the court quickly to prevent opponents from sending their whole team to the basket for an offensive rebound on a shot attempt instead of keeping some players back to defend against the fast break.

Players usually like to fast-break, so it should be easy to motivate them to concentrate on defensive rebounding: no rebounds, no fast break. Defensive rebounds provide more fast-break chances. The fast-breaking Boston Celtics of the 1960s were at their best when triggered by a defensive rebound and an outlet pass from Bill Russell, one of the best college and professional rebounders in history. Russell excelled at this blue-collar basketball skill for his entire career and is considered one of the greatest leaders in the history of the game, both as a player and as a player-coach. His example as a defender and rebounder was integral to his leadership.

Winning Perhaps the strongest evidence of the importance of rebounding lies in its high correlation with winning games. In one U.S. study (National Association of Basketball Coaches 2000) of rebounding and winning over a 10-year period, teams that outrebounded their opponents won the game 80 percent of the time. In addition, national leaders in team rebounding in the United States win more of their games and list rebounding as the third-most-important factor related to winning. More games are also won by teams that lead the nation in fewest turnovers (the second-most-important factor at both ends of the floor) plus field-goal and free-throw accuracy (the most important factor). These statistics suggest that teams that gain possession of the ball only after their opponents score are, at best, trading baskets. In contrast, effective rebounding allows a team to create a winning edge at both ends of the floor.

Work Ethic Rebounding is a blue-collar skill that depends mostly on hard work. It requires players and teams to get down in the trenches and do the physical dirty work. Among other reasons, then, players should develop the tradition of rebounding (for themselves and for their team) because it enhances the core value of working hard.

Reinforcing the Motivation

To review, coaches can convince players to rebound by helping them understand that rebounding is not only essential for ball possession and for the fast break but also crucial to winning. With this understanding established, coaches can praise and encourage players who give maximum effort in rebounding and single out individual players for particular rebounding accomplishments—for instance, most rebounds for the half, most defensive rebounds for the game, most rebounds per minute, best blockout, most consistent rebounding, and highest rebounding efficiency. Coaches should make sure that players know how much their coach and teammates value rebounding as a team skill and that their efforts to rebound effectively will be rewarded. Once all players feel responsible for rebounding and understand why they must rebound, coaches can explain and demonstrate the fundamental rebounding skills.

REBOUNDING RULES

Offensive and defensive rebounding hinge on four concepts—the "big bullets of the boards"—that are critical to any player or team that wants to succeed at rebounding:

1. *Assume* that each shot will be missed and do the assigned job at both ends of the floor.

2. *Keep hands up* (hands above the shoulders) when in rebounding areas, whether on offense or defense.

3. *Use 2-and-2 rebounding.* When going for any rebound (on offense or defense), rebound from two feet with two hands. Go up tall and small; come down big and wide.

4. *Capture and chin the ball and turn away from pressure.* On all rebounds, use two hands to capture the ball and chin it to protect it. To chin the ball, use two hands, with the fingers pointing up, to bring the ball up under the chin or move it from shoulder to shoulder (the power position); the elbows should be out and up (big and wide). The last step of rebounding is to pivot and turn away from the opponent's pressure to protect the rebound while clearing the ball to an open area on the court.

CRITICAL CUES FOR REBOUNDING

1. Assume a miss.
2. Keep hands up.
3. Use 2-and-2 rebounding technique.
4. Capture, chin, and turn.

The *assume a miss* prompt reminds players and coaches to assume that *every* shot will be missed. When that assumption becomes habitual, players are conditioned to focus on carrying out their rebounding assignment on every shot attempt. Even on an uncontested layup by a teammate, players should always assume a miss—then they will develop the habit of rebounding consistently or carrying out their team-rebounding assignment.

The verbal prompt *keep hands up* provides a reminder of an essential skill in rebounding, especially when players are blocking out on defense or near the offensive basket. In fact, this point was viewed as the most important rebounding reminder by John Wooden during his time at UCLA. The correct arm position is shown in many of the figures included in this chapter. Players should start in quick stance, ready to jump (sitting into the stance with the legs bent) and with the hands up and ready to rebound the ball (upper arms horizontal and level with the shoulders; forearms vertical and slightly forward). The rationale for the hands-up arm position is as follows:

- It keeps players ready for a quick rebound (e.g., ball hits the rim and bounces directly to the player with no time to respond).

- It allows players to prevent the opponent from rebounding—just get close to the opponent, with the hands up. Doing so prevents the opponent from getting the hands up to rebound the ball without lifting the defender when going up for the ball.

- It makes a difference when players are blocking out on defense. The hands-up technique (figure 8.1a) prevents the defensive rebounder from using the illegal method of locating and grabbing the opponent in the hands down behind position to feel and control and to hold and control the offensive rebounder (figure 8.1b). When blocking out on defense (figure 8.1a), the defender blocking out with "rigid arms of steel" creates a larger area that the offensive opponent must get around (from elbow to elbow) and creates a more effective legal blockout technique.

The prompt "use 2-and-2 rebounding" refers to the important skill of rebounding from two feet with two hands. This concept was popularized by hall of fame coach Jim Brandenburg, formerly the University of Wyoming's men's basketball coach. Because rebounding is a contact skill, players should use a quick stance (sit into the game) with the feet shoulder-width apart before and after jumping into the air for a rebound. To be effective, rebounders also need to capture the ball securely with both hands, preferably at the peak of the jump.

The teaching technique for 2-and-2 rebounding is as follows:

- Get into a rebounding ready position (quick stance, hands up).

- Execute the 2-and-2 rebound. Go up tall and small and come down big and wide (figure 8.2). Use an angle jump (between vertical and horizontal) to the ball to get rebounds out of your area.

- *Capture and chin.* Grab the ball with two hands and rip it to a position under the chin or into the power position and against the chest. The fingers should be pointed up (not out), the elbows should be out and up, and the ball should be forcefully squeezed under or near the chin to protect the ball. It is necessary to use a turn or pivot away from nearby opponents to then clear the ball while protecting the ball using the trunk as a barrier.

- Protect the ball (chin it or squeeze it tightly); see figure 8.2b.

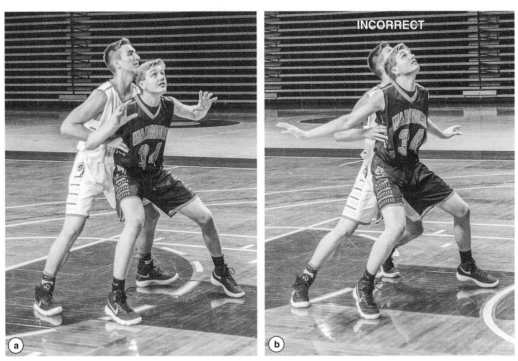

Figure 8.1 Hands-up rebounding: *(a)* correct, *(b)* incorrect and illegal (hands down to hold or wrap opponent).

Figure 8.2 2-and-2 rebounding: *(a)* Go up tall and small; *(b)* come down big and wide (capture and chin the ball).

All players need to learn these "big-bullet" principles that are essential to successful rebounding: *assume; hands up; 2-and-2;* and *capture, chin, and turn.*

DEFENSIVE REBOUNDING

The suggested rebounding technique requires that players gain the inside position on an opponent, block out the opponent, and then get the rebound. Getting a position between the basket or the ball and the opponent enhances the defense's positional advantage to secure a rebound bouncing from the rim or the backboard. Although rebounding seems to consist of three distinct phases, they occur very quickly as if they were a single action. The rebounding technique is commonly referred to as *blocking out* but is sometimes called *boxing out* or *checking* an opponent (the first phase).

All players should understand the following fundamental rebounding principles associated with blocking out:

- See or hear the shot (either the defender guarding the shooter or another defender calls *shot*).

- Assume that the shot will be missed (all players).

- Locate the opponent.

- Go to the opponent and block out (only when the opponent is inside the three-point field-goal arc and is rebounding).
- Go to the ball.
- Get and keep the ball.
- Move the ball out or down the court by pivoting and turning away from pressure.

See or Hear the Shot

Players must be aware of when and where a shot is taken. Whether they are guarding an opponent on defense or attempting to get open on offense, they should know where the ball is at all times. Therefore, coaches should emphasize to players the need to position themselves so that they can see both their assigned player and the ball on defense and use their peripheral vision (big vision) to see the ball while moving to get open on offense. Players who are blind to the ball usually have other problems with fundamental skills, such as positioning and movement, which should be corrected. *See the opponent; guard the ball.*

Once players see a shot being taken, they call out *shot* to alert teammates (who may have momentarily lost sight of the ball) that they should get in position to rebound (*hear the shot*). The defender guarding the shooter has the primary responsibility for making the defensive call. However, no verbal alarm works as well as a player's own observation of the shot being released.

CRITICAL CUE
Visual contact until physical contact on rebounds.

Assume a Miss

Every shot attempt means a potential rebound. Players must learn to assume that every shot will be a miss and to go to their rebound assignment. When players develop this habit, they will be conditioned to perform their assigned rebound task every time a shot is taken, regardless of the outcome. This habit must be implemented, especially on offense, where offensive rebounding is such a low-percentage individual play (a good *team* goal on offense is to get 30 percent of the available offensive rebounds from missed shots).

CRITICAL CUE
Assume a miss is the most important rebounding principle

Find the Opponent

Almost without exception, young players fall into the habit of watching the flight of the ball when shots are in the air—the most common defensive rebounding mistake. This error can prevent players from gaining an advantage in rebounding position. Once the ball is in the air, their first reaction should be to locate the opponent they are supposed to block out or the opposing player nearest to them (visual contact before physical contact).

This principle does not mean that players should be unaware of the direction and distance of the shot; however, they must avoid becoming mere spectators when the ball is in the air. Coaches should train players to be active rebounders by teaching them to locate an opponent while maintaining a sense of the direction and timing of the shot. *Move the feet; rebound with the feet.*

To determine whether players are watching only the ball in flight, use a simple rebounding drill in which the opposing player holds up a given number of fingers after the shot is released by another player. After rebounding the ball, the player guarding that offensive player should be able to report the number of fingers that were held up. If not, the defensive player was probably focusing too much on the ball in the air and not enough on the opponent.

Go to the Opponent and Block Out

At this point, the defensive player has set the stage for the next step—the actual blocking out of the opponent. Players may not have difficulty with the first three steps, but blocking out is challenging for almost all players, especially for beginners.

The purpose of blocking out, or boxing out, is to gain an inside positional advantage (usually closer to the basket) over an opponent for a rebound. Normally, a player is more likely to rebound a missed shot if positioned closer to the basket than the opponent. This location is called *inside* position because the player is between the basket and the opponent (opponent–rebounder–basket). However, it is best to get that inside position farther away from the basket and the associated congestion (i.e., to form a deep defensive rebounding pocket).

Occasionally—when an opponent is far underneath the basket and a shot is taken from a long distance, for example—outside position (with the opponent between the player and the basket) is preferable. But the inside position is generally the desired position for a player when blocking out an opponent. The difference between inside and outside positions is illustrated in figure 8.3.

Before blocking out, a player must go to where the offensive opponent was previously located, as shown in figure 8.4 (visual contact, then physical contact). The player should move quickly and prevent the opponent from gaining a positional advantage. To help players gain inside position for the blockout, coaches should teach them to use pivots and turns.

When blocking out an opponent, a player must be in a stance similar to a quick stance with the following modifications. The feet should be parallel and shoulder-width apart; the arms

Figure 8.3 Inside (right) and outside (left) rebounding positions.

Figure 8.4 Go to the offensive player to block out. Make contact with the hands up.

should be raised, with the upper arms parallel to the floor and bent at the elbows; and the hands should be forward with the palms up. The standard blockout position is shown in figure 8.4. *Make rigid arms of steel when blocking out.*

The boxout or blockout is the phase of rebounding in which players usually make contact with an opponent. Contact is normally initiated by the player with the inside position. Because players must turn to the basket and be in quick stance in order to rebound the ball (having already located the designated opponent after the shot was released), they can no longer see the opponent being blocked out. Therefore, they must use the sense of touch to keep track of the opponent's location. The body parts most often used for this purpose are the buttocks, back, upper arms, and elbows. Players should sit into the game and make contact using radar bumpers and active feet. Feel with the radar bumpers, not the hands. Keep the hands up with rigid "arms of steel."

Figures 8.5 and 8.6 illustrate the preferred technique for beginning and intermediate players: Go to the opponent, use a front turn to step into the opponent's path (right foot to right foot or vice versa) followed by a rear turn to make contact, and take away the opponent's momentum and remaining path. *Be proactive—go to the opponent.* Elite players can use an advanced technique, *blast and box*, which is shown in figure 8.7. In this approach, the defender blasts the offensive player with a forearm shiver (figure 8.7*a*) and then slides into a regular blockout with rigid "arms of steel" (figure 8.7*b*) before pursuing the ball or rebounding (boarding the ball; figure 8.7*c*). More specifically, the defender locates and meets the opponent with the forearm-shiver blast to take away the opponent's momentum to the basket. This blast is followed by a front-turn move to slide into a box or blockout position with active feet. In short, go to the opponent, blast and box, and then board (pursue the ball). This technique is sometimes referred to as the *hit-and-get* core of rebounding (go to the assigned player to *hit* or block out, then *get* the ball and capture and chin it and turn or pivot away from the opponent).

Figure 8.8 illustrates why it is so important for players to make contact with the opponent. In figure 8.8*a*, no contact is made, and the opponent has a clear lane to the basket and an advantage for the rebound. In figure 8.8*b*, however, the inside player establishes contact with active feet and prevents the opponent from gaining an inside position for the rebound. Turns and pivots are not always viable options for defensive rebounders, so it is important for coaches to emphasize that the key concern in defensive rebounding is not so much the technique used to block out the opponent but the sheer fact of whether or not the opponent is effectively blocked out. Effective blockout technique forces an offensive rebounder to rebound with a positional disadvantage and commit over-the-back rebounding fouls.

Against an exceptional offensive rebounder, players might use the "face-block" technique: Face the player and use a two-forearm shiver to get and maintain contact. This move has the disadvantage of preventing the defensive rebounder who uses it from pursuing and capturing the ball—teammates must do so. The scouting report on an

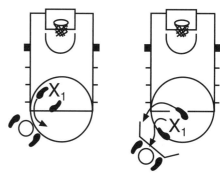

a. Front turn   b. Rear turn

Figure 8.5 Front-turn–rear-turn technique for blocking out.

Figure 8.6 Rear-turn completion of blockout with contact.

CRITICAL CUE
Defensive rebounding: Go to the opponent and make contact with a front-turn–rear-turn move or a hit-and-get rebound technique.

Figure 8.7 Blast and box, then go to the ball to board: *(a)* Deliver a forearm blast, *(b)* use a radar bumper block (rear turn into a blast-and-blockout), and *(c)* get the ball.

opponent may identify an aggressive, disciplined rebounder that necessitates using the "face-block" technique to negate this type of offensive rebounder.

Despite widely held perceptions, basketball is a contact sport. Coaches know that some players are better prepared than others for the physical side of rebounding. In drills and games, coaches should match up players according to size, strength, and readiness for contact.

Figure 8.8 Blockout contact: *(a)* Contact is not made, and the opponent (#52) has an advantage for the rebound. *(b)* Contact is made, effectively blocking out the opponent and possibly leading to an over-the-back offensive-rebounding foul.

Go to the Ball

The old saying that certain players have a "nose for the ball" may be true. Some rebounders seem to be in the right place for a rebound on every missed shot. In reality, these apparently instinctive rebounders have probably studied where shots taken from various spots on the court are likely to go when missed; furthermore, they hustle and actively pursue the ball. This combination produces effective rebounders who just go to *get* the ball (the desired final product).

Coaches can help players develop this kind of rebounding instinct by pointing out the rebounding distribution diagrammed in figure 8.9. Shots taken from the side of the court are much more likely (70 to 75 percent) to rebound to the opposite side. Therefore, players should learn to take a position on the opposite side of the basket from where the shot was taken (the weak-side or help-side position). From a team perspective, at least two rebounders should be sent to the weak side on all shots from the side of the court. Low- or medium-post offensive players are instructed to rebound to the middle when shots are taken from their side of the floor where posting. In contrast, shots taken from the middle of the court tend to rebound to an area in the middle of the lane.

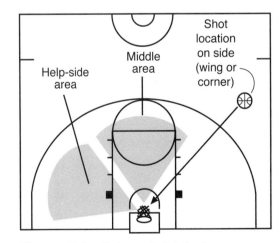

Figure 8.9 Rebound distribution areas.

Players should also know that shots taken from close range tend to rebound closer to the basket than do shots launched from longer distances (long shots produce long rebounds). For instance, three-point field-goal shots rebound farther from the basket, whereas shots taken from in front (the top of the key) rebound near the free-throw line. Finally, players should be aware that some rims tend to make the ball rebound farther away from

Figure 8.10 Angle jump to the ball.

the basket, whereas others seem to cushion the impact of shots and produce much shorter rebounds. For that reason, players should test the bounce of the rims during warm-up (except for NCAA Division I games where impact–rebound ball interaction is controlled by the rules).

Another reason that some players seem to get to the ball is sheer hustle. Players who are good rebounders take the approach that every free ball is theirs, effectively telling opponents, "I want the ball more than you do." Coaches can instill this mentality in players by giving praise and other rewards for coming up with the most rebounds, loose balls, and steals (sometimes called *garbage plays*). Remind players to *find a way* to go and get the ball with two hands.

Rebounding can certainly be aided by timing and jumping ability, but all the spring in the world means nothing if a player does not know when or how to use it. Fortunately, several drills can help players get a feel for when they should leave the floor for a rebound. One especially effective drill is to have players repeatedly toss the ball off the backboard and attempt to grab the rebound at the maximum height of the jump each time (additional drill ideas are presented later in this chapter). Coaches must also instill in players the concept of angle-jumping to the ball and rebounding out of their area (to the side or forward); players should pursue and board the ball (see figure 8.10).

Get and Keep the Ball

Too often, players make perfect rebounding plays only to lose possession because of poor ball protection. Therefore, when teaching rebounding, coaches should emphasize that all players' efforts to gain possession of the ball will go for naught if they fail to protect it afterward.

As discussed earlier, rebounding from two feet with two hands (2-and-2 rebounding) is a strong, balanced technique. Specifically, two-foot jumping and two-handed grabbing of the ball reduce the chances of letting the ball slip away or get dislodged by an opponent. Coaches can help players develop this skill by insisting that they use it for every rebound they pursue. Because rebounding contact often causes young players to close their eyes when capturing the ball, coaches should train young players to keep their eyes open and focused on the ball as they capture the rebound.

Occasionally, the ball may come off the rim in an area where the player is unable to grasp it with both hands. In such cases, players should gain control using only one hand (block it and then tuck with two hands) or tap the ball to a nearby teammate.

Maintaining possession of the rebound once it is captured is frequently more difficult than it might seem. Opposing players try to knock the ball from the rebounder's hands. In addition, they often trap the rebounder with two or even three players, thus making it nearly impossible for the player to pass or dribble the ball. Therefore, players need to learn to handle such situations and protect the ball with proper technique.

When players rebound the ball in the vicinity of an opponent or opponents, their first move should be to bring the ball in under the chin with the elbows out and a hand (with the fingers pointing up) on each side of the ball, squeezing it tightly (see figure 8.11). The best position for the ball is directly under the chin, but it may also be moved from shoulder to shoulder anywhere in the power position to keep it away from opponents.

The teaching points are as follows: The fingers are pointed up (to prevent dangling the ball and exposing it away from the body); the elbows should be out and up to clear space for a low, wide-base 2-and-2 rebound space; and the player should squeeze the ball and make herself big. Coaches should tell players to use two hands to capture and chin the rebound (and whenever handling the ball in a congested area) in order to protect and retain the ball. Players should not swing the elbows around to ward off an opponent; doing so can constitute a violation or foul. Players may, however, take up space to clear their area with the elbows out (make themselves big). In addition, a rebounder chinning the ball can always use a pivot or turn to move away from pressure (danger) in order to protect and shield the ball. This move can involve either a front or a rear turn to protect the ball away from the opponent. Players should always keep the head up with big vision and look for teammates breaking downcourt, to an open spot in the backcourt, on a defensive rebound situation, or for an offensive rebound in an open area to protect the ball.

When a rebounder gains possession of the ball after a missed shot, a single opponent (usually one that the rebounder has blocked out) is often nearby and attempts to steal the ball or pressure the rebounder. Coaches should teach players to pivot away from the opponent (using EPF footwork), as shown in figure 8.12. The player should

Figure 8.11 Chin it—elbows out, fingers up: *(a)* side view and *(b)* front view.

Figure 8.12 Pivot away from pressure *(a)* secure possession of the ball and *(b)* turn and pivot away from the opponent to keep the ball.

have an open passing lane to a teammate or be able to dribble without losing the ball to a steal. Players should be cautioned, however, not to put the ball on the floor immediately after rebounding a shot in traffic; doing so creates an opportunity for an opponent to steal or deflect the ball. Players should see or feel pressure from opponents and use pivots to turn away from that pressure and safely clear the ball.

When rebounders find themselves surrounded by two or more opponents, they should not panic. If they are trained to remain calm—to keep the ball in the protective power or chin-it position and look over the entire court—then options will present themselves. One escape move that coaches can teach players is the step-through technique shown in figure 8.13. This move can be followed by a pass or a two-dribble push to advance the ball up the floor. Big players can then quick-stop, chin the ball, and look for a pass to an open teammate, whereas perimeter players can continue dribbling up the floor. This technique can be used when the trapping defenders leave an opening large enough for the ball handler to slither through. Sometimes an overhead pass fake causes defenders to leave their feet and creates an opening for the offensive player to step or dribble through. Players should not, however, force their way through the defenders, which may result in a charging foul.

Another option for a rebounder surrounded by opponents is to throw a pass over them. Even smaller players can use this approach if they make the proper fakes before making the pass ("fake a pass to make a pass," as advocated by Morgan Wootten, Naismith Hall of Fame coach from DeMatha Catholic High School). If the rebounder is trapped by two or more opponents, a teammate should be open or be able to break open to receive a pass. Also, one of the defenders may reach in and foul the rebounder. Given these options, coaches should tell players to keep their composure when they are trapped by opponents after a rebound and wait for an option to appear.

Figure 8.13 Trapped rebounder step-through move: *(a)* outlet pass or *(b)* two-dribble push.

Move the Ball

Once possession is assured, the player with the defensive rebound must choose one of the following options: pass to an open teammate up the floor, use a two-dribble push to clear the ball, or wait for a ballhandling perimeter player to come for the ball. Whatever action the player takes should begin with the head up, using big vision, and the ball in a protected power position. Remember, there is *no* 5-second count in the backcourt (defensive rebound location).

Passing the Ball The preferred method for moving the ball after a defensive rebound is to make an outlet pass. No opponent can outrun a sharp pass down the court. Thus it is the first option to look for after a defensive rebound regardless of whether game strategy calls for a fast break or simply moving the ball quickly and safely up the court.

Several types of passes can be used to get the ball to a teammate breaking down the court. The long air pass (baseball or one-handed pass) is used when a teammate outlet is open at the other end of the court. The two-handed overhead pass is used when a teammate is positioned from the free-throw lane to the midcourt area and no opponent is in the line of the pass; the overhead pass is the most common outlet pass. The two-handed chest pass is used to get the ball to a teammate who has broken open to the side or the middle of the court within 10 to 30 feet (about 3 to 9 meters) from the passer. Because there is often less traffic on the sides of the court than in the middle, players should be taught to look first for open teammates in this area, on the rebound side of the court, before looking to the middle.

Successful passing is the responsibility not only of the passer but also of the catcher, and coaches should teach players to get open after a teammate has claimed a defensive rebound. If the opportunity to beat an opponent down the court is available, a player should take advantage of it. Guards should be instructed to move quickly to a spot where the rebounder can get the ball to them. A particularly good spot for guards to position themselves for an outlet pass after a rebound is on the rebound side of the court—between the opponent's free-throw line and the half-court line—with their backs to the sideline to allow them to see the whole floor (especially defenders) with big vision. See figure 8.14.

Good basketball teams retain possession of the ball after defensive rebounds. Coaches must emphasize that the transition from defense to offense can lead to either a successful offensive possession or a return to defense, depending on how players handle the ball.

CRITICAL CUE
Use an outlet pass or a two-dribble push to start the fast break or clear the ball.

CRITICAL CUE
Perimeter players move quickly to receive an outlet pass:
- Between the opponent's free-throw line and the half-court line
- With the back or butt to the side-line to enable big vision of the perimeter player receiving the outlet pass.

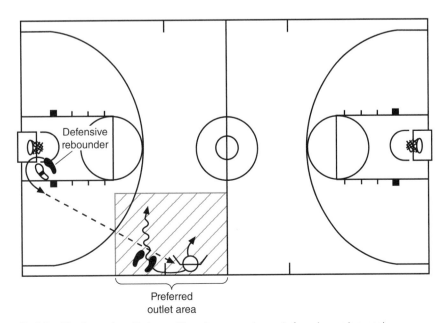

Figure 8.14 Preferred outlet position for guard on defensive rebound.

Dribbling the Ball Certain players should not be put in the position of dribbling the ball from one end of the court to the other. However, it has recently become more common for coaches to allow players to take a rebounded ball the length of the court using the dribble. As bigger and better players develop the ability to rebound and dribble safely, the benefits of this full-court maneuver have become apparent.

One major advantage of having a defensive rebounder dribble the ball to the other end of the court is that it eliminates the possibility of passing errors; there can be no errant pass if there is no outlet pass. In addition, the rebounder or dribbler can quickly assume the middle position on the fast break without having to wait for a teammate to get open. Players must be able to respond to this situation quickly. Therefore, teammates should practice spreading out quickly and filling the passing lanes as they run down the court.

Having defensive rebounders dribble the ball usually creates a numerical advantage over the opposition. Because one or more opponents are often slow to react in making the transition from offense to defense, a defensive rebounder or dribbler can get down the court ahead of them. If players are trained to recognize the situation quickly and hurry down the court, the team can frequently create a 5-on-4 or even 5-on-3 advantage. Almost all big players can be taught to rebound, pivot and face up the court, use one or two dribbles (two-dribble push) to clear the ball, use a quick stop, chin the ball, and look for a clear pass ahead to a better ballhandling teammate to continue the fast break.

OFFENSIVE REBOUNDING

A coach must decide on a rebounding philosophy, especially on offense. Generally, all players should have the same assignments and use the same rules as for defensive rebounding. On offense, coaches decide which offensive players should be assigned to go to the boards (go to a gap) as offensive rebounders and which players should transition back to defense. Most teams have three players rebound and two players get back on defense (one as a full safety and one to stop the advancing of the ball). For a more aggressive approach, a team could send four players to rebound and assign only one safety or fullback to get back on defense.

Offensive rebounding is especially difficult in a successful ball–defender–basket defense because defensive players have an advantage in the contest to get inside position. However, offensive players can gain an edge by knowing when and where a shot is going to be taken. Therefore, coaches should emphasize the need for players to anticipate shots by teammates, as well as to react to their own shots. Otherwise, offensive players have difficulty succeeding against good defensive rebounders. It is not always possible to get around a rebounder who is in proper position for blocking out; moreover, players should not go over the defensive rebounder's back when trying to get an offensive rebound because doing so can lead to being called for a foul. With both hands up, however, an offensive rebounder may be able to tip the ball out to a teammate and thus keep possession of the ball.

The primary positioning objectives for an offensive rebounder are as follows (in order of importance): Players should go to a gap, not a back (figure 8.15); get an inside position and block out the defender; get at least even with the defender by going to one side and around to the basket; make contact with and

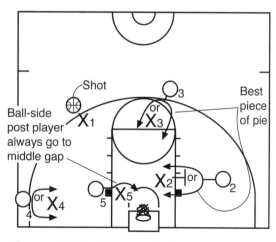

Figure 8.15 "O" boards: Go to a gap—know where the shot is taken and go to the best gap where more rebounds are likely to fall (i.e., get the best piece of pie). For example, on help side (weak side), go to the gap toward the baseline, and on shots from the middle, go to either gap; ball-side post player always goes to middle gap (get two rebounders to the weak side).

nudge the inside defender under the basket, pinning the defender inside by chesting with the hands up (figure 8.16); and tap to self or a teammate only to keep the ball alive if they can't get both hands on the ball.

The techniques for going to a gap are the V-cut and swim move (primary) and the rear-turn roll. On the shot, the offensive rebounder selects the best gap by the defender (depending on position and predicted rebound location) and makes a V-cut to the gap. When blocked out, the offensive rebounder executes a tap with the outside hand or arm, followed by a forceful, quick overhead swim stroke with the near hand or arm to get at least even with the defender in the hands-up position (figure 8.17). Another move for getting by or at least even with a defender is the rear-turn roll, which is best used against a physically aggressive defender who actively blocks out. The offensive player meets the contact with the forward leg in the direction of the desired gap. Using that foot to make contact and as the turning foot, the offensive rebounder makes a 180-degree rear turn to get the stepping foot outside the defender's foot in the desired gap (figure 8.18, *a* and *b*). Then, using that stepping foot as the new turning foot, the rebounder uses a 180-degree front turn to get by the defender at the gap in a hands-up position (figure 8.18*c*). This technique requires using the EPF turning skill, as shown in figure 8.18.

To review, offensive rebounding is important because it gives the offensive team another opportunity to score. This new life also discourages defensive players, who have lost a chance to gain possession of the basketball. Many options are available to the offensive rebounder.

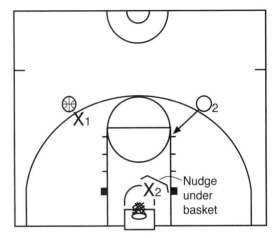

Figure 8.16 "O" boards: Block in when the defense is too close under the basket.

Figure 8.17 Offensive rebound techniques for going to a gap: *(a)* V-cut to the gap, tap with the outside hand, and use the inside hand to swim through with an overhand stroke; *(b)* move to the inside position with the hands up. (*Note:* Offensive player's hands should be up in photo *b*.)

Figure 8.18 Rear-turn roll for offensive rebounding: *(a)* Meet blockout contact with the turning foot, *(b)* use a 180-degree rear turn to get outside, and *(c)* use a 180-degree front turn into the gap with the head up.

Shooting After Rebounding

When a player gets an offensive rebound, the first option is to quickly shoot the ball with a power move to the basket. Players should first look to shoot, and then, if this is not possible, pass to an open teammate (passing outside for a three-pointer is a good option) before finally exercising the option of dribbling (choose action over reaction). Coaches should emphasize that the moment after a rebound is a very good time to take advantage of the defense. Because the defensive opponent was unable to prevent the offensive player from getting in position for the rebound, the defender may also be in a poor position to defend against a shot. In addition, the defense is packed inside to block out, and the three-point field-goal area is usually open after an offensive rebound, especially near the rebound area. An offensive rebounder can take a shot either without dribbling (preferred) or after dribbling.

Tips If players are skilled enough and big enough, they should tip the ball back toward the basket or out to a teammate outside the rebound area. *Tipping* is a misleading term for a leaping player who shoots a rebounded ball before returning to the floor. Tips that involve slapping at the ball with one hand are usually unsuccessful. Instead, coaches can teach players to catch the ball with the elbows locked and shoot it with both hands if possible (tip with two hands). Tipping the ball outside to an open teammate away from the congested rebound area is also a viable offensive rebound option.

Tipping the ball is the most efficient way to take advantage of defensive players who are out of position. By not bringing the ball down from the jump, offensive rebounders take away the defenders' opportunity to recover and give them almost no chance to block the tip attempt. However, before coaches suggest the tip as a rebounding option, they should make sure that their players are physically mature and sufficiently skilled.

The tip is often too difficult for beginning players but provides an excellent option for more skilled players.

Shots Without Dribbling Coaches should encourage players to go up with the shot after a rebound without putting the ball on the floor. Dribbling takes time and allows the defense to recover. It also exposes the ball to the defense, making it more likely that a defender will steal or deflect the ball. If players have learned the correct rebound-jumping technique, they should land with the ball ready to go back up for the shot. They can shoot the ball from either an overhead position (explode to score from the forehead) or from a chin-it position, but they should always keep the ball up.

Players often develop the bad habit of dribbling the ball right after they get it from a pass or a rebound. To counter this tendency, coaches should highlight instances when players do *not* put the ball on the floor after rebounding and praise them for it.

A good time to help players develop the habit of going back up with a shot after a rebound is during individual shooting practices. On every missed shot, players should hustle for the rebound, get their balance, and, with the shoulders square to the basket, go back up for another shot: Keep the ball overhead and explode to the basket; chin the ball and explode; or chin the ball, do a shot fake, and explode. Players should continue to shoot and rebound until they make the basket and then start over from a new spot on the court. In this way, shooting without dribbling after an offensive rebound can become an automatic response.

Shots After Dribbling Although it should be avoided whenever possible, it is occasionally acceptable for a player who has grabbed an offensive rebound to dribble before shooting. One obvious example is when a player grabs a rebound far away from the basket and has an open lane to the goal. Because this situation presents an easy scoring opportunity, the player should dribble the ball in for the layup (attack the basket with one power dribble). Another option is to dribble out of the lane in order to clear the ball from a congested area.

Passing After Rebounding

The player who has captured an offensive rebound can also pass the basketball to a teammate. The pass is the second option (after shooting) that players should look for after getting an offensive rebound. When they turn to the basket to look for the open shot after the rebound, they should also locate any open teammates (big vision) to whom they could pass the ball for an easy shot, especially a three-pointer. Coaches can encourage offensive players to take advantage of defenders' having to recover after the rebound, either by taking a shot or by passing to a teammate (usually outside) who has a good shot. Coach John Wooden believed that a good option is to pass out of the collapsed defense that results from an offensive rebound and set up a teammate for a trey.

Sometimes an offensive team chooses to reset the offense, either to run a play or to take more time off the clock. In that case, the option to shoot is the lowest priority for the offensive rebounder, and passing and dribbling are the more preferred options.

Dribbling After Rebounding

In most situations, the offensive rebounder should dribble only if a shot or a pass is impossible. Usually, dribbling only gives the defensive players an opportunity to recover and possibly steal the ball, especially since the offensive rebounder is often surrounded by defenders. Therefore, coaches should continually advise players to look first for a shot and then for a passing opportunity before dribbling after they get an offensive rebound.

CRITICAL CUE Offensive rebound options—score, pass, or dribble (in that order).

COACHING POINTS FOR REBOUNDING

- Rebounding is the responsibility of all players on the team.
- Good rebounding is closely associated with ball possession, fast breaks, and winning.
- The most important principle of rebounding is to assume that the shot will be missed; this assumption initiates an automatic response to do the assigned task in *that* situation (offense or defense).
- The 2-and-2 rebound technique is most effective: Rebound from two feet with two hands.
- The hands should be kept up when players block out or are positioned near the basket (offense or defense).
- The best overall rebounding technique emphasizes blocking out the opposing player as follows:
  - Be aware when a shot is taken and assume that it will miss.
  - Find, go to, and block out an opponent (*blast and box*) while attending to the direction and distance of the shot. *Hit* the opponent.
  - Go to (pursue) and capture the ball and get it into the protected position under the chin (pursue the ball; capture and chin the ball). *Get* the ball.
- The most important specific technique of rebounding is to chin the ball (*chin it— protect it when you get it, and then pivot (turn) to protect and clear the ball from congestion*).
- Offensive rebounders should assume a miss and *go to a gap (not a back)* with the hands up.
- Offensive rebounders should use the 2-and-2 technique and look to shoot, pass, or dribble—in that order.
- Defensive rebounders should *blast, box, and board* (pursue the ball); some coaches prefer the *hit and get* terminology.
- Defensive rebounders should either pass, dribble, or hold the ball, depending on their skills and the situation.

REBOUNDING ASSESSMENT

Coaches should keep rebounding statistics for each player and for the team as a whole. Offensive and defensive rebounds should be recorded separately to help identify players who have success or difficulty in rebounding at a particular end of the court. This information may reveal a problem with a player's offensive or defensive rebounding technique or indicate that a player is not hustling enough at one end of the court. Individual rebounding statistics are just some of the many pieces of information that coaches can use to evaluate the contribution of each player, particularly those positioned nearest the basket.

An excellent team goal is to get 60 percent of all rebounds—30 percent in offensive rebounding situations and 80 percent in defensive rebounding situations. Goals based on percentages are generally better than goals based on number of rebounds because they are valid for all styles of play (e.g., slow or fast).

Assessment of individual rebounding can also be carried out in terms of a percentage by comparing the number of times a player did the *assigned job* with the total number of rebounding opportunities. This approach to assessment measures the *process* that leads to the desired outcome of obtaining rebounds. For instance, a player with an offensive rebound efficiency of 70 percent might have done the job correctly 14 times in 20 situations (i.e., 20 shot attempts by the team), thus requiring a coach or program assistant to define and evaluate all 20 possessions and decide whether the player passed or failed on each. For instance, on a given shot attempt, did the offensive rebounder go to a gap (V-cut and swim move or rear-turn roll or nudge under the basket), make a 2-and-2 attempt to capture the rebound and (if captured) chin the ball, and, finally, protect or turn away from danger? In another example, if a player is a designated safety on the shot attempt, did he or she sprint back to half-court before the shot hit the rim in order to prevent the layup and organize the defense? In this way, the whole *process* of individual rebounding is graded on a pass-fail basis; in other words, a player is graded (pass or fail) on the whole process of meeting assigned responsibilities in each offensive or defensive rebound situation.

Assessment of individual defensive rebounding is more challenging, and coaches must remember that each player should be graded on each attempt; grade the *process*. For example, when an assigned offensive player is inside the three-point arc, did the defender blast, box, and board; put the hands up on the blockout near the basket; and actively pursue, capture, and chin the ball with a 2-and-2 rebound move (*hit and get*)? Defensive rebounding efficiency can be expressed as a percentage by dividing number of successful rebound attempts (i.e., instances of performing the assigned task) by the total number of shot attempts by the opponent. A goal of 80 percent is a reasonable but challenging target for defensive rebounding efficiency (again, as a measure of player *process*). If players do their rebounding job 80 percent of the time, the team will be a successful rebounding team. Remember: This efficiency does not require getting the rebound (although doing so certainly enhances a team's chances of winning!).

Rebound percentages can be tracked in practices and in games; in either setting, one evaluator can directly rate two players at a time. In practices, evaluators can chart any competition situation that involves offense and defense (1-on-1, 2-on-2, and so on up to 5-on-5). The two players selected should remain anonymous during each practice, and the results should be totaled, announced, and posted after each practice. For games, video analysis allows a coach (given enough time) to assess each player on each possession in order to determine percentages for offensive, defensive, and total rebounding efficiency. Assessment should be performed at least every fifth game to ensure realistic feedback in order to change players' behavior and enhance learning. Assessment experts advise that regular, periodic assessments—as well as status and progress reports—are needed in order to enhance learning and change players' rebounding behavior. The totals for all individual players can be used to obtain team percentages for rebounding efficiency (offensive, defensive, and total).

TROUBLESHOOTING

The following list identifies common rebounding errors and possible remedies. Coaches should provide appropriate feedback in order to change players' behavior and enhance their learning.

- **Problem:** Lack of motivation to rebound

  Correction: Review the importance of and rationale for rebounding and sell players on technique, effort, and the benefits of rebounding success.

(continued)

- **Problem:** Errors in rebounding in terms of the "big bullets" of rebounding

  Correction:

  - Assume: Evaluate to ensure that each shot attempt prompts each player to know, understand, and try to carry out his or her rebounding responsibility.
  - Hands up: Practice and correct or reinforce this position until it becomes automatic. For this purpose, an assistant coach can stand on the baseline under the basket to provide feedback on the hands-up skill for either offensive or defensive players.
  - 2-and-2: Penalize players for losing the ball on one-foot or one-handed rebounding (unless they are tipping to self or a teammate).
  - Remind players to capture, chin, and turn away from danger: Reinforce these points, and (as a last resort) levy penalties for losing possession of the ball.

- **Problem:** Losing or failing to capture the ball

  Correction: Check 2-and-2 technique. Stand under the basket to see if players are capturing the ball with a *click* (using both hands) and with both eyes open and focused on the ball. Beginners often close their eyes during contact rebounding.

- **Problem:** Small rebounding pocket on defense (defenders not going quickly to the assigned player to block out—blast or make contact—first)

  Correction: This problem often results from defenders following the flight of the ball on a shot attempt (i.e., being ball watchers or rebound spectators). Teach them to see the defender first (make visual contact after a shot attempt). In other words, they must locate the assigned offensive player both visually (see the player) and then physically (block the player). Visual contact comes before physical contact.

- **Problem:** Hands down (feeling or holding the opponent with the arms down behind when rebounding)

  Correction: Caution players that it is illegal to hold when blocking out and impossible to capture the quick rebound in a hands-down position (on offense or defense). Players should keep the hands up for the quick rebound, make contact with radar bumpers, and use active feet to maintain contact until pursuing the ball. They should get the elbows level with the shoulders and make "arms of steel" when blocking out.

- **Problem:** Rebounding only overhead or near the basket

  Correction: Focus on angle-jumping out of the one's area at less than vertical angles (60 to 85 degrees), as well as using 2-and-2 technique to capture the ball with balance and protection. Emphasize that the only rebounds available *under* the basket come from made shots.

- **Problem:** Dangling the ball or putting it overhead and away from the power or chin-it position

  Correction: Losing the ball after a rebound typically results from failing to capture and chin the ball. Have players attack rebounders in practice: slap from under, pressure, reach over, or bat the dangling ball.

- **Problem:** Failure to use a pivot or turn away from danger after a rebound is secured

  Correction: On defensive rebounds, add a two-dribble push move to clear the ball up the floor. On offensive rebounds, add a rear turn and crack-back pass for a three-point field-goal attempt by a teammate.

REBOUNDING DRILLS

Effective rebounding requires players to be aggressive and make legal contact with opponents; therefore, players should be given drills that progressively develop the trait of aggressiveness.

LINE DRILL: 2-AND-2 REBOUND PROGRESSION ▶

Purpose: To teach 2-and-2 and capture-and-chin-it rebound techniques

Equipment: Half court, one basketball per line

Procedure: The drill begins without the ball as players use the 2-and-2 rebound technique to get an imaginary rebound at the free-throw line, the half-court line, the opposite free-throw line, and the opposite baseline. Next, the first player in each line has a basketball and creates a simulated rebound with a two-handed underhand or overhead toss, uses 2-and-2 rebound technique, captures and chins the ball, and uses an EPF turn technique away from an imaginary defender to pass to the next person in line, who repeats the sequence.

Here is the learning progression:

- Get an imaginary 2-and-2 rebound.
- Toss the ball directly overhead and get a 2-and-2 rebound.
- Toss the ball to the right, left, or in front to force rebounders to use 2-and-2 technique to rebound out of their area—that is, to angle-jump to the left, right, or forward to capture and chin the ball.
- A variation is to use a coach at the top of the key level as the tosser for each line for the first three progressions (see previous bullets).
- Toss the ball overhead in pairs. The second person can contest the rebound and pressure the rebounder to check the chin-it position and turn move. The rebounder must pivot away from pressure and execute an outlet pass back to the next person in line.
- Practice a two-dribble push upcourt. The rebounder can get a 2-and-2 rebound, capture and chin the ball, pivot away from pressure, and practice the two-dribble push toward the half-court line. After completing the sequence with a quick stop, the rebounder can pivot and execute an outlet pass back to the next person on the baseline.

LINE DRILL: DEFENSIVE REBOUND PROGRESSION ▶

Purpose: To teach the techniques of defensive rebounding through simulation

Equipment: Half court (minimum)

Procedure: Players are organized in four lines on the baseline. When the coach gives the verbal command *shot*, the first player in each line sprints onto the court 6 to 15 feet (1.8 to 4.6 meters) from the basket in defensive closeout position and then uses the blast-box-board (hit-and-get) technique to obtain an imaginary defensive rebound. Each player simulates the blockout, captures the imaginary rebound, chins the ball, and makes an outlet pass using EPF technique. Then the next four players sprint onto the floor in basic position or quick stance for defense.

Variations

- *"D" boards help-side box:* The first four players sprint onto the floor in an offensive basic stance near the free-throw line extended, and the next four assume a proper defensive basic position to support the defender (who is *pointing pistols* at the imaginary ball and the player being guarded) while facing a sideline. On the *shot* command, all four defenders carry out defensive rebounding assignments, and all must make contact at the free-throw line. No ball is needed for this variation.

- *"D" boards with a ball (blocking the shooter):* The four defensive players on the baseline each have a ball in triple-threat position. They each pass to the corresponding offensive player at the free-throw line, then close out from off-the-ball to on-the-ball position to prevent the drive and contest the shot. The offensive player catches the ball with the feet in the air and ready to shoot, executes a shot fake, and then shoots a short shot to an imaginary basket from 12 to 15 feet (3.7 to 4.6 meters) away by focusing on shooting up (not out) and holding the follow-through until the ball hits the floor. The shooter then serves as the buddy coach for defender by checking his or her defensive rebounding technique. The shooter coaches the buddy, who becomes the next shooter and then goes to the back of the line. This variation can be used to practice many "D" board repetitions in a short time.

LINE DRILL: OFFENSIVE REBOUND PROGRESSION

Purpose: To teach players the techniques of offensive rebounding—getting past the defender to block out, getting to a gap (getting at least even with the defender), and making contact to move the defender closer to the basket (when the defender doesn't move away from the basket to block out)

Equipment: Half court

Procedure: Players are organized in four lines on the baseline. The first four players are positioned at the free-throw line, facing away from the baseline in quick stance with hands up. (For a more realistic perspective, place the lines at the half-court line and the first four players at the top of the key, facing the baseline.) The coach controls the drill with the following commands:

- Swim-move by right or left and block out with hands up.
- Swim-move by right or left and go to a gap.
- Go to a gap with hands up and return to the baseline.

The first player in each line near the free-throw line extended learns the feeling of the hands-up, ready-to-rebound position, then moves to the back of the line; the second person in line practices offensive rebounding technique past them and then becomes the first in line (*hands up, ready to rebound*). The drill is performed without a ball and allows many repetitions of basic offensive rebounding technique in a short time. The same procedure can be carried out to practice the rear-turn roll. The offensive player approaches the defender from behind, places one foot or knee in the middle of the defender (split legs), and performs a rear turn and then a front turn to get to the gap and by the defender.

LINE DRILL: PIVOT-AND-PASS PROGRESSION

Purpose: To teach basic rebounding rules with special emphasis on the pivot-and-pass to avoid committing an offensive foul while clearing the defender with the elbow

Equipment: Half court, one ball per line

Procedure: Players are organized in four lines on the baseline. The first four players step onto the court from the baseline to start the drill.

- *Toss-and-turn:* The first player in each line starts with the ball and uses a two-handed underhand toss out of the area (not overhead) high enough to allow the same player to get a 2-and-2 rebound, capture and chin it, and finish with a pivot-and-pass EPF move to pass to the next player in line, who catches the ball with the feet in the air while moving onto the court. The catcher then repeats the toss-and-turn sequence and passes to the next player in line, and so on.

- *Bounce-and-turn:* This is a similar drill starting from four lines, but in this version the next person in line starts the drill with a two-handed bounce pass off the floor to a simulated rebound spot above and out of the rebounder's area. The rebounder gets a two-handed capture-and-chin rebound followed by a pivot move and pass to the next person in line.

REBOUND AND OUTLET ⊙

Purpose: To teach players the skill of taking a defensive rebound off the backboard and making an outlet pass (or dribble)

Equipment: One ball per basket (option: two lines operating simultaneously, one on each side of the basket)

Procedure: Have the receiver call the passer's name while breaking to get open. All passes should be caught with the feet in the air. The first player, X_1, passes to X_4, gets open for a return pass, receives it with a quick stop in the free-throw lane, and tosses the ball underhand above the rectangle level to simulate a defensive rebound (figure 8.19). Player X_1 angle-jumps to the ball, captures it with two hands, brings it to the forehead, makes a front turn on the right pivot foot, makes an outlet pass to X_4, and takes the place of X_4.

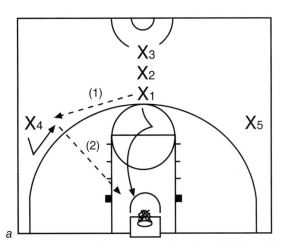 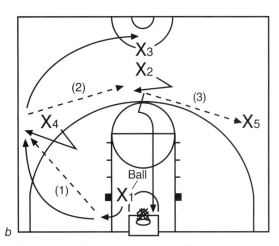

Figure 8.19 Rebound-and-outlet drill for defensive rebounding: *(a)* start and *(b)* continuation (changing sides).

Player X_4 passes to X_2 and goes to the back of the line. The sequence is repeated on the other side with players X_2, X_5, and X_3.

Variation: The outlet lines can be placed at the half-court line, and the defensive rebounders can use a two-dribble push, make a quick stop, and deliver an outlet pass.

REBOUND NUMBER

Purpose: To practice seeing the opponent and the ball when a shot is taken

Equipment: Ball and basket

Procedure: Divide players into pairs and assign two or three pairs per basket. Put two players on offense and two on defense—one offensive–defensive pair on each side of the lane, halfway between the baseline and the free-throw line. A coach is positioned at each free-throw line with a ball. The defensive player on each side of the lane assumes a basic position and guards the offensive player. The offensive players begin to move to get open, and the coach can pass to them if they get free. Otherwise, the coach takes a shot, and each offensive player immediately raises a hand and holds up a certain number of fingers as they rebound. The defensive players try to block out the offensive players and get the rebound. If one of the defensive players gets the rebound and both defenders correctly name the number of fingers held up by their offensive opponent, then the offensive players switch to defense during the next repetition of the drill as defense switches to offense.

CLOSEOUT AND BLOCKOUT

Purpose: To simulate team competition in a controlled 1-on-1, 2-on-2, or 3-on-3 rebounding situation that includes on-the-ball and off-the-ball blockouts

Equipment: Ball, basket, and half court

Procedure: To start the drill, one, two, or three offensive players are positioned 15 to 18 feet (4.6 to 5.5 meters) from the basket, and the corresponding number of defensive players are positioned under the basket. The drill is played as a competitive make-it-take-it exercise that is restarted only when a basket is made. In defensive rebounding situations, the defense must clear the ball above the top of the key area before changing to offense. The coach may require the three defenders to stay on defense whenever an assignment is missed.

LINE DRILL: FULL-COURT OFFENSIVE BOARDS WITHOUT THE BALL

Purpose: To teach offensive rebounding skills by simulation

Equipment: Half court (minimum)

Procedure: Players are in four lines at baseline. The first four players make a get-ahead-or-get-even move from basic position, move to the free-throw line area, jump quickly, simulate capturing the ball, land in the chin-it position, and use a designated scoring move. They repeat this process at the half-court line, the opposite free-throw line, and the opposite baseline. The return is made when all groups of four reach the end line. Players should maintain proper offensive spacing (15 to 18 feet, or 4.6 to 5.5 meters) from the player immediately ahead.

HANDS-UP, FIGURE-8, BACKBOARD-PASSING REBOUND

Purpose: To teach players to control the rebound and *always* keep both hands up when rebounding

Equipment: One ball per basket

Procedure: The drill starts with three players at a basket—two on one side of the basket and one on the other side. On the overloaded side with two players, the first player starts the drill with a pass off the backboard (above the rectangle) to the next player on the opposite side of the basket. The object is for the group to perform continuous, controlled, two-handed tipping or chin-it rebounding for a given number of repetitions. Players tip or rebound and then go behind the next player on the opposite side of the basket while keeping their hands up throughout the drill.

Most players need to rebound the ball with a two-footed, two-handed approach and a chin-it or "ball-to-forehead" move and then go back up with an offensive scoring move designated by the coach (ball overhead, power shot, or shot fake and power shot). Rebounders should keep the feet at right angles to the baseline (point the toes at the baseline) and shoot the ball above the rectangle so that it rebounds from the backboard to the next rebounder. All players keep their hands up as they move continuously in a figure-eight movement pattern back and forth across the lane (2-and-2 rebound, shot across backboard and above rectangle, and going behind the player on the other side with the hands up). After a coaching goal is met—for instance, 10 passes and the last one makes a basket—the coach can have players each make one-and-one free throws before continuing; a free-throw miss by any player restarts the drill.

GARBAGE ▶

Purpose: To teach players to score on an offensive rebound

Equipment: Two balls per basket

Procedure: Two lines of players are positioned at the free-throw line area while facing the basket; each line has a ball. The first player in each line passes the ball to the backboard with a two-handed underhand toss, rebounds the ball, and then uses a designated scoring move. After scoring (and only after scoring), the player passes the ball to the next player in line and goes to the end of the opposite line. Each player assumes a miss and continues rebounding until the basket is made. Players use the following scoring moves:

- Two-handed tip and score
- Overhead (ball on the forehead with two hands), quick jump to score
- Chin-it and score
- Chin-it, fake (lifting the ball head-high and keeping the legs locked), and score
- Chin-it, pass to an outlet (player in line) for a trey

A final competition phase of the garbage drill can be added to teach aggressiveness and scoring in the lane. The coach has one ball at the free-throw line and works with two players at a time, one from each line. The coach usually shoots the ball and players rebound until one captures the ball and scores. On a loose ball, players should use a two-handed rebound or two-handed pickup and chin it. The player with the ball must score in the lane without dribbling while the other player defends. There are no out-of-bounds areas, and the ball handler may use the coach for a release pass (which is returned if a quick move to get open is used).

NO-BABIES-ALLOWED (NBA) OR SURVIVAL REBOUNDING ▶

Purpose: To teach aggressiveness

Equipment: One ball per basket

Procedure: Groups of four to eight players are positioned at each basket; three players from each basket are in the game at any given time. If six to eight players are used, extra players should be shooting free throws until they are rotated into the game. The next player rotating in waits inside the arc ready to replace one of the three players in the drill as they meet the goal and rotate out. See figure 8.20. A coach or manager is positioned at each basket to shoot the ball (intentionally missing) and act as a passing outlet for the rebounder. The rules of competition are as follows:

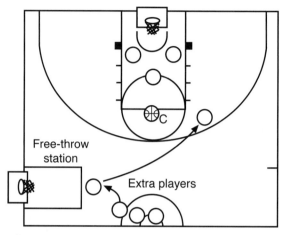

Figure 8.20 No-babies-allowed (NBA) rebounding.

- Play starts with a missed shot.

- All three players try to get the rebound.

- The player who obtains the rebound is on offense, and the other two players become defenders. Rebounders use scoring moves; all shots must be taken in the free-throw lane without dribbling.

- The rebounder may outlet to the coach and get open for a return pass in the lane.

- There is no out-of-bounds area.

- Scoring three baskets allows a player to rotate out (the other players retain their totals). When starting, the best variation is one scored basket to move out of the drill and into the line that feeds players into the drill.

- Significant fouls are the only ones called by the coach; a player may lose a score by fouling or by not playing defense.

INDIVIDUAL REBOUNDING

Purpose: To have players practice rebounding skills on their own

Equipment: Ball, basket, and toss-back rebounding device (or a partner)

Procedure: Players carry out rebounding options at game speed using the two-footed, two-handed rebounding technique.

Options

- Toss the ball against the backboard or above the rim with a two-handed underhand toss to create a rebound, then use an angle jump to capture the ball and make an offensive scoring move (overhead; chin and score; chin, shot fake, and score). Assume a miss.

- Toss the ball to create a defensive rebound. Make a quick outlet pass to the toss-back or the partner or use a two-dribble push to clear the ball.

- Advanced: Players jump as high and as quickly as they can and pop the ball against the backboard with two hands on each jump.

- Place the ball on the free-throw lane block. Players grab it with two hands, explode to the backboard, and score from 2 feet (0.6 meter) without gathering: Capture, chin, and explode to the basket. Then place the ball on the opposite block and repeat the drill.

- Super rebounds: Players start outside the lane and pass the ball off the backboard above the rectangle to the other side of the lane. They take one step into the lane, jump over to get the rebound, and land on two feet outside the lane on the other side. Repeat five times and finish with a power-move score.

REBOUND PROGRESSION: 3-ON-0, 3-ON-3

Purpose: To provide a three-player format to review and practice rebounding skills as a team and as part of a practice or a game warm-up

Equipment: Ball, basket, half court, and three air dummies (if available)

Procedure: Half of the team performs the drill near the basket while the other half stretches or performs other skill work. The drill includes two sections:

1. In the offensive (3-on-0) team-rebounding section, the coach controls the drill and shoots the ball from one side of the court to create the rebound. Variations include the following:

   - Regular 3-on-0 at any three positions: On the shot, the low-post player rebounds to the middle toward the weak side to get two rebounders to the weak side.
   - Tip up (to keep alive) and tip out.
   - Out-of-bounds save: The coach bounces the ball toward the out-of-bounds area; a *saver* and a *savee* (a teammate not pursuing the ball) communicate verbally (*ball* and *help*).
   - 3-on-3 with air dummies or dummy defenders: Offensive players must go to a gap and rebound.
   - No babies allowed: The player who gets the rebound tries to score while the other two players harass. All three offensive rebounders assume a miss, rebound until a score, and then sprint toward the half-court line (or to the top of the key) with vision on the ball and the basket over the inside shoulder.

2. The defensive (3-on-3) team-rebounding section uses three air dummies or dummy offensive players to block out. When the coach shoots, the three defenders blast and pursue (*hit and get*) and either outlet the ball to the coach or execute a two-dribble push outlet and then pass to the coach. Follow the BOPCRO sequence: *Block out* (or blast), *pursue* and *chin*, *rebound*, and *outlet*.

CUTTHROAT REBOUNDING: 3-ON-3, 4-ON-4 ▶

Purpose: To simulate gamelike offensive and defensive rebounding in a continuous, coach-controlled drill

Equipment: Ball, basket, half court, three groups of players (three or four per group) separately identified (e.g., red, white, and blue)

Procedure: Begin with a group on offense, a group on defense, and a group behind the baseline underneath the basket. The coach has the ball and is underneath the basket behind the baseline to start and control the drill. Two outlet receivers are positioned near the sideline near half-court. The rotation is as follows: As a shot is missed, both offensive and defensive groups rebound. If the defensive group gets the ball, the players use the BOP-CRO sequence to the outlet and move to offense, and the baseline group comes in on defense. If the offensive group gets a rebound, the players stay on offense (after a score, they transition to half-court and stay on offense). The baseline group again comes in on defense. The ball is always returned to the coach to continue the drill for the designated period of time. Winners can be determined by getting the most defensive rebounds, the most offensive rebounds, or the most points scored; any of these options can be emphasized by the coach.

WAR REBOUNDING

Purpose: To emphasize aggressive defensive or offensive rebounding in a 5-on-5 situation

Equipment: Ball, basket, half court

Procedure: This live drill begins with the coach shooting the ball (and missing most of the time). The drill is played on live, made, or missed shots without regard to out-of-bounds lines in order to get players to capture, secure, and chin the ball in all circumstances. The usual scoring scheme is 1 point for a defensive rebound, 2 points for a score, and 3 points for an offensive rebound. Coaches can emphasize offense or defense by giving points to that phase only and allowing a team to stay in the scoring mode when players score; for instance, if a group makes a defensive rebound score, it stays on defense. The drill can be done for a certain time period or played to a certain score. It can be started with many variations, such as the following:

- Closeouts: Defenders start on the baseline, pass to an offensive player or pass to the coach for the shot.
- Make a skip pass, then shoot.
- Use a secondary fast-break set, swing the ball, and then shoot.
- Start from a zone defense.
- Use any special offensive set or situation, then shoot.

Wooden Wisdom

"Be more concerned with your character than your reputation, because your character is what you really are, while your reputation is merely what others think you are."

—John Wooden

CHAPTER 9

TEAM OFFENSE

"Basketball is a game of finesse and reason, especially on offense."

Phil Jackson, Naismith Hall of Fame coach, Chicago Bulls and Los Angeles Lakers
(Jackson used a concept from a Lakota Indian war chant: "Don't overpower; outsmart the opponent.")

oaches should instill in players the confidence to go all out—to have fun, to learn and improve, and to take chances and make mistakes, especially on offense. By preparing players to handle all situations and helping them improve their basketball IQ, coaches can strengthen their confidence in their ability to succeed. To accomplish this goal, coaches and players must focus on teaching and learning not just plays but *how* to play on offense.

Specifically, in order to prepare the team for all situations, the following areas should be covered: general offensive principles, responsibilities of players at each offensive position, offensive team tactics, and special situations for team offense. As these areas are taught and learned, players and coaches should always remind themselves that every offense is based on fundamentals and that quick and proper execution of those fundamentals is the key to any successful offense.

GENERAL OFFENSIVE PRINCIPLES

Unless coaches are familiar with the offensive strengths and weaknesses of team members, they should select a basic offense that can be adapted to a variety of players and is flexible enough to allow team members to use their individual strengths. The coach's basic philosophy should be stable and should evolve slowly, but the offensive and defensive styles of play should change to fit the players.

Offense depends heavily on proper spacing and timing; all five players should be spread out on the court area, moving and cutting together with the right timing. Any offense should have court balance; that is, it should maintain proper court spacing—about 15 to 18 feet (4.6 to 5.5 meters)—between offensive teammates (unless cutting and screening). Balance also involves producing high-percentage shots with assigned offensive rebounders and assigned players to prepare for defense when a shot is taken. Making the quick transition from offense to defense (and vice versa) is referred to as the transition game—going to get the offensive rebound or to return to defense quickly. In addition, balanced scoring from several players is always better than dependence on a scoring star in a team game. Offensive players need to use their strengths to produce a balanced offense.

A good offense includes both player movement and ball movement and may, with more experienced players, include screening. Scoring should come from the inside (close to the basket) as well as the outside (on the perimeter of the defense). The offense should be developed from the inside out: Establish an inside game and a complementary outside game, thus preventing the defense from concentrating on one area or one player. The *execution* of any system is much more important than the system itself. What a team does is not as critical as how well the players do it; therefore, focus on execution.

PLAYER POSITIONS AND RESPONSIBILITIES

Each player on a basketball team has a position to play that is related to role, ability, and skill. The three basic positions are guard, forward, and center or post (figure 9.1). Some coaches use other names, such as *point*, *wing*, and *inside player*. The authors favor equipping all players with all fundamental skills so they have the flexibility to play positionless basketball where there is more flexibility for players to be interchangeable.

The center is usually the tallest player, with forwards coming next, and guards being the smallest. Centers and forwards tend to be the best rebounders, whereas guards are often the best ball handlers. Guards also tend to play outside more than forwards and

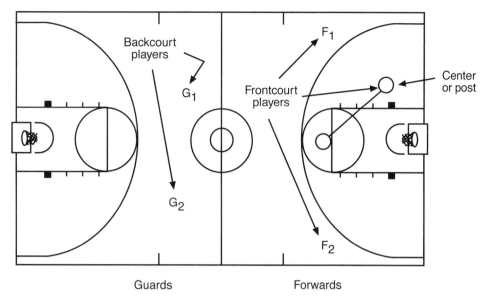

Figure 9.1 Player positions.

centers. No matter what term is used, all perimeter players and all inside players should learn the basic skills so that they can be interchangeable in selected situations. In addition, some coaches favor "positionless" basketball, in which all players are expected to be prepared to play various aspects of the game, regardless of position and skills required.

Guards Grouped together, guards are usually referred to as the team's *backcourt*. This grouping can be broken down further into the point guard (normally the best ball handler and often the player who directs the team on the floor) and shooting guards (also called *big guards* or *off guards*). Because of their dribbling ability, point guards can often create a scoring chance for a teammate (such as the shooting guard) by penetrating and passing—that is, by driving past defenders to the basket and then passing to an unguarded teammate (a move known as a penetrate-and-pitch or drive-and-dish). Thus point guards are called *playmakers* because they direct teammates and create scoring opportunities. The point guard is usually among the best ball handlers on the team and should also be a leader who can serve as a coach on the floor. Shooting guards, on the other hand, should be chosen from the best ball handlers, shooters, and scorers on the team.

Forwards Forwards are sometimes called *corner* players because their normal offensive position is in the corner of the frontcourt. Most teams play a small forward and a big forward (sometimes called the *power forward* or *strong forward*). The small forward is more of a swing player who can play guard or forward and who plays facing the basket, where good ballhandling and outside shooting are essential. In contrast, the big forward is often a strong rebounder who swings from outside to inside (back to the basket). Small forwards should be able to play as a combination guard-forward, handle the ball well, play on the perimeter, and rebound. Big forwards must be able to play as a combination forward-center.

Center or Post Player Players for the center position should be chosen from among the biggest players and those who relish playing inside, near the basket, where contact and congestion are readily accepted. Usually *the* biggest player, the center plays inside, either around the free-throw lane in the high post (near the foul line) or in the low post (close to the basket) and outside the free-throw or three-second lane with the back to the basket. Post players may also play facing the basket on offense—getting the ball in the high post (free-throw lane area) or in the short corner when stepping out from the low or medium post to face the basket (see chapter 6). The center and the two forwards are known collectively as the *frontcourt*. It is recommended that all players develop all fundamental skills, equipping them to crossover positions and enhancing team flexibility.

OFFENSIVE TEAM TACTICS

Coaches develop team tactics to prepare the team to face all basic defensive situations; these tactics include the following essential elements:

- *Defense-to-offense transition game*—primary fast break to keep the defense honest and put immediate pressure on the defense; secondary fast break for use when the defense is back but not fully organized

- *Press offense* to handle ball safely and attack against defensive presses (ranging from half-court to full-court)

- *Player-to-player set offense* for situations in which opponents guard offensive players individually

- *Zone set offense* to be used against zone or area defenses

- *Combination set offense* to be used against combination defenses (which mix zone and player-to-player defenses)

- *Delay or control offense* to use when time and score dictate controlling the game and maintaining ball possession for longer periods before a shot and forcing the opponent to defend a larger court area (with or without a shot clock)

- *Special-situation plays*—for example, jump balls, out-of-bounds plays, free throws, and last-second plays

- *Offense-to-defense transition game* (providing offensive rebounders while preventing easy scores and fast breaks by the opponent)

Primary Fast Break: Transition From Defense to Offense

A team can set up a good shot by running the fast break when it gains possession of the ball and brings it up the court before the opposing players get into a good defensive position. This situation, in which the defense is outnumbered, is called a *primary* fast break (figure 9.2a). The fast break, which usually develops after a rebound or steal (and sometimes after a made basket), is the fastest way to make the transition from defense to offense. As soon as the defense gains control of the ball, it uses an outlet pass or dribble to start the break; passing is the first option and dribbling the last when moving the ball up the court. Then teammates try to beat the defenders up the court while staying spread out; thus they should run at top speed under control. For balance, one player should stay a few steps behind the action in a defensive safety role (often called the fullback).

A typical three-lane fast-break pattern is shown in figure 9.2. A team can effectively use a three-lane fast break (with the ball in the middle) when its players outnumber the opponents in a 3-on-2 situation. In a 3-on-1 scenario, the offense should convert to a two-lane fast break (2-on-1 plus a trailer), as shown in figure 9.3. In a two-lane fast

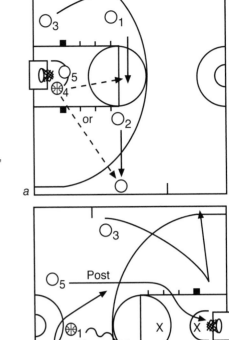

Figure 9.2 Primary fast break: *(a)* starting after a defensive rebound, *(b)* spreading out and filling the lanes, and *(c)* completing a three-lane fast break.

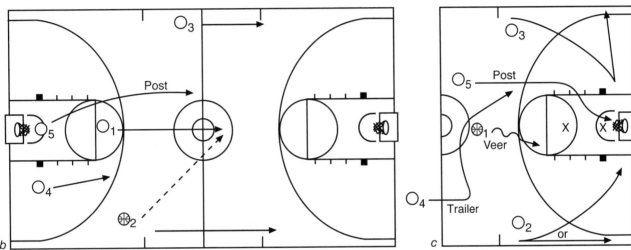

break, the offensive players should split the floor (stay at least as wide as the free-throw lane) to make the defender commit. The best ball handler should handle the ball at the completion and *go to the glass unless forced to pass.* The dribbler always needs to offset the middle staying to the side of the lane, preferably dribbling with the outside hand in the 2-on-1 situation. Advanced players can dribble with the inside hand (which makes it easier to push a bounce pass by the defender) or shoot the reverse layback shot if the defender doesn't pick up or guard the dribbler on defense.

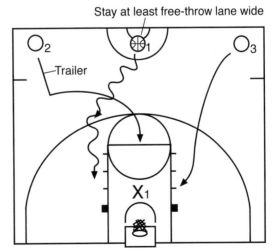

Figure 9.3 Primary two-lane fast break finish: Offensive players should stay at least as wide as the free-throw lane, attacking the basket from the edges of the free-throw lane— (i.e., stay out of the middle of the free-throw lane with the ball).

Secondary Fast Break: Transition From Defense to Offense

If a primary fast break (outnumbering the defense 3-on-2, 3-on-1, or 2-on-1) is not available, then the team should employ a secondary fast break. This tactic keeps pressure on the defense by taking the ball up the side to the baseline (which flattens or collapses the defense), posting a player inside, and reversing the ball from a 4-out–1-in formation to the second side before flowing into the set offense (figure 9.4).

Transition Game (Alternative Secondary Fast-Break System) This alternative fast-break system is used by coach Craig Nelson with his team at Washington High School in Sioux Falls, South Dakota. It employs the following patterns in which players run the floor from defense to offense every time down the floor:

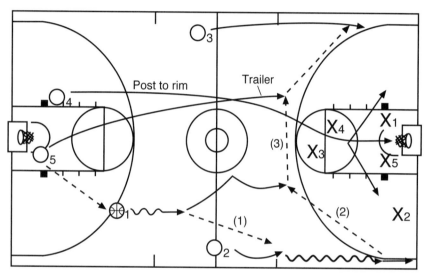

Figure 9.4 Secondary fast break (four out, one in).

- Player 1 (point guard) tries to get all outlets on the side of the floor where the rebound is taken while getting as high and wide up the floor as a safe outlet will allow.

- Player 2 (shooting guard) always runs the right wing, making sure to get within 3 feet (1 meter) of the sideline when crossing half-court.

- Player 3 (small forward) always runs the left wing, getting as wide as possible before crossing half-court—within a couple feet (0.7 meter) of the sideline.

- Players 4 and 5 (the "bigs") are interchangeable. The one who gets the rebound becomes the trailer, and the other one sprints from rim to rim. After throwing the outlet pass, the trailer stays at least two or three steps behind the point guard and usually runs directly down the middle of the court to maintain proper spacing (15 to 18 feet, or 4.6 to 5.5 meters) from the point guard. If the point guard is unable to pass the ball ahead to player 2 or player 3 on the wing, then the trailer will need to throw a quick reversal pass to get the ball to the other side of the court. If neither player 4 nor player 5 gets the rebound, then they are in a race to become the first one down the floor and get a layup or set up in good posting position. Whichever one is *not* first down the court automatically slows down and becomes the trailer.

Drills for this approach are provided in the drills section later in this chapter.

Press Offense

Any specific press offense is less important than fundamentals such as spacing, cutting, meeting the pass, catching and facing, and passing first and dribbling last. Still, if the defense is defending on a full-court basis (i.e., all over the court), then coaches need a press offense to help the team get the ball inbounds safely. Players should get the ball inbounds before the defense gets set (i.e., use the transition fast break to beat a pressing defense before it is set). Therefore, coaches should designate a frontcourt player to take the ball out after all made baskets and quickly inbound the ball to a guard (figure 9.5*a*). The catcher of the inbounds pass should stay out of the corners and not get too close to the sideline, all of which are prime trapping areas.

Against any zone press, coaches should teach players to attack the defense in the backcourt or frontcourt by establishing a sideline pass outlet, two middle pass outlets (short and long to attack the middle of the defense), and a safety valve pass outlet slightly behind the ball handler (figures 9.5*b* and 9.6). Coaches should emphasize to players the need to use good passing and catching fundamentals and remind them to move to get open and to keep their poise. Pressing defenses take chances, and offensive players should be prepared to take advantage of those overcommitments. For example, in figure 9.6, by attacking the middle of the defense (X_4 and X_5), the offense can get the ball to O_5 or O_4, especially where O_5 can catch and face without dribbling and look for the best option, usually with a pass ahead or a dribble drive through the defense.

Generally, players need to attack a pressing defense. They should be aggressive and look to score layups by getting the ball up the side or to the middle of the pressing defense.

As a last resort, the offense can use the safety valve to reverse the ball and attack on the second side (figure 9.7). In extreme emergencies, when the ball handler is trapped

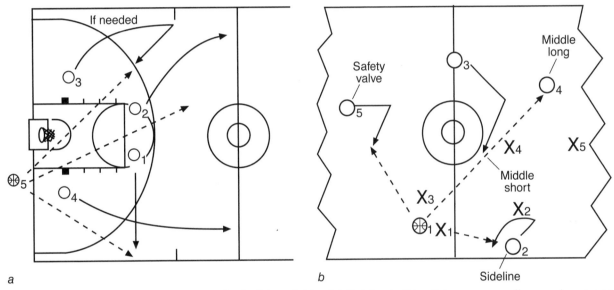

a   *b*

Figure 9.5   Press offense—getting the ball in quickly: *(a)* Get the ball in; *(b)* use press offense when trapped.

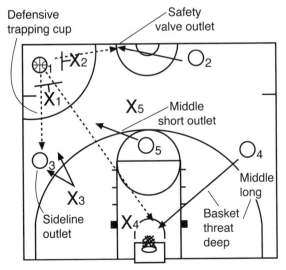

Figure 9.6   Beating the trap: Form the three-player cup (O_3, O_5, O_2) with a basket threat deep.

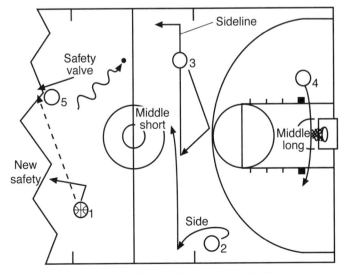

Figure 9.7   Press offense: Reverse the ball.

or double-teamed, the nearest teammate (usually the safety valve) can come to the ball directly behind the trap (an area that is usually undefended) for a pass. In this case, the ball handler can use a rear turn to protect the ball and make the pass. The safety-valve player should then attack the press immediately on the second side.

Set Offense

If the defense is set and waiting after the primary and secondary fast breaks, a set offense should be used to get a good shot. The team should get into a basic starting formation and then use fundamental skill moves with and without the ball to create scoring opportunities. This basic set or formation may take a variety of starting positions. Coaches should select a preferred starting formation that fits personnel and favored tactics.

2-2-1 Give-and-Go Offense This offense is based on the first team play used in basketball—the two-person play called *give-and-go* or *pass-and-cut*—in which the ball handler passes to a catcher and cuts to the basket for a possible return pass. This play is started from a four-out–one-in, two-guard–two-forward set (see figure 9.8, which also shows possible give-and-go, or pass-and-cut, options). It can be initiated by any two players at any time. Basic rules of this offense are as follows:

1. The middle of the court is the cutting highway. Cutters must cut through the middle after a pass, go toward the basket, pause, and face away from the baseline, clearing the middle quickly after using big vision to see the whole court. This cut controls the offense.

2. Players should read and react to defenders: Pass and cut against the sag (soft) defense, cut in front of defenders when possible, and use the backdoor (back cut) on defensive overplays.

3. Cutters can post up briefly but must clear the middle area after 2 seconds.

4. Players should make a catching spot (open hand) available to the passer, space themselves 15 to 18 feet (4.6 to 5.5 meters) away, and meet the pass.

5. Against zone defenses, players should cut through the middle of defensive gaps or holes and drive into gaps after a catch to explore drive-and-dish or penetrate-and-pass options.

6. This offense is player generated (i.e., players have much freedom) and rule based. The key is the penetrating cut.

7. The post player is stationed on the low post near the block and is responsible for rebounding on the weak side and being ready for the strong-side 2-on-1 dumpdown on cut-or-pass penetration by a player with the ball. The post player may post up when the ball is on that side and flash-post for a layup only occasionally when the defender is not alert or loses vision.

8. Some optional moves can be used by verbal call:
   - Perimeter screen on the ball
   - Perimeter pass and screen off the ball
   - Perimeter drive after a clearout on one side of the floor
   - Flash post by cutters (2-second rule) and clear to an open area

9. On traps or double teams, players should pass to the middle cutter in a hole or to another player coming to the ball (emergency).

10. The offense can be run full-court, three-quarter-court, or half-court. The movement of the ball and the cutters is more important than the formation or

the set. Coaches should teach player spacing. Players should cut with a purpose; they may go on the same side or on the opposite side on the middle clear.

11. Here is the offensive teaching progression:

- 2-on-0, 2-on-2 (guard, forward)
- 3-on-0, 3-on-3, 3-on-3 with weak-side post
- 5-on-0, 5-on-5 half-court, 5-on-5 full-court

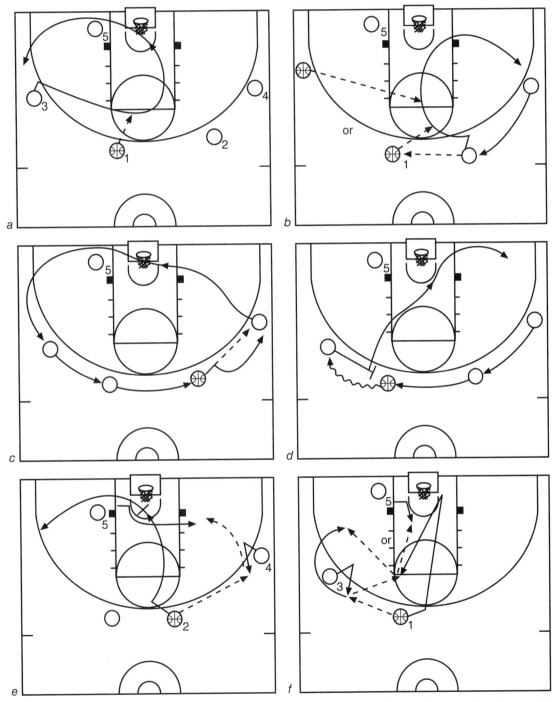

Figure 9.8 Pass-and-cut offensive variations: (a) forward go—forward cut and replace self; (b) guard go—guard cut and rotate; (c) guard around—guard around and follow through; (d) forward on-ball screen, roll, and clear; (e) guard to forward pass-and-cut, clear (and post flash); (f) guard to forward pass-and-cut to post up.

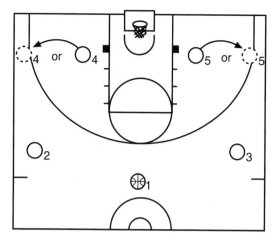

Figure 9.9 A 1-2-2 double low-post set (or open post).

1-2-2 Give-and-Go Another offense for beginning players is the 1-2-2 give-and-go, which can be used effectively against player-to-player defenses. This simple team offense uses passing, catching, basic moves without the ball, and individual moves with the ball. The 1-2-2 double low-post or open-post set is a one-guard, open-post formation that allows any player to V-cut into the post area and keeps the middle open for individual offensive moves plus give-and-go options (figure 9.9). The give-and-go offense from the 1-2-2 open-post formation can also be used against zone defenses and combination defenses (zone and player-to-player) by depending less on cutting and emphasizing more individual moves from stationary spots.

The rules for this offense are as follows:

1. The give-and-go from the point-to-wing pass is a pass-and-go-to-the-basket move after a V-cut is made by O_3 (figure 9.10). Cutting players who don't receive the return pass should balance the floor opposite the first pass (figure 9.10a). The give-and-go from the wing position to the corner position is shown in figure 9.10b. Notice how floor balance is regained.

2. If a wing player is overplayed or denied the pass by a defender, then offensive players should use a backdoor cut to the basket and replace on the same side (figure 9.10c). A corner player who is overplayed should make a backdoor cut and come back to the same side (figure 9.10d).

3. A wing or forward may V-cut into the post area (high or low). Players who make ball cuts and don't receive the ball within 2 seconds should return to their starting position (figure 9.10e).

4. When a shot is taken, the point guard (O_1) should go to defense near the half-court line as the safety (fullback), and the other four players should go to offensive rebounding positions.

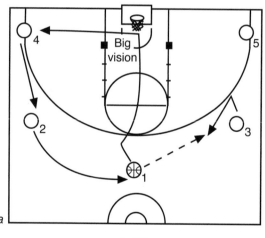

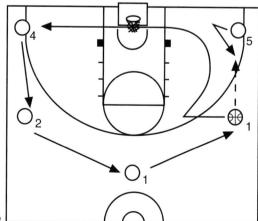

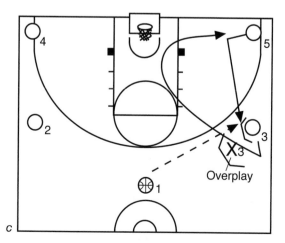

Figure 9.10 1-2-2 offense: (a) give-and-go from the point, (b) give-and-go on wing-to-corner pass, (c) backdoor cut by the wing. (continued)

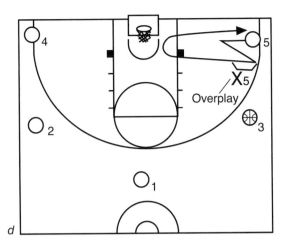

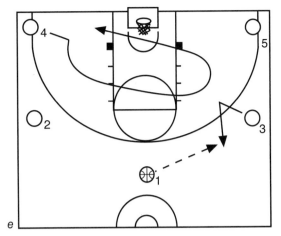

Figure 9.10 *(continued)* 1-2-2 offense: *(d)* backdoor cut by the corner, *(e)* V-cut to the post area and return.

This rule applies to all offensive situations: The offensive team should always maintain defensive balance and make a quick transition to defense. Coaches may prefer to have two players change to defense as "fullbacks" when a shot is taken.

1-4 Offense The 1-4 double high-post set requires a good point guard and two accomplished inside players. It is difficult to press, and there are four possible entry passes (figure 9.11).

1-3-1 Offense The 1-3-1 high-to-low-post set locates a point guard in front, positions forwards for individual moves, and requires two inside players (the high-post player must be able to face the basket); see figure 9.12.

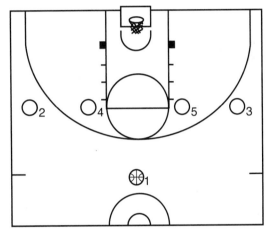

Figure 9.11 A 1-4 set or formation (point O_1, wings O_2 and O_3, and posts O_4 and O_5), sometimes called a *double high post*.

1-2-2 Stack Coaches may consider using a 1-2-2 stack formation, which calls for a point guard in front, one open side for individual moves, and a stack on the other side. This set may be used with one player (O_4) cutting to any position while the other stack player acts as a screener and then takes up a single-post position (O_5). The stack allows a variety of cuts by player O_4 (figure 9.13) and allows excellent open-entry passes to initiate offense.

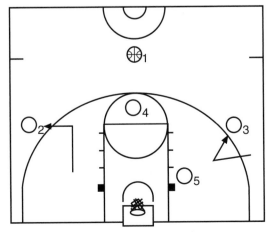

Figure 9.12 A 1-3-1 high-to-low-post set.

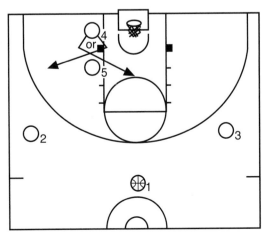

Figure 9.13 A stack set with a one-player front.

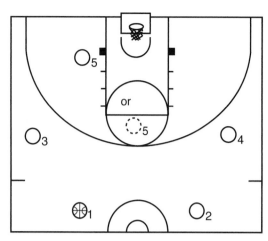

Figure 9.14 A 2-2-1 or 2-3 set (high or low post).

2-2-1 or 2-3 Set The final suggestion for an offensive formation is the traditional 2-2-1 or 2-3 set (figure 9.14). It uses a two-guard front with a single post (high or low). The sides and corners of the court are open for forward moves. The 2-3 formation is more vulnerable to pressing defenses.

Zone Offense

Against a zone defense, coaches can opt for the modified, recommended give-and-go offense or select another formation. In any case, they should teach players to use the following zone offense rules:

- Perimeter players align in the gaps on the perimeter and step up into shooting range (figure 9.15).

- Attack the defense, but be patient. Look for opportunities for dribble or pass penetration inside the zone after quickly passing around the perimeter. Dribble penetration best occurs right after a catch and after second perimeter passes.

- Watch floor spacing between teammates. Proper spacing spreads the defense and makes it difficult to cover offensive players.

- Cut through the zone. Test the zone by moving players and relocating (figure 9.16).

- Screen the zone. Beat a zone defense by screening inside or outside (figure 9.17).

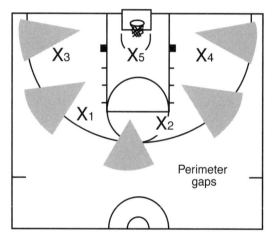

Figure 9.15 Against a zone defense, align in the gaps.

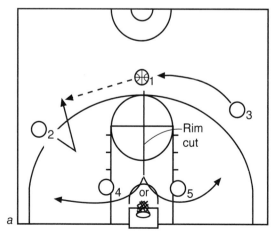
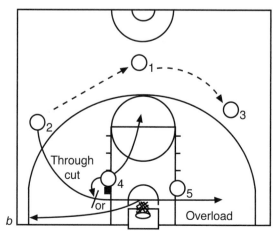

Figure 9.16 Zone offense: (a) Point cuts through the zone; (b) wing cuts through the zone.

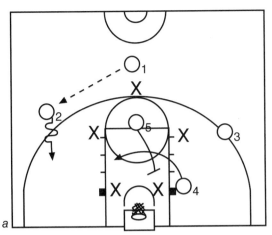 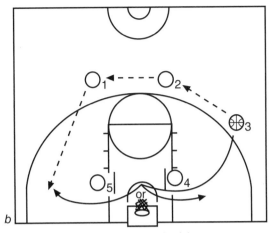

Figure 9.17 Zone offense: *(a)* Screen the zone low; *(b)* screen the zone inside.

Coaches should encourage player and ball movement. Because most zone defenses are ball oriented, ball fakes are effective. Players should put the ball overhead in order for defenders to see it and react to a fake (pass or shot): *Fake a pass to make a pass.* However, players should place the ball overhead only after properly catching it and putting the ball in triple-threat position.

Offense Against Combination Defenses

When the opponent uses a combination of player-to-player and zone defense (e.g., triangle-and-2, box-and-1, or diamond-and-1), the offense needs an organized approach to attack the defense. It can do so by using either the regular player-to-player offense or the zone offense. Coaches need to choose an offense that involves player movement, ball movement, and screening action. Analyze the defense and use an offense (play or set) that exploits it. For example, in the set shown in figure 9.17*a*, the offensive player being guarded one-on-one could serve as the baseline runner using the screens.

Control or Delay Game Offense

When a team has a lead late in a game, the coach may decide to have players spread out on the court and use the whole frontcourt to make the defense cover a larger area. This approach, called a *delay* game (or *control* game), usually involves taking only close-to-the-basket shots. In such situations, it may be best to run a normal offense with greater spacing modified by stricter rules for shot selection or for making a certain number of passes before a shot is taken (unless the shot is a layup). This offense can be used with or without a shot clock. When a delay-game shot rule calls for waiting until only 8 to 10 seconds remain on the shot clock, the ball handler looks for dribble penetration and other players start individual moves to set up a good shot. The decision of when to use delay-game tactics to control the ball and use the clock should be dictated by time and score.

The most common formation for this offense is shown in figure 9.18, in which

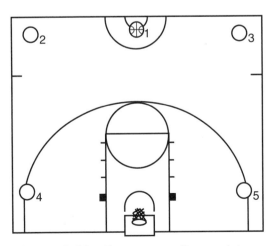

Figure 9.18 Four-corner offense: delay- or control-game set.

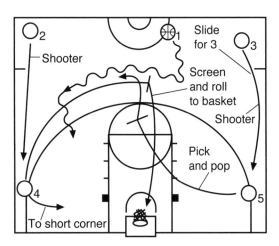

Figure 9.19 Last-second play.

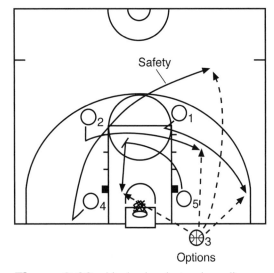

Figure 9.20 Under-basket or baseline out-of-bounds (BLOB) play: O_5 and O_2 run a pick-and-roll.

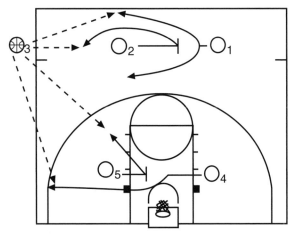

Figure 9.21 Sideline out-of-bounds (SLOB) play: O_2 screens for O_1, O_5 screens for O_4, and O_3 has four passing options.

four offensive players are placed in the four corners and the best dribbler or ball handler is out front in the middle of the court. Player O_1, usually the point guard or playmaker, constantly looks for chances to penetrate and pass. All offensive players should read and react to the defense and wait for their defender to make an error on which they can capitalize. When using the control game, coaches should put good free-throw shooters on the floor, because defenders may foul more, either out of frustration or by design.

Players should not get passive or lose momentum; to the contrary, they should stay on the attack. They can decoy the defense by appearing to delay while always looking for chances to score. If they don't want to shoot, they can also run a normal offense and act as though they are attacking.

With 8 to 10 seconds left on the shot clock, a special play may be used (figure 9.19). The options are for O_1 to use the pick, for O_2 or O_3 to move for the penetrate-and-pitch three-pointer, for O_4 to use the backpick by O_5, and for O_5 to step out after the screen.

Special Situations for Team Offense

Offensive players should be prepared to face a variety of special situations, including out-of-bounds plays, free throws, jump balls, and last-second scoring plays. The purpose is to prepare the team for any game situation.

Bringing the Ball Inbounds Every team must have a plan for bringing the ball into play underneath its own basket and on the sidelines. The sample formations and plays shown in figures 9.20 and 9.21 can be used against any defense. Most important, the team must be able to get the ball inbounds safely against all defensive tactics on baseline out-of-bounds (BLOB) plays.

Free Throws Free-throw situations must also be planned carefully. For the offense, the two best rebounders should occupy the second lane spaces and try to gain an offensive rebound in the middle of the lane or to the baseline side of the defender. In figure 9.22, player O_3 is stationed in a position to be alert for any long rebound or loose ball that might be tipped out, and O_1 has safety (fullback) responsibilities on defense and must not let any opponent get behind him or her for a long pass reception, while shooter O_2 assists in transition defense. For the defensive free throw, as shown in

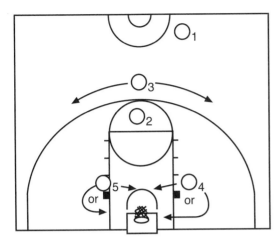

Figure 9.22 Offensive tactics on free throws: O_2 is shooting, O_4 and O_5 occupy the second lane spaces, O_3 is at the top of the circle (the key), and O_1 serves as the defensive safety with O_3 assisting after the basket.

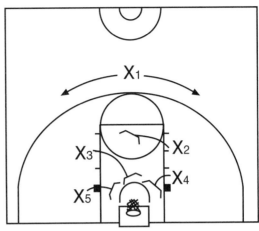

Figure 9.23 Defensive tactics on free throws: Four defenders block out or check their opponents on the free-throw lane, while X_1 is alert for an opponent's offensive tip out.

figure 9.23, player X_1 must be alert for a loose ball or long rebound. Player X_2 blocks out or checks the shooter by getting between the shooter and the basket. Players X_4 and X_5 check the opponents on their respective sides of the lane (from the second lane spaces), while player X_3 rebounds in the middle area. When a defensive rebound is captured, all team members transition to the fast break.

Jump Balls Special plays should be developed for the jump balls that start games and overtime periods. Regardless of the formation used, the ball should be tipped to an open spot—that is, a spot where two teammates are next to each other without an opponent between them. Smaller, quicker players should defend the basket. See figure 9.24.

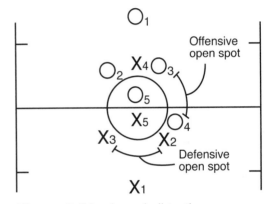

Figure 9.24 Jump-ball tactics.

Last-Second Shots The last-second-shot play diagrammed in figure 9.25 can be used in the delay game or in any situation where a move to the basket is made with 8 to 10 seconds remaining. Use of the play should depend on the level of play (younger players need more time) and allow time for a good shot opportunity, a possible offensive rebound, and a second shot—but not enough time for the opponent to get a good shot at the other end of the court.

No matter what offensive situation, formation, play, or system is chosen, the key is execution—not what players do but *how well* they do it. Practice these special situations using the game clock so players can execute well with proper offensive timing.

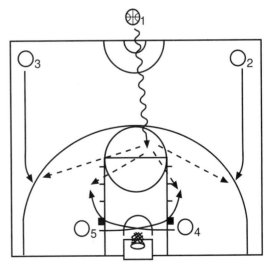

Figure 9.25 Last-second shot: O_4 and O_5 cross under the basket while O_2 and O_3 slide into scoring position and are ready to shoot. O_1 has four passing options, as well as penetration options for a shot.

Defensive Transition: Offense to Defense

Offensive players should make the transition to defense *quickly*, without getting outnumbered on the fast break, in order to set the defense. One way to achieve this goal is for the coach to create transition roles for all offensive players.

• **Fullback—the designated safety, usually the point guard, who is responsible for preventing easy scores (no layups).** As a teammate takes a shot, the fullback sprints to the half-court center circle, then retreats by running backward to the basket with big vision, and directs the defense from there (figure 9.26). If the fullback is the shooter, then another player makes the call and switches assignments. On an offensive fast break, the last player down the floor serves as the fullback and never crosses the half-court line until a score is made or a secondary fast break begins.

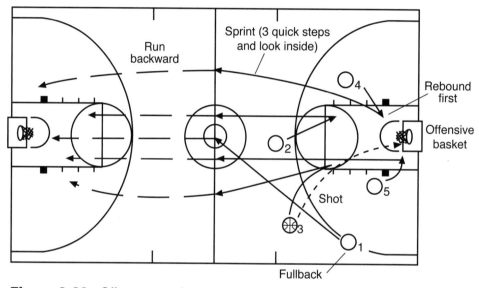

Figure 9.26 Offense-to-defense transition.

• **Tailbacks—all other players.** When the shot is taken, tailbacks are responsible for going to the offensive boards (*assume a miss*) until a basket is made or the opposing team gets the ball. At that point, all four tailbacks sprint to half-court, seeing the ball over their inside shoulder while running backward to their defensive assignment (i.e., getting their *tails back* on defense) if they are not outnumbered. When outnumbered (3-on-2, 2-on-1), the top priority is to protect the basket (no layups) while teammates transition to defense to help. Most teams use three tailbacks, while the fourth player (usually the shooter) serves as a rebounder at the free-throw line or as a long rebounder. With this tactic, this player then transitions to defense early and becomes a halfback who is responsible for stopping the ball coming up the court.

Variations of the plan can be developed for special situations—for instance, to pressure the rebounder or stop the ball from coming up the floor.

TROUBLESHOOTING

Most offensive errors result from a lack of proper sequential and progressive development. Therefore, it is critical to start by going slowly and carefully with no defenders, then progress to 5-on-0 at game speed to get spacing and timing. Only then can defenders be added to simulate game conditions; first use a dummy defense, then live defense in all variations so that offensive players learn to read and respond properly to all defensive situations.

COACHING POINTS FOR TEAM OFFENSE

- Tell players to be quick but not to hurry—focus first on execution and timing, then on speed.
- Maintain balance in all areas:
    - Individual (physical and emotional)
    - Offensive and defensive
    - Offensive rebounding and defensive coverage (on all shot attempts)
    - Floor spacing (spreading out and moving the ball)
    - Inside and outside scoring
    - Passing and scoring
- Teach players to strive for good spacing and timing.
- Teach intelligent teamwork on offense.
- Teach players to put the team first and individual plays second.
- Encourage players to play fearlessly—to make mistakes and learn from them.
- Develop individual play within the team context.
- Both the ball and players should move on offense; players should move with a purpose.
- Be patient with team offense. Play must be coordinated with player movements; as a result, learning progress is slower than with team defense.

CHECKLIST FOR TEAM OFFENSE

- Development of general principles
- Definition of positions and responsibilities
- Offensive fundamental skills
- Body control
- Ballhandling
- Shooting
- Perimeter play
- Post play
- Rebounding
- Press offense
- Transition to offense (primary and secondary fast break)
- Player-to-player set offense
- Zone set offense
- Combination set offense
- Delay (control) offense
- Special situations: jump balls, offensive free throws, out-of-bounds plays
- Transition to defense

DRILLS FOR TEAM OFFENSE

Team offense should first be executed slowly and correctly. Then moves are carried out at game speed to develop team coordination and timing. Emphasize proper spacing and timing unless players are screening or cutting to the basket.

SKELETON OFFENSE: 5-ON-0 (DRY RUN) ▶

Purpose: To teach movements and assignments for basic team offensive formation

Equipment: One ball and half court

Procedure: Five players at a time take the court to practice team offensive formations, plays, or movements, as well as individual assignments within the team offense. The offense should be initiated in all situations: backcourt, frontcourt, out-of-bounds, and free throws. Offensive play should be completed with a score each time (rebound each shot), and transition should be made to half-court by all five players after a made basket. This drill includes five offensive players at a time and no defenders.

Options

- Half-court offense—all sets
- Half-court to full-court (defense to offense)—after made or missed baskets, press offense, secondary fast break, set offense
- Half-court defense to full-court offensive options to defensive transition

On all offensive shots, assume a miss and make a transition (always rebound until the basket is made). Players should always make a transition to half-court on all drills, regardless of whether the shot is made or missed. Coaches should ensure that transitions on missed shots are also practiced at least weekly in this drill.

TEAM OFFENSE AND DEFENSE: 4-ON-4, 5-ON-5 ▶

Purpose: To teach team offense and defense in a progressive manner that culminates in 4-on-4 competition or 5-on-5 gamelike competition

Equipment: Ball, basket, and half court or full court (when practicing full-court transition)

Procedure: Four defenders and four offensive players practice team play. They should practice all offensive situations in order to prevent surprises at game time. The progression is for defenders to play dummy position defense and then no-hands defense (players may grasp the front of their own jersey) before going to gamelike offense and defense with no restrictions and various defensive tactics. Play should continue until the defense-turned-offense (after a miss) transitions to the other end of the floor (i.e., go from half court to full court). The drill may also be run as a 5-on-5 gamelike format.

Options

- Half court only
- Half-court make-it-take-it with full-court transition on misses
- Half court to full court (defense to offense transition—press offense, fast break, set offenses)
- Full court—stopping for corrections and shooting drills (field goals, free throws)

BLITZ FAST BREAK ▶

Purpose: To teach fast-break fundamentals (two-lane and three-lane) for offense and defense

Equipment: One ball and a full-court space

Procedure: A full team (10 to 16 players) is divided into two teams aligned as shown in figure 9.27, with opposing teams at half-court. One team is selected to start on defense at one end of the court; the other team starts on offense at half-court.

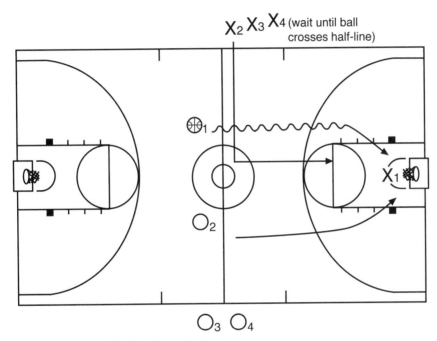

X_2 X_3 X_4 (wait until ball crosses half-line)

Figure 9.27 Blitz fast break: 2-on-1.

The drill begins when player O_1 crosses the half-court line with the ball for a 2-on-1 fast break. Player X_2 is allowed to help X_1 in the outnumbered situation after touching the center circle. Defender X_1 should bluff, anticipate, and delay the offensive duo in the two-lane fast break until X_2 can recover to help. The defenders should talk and get both players covered if they don't complete the break.

When the basket is made or missed, X_1 or X_2 captures the ball and advances it in a two-lane fast break toward the other basket. As soon as the X team gains possession of the ball, the next O player, O_3, touches the center circle and becomes the defensive safety (figure 9.28). When X_2 crosses the half-court line with the ball, O_4 can sprint to join the defense after touching the center circle. The drill usually continues to 9 baskets by one team. Score can be kept on the scoreboard. Coaches should officiate.

The other blitz fast-break option is the three-lane fast break, 3-on-2, which requires at least 12 players to form the two teams; the alignment is shown in figure 9.29. The two defenders usually align in tandem, with the inside player (X_4) positioned forward and the outside player (X_1) covering the basket and taking the first pass on a closeout. The other defender sprints to help as soon as the middle ball handler crosses the half-court line. Then dribbler O_1 veer-dribbles to one side after reading the back defender X_1 and passes to the open teammate.

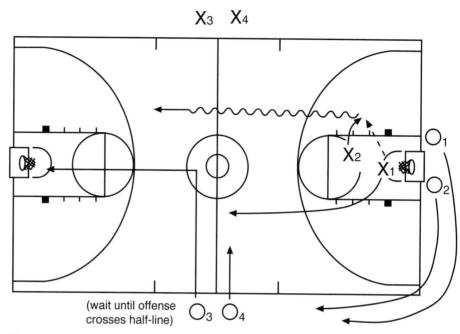

Figure 9.28 2-on-1 blitz fast break (part 2).

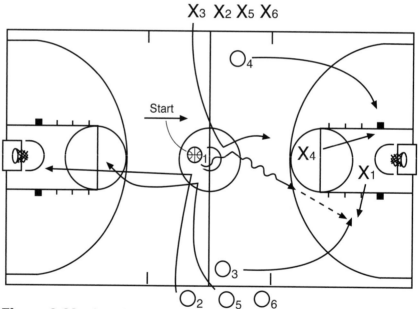

Figure 9.29 3-on-2 blitz fast break.

When defenders on the X team get the ball, they form a three-lane fast break to the other end, with the ball in the middle. As soon as the X team gains the ball, the next two O players, O_2 and O_5, sprint to join the defense after touching the center circle. The drill runs continuously until one team reaches 10 baskets.

Options

- Use the 2-on-1 blitz.
- Use the 3-on-2 blitz.
- Sideline players start at the top of the key; the defender touches the top-of-the-key circle before going to the other end.

TRANSITION FAST BREAK ▶

Purpose: To teach transition basketball from a structured start with an unpredictable finish

Equipment: Ball, two opposing teams, and a full court

Procedure: The drill begins at one end of the floor (figure 9.30). The coach begins by passing to any offensive player (O_4 in this case) and calls numbers or names for one or two defenders. When a name is called, that player touches the baseline before going to play defense, thus creating an outnumbered fast-break situation. The defensive team sprints back and talks to protect the basket, stop the ball, and quickly cover all offensive players. The offensive team attacks, reads the defense, and runs the primary or secondary fast break. Play continues for one, two, or three transitions before starting over.

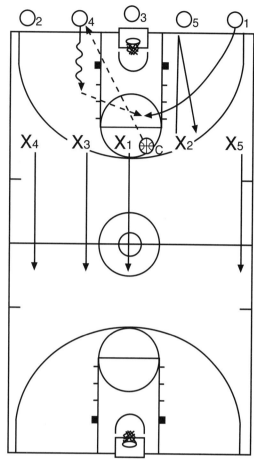

Figure 9.30 Team transition fast-break drill (5-on-4, 5-on-3, or 5-on-2).

DEFENSE-TO-OFFENSE TRANSITION

Purpose: To teach defense-to-offense transition with a sequenced, progressive method (two-person, three-person, five-person)

Equipment: Ball, full court

Procedure: Follow the drill progressions (2-on-0 and 3-on-0) and the 5-on-0 options in the scripted format. The advanced completion option may be added as needed during the season. Coaches pick the core transition package and then add options that fit their personnel.

Before using all five players in the same transition drill and going through the 5-on-0 script which follows, run a series of drills with fewer players involved so that you can pay special attention to how each part of the drill breaks down for this team transition plan.

Two-Person Transition Progression

- Player 4 or 5 (i.e., an inside player) throws the ball up to self off the glass to simulate a rebound. The rebounder then practices pivoting on the outside foot (closest to the sideline on the rebound side of the court) and throwing the outlet to player 1 (point guard). Player 1 practices getting to the sideline, getting out wide on the court, and then working up the court to start the fast break. The higher and wider the outlet pass can be received, the better the chance of creating a fast-break scoring opportunity.

- Player 1 starts at about the 28-foot (8.5-meter) mark beyond half-court, simulates catching an outlet pass, and then passes the ball ahead to player 2 or 3. Practice on each side of the court. Also, practice throwing the diagonal pitch-ahead pass, which is longer and more difficult to throw on time and on target.

- Player 1 practices the correct pass to player 4 or 5, who is outrunning the defense for a layup. This pass requires using the proper arc to go over the defense but still catchable by player 4 or 5 to set up the layup finish.

Three-Person Transition Progression

- This drill will quickly simulate many reps to work on the outlet pass and pitch-ahead pass. Player 4 or 5 simulates the rebound (thrown off the glass), then throws the outlet to the point guard, who uses either no dribbles or one dribble and pitches the ball ahead to player 2 or 3, who in turn shoots or drives to a finish. This drill can be practiced simultaneously in both directions to keep six players active. Players should switch sides and practice the outlet and pitch-ahead pass up the other side of the court as well.

- This drill also works on the quick pitch ahead into a post feed. Set up the drill with a point guard, a wing player (2 or 3), and a big (post). The point guard starts the drill with ball near midcourt by simulating an outlet pass to self and quickly pitching the ball ahead to player 2 or 3, who works on a quick shot fake and pass to the big. The big is either running to the rim and catches the pass on the run into a layup or has run ahead of the ball and is already in posting position, sealing off the defender and waiting for the post-feed pass from the wing.

5-on-0 Defense-to-Offense Transition Options

Use a progressive team format to practice from a missed shot or rebound.

- 1-2-1-4-3 give-and-go 4
- 1-2-1-5 backdoor 4
- 1-2-1-4-3 screen-and-roll with 4
- 1-2-1-4-3, 5 backpick for player 2
- 1-2-1-4-3-2 coming off staggered double screen from 1 and 4 (as 4 or 5 gets rebound and throws outlet but also needs to be practiced with guards or wings as rebounder)
- 4/5-1-2 layup or three-point shot
- 4/5-1-3 layup or three-point shot
- 4-1-5 layup
- 5-1-4 layup
- 4-1-2-5 layup
- 4-1-3-5 layup
- 4-1-2-4- top-down pass to 5 for layup
- 4-1-3-4- top-down pass to 5 for layup
- 4-1-2-1 three-pointer
- 4-1-2-4 trailer three-pointer
- 4-1-2-skip pass to 3 for three-point shot

- 4-1-3-skip pass to 2 for three-point shot
- 4-1-2-3-5
- 4-1-2-1-4-3 drive or feed to 5 for shot
- 4-1-3-1-4-2 drive or feed to 5 for shot

Advanced Completion Options

- 1-2-4-3, then 5 backpick for 4 and bigs interchange spots to work on high–low post game
- 1-2-1, trailing 4 high-ball screen for point guard 1 to attack toward basket
- 1-4-3, 5 diagonal backpick for 2 to cut across lane
- 1-2-1-4-3, 5 swing cut for 2 once ball crosses midline
- 1-2-1-4 backdoor cut to 3 as reversal pass gets denied

Wooden Wisdom

"It isn't what you do, but how well you do it." (This is especially true on offense.)

—John Wooden

CHAPTER 10

TEAM DEFENSE

"Team defense and ballhandling are the cornerstones of successful teams."

Henry "Hank" Iba, Naismith Hall of Fame coach, former head coach at Oklahoma State University, U.S. Olympic coach (1964, 1968, and 1972)

Coaches should build a team on a solid foundation. That foundation should begin with defense, which is one of the most concrete and unchanging elements of the game and can be the most consistent phase of team play. A team that prevents its opponents from getting good shots is tough to beat. Sound defense depends on coaches to develop a team of individuals who play hard, smart (with purpose), and together (putting team first) while having fun. In a prime example, Bill Russell, the cornerstone of the Boston Celtics dynasty in the 1960s, has been called the first person who ever dominated his team sport by being a great defender. He was the quintessential defensive player who rebounded, defended, and competed. Moreover, he was the complete team player who played for others and made everyone else better.

Team defense can be even more dominant among beginners, because younger players possess limited individual and team offensive skills. Therefore, coaches should strive to convince them that defense is the key to building a foundation for team play. Beginners may have trouble understanding the relationship between defense and winning (doing their best), and they may need to be convinced that preventing a score by the opponent is just as important as scoring for their own team.

CRITICAL CUE
Prevent easy scores by allowing only one contested shot.

Untrained defenses tend to be reactive rather than proactive—a defender usually reacts to the moves of an offensive player. Players must learn instead to be aggressive and to initiate action on defense. Coaches must teach players to act—not react—when playing defense. A team can develop effective defensive play that is more proactive than reactive through encouragement, determination, and practice.

Team defenses are based on fundamental individual skills, and coaches should motivate players to develop pride in their ability to play defense. Any team can be made better by developing a sound team defense—one in which each defender can count on defensive help from teammates. *Don't let your teammates down.*

One precept of team defense is to prepare players for action and prevent problems before they happen. For example, a player in quick stance can often anticipate moves by an offensive player before they are made and then take those moves away. Coaches should teach players to be ready for anything, which means being prepared to defend against an opponent's best offensive moves. This preparation makes the defender mentally and physically ready for secondary offensive moves by an opponent. Players should get in a defensive quick stance and stay in that stance—a measure of team defense and dedication to the principle of being ready and prepared to help one's teammates as well as defend your assigned player.

One main objective of any defense should be to make the other teams do things that it does not want to do. Offense depends on confidence and rhythm, both of which can be disrupted by an effective defense. Defenders should take away opponents' strengths and make them learn how to play differently during games. This approach forces offenses to resort to secondary moves and options, which is especially difficult to do during a game. In short, a good defense makes the offense play to its weaknesses by taking away its strengths. Defense is a game of give and take; if players take something away, they will likely give an opponent access to an alternative (secondary) move—which is usually a good tradeoff. This reality applies to strengths and weaknesses, as well as each defensive level and category of defense. Defenders should always be prepared to take away opponents' strengths or best offensive moves—for example, preventing a dribbler from using the preferred hand to go by a defender.

CRITICAL CUE
Take away the offensive player's best move or strength.

The glue that holds team defense together is communication. To be effective on defense, teams need to develop and implement excellent communication skills—both verbal and nonverbal, and both talking and listening. In the team sport of basketball, players cannot communicate too much, and coaches cannot emphasize communication too much. This point is especially important to emphasize in the current digital era, in which face-to-face communication is less common than in the past.

Team defense also depends on the effectiveness of your team offense, including ball-handling and good shots. Efficient offense tends to energize and complement team defense; it also reduces the pressure on the defense and enables the defense to be more aggressive and confident.

DEFENSIVE COURT LEVELS

The many varieties and styles of defense can be played at various levels of the court (figure 10.1). Coaches can instruct players to begin defending the opposing team at any point (level) on the court.

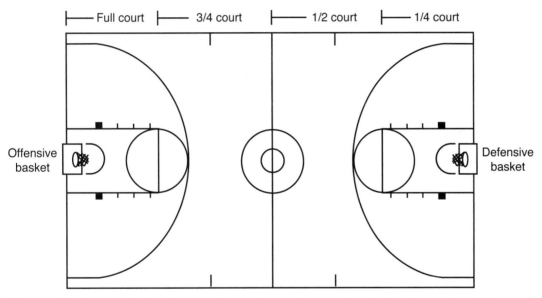

Figure 10.1 Levels of defense—defending and protecting the basket on the right.

Full-court team defense is a pressing defense in which defenders guard or pick up opponents as soon as possible all over the court. In a three-quarter-court defense, defenders usually allow the first inbounds pass and then pick up offensive players near the free-throw line or the top of the offensive circle. The most common pickup point is at midcourt; in fact, half-court, player-to-player team defense is recommended for all players of upper-elementary age in the United States (i.e., ages 10 to 14). Coaches can also activate team defense at the top of the defensive key. This quarter-court defensive level is used if the other team has greater individual talent; it is the foundation level. A team can increase its level of defense as it gets better at defense or develops better team defense.

A team defensive level that is set at full-court or three-quarter court puts more pressure on opponents but also forces the defensive team to cover more of the court. Thus it takes away the opponent's opportunity for free movement in the backcourt but also gives the opponent the possible advantage of beating the pressure, gaining a numerical advantage over the defense, and getting an easy score. With this trade-off in mind, coaches should select a starting defensive level at which the team can succeed in preventing the opponent from getting good shots.

DEFENSIVE CATEGORIES

Team defenses fall into three general categories: player-to-player, in which each defender is assigned to a specific offensive player (strongly recommended for all players from age 7 through 14); zone, in which each player is assigned a specific area of responsibility depending on the position of the ball and the positions of the offensive players; and combination, which includes elements of both player-to-player and zone defense. All defenses can be started at different levels and with various amounts of pressure (proactive pressing versus reactive sagging).

Player-to-Player Defense

Coaches should emphasize player-to-player as the basic defense for all teams. This defensive approach is valuable because its techniques can be applied in all defenses. It should be the primary defense, and really the only one, used in elementary-school levels of play in the United States (ages 7 through 14).

Contrary to this advice, elementary, middle, and junior high school (U.S.) teams often use defenses and pressing tactics that take advantage of young players' lower skill levels in ballhandling and perimeter shooting. This approach hinders the player's long-range development and should therefore be discouraged. Players at these age levels should focus instead on fun and fundamentals. Everyone should get a chance to play in every game in order to use strengths, work on weaknesses, and develop fundamental skills.

Moreover, if players in this age group learn the basics of player-to-player defense, then they can adapt to other defenses later.

Player-to-player defense is also the most challenging and most personally rewarding type of defense. No defender can hide: The offense is likely to score an easy basket after any defensive lapse, thus ensuring specific personal accountability. As a result, player-to-player defense promotes individual responsibility to the team as well as team cohesion. The basic principles of this type of defense are explained in chapter 7.

Zone Defense

Zone defense assigns each defensive player the responsibility not for an individual offensive player but for a certain area or zone; it also focuses more on the ball. A zone defense usually changes as the ball moves and is designed to protect a limited area of the court. Zone defenses are often weaker in the gaps or seams between defenders and on the outside, but they can be modified to disguise those weaknesses.

Zone defenses can also be designed to give and to take away. For instance, sagging zones give up more outside shots but take away the inside, whereas lane or pressure zones take away outside shots but may be vulnerable inside. Zones can also be changed to lane defenses designed to intercept passes, trapping defenses (in which two players double-team an offensive player who has the ball), and sagging defenses that heavily protect the inside area near the basket.

The 2-3 Zone The 2-3 is the most commonly used zone defense. Its basic coverage areas are shown in figure 10.2*a*, and its weak areas are shown in figure 10.2*b*. Coaches can use this defense when playing a team with a good post player or when

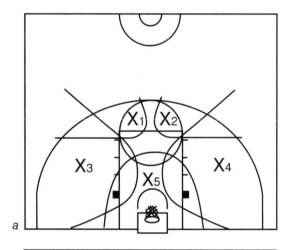

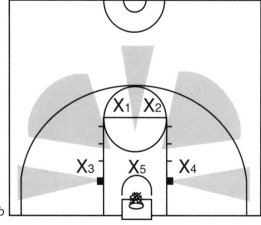

Figure 10.2 The 2-3 zone defense: *(a)* coverage and *(b)* weak areas.

they need to ensure good corner coverage. As shown in figure 10.3, players using this defensive scheme shift with the ball in various positions.

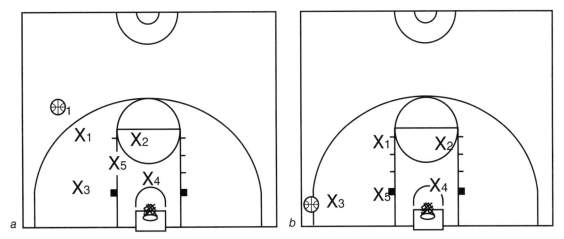

Figure 10.3 The 2-3 zone: *(a)* ball on the wing and *(b)* ball in the frontcourt corner.

The 1-3-1 Zone The 1-3-1 zone defense is also commonly used to cover the high post and wing areas. It is strong in the center, on the wings, and at the point. Its coverage and gaps are shown in figure 10.4, and its shifts are shown in figure 10.5, with the ball in the corner and on the wing, respectively (when the ball is in the corner, most zones revert to a 2-3 formation).

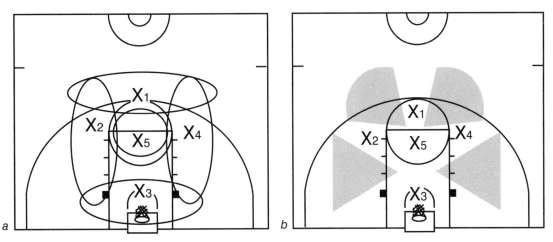

Figure 10.4 The 1-3-1 zone defense: *(a)* coverage and *(b)* weak areas.

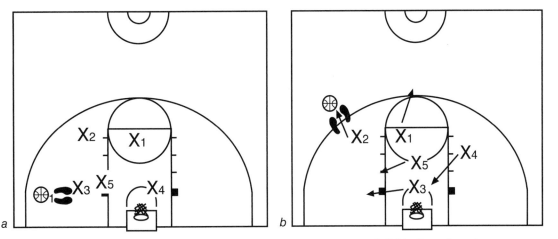

Figure 10.5 The 1-3-1 zone defense: *(a)* ball in the corner and *(b)* ball on the wing.

The 1-2-2 Zone The 1-2-2 zone defense provides good coverage on the perimeter but is vulnerable inside. Its coverage and weak areas are indicated in figure 10.6. Its movement and shifts (figure 10.7) are similar to those of the 1-3-1 zone.

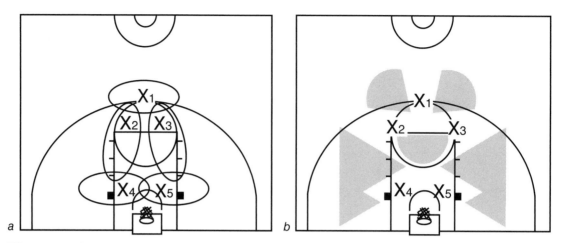

Figure 10.6 The 1-2-2 zone defense: *(a)* coverage and *(b)* weak areas.

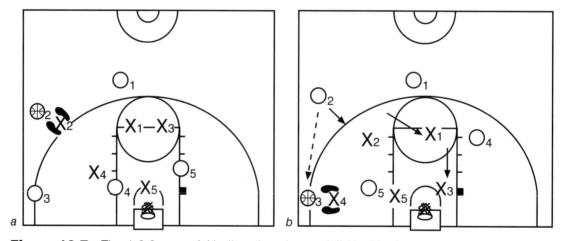

Figure 10.7 The 1-2-2 zone: *(a)* ball on the wing and *(b)* ball in the corner.

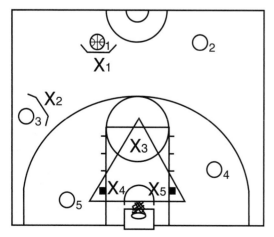

Figure 10.8 Triangle-and-2 (combination zone and player-to-player defense): triangle zone plus two player-to-player defenders (X_1 and X_2).

Combination Defense

Combination defenses are used to take away an opponent's strength and confuse the offense. They may take several forms. For example, a triangle-and-2 defense might be used against a team with only two good scorers, whereas a box-and-1 could be used against an opponent with one key scorer or ball handler.

Triangle-and-2 Two defenders are assigned player-to-player responsibility for selected opponents while the other three defenders play a triangular zone (figure 10.8). To use this defense effectively, coaches must decide on the extent of floor coverage and shifts for the triangle zone defenders. They must also decide how they want the two player-to-player defenders to play (e.g., tight, loose, denying the ball). Although this defense undercuts the effectiveness of the two focal offensive players (usually perimeter players), it is vulnerable in other outside shooting areas.

Box-and-1 or Diamond-and-1 In this approach, one defender has player-to-player responsibility while the other four play a zone defense near the basket. This defense works well against a team with one outstanding scorer or ball handler. Two forms of this defense are shown in figure 10.9. Coaches using this approach should assign their best player-to-player defender to the opposing player who is the best scorer, ball handler, or team leader. After determining the key player for the other team, determine how to take away that player's strength, either through ball denial or by assigning that player to the best defender on the team. Although this defense undercuts the effectiveness of one player and uses the other four zone players to help and protect the basket, it can be vulnerable to outside shooting.

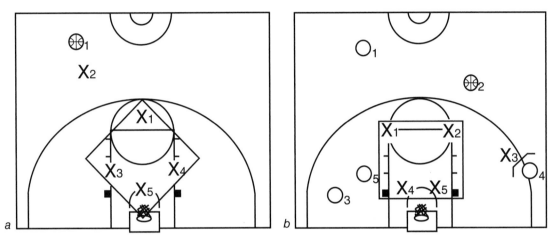

Figure 10.9 Combination defenses: *(a)* diamond-and-1 and *(b)* box-and-1.

Pressing Defenses

Player-to-player pressure defenses can be played at the half-court, three-quarter-court, or full-court level. All basic principles apply, but helping situations are much more challenging as the defense expands to cover the full court. Therefore, this approach places a premium on individual defenders' ability to stop and pressure the ball handler. This type of pressure defense was first developed in the 1940s in the men's game and has become commonplace, especially on teams that have greater athletic ability than the opposition.

Zone pressure defenses can be played at all levels. Probably the most famous instance of a full-court zone press was popularized in the unprecedented success experienced at UCLA under John Wooden. The staple of his first national collegiate championship team was the full-court 2-2-1 zone press (figure 10.10). Zone presses tend to speed up the game by forcing opponents to pass more because of the use of traps or double teams as offenses tend to use more dribbling tactics, whereas player-to-player pressure defenses tend to slow the tempo.

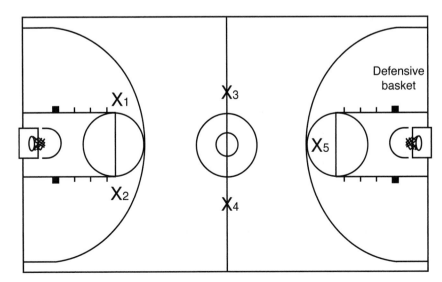

Figure 10.10 2-2-1 zone-press starting set.

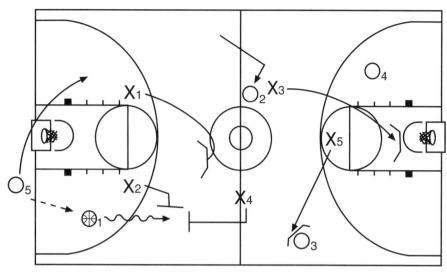

Figure 10.11 2-2-1 zone-press trap.

This press is usually used as a containing tactic to keep the ball out of the middle, and it tends to set at least one sideline trap before half-court. In the trapping sequence shown in figure 10.11, player X_1 covers the middle, X_5 covers the sideline, and X_3 protects the basket.

Coaches need to make decisions about when and where to trap (usually when the dribble comes to the defense and near the half-court line), how to rotate, whether to use continuous trapping, when to drop back to the regular half-court defense, and what type of defense to transition into on the half-court. With player-to-player defense, one method is to retreat to the basic defense after one trap—specifically, protect the basket, stop the ball, and pick up all open players (in that order). During the transition to half-court defense, communication is crucial as teams can transition into another type of defense after one trap (e.g., from a full-court zone press into a half-court player-to-player defense).

A half-court zone press is exemplified by the 1-3-1 defense used by the Kentucky team that won a national championship in 1978 with coach Joe B. Hall. The basic set is an extended 1-3-1 (figure 10.12).

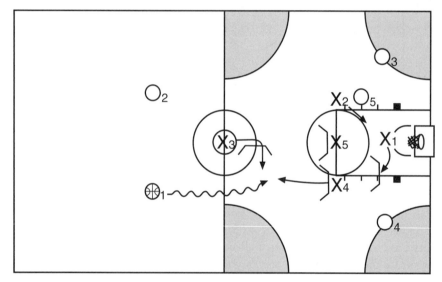

Figure 10.12 1-3-1 half-court zone press.

In this approach, the perimeter players (X_3, X_4, and X_2) play in the passing lanes and force the offense to pass over the top (i.e., to use slower passes). The ball is then forced into the corners and trapped (figure 10.13).

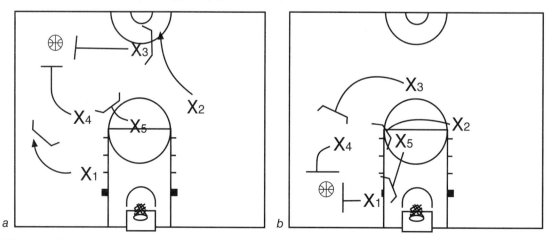

Figure 10.13 1-3-1 corner traps: (a) near the half-court line, (b) near the baseline.

COACHING POINTS FOR TEAM DEFENSE

- Select one defense as the primary team defense. The half-court player-to-player defense is recommended for young players (ages 7 through 14, or through upper elementary school in the United States).
- Treat attitude and motivation as major concerns when developing team defensive play. Teach players why defense is important to success.
- Focus on practicing against all offenses. Prevent surprises for the defense during games by preparing the team fully in practice for all game situations.
- Place equal emphasis on offense and defense (while spending more time on offense because it requires ballhandling and shooting).
- Require defenders to play hard—all five players must move with every pass or dribble.
- Begin with an effective transition from offense to defense.
- End with a defensive rebound, a steal, or an opponent's turnover.
- Require communication—both verbal and nonverbal and both talking and listening.

CHECKLIST FOR TEAM DEFENSE

- Development of general principles
- Development and use of fundamental defensive skills
- Fundamental stance and steps
- On-the-ball defense (live-ball, dribble, dead-ball)
- Off-the-ball defense (closed or open stance)
- Defensive closeouts (off-the-ball to on-the-ball)
- On-the-ball to off-the-ball defense (jumping or exploding to the ball)
- Special situations for defense
- Post defense
- Help-and-decide (bluffing, switching, trapping)
- On-the-ball screens
- Off-the-ball screens
- Double screens
- Defensive charge
- Pressuring the shot
- Loose ball
- Defensive rebounding
- Team defense
- Player-to-player (ages 7 through 14)
- Zone
- Combination
- Levels of defense
- Zone press
- Out-of-bounds, under the basket (defense against baseline out-of-bounds plays [BLOB])
- Out-of-bounds, side (defense against sideline out-of-bounds plays [SLOB])
- Defensive free throws
- Transition to offense

TROUBLESHOOTING

The biggest challenge on defense is to get players to play as hard as possible at the defensive end of the floor. Especially on defense, coaches cannot coach well unless players play extremely hard with maximum physical and emotional effort. Therefore, coaches must convince players that they cannot succeed without an all-out effort. Part of that effort involves giving maximum mental effort, which requires high levels of communication for defensive effectiveness. Coaches should encourage players to be their best on defense, both physically and mentally. The "mad dog in a meathouse" approach does work on defense: *Play as hard as you can for as long as you can.* Teams must learn to play hard with a purpose.

DRILLS FOR TEAM DEFENSE

Defense needs to be learned for all situations and built up progressively from individual play (1-on-1) to team play (5-on-5). To lay the foundation for developing team defense, see chapter 7 for the following individual defensive drills:

- Moving Stance and Steps
- Line Drill: Individual Defense (especially 1-on-1 for live ball, dribble, passer, and dead ball)
- Closeout: 1-on-1, 2-on-2, 3-on-3, 4-on-4
- On-the-Ball and Off-the-Ball: 2-on-2
- Defensive Slide: Moving Stance and Steps

HALF-COURT BASIC DEFENSE: 3-ON-3, 4-ON-4 ⏵

Purpose: To break down all situations of two-person and three-person offensive play and learn to defend them in a team situation (to prepare the team for all situations—no game surprises). This is the basic defensive drill for practicing all basic defensive tactics; most offensive team plays are one- or three-person tactics.

Equipment: Ball, half court, and 8 to 12 players

Procedure: Each practice can emphasize a selected offensive situation to defend. Set up a drill rotation—offense to defense to off-court.

Options
- On-the-ball screens
- Off-the-ball screens
- Double screens
- Use of traps
- Two out, two in (perimeter, post)
- Four outside players, flash post on the cut
- Give-and-go moves
- Dribble penetration

- Post play (single, double)
- Three out, one in
- Three in, one out
- One-guard front or two-guard front

HALF-COURT TO FULL-COURT: 3-ON-3, 4-ON-4, 5-ON-5

Purpose: To practice basic half-court defense and transition to offense and vice versa

Equipment: Ball, full court, and at least two groups of players

Procedure: Set up selected offensive situations to defend and then transition to offense on missed shots. Work on selected offensive situations, then carry out an effective defensive transition on made or missed baskets.

Options

- 3-on-3 (the most basic and efficient team-defense drill)
- 4-on-4
- 5-on-5 team offense and defense

FULL-COURT: 3-ON-3, 5-ON-5

Purpose: To teach all phases of defense progressively—3-on-3 breakdowns and 5-on-5 with full teams. This drill is one of the best, most taxing drills for offense and defense because players must play full-court offense and defense while executing all fundamental skills.

Equipment: Ball, full court, and at least two groups of players

Procedure: For 3-on-3 full-court play, players or groups should change (switch offense and defense [and off-court]) after no more than three circuits up and back. The ball must be dribbled over half-court, and no breakaway lob passes are allowed in an early use of this full-court defensive drill.

Variation: Play full-court 3-on-3 games to two baskets using the following rules:

- Offense calls fouls (which count as a score).
- No lob passes are allowed over half-court (i.e., no breakaways).
- No dribbling is allowed on offense (use pass-and-cut and pass-and-pick away from the ball).
- New team is waiting to come in (to face the winner, who stays).

2-ON-2 AVOID THE SCREEN

Purpose: To simulate defensive schemes against a down screen

Equipment: Four players, one passer (coach or player), one ball, half court

Procedure: As shown in figure 10.14, two defensive players align themselves with O_1 at the top of the key and O_2 on the wing. O_1 starts with a ball and delivers a pass to the opposite wing (a coach or extra player) away from teammate O_2. On the pass to the wing, both defensive players jump to the ball in order to be about halfway between their respective assigned players and the ball. With this proper defensive alignment, they have the

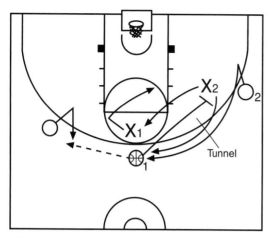

Figure 10.14 Avoid-the-screen drill.

best opportunity to react to what the offense is doing and avoid any potential screens that may be set.

The offensive players now begin the process of setting a down screen—specifically, O_1 setting a screen for O_2. X_1 follows O_1, providing a tunnel for X_2 to get through in order to avoid the down screen and defend O_2. The coach (or extra player) passes the ball to O_2, who is coming to the top of the key. For purposes of the drill, O_2 takes a quick look at the rim from the quick-stance triple-threat position, then passes the ball right back to the coach.

Now all players are located at different positions from their starting points, and O_2 will set a down screen for O_1. After this rotation, the drill is reset with a new set of defenders.

SPRINT TO LOW-I HELP POSITION

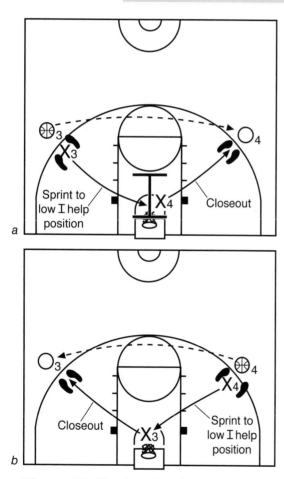

Figure 10.15 2-on-2 sprint to low-I help position: *(a)* skip pass closeout and cover low-I help; *(b)* return skip pass.

Purpose: To practice closeout technique

Equipment: Four players, one ball, and half court

Procedure: As shown in figure 10.15, player O_4 starts on the left wing with the ball while being guarded by defender X_4, and player O_3 is positioned on the opposite wing while being guarded by defender X_3. Defender X_3 uses proper on-ball defensive stance, and defender X_4 is located with two feet in the key and with his or her head right under the rim in the proper low-I (where the off-side defenders are aligned vertically with the basket and ready to help on the ball-side; the 2 defenders in the vertical line help position are called *low-I* and *high-I* defenders) help-side defensive position. Player O_3 then throws a skip pass to player O_4, which forces defender X_3 to sprint from on-ball defense to getting two feet in the paint with his or her head under the rim (the low-I spot). Defender X_4 must use proper closeout technique to go out from the rim to player O_4, who is catching the ball and looking for a shot or drive. The offensive players continue to throw skip passes back and forth. On the fifth skip pass, players finish the drill with live play to either a score or a rebound. On each catch, the offensive players should look at the rim and perform a couple of fakes or attack moves, essentially holding the ball for 2 or 3 seconds, rather than immediately throwing the next skip pass.

Wooden Wisdom

"Failure is not fatal, but failure to change might be."

—John Wooden

Boling, D. 2004. *Tales From the Gonzaga Hardwood*. Champaign, IL: Sports Publishing LLC.

Bunn, J. 1955. *Scientific Principles of Coaching*. Englewood Cliffs, NJ: Prentice Hall.

Carter, J. 2006. *Noah's Arc—Building the Perfect Shot*. Palo Alto, CA: Self-published.

Gladwell, M. 2011. *Outliers: The Story of Success*. New York: Little, Brown and Co.

Harle, S., and J. Vickers. 2006. *Quiet Eye Improves Accuracy in the Free Throw*. Calgary, AB: University of Calgary.

Hays, D. 2006. *Developing Your Shot and Offensive Moves*. Oklahoma City: Self-published.

Jaimet, S. 2006. *The Perfect Jump Shot*. Indianapolis: Elemental Press.

Krause, J., and B. Brown. 2006. *NABC's Youth Basketball Coaching Handbook: Beyond the Backboard*. Monterey, CA: Coaches Choice.

Krause, J., C. Janz, and J. Conn. 2003. *NABC's Handbook for Teaching: Basketball Skill Progressions*. Monterey, CA: Coaches Choice.

Krause, J., and R. Pim. 2002. *Coaching Basketball*. New York: McGraw-Hill.

Krause, J. 2005. *Lessons From the Legends: Basketball Offense Sourcebook*. Monterey, CA: Triumph Books.

Krause, J. 2005. *Lessons From the Legends: Basketball Defense Sourcebook*. Monterey, CA: Triumph Books.

Krause, J. 2005. *Lessons From the Legends: Beyond the X's and O's*. Monterey, CA: Triumph Books.

Krause, J., and M. Harkins. 2014. *Zone Offenses for Men's and Women's Basketball*, 2nd ed. Monterey, CA: Coaches Choice.

Krzyzewski, M. 2000. *Leading With the Heart*. New York: Warner Books.

Martens, R. 1997. *Successful Coaching*, Updated 2nd ed. Champaign, IL: Human Kinetics.

Marty, R., and S. Lucey. 2018. *A Data-Driven Method for Understanding and Increasing Three-Point Shooting Percentage*. Boston, MA: MIT Sloan Sports Analytics Conference.

Medina, J. 2014. *Brain Rules: 12 Principles for Surviving and Thriving at Work, Home, and School*, 2nd ed. Seattle, WA: Pear Press.

Nater, S., and R. Gallimore. 2010. *You Haven't Taught Until They Have Learned: John Wooden's Teaching Principles and Practices*. Morgantown, WV: Fitness Information Technology.

National Association of Basketball Coaches. 2000. *1999-2000 Annual Research Report of the NABC Research Committee*. Atlanta, GA: National Association of Basketball Coaches.

National Collegiate Athletic Association. 2016. *Division I Men's Basketball Statistical Trends*. www.ncaa.org/championships/statistics/division-i-mens-basketball-statistical-trends.

NCAA Basketball Trend Statistics, 2017. *Team Statistics*. www.NCAA.org.

Nielson, J. 1988. "The Shot That Reigns Over the Rim." *The New York Times*, March 8, 1988, A00025. https://www.nytimes.com/1988/03/08/sports/the-shot-that-reigns-over-the-rim.html.

Noah Basketball. www.noahbasketball.com.

Reger, J. 2012. *Quotable Wooden: Words of Wisdom, Preparation, and Success by and About John Wooden, College Basketball's Greatest Coach*. Lanham, MD: Taylor Trade Publishing.

Withers, B. 2002. *Bravehearts: The Against-All-Odds Rise of Gonzaga Basketball*. Chicago: Triumph Books.

Wolff, A. 2002. *Big Game, Small World*. New York: Warner Books.

Wooden, J.R. 1998. *Practical Modern Basketball*, 3rd ed. Redwood City, CA: Benjamin Cummings.

Wooden, J., and S. Jamison. 2004. *My Personal Best: Life Lessons From an All-American Journey*. New York: McGraw-Hill.

INDEX

Note: Page references followed by an italicized *f* or *t* indicate information contained in figures or tables, respectively.

ABOUT THE AUTHORS

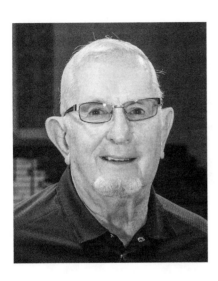

Jerry Krause has been a part of Gonzaga University's men's basketball program for over 25 years. In 2001, he returned to the university as the director of men's basketball operations after serving a five-year civilian term at the U.S. Military Academy at West Point. There he was a professor of sports philosophy and director of instruction for the department of physical education.

Krause's legendary career includes many highlights. He served as head coach at Eastern Washington University (EWU) for 17 years, where his Eagle teams posted a 262-196 record and a .572 winning percentage and attained a graduation record of 84 percent. He has coached at all levels—youth sport through Olympics—and for both men and women. He took a sabbatical from EWU to assist the late Ralph Miller at Oregon State University in writing his first book (*Better Basketball Basics*) and then returned to EWU to lead the Eagles from the NAIA into the NCAA Division I ranks.

He is one of the most prolific authors of basketball books, having written 34 titles, and has also produced 33 instructional videos. For 50 years he has been research chairman for the National Association of Basketball Coaches and was a long-standing member of the NCAA Basketball Rules Committee. He was involved in rule changes that brought about the 45-second (and later 30-second) shot clock, the three-point shot, and the breakaway rim as well as inventing the NCAA/NBA approved basketball rim tester to standardize ball-rim rebounds and make the game the same around the world. He is a member of the NAIA Basketball Coaches, SHAPE America (formerly National Association for Sport and Physical Education), New York State AHPERD, SHAPE Washington (formerly Washington AHPERD), and the Inland Northwest Sports Halls of Fame.

Craig R. Nelson is the boys' basketball head coach at Washington High School in Sioux Falls, South Dakota. In his six seasons at Washington, he has guided the team to four state AA tournament appearances. Nelson graduated from Northern State University in Aberdeen, South Dakota (2008), where he played for legendary coach Don Meyer. During his college career, Nelson started in all 121 games and helped lead the team to 98 wins. In his senior season, he ranked fourth among all Division II players and ranked first in the Northern Sun Intercollegiate Conference (NSIC) in three-point shooting. At the end of his senior season, he was one of the top five free-throw shooters in the country (93%). In high school, Nelson played in back-to-back state tournament titles and was named the North Dakota Class B Basketball Player of the Year in 2003. Coaching is part of Nelson's heritage—his father, Dave Nelson, led teams to multiple high school state tournaments (including the years he was coach to Craig), and Craig's grandfather, Ed Beyer, is the all-time winningest coach in North Dakota high school history.